The Pearl

The Pearl

A True Tale of Forbidden Love in
Catherine the Great's Russia

Douglas Smith

To Cynthia & Bob,
To fellow
Russianists!
Best wishes,
Doug

Yale University Press   New Haven & London

Library of Congress Cataloging-in-Publication Data
Smith, Douglas, 1962–
The Pearl : a true tale of forbidden love in Catherine
the Great's Russia / Douglas Smith.
p. cm.
Includes bibliographical references (p.) and index.
ISBN-13: 978-0-300-12041-7 (alk. paper)
ISBN-10: 0-300-12041-9 (alk. paper)
1. Kovaleva-Zhemchugova, P. I. (Praskovia Ivanovna)
2. Singers—Russia—Biography. 3. Opera—Russia—
18th century. 4. Sheremetev family. I. Title.
ML420.K875S65 2008
782.1092—dc22
[B]
2007045563
A catalogue record for this book is available from the
British Library.
The paper in this book meets the guidelines for
permanence and durability of the Committee on
Production Guidelines for Book Longevity of the
Council on Library Resources.
10 9 8 7 6 5 4 3 2 1

To Stephanie

Remember that what you are told is really threefold: shaped by the teller, reshaped by the listener, concealed from both by the dead man of the tale.

—VLADIMIR NABOKOV, *The Real Life of Sebastian Knight*

Contents

Contents

Contents

Acknowledgments

It is a pleasure to acknowledge the individuals and institutions without whose help this book could not have been written. Members of the Sheremetev family greeted me warmly when I told them of my plans to write a book on their ancestors. Kyra Cheremeteff, a direct descendant of Nicholas and Praskovia, responded with generosity to my inquiries. Her parents, Nikita and Maïko Cheremeteff, took me in on a cold December night and shared with me family lore, books, and a wonderful meal. I am both touched by their gracious hospitality and grateful for their help. Other family members have kindly responded to my requests for information: Catherine Davison, Xenia Cheremeteff Sfiri, Yevdokia Sheremeteva and her husband, Stepan. Varvara Pavlina and her brother Nikolai allowed me to visit them in Moscow on several occasions and spent hours answering my many questions.

I am grateful to Emma Parry for all her enthusiasm, advice, and hard work and to everyone else at Fletcher and Parry, especially Kate Scherler and Melissa Chinchillo. Steven Hanson, Glennys Young, Dan Waugh, Michael Biggins, Simon Werrett, and Ben Schmidt at the University of Washington have welcomed me and my research and offered considerable support. I wish to express my gratitude to the staffs of the Library of Congress, the University of Washington's Suzzallo and Allen Libraries, the New York Public Library, the Charles E. Young Research Library at UCLA, and the University of Kansas Libraries.

Acknowledgments

I received generous help at various stages of my work from Roland Merullo, John Brewer, Stella Tillyard, John Crosby, Christopher Merrill, Brian Burt, Frances McCue, Jeff Deutsch, Simon Sebag Montefiore, Andrew Kahn, Rachel Polonsky, Rosamund Bartlett, Andrea di Robilant, Jessica Ring, Dominique Posy, Roy Robson, Geoffrey Symcox, Celine Dauverd, Janet Hartley, Dominic Phelps, Benedikt Wagner, Marc Mariani, Stephanie Camp, Glynis Ridley, Gabriele Lehman-Carli, R. D. Zimmerman, Ann Goldstein, Andrew Solomon, Mary Bisbee-Beek, Robin Davis Miller, Paul Worth, Julie Cassiday, Kathy Connelly, John T. Alexander, Eve Levin, David Moon, Michelle Cuttright, Frances Devlin, Geoffrey Husic, Harold Leich, Dan Newton, Mary Lincoln, Sofiya Yuzefpolskaya, Anthony Cross, Stephanie Davis, Steven Englund, Jean-Claude Lachnitt of the Fondation Napoléon, Peter Pozefsky, Jacquelyn Miller, Tracy Dennison, Audra Kelly of the Hillwood Musuem, Ryan Brown, Jacqueline Letzter, Robert Adelson, Olga Glagoleva, Michelle Anderson, Ed Marquand, Gary Hawkey, Stephanie Lock, Suzan-Lori Parks, William Brumfield, Richard Stites, and Valerie Kivelson. As she did with my previous books, Elise Wirtschafter offered much encouragement and many helpful comments. Drs. Thomas Pozefsky and Michael Kimmerling graciously consulted with me on my subjects' medical histories. I wish to thank Jonathan Brent, Sarah Miller, Annelise Finegan, and Lawrence Kenney at Yale University Press.

A draft of the book was written at the Villa Serbelloni in Bellagio, Italy. I am most thankful to the Rockefeller Foundation for the opportunity to spend a month at the villa and to everyone who helped make my stay so productive and enjoyable: Susan Garfield, Amanda Sevareid, Pilar Palacia, Elena Ongania, Nadia Gilardoni, and the rest of the remarkable staff. Vicky Lettmann, Priscilla Roosevelt, Annette Smith, Willard Sunderland, Hilde Hoogenboom, and Simon Dixon read drafts of the book and offered much-needed suggestions for improvement.

In Russia, I have been helped by many friends and colleagues. Nikita Sokolov, Tatiana Safronova, Alexei Kovalchuk, Lena Marasinova, Alexander Bobosov, and Andrei Zorin have provided invaluable support, encouragement, and hospitality. I was extremely fortunate to have an indefatigable research team in Yekaterina Pravilova, Arina Belozerova, Dmitry Belozerov, Yurii Nikiforov, Mikhail Miagkov, Andrei Kurilkin, Natalia Bolotina, Yelena Perezhogina, and Yelena Savitskaia. Aided by their truly herculean efforts, I was able to conduct the most thorough search of the Sheremetev archives to date and uncover much new information on the lives of Praskovia and Nicholas. Alla Krasko has freely given of her time and thorough knowledge of the Sheremetev family. Yurii Piriutko allowed me to visit Praskovia's and Nicholas's graves, and Olga Velikanova and Yelena Tsesevich gave me a tour of the Fountain House that included a rare opportunity to see Praskovia's rooms. Father Boris Mikhailovich opened his library and went so far as to perform Praskovia's folk song for me over dinner.

I gratefully acknowledge the assistance of the following Russian museums, libraries, archives, and individuals. At the State Hermitage Museum: Mikhail Piotrovsky, Georgy Vilinbakhov, Galina Komelova, Yelena Obukhovich, Galina Printseva, and the entire Department of Russian Cultural History; at the Russian State Historical Archive: Alexander Sokolov, Galina Lisitsyna, Tatiana Furaeva, Larisa Sinitsyna, Galina Ippolitova, Serafima Varekhova, and especially Valentina Lupanova; at the Russian Institute for the History of the Arts: Tatiana Kliavina and Galina Kopytova; at the Russian National Library: Liudmila Buchina and Natalia Rogova; at the Russian State Library: Viktor Molchanov; at the State Historial Museum: Alexander Shkurko and Andrei Yanovsky; at the Kuskovo Estate Museum: Yelena Eritsian, Emma Zhuravskaia, Liudmila Sinelnikova, Irina Polozova, Tatiana Panova, Yekaterina Gorbatova, Galina Kholodnykh, and Liudmila Siagaeva, my marvelous tour guide; at the Ostankino Estate Museum: Gennady Vdovin, Irina Saprunova, and Lia Lepskaia; at the Bakhrushchin Theater Museum: Valery Gubin, Svetlana Semikolenova, Inesa Preobrazhenskaia, Nina Vydrina, Irina Duksina, and Yelena Yershova; at the Russian State Archive for Ancient Acts: Mikhail Lukichev, Yurii Eskin, Galina Borodulina, Alexander Gamiunov, and Svetlana Dolgova; at the State Literary Museum: A. Nevsky.

I owe a special debt to Valentina Fyodorova of the Hermitage Museum and to Varvara Rakina and Olga Solomodenko of the Ostankino Estate Museum. For the past six years they have hosted me repeatedly at their respective museums and gone out of their way to provide me with materials that might help in my research. We have discussed Praskovia and Nicholas for hours, and their ideas have shaped my thinking about my subjects in important ways. I cannot thank them enough.

Acknowledgments

My wife, Stephanie, has listened to me talk about Praskovia and Nicholas since my first encounter with them on a visit to Kuskovo in 1992, and over the years she has added her perceptive insights to my understanding of their lives. She read a draft of the book, catching many errors and making important recommendations. This book is dedicated to her with love and profound gratitude.

Note on Style

Dates are given here according to the Old Style (Julian) calendar used in Russia until 1918. In the eighteenth century this calendar was eleven days behind the New Style (Gregorian) calendar used in the West and twelve days behind in the nineteenth century.

Money: 1 ruble comprises 100 kopecks. In 1800, a single man could live comfortably in St. Petersburg on 300 rubles a year. In the reign of Catherine the Great (1762–96) persons with an annual income of 9,000 rubles were considered rich. Count Nicholas Sheremetev's income in 1798 exceeded 630,000 rubles.

Distances and weights: 1 *verst* equals approximately 2/3 of a mile (or 1.06 kilometers). 1 *pood* equals thirty-six pounds.

Spelling: To help readers not familiar with Russian, I have anglicized most of the personal names and simplified their spellings (Nicholas not Nikolai, Michael not Mikhail). I have largely omitted patronymics, a Russian's second name derived from his or her father's given name (Ivan *Ivanovich*, Varvara *Ivanovna*), except in cases were it seemed necessary to help distinguish individuals with the same first and last names. I use the more widely accepted Sheremetev in favor of Cheremeteff or Chéréméteff and have kept the feminine ending for Russian surnames (e.g., Sheremeteva, Kovalyova). The titles of dramatic works have been translated into English, except in those instances when they are already well known in the original languages.

THE SHEREMETEV FAMILY

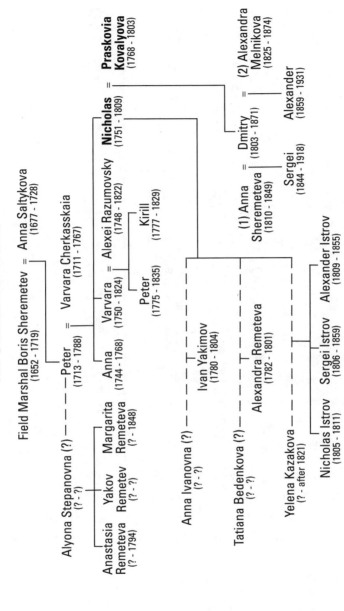

THE KOVALYOV FAMILY

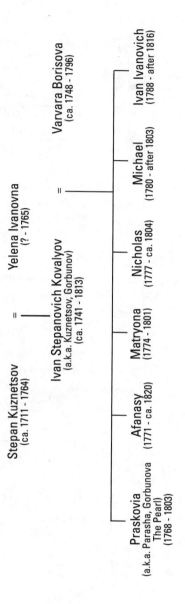

Stepan Kuznetsov
(ca. 1711 - 1764)

=

Yelena Ivanovna
(? - 1765)

Ivan Stepanovich Kovalyov
(a.k.a. Kuznetsov, Gorbunov)
(ca. 1741 - 1813)

=

Varvara Borisova
(ca. 1748 - 1796)

Praskovia
(a.k.a. Parasha, Gorbunova
The Pearl)
(1768 - 1803)

Afanasy
(1771 - ca. 1820)

Matryona
(1774 - 1801)

Nicholas
(1777 - ca. 1804)

Michael
(1780 - after 1803)

Ivan Ivanovich
(1788 - after 1816)

Prelude

Late in 1918, amid the chaos of revolution and civil war engulfing Russia, the poet Anna Akhmatova moved into the Fountain House, the grand St. Petersburg palace of the Sheremetev family recently appropriated by the fledgling Bolshevik government. For the next three decades the Fountain House would be her main residence and a powerful source of artistic inspiration. From her earliest days there Akhmatova fell under the palace's spell, entranced by its history and the many stories, myths, and legends surrounding its generations of inhabitants.

Of all the stories, she was most fascinated by that of Countess Praskovia Sheremeteva. In Praskovia, known for nearly all her life as Parasha, whose ghost appeared to inhabit the empty halls of the Fountain House, Akhmatova glimpsed her double and in her tragic life, a reflection of her own. Like Akhmatova, Praskovia had been a brilliant artist forced to create her art in extreme conditions. Like Akhmatova, Praskovia had been a social outsider, the object of suspicion and cruel gossip. And like Akhmatova, Praskovia had been the other woman, the unlawful wife.

Akhmatova paid tribute to Praskovia's spirit in a sketch to her epic "Poem without a Hero":

> What are you muttering, midnight?
> In any case, Parasha is dead,
> The young mistress of the palace.

The gallery remains uncompleted—
This capricious wedding gift,
Where, prompted by Boreas,
I am writing all this down for you.
Incense streams from every window,
The beloved lock has been cut,
And the oval of her face grows dark.[1]

The young mistress of the palace had died in the Fountain House early on the morning of 23 February 1803 at the age of thirty-four, three weeks after having given birth to her first child, a son named Dmitry. She was buried three days later at the Alexander Nevsky Monastery in a lavish funeral.

Along the route, crowds gathered to witness the procession. As the cortege made its way down Nevsky Prospect, more police had to be summoned to hold back the throng. One group, however, was strangely absent. The city's nobles did not attend the funeral even though the Sheremetevs were one of Russia's richest and most distinguished families. They stayed home because they knew the secret about Praskovia's past that this blinding splendor had been intended to obscure. She was not the descendant of Polish nobility, as the silver plate on her coffin proclaimed. Rather, she had been one of the count's serfs, the daughter of his illiterate blacksmith, and his longtime mistress.

The nobles weren't the only ones who stayed away that day. Praskovia's husband, Count Nicholas Sheremetev, also didn't attend. He remained at the Fountain House crushed with grief, unable to rise from his bed.

Praskovia's death nearly killed Nicholas, and for months his thoughts dwelled on his own end as the only solution to his misery. Guilt fed his despair. He and Praskovia had wed, in secret, a year and a half earlier, yet it was only now that he had found the courage to inform the tsar and his family about the truth of their relationship. In his heart Nicholas knew he had wronged Praskovia. He should have revealed their secret sooner. It took her death for him to realize that society's prejudices about noble birth and the sanctity of lineage, prejudices that Nicholas had struggled for decades to free himself from, amounted to nothing alongside his love.

Prelude

In the end, Nicholas learned this truth, yet it had come at a terrible price.

Praskovia and Nicholas had known each other since the late 1770s and been lovers since the mid-1780s. In December 1798, Nicholas gave Praskovia her freedom, and three years later they married. Practically from the time of their meeting, Praskovia and Nicholas were bound to each other not only as master and serf, but by a shared passion for music. Music, opera in particular, was at the center of their lives, and it was Praskovia's rare talent as a singer and Nicholas's vision of creating the finest opera company in Russia that brought them together.

Praskovia debuted as a child and quickly became the star of the Sheremetev theater. While still a teenager, Praskovia, performing under the name "the Pearl," achieved acclaim, establishing herself as one of Russia's greatest singers. Empress Catherine the Great, her son, Tsar Paul I, and Stanislaw August Poniatowski, the last king of Poland, all came to hear her sing. The nobility flocked to Sheremetev's theater, which at its high point rivaled the opera companies of Vienna, Berlin, and Paris.

Her career ended suddenly. In the late 1790s, Praskovia contracted a mysterious illness and was forced to retire. Without Praskovia, Nicholas saw no point in continuing and closed his theater. His lifework came to an end. The couple left Moscow for St. Petersburg, where Nicholas had been summoned to serve at court. Marriage offered a degree of solace to Praskovia, whose devout nature had caused her to suffer for years over the sinfulness of her relationship with Nicholas. But it did nothing to fill the emptiness she felt upon her retirement from the stage, nor did it stop the gossip that had hounded them ever since Nicholas took her to his bed.

After her death, Praskovia passed into legend. The story of her improbable journey from serf to countess inspired a folk song sung by millions of peasants across Russia. Penny prints depicting a romanticized first meeting with Nicholas hung in many Russian homes. In smoky taverns and roadside inns gypsy musicians performed a song about how "the church bells were calling, our sweet Parasha is to be married to the master."[2] Praskovia's tale was recalled in poems and novellas. By the end of the nineteenth century, nearly everyone had heard of the poor serf girl who had married Russia's richest aristocrat.

Under the Soviets, Praskovia was transformed into a quasi-socialist celebrity. She became a symbol of the worker-peasant class whose talents had been exploited by their masters. Her image was put on postcards, and a crudely politicized version of her life fed to Soviet schoolchildren. The Sheremetev estates of Kuskovo and Ostankino were reopened as shrines to Praskovia and the genius of the Russian peasant. As for the Sheremetevs, visitors were instructed to gaze upon their palaces so that they might "better know their enemy, and consequently develop a deeper and more conscious hatred toward him."[3] Writers cranked out books and brochures full of distortions and half-truths about Praskovia and Nicholas, and their story became the subject of a popular made-for-television movie. Praskovia remains today among the more recognizable female faces from Russia's imperial past, a figure about whom most Russians and even many foreign visitors have heard but few know much about.

In the spring of 1872, Peter Bezsonov, an ethnographer, folklorist, and Praskovia's first biographer, arrived at Kuskovo on the southeastern edge of Moscow. Bezsonov had long been interested in Praskovia's folk song and had come to do research for a book he was writing on it and its heroine. Count Sergei Sheremetev, the grandson of Praskovia and Nicholas, warmly received Bezsonov and set him up in a comfortable dacha on the estate grounds.

Some of the family papers were stored in Kuskovo's old wooden theater, the site of Praskovia's dramatic triumphs, which now sat forgotten, its exterior flaked with brittle, chipping paint, its interior stripped of its sumptuous velvet seats, its luxurious taffetas, and gilded archways. Bezsonov was dismayed to find the condition of the archive no better. Documents lay about in large messy piles without any guide or index. Water from the hundred-year-old roof had leaked onto the papers, leaving behind rot and mold and rendering many of them illegible.[4]

As he worked his way through the surviving papers that summer, Bezsonov began to feel as if he were in search of a ghost; but for the occasional reference, Praskovia simply wasn't there. She appeared to have mysteriously vanished. He suspected that someone had gone through the archive, carefully removing and presumably destroying anything on Praskovia that might have reflected poorly on her, Nicholas, or his family. His suspicion fell on Nicholas.[5]

After Praskovia's death, Nicholas became the guardian of her memory and the author of her life story. Nicholas turned Praskovia's rooms in the Fountain House into a holy shrine. He completed the almshouse in Moscow begun many years earlier with Praskovia's encouragement and gave generously to numerous charities in her name. And he wrote a few brief accounts of Praskovia's life for their son, Dmitry. More hagiography than biography, these writings present Praskovia as Nicholas wished their son to think of his departed mother and as Nicholas himself wished to remember her.[6] All of these efforts were an attempt both to memorialize Praskovia and to create an image of her as a woman of near saintly purity, devoid of the slightest frailties.

It is tempting to think that Nicholas got rid of any evidence that contradicted this image. We know he was not above falsifying Praskovia's past in order to make her more acceptable to polite society as well as to the weaker elements of his own character. But did he go so far as to burn whatever letters, diary, or testimony she may have written? It is impossible to say for certain.

Praskovia's papers may have indeed been burned, though not by Nicholas. Both the theatrical warehouse and the Sheremetevs' mansion in the heart of Moscow were consumed by the great fire of 1812 during Napolon's invasion, which destroyed much of the city. The mansion housed the family's magnificent library and may have been the repository of Praskovia's papers as well.[7]

It's more likely, however, that there were never any papers to destroy. In the eighteenth century it was rare even for Russian noblemen and women to keep diaries or write memoirs. Few serfs were literate, and none are known to have left any substantial accounts of their lives. Even in England, which had higher literacy rates and a more developed theatrical life than Russia, none of the leading actresses of the time wrote memoirs.[8] Bezsonov's assertion was most likely motivated by a desire to cast the Sheremetevs in a bad light. His relations with Count Sergei Sheremetev had become strained, and he never had much sympathy for the nobility. After Bezsonov left Kuskovo and published his book, Sergei was outraged at the depiction of his grandfather and even accused Bezsonov of having stolen documents from the family archive.

This dearth of personal material is exacerbated by the attitudes of the day that saw little value in recording the lives of serfs. Even an artist of exceptional talent such as Praskovia did not receive nearly the attention given free performers. That we possess as many references as we do to Praskovia's career testifies to her greatness, a greatness that helped chip away at the barrier between free and serf artists so that in the nineteenth century serf actors, singers, dancers, and musicians did begin to receive their due recognition. It is a sad irony that one of the greatest voices in Russia was denied the voice to tell her story. Everything we know about Praskovia comes from the words of others.

The challenges of telling the story of Praskovia and Nicholas are more general, however, and confront any historian seeking to remove the veils that shield private life. As the literary biographer Richard Holmes has observed, "That ordinariness, and that family intimacy, is the very thing that the biographer—as opposed to the novelist—cannot share or recreate. Tolstoy in the opening of *Anna Karenina* writes that all families are happy in the same way; he might have added that they leave little record of that happiness, even though it is the stuff of life. The very closeness of husbands and wives precludes letters between them, and often the keeping of journals (unless one party is secretly unhappy). The private domestic world closes in on itself, and the biographer is shut out."[9]

For the biographer to enter the confidential space of couples, distance is required, either physical distance, which produces letters, or emotional, which produces revelations to one's diary or, in the extreme, court proceedings in which the intimate details of human life are brought before the world. We have nothing of the sort in this instance. Nicholas and Praskovia were rarely apart and so had no need of letters; what's more, Praskovia was rarely apart from her closest friends. It was only after her death created the greatest distance imaginable that Nicholas began to write about their lives together.

The one person who knew their story better than anyone else, Tatiana Shlykova, once the prima ballerina of Nicholas's troupe, Praskovia's best friend, and a witness to their secret wedding, lived to the age of ninety. As a boy in the 1850s, Count Sergei Sheremetev would sit at Tatiana's feet in her room in the Fountain House and listen to her tell of her life. Tatiana loved to reminisce about her past, but she was always careful not to disclose too much about Praskovia and Nicholas. "Much of the past in Tatiana Vasilievna's life remained forever secret," Sergei wrote, "about much we can only guess, but it is beyond doubt that a deep, resolute, and loyal friendship bound her to my grandmother Praskovia Ivanovna, and her words about my grandfather, and even the sound of her voice, spoke of a grateful memory. When she would talk about them, one could feel that her entire soul was with them."[10] Tatiana died in 1863, taking these secrets with her to the grave.

For over five years I have searched the archives in Moscow and St. Petersburg, interviewed Praskovia's and Nicholas's descendants in Russia and abroad, and written to members of the extended Sheremetev family throughout the world in the hope of discovering some long-lost papers of Praskovia. At times I thought I was on the verge of making a startling discovery. While working at the Russian State Historical Archive in St. Petersburg, I was handed a file of documents dated 1809, the year of Nicholas's death. Among the faded papers was a report titled "File Describing the Documents found at Ostankino in the Room of the Late Countess Praskovia Ivanovna." With a racing heart I read the accompanying letter by one of Nicholas's secretaries describing how the papers had been found in a dusty wardrobe in ten bundles held together by Dutch string and red ribbon. Weeks passed before I recovered from the disappointment of finding here nothing more than a collection of administrative reports compiled by Nicholas's estate managers.[11] My searches did uncover, however, considerable new information that has eluded biographers until now, most notably a cache of documents in the State Hermitage Museum that held the answers to the mystery of their secret marriage. Nonetheless, I have found no misplaced diary or letters that would afford access to Praskovia's inner world. So much of her life remains out of sight, irretrievable, frustratingly unknowable.

In my search for Praskovia, I have had to adopt strategies that while not widely employed by historians are common among biographers. I have been to the places Praskovia and Nicholas lived to get a sense of the physical world they inhabited. I have explored the palace and grounds at Kuskovo, attended a concert in the Ostankino theater, witnessed a service in the church where they married, stood in reverent silence in the room where Praskovia gave birth to Dmitry and later died, and visited their graves. I have held in my hand Nicholas's and Praskovia's marriage certificate, which bears their signatures, and a lock of Praskovia's auburn hair. I have spent hours examining Nicholas's and Praskovia's portraits for the faintest clues to my subjects' emotional histories.

Biography is impossible without the life-giving breath of fiction. When one writes a life it is never enough merely to string together along a chronological continuum the grubby facts retrieved from the archive. Lives don't reside in bundles of faded letters or in the foxed pages of old diaries patiently waiting for the biographer to come along and copy them down. Rather, they are actively created, shaped, and imbued with meaning and coherence in ways that have much in common with the work of the novelist. For a biography to be believable and true, imagination is required, imagination, the biographer Michael Holroyd reminds us, to capture the "dreams and fantasies, the shadow of the life that isn't lived but lingers within people."[12] The biographer must be a conjurer.

In writing the lives of Praskovia and Nicholas, I, too, have relied on the conjurer's tricks. I have had to summon my subjects' spirits and engage them in imagined conversations across the centuries for insights into the hidden pathways of their hearts. This has led me into the realm of speculation, especially with regard to Praskovia's story, yet, unlike the novelist, I have delivered all my findings from that shadowy landscape with a qualifying *perhaps*, a cautionary *maybe*. I have marked for the reader the doors that have withstood my attempts to open them and behind which so many secrets remain. Nonetheless, there are no imagined scenes in this book, no made-up characters, no invented dialogue. This, as best I know, is what happened.

I first learned about Praskovia and Nicholas on a visit to Kuskovo in the autumn of 1992. Like so many before me, I was immediately struck by the tragic beauty of their story. It is one of the most poignant love affairs in Russian history. Of course, masters had been taking serfs as their mistresses long before Nicholas, yet there is something new and different in Nicholas's and Praskovia's story. This difference is expressed not only by the fact that Nicholas married Praskovia, an unprecedented act for someone of his high social standing, but, more important, by the fact that he loved, indeed worshiped, her. Despite her lowly birth, Nicholas accepted Praskovia as his equal, worthy of his honor and respect. He saw in her the embodiment of goodness, sincerity, and Christian virtue. He called her his "tender friend and trusted companion," words that reveal an unmistakably modern sensibility toward marriage and the nature of a husband's and wife's affections.[13]

Today, such feelings appear uncontroversial, banal even, yet in eighteenth-century Russia they were revolutionary. For centuries, Russia's millions of serfs had been considered inferior beings, barely human, especially in relation to the aristocracy. Like all Russian noblemen, Nicholas was raised to hold these assumptions and educated to believe that his proud lineage constituted an unbridgeable chasm sanctioned by God, the emperor, and tradition separating him and the rest of his class from the dark peasant masses. Nicholas never completely freed himself of such beliefs. He was a reluctant revolutionary, someone who, when faced with the contradiction between what he had long held to be true and what he saw before him in the person of Praskovia, chose to renounce society's norms for the promise of an unknown future.

Nicholas's personal journey of moral transformation was one that Russian society as a whole had to undertake before serfdom could be ended. His relations with Praskovia showed Nicholas to be years ahead of his fellow nobles in his thinking, and his life issued a challenge to society that declared the common humanity in all people, nobles and serfs alike. Nicholas's actions reverberated throughout society, eventually inspiring others to change their beliefs as well. In the end, the example of their lives served to cast a harsh light on the gross injustice of serfdom and to help hasten its demise.

But theirs is not just a Russian story. It is a universal one of the power of love to transcend social convention and transform the human heart. Reflecting back on his life with Praskovia, Nicholas wrote in a letter to their son, "Tradition is not law. One mustn't submit one's mind and will to it, especially in those instances when one can free oneself from our age-old errors." These errors insisted on human inequality, what Nicholas had come to recognize as nothing more than "the transitory prejudices of this world."[14] Nicholas instructed his son to ignore society's prejudices and to listen only to his heart and the voice of his conscience. His advice is just as sound today as it was two centuries ago, and the story of Praskovia and Nicholas just as moving.

I

KUSKOVO

A luxurious grandee's palace, Moscow's favorite garden,

Where, amid infinite pleasures, one day was worth more

Than a year in any other wondrous land!

—PRINCE IVAN DOLGORUKY, *A Walk at Kuskovo*

ONE

An Aristocratic Boyhood

Nicholas Petrovich Sheremetev was born on 28 June 1751 at the Fountain House, the family's summer residence that in those days lay just beyond the St. Petersburg city limit. His birth did not exactly overwhelm his father, Count Peter Sheremetev. The count first mentioned it, in passing, three days later in a letter to his stewards in Moscow, and then only after informing them that the dogs and four flasks of rosewater they had sent two weeks earlier had arrived in good condition.[1] His father's reaction is somewhat understandable. Not only was Nicholas not the much-awaited first son, but he was also, depending on which sources one believes, the last of six or seven children. The eldest, Anna, was born in 1744, followed by Boris a year later. Three more children appeared in rapid succession: Alexei, Maria, and Varvara. Nicholas, named for the Russian St. Nicholas Mirlikisky, was baptized, according to custom, three days after his birth in the Fountain House's chapel of St. Varvara the Great Martyr. This was the same chapel where, fifty-two years later, Praskovia's and Nicholas's son would be baptized and, three weeks after that, Praskovia's coffin would lie for its final blessing before her burial at the Alexander Nevsky Monastery.

The Sheremetevs were one of Russia's great noble families. For centuries they served the grand princes of Muscovy as military commanders and counselors. A Sheremetev was married to Ivan the Terrible's ill-fated son, the tsarevich Ivan, murdered by the mad tsar supposedly after being provoked by the sight of his daughter-in-law in immodest dress. In 1613, the Sheremetevs played a decisive role in the election of Michael Romanov, a blood relative, thus establishing Russia's imperial dynasty. Nicholas's paternal grandfather, Boris Sheremetev, a diplomat and celebrated general under Peter the Great, was renowned for defeating Charles XII of Sweden at the Battle of Poltava in 1709. Peter amply rewarded Boris for his service, making him both the first Russian field marshal and count of the Russian Empire. When he was laid to rest in St. Petersburg's Alexander Nevsky Monastery in 1719, the tsar attended the funeral and made sure he received a hero's burial.

Standing in respectful silence with Peter the Great that day was Count Peter Sheremetev, a cross-eyed six-year-old boy, born on 26 February 1713 in the provincial town of Priluki a few hundred versts east of Kiev. He was the second son of the Field Marshal, as Count Boris was usually called, born to his second wife — Anna Naryshkina (*née* Saltykova); his elder half brother Michael had died in 1714, and so Peter became the sole heir to his father's fortune. The Field Marshal's other children — Anna, from his first marriage, Natalia, Sergei, Vera, and Catherine, from his second — were cut out of any inheritance, which was to be the cause of a family feud that would rage into the next century.

With the death of the Field Marshal, Peter and his siblings were left to be raised by their mother. Strong-willed, smart, and extremely capable, Anna was warmly received by Tsar Peter when she arrived in the capital, children in tow, to bury her husband. Peter promised to look after Anna and her children like a father, and he did. The tsar, and later his wife and successor, Catherine I, opened the royal palaces to Anna's family.

No Russian nobleman in the eighteenth century had as long and as enriching, if not particularly accomplished, a career as Count Peter Sheremetev. He proved himself the most adroit of courtiers, possessing that rare talent of being both fully attuned to the intricate and often dangerous machinations forever brewing at court and, at the same time, seeming to float above it all, dispassionate, disinterested, and preternaturally cautious, beholden to no one. No other nobleman could say upon his deathbed that he had served eight consecutive rulers, beginning with Peter the Great and ending with Catherine the Great.

Along with a list of lofty titles (general-in-chief, senator, chief chamberlain of her majesty's imperial court), Peter boasted wealth of almost fairy-tale proportions. From his father he inherited a massive estate of over sixty thousand serfs, which placed him among the biggest landowners in Russia at the time. Croesus, his countrymen called him, after the fabulously wealthy fifth-century BC king of Lydia, and, in his later years, the rich Lazarus of Moscow.[2] His status and wealth induced envy in many: "Count Peter Sheremetev is a man of extremely mediocre intellect, lazy, ignorant of affairs and, in a word, a man who drags down rather than raises up his name, and only takes pride in his riches," opined Prince Michael Shcherbatov. "He lives with all possible magnificence, and always with the monarch's approval. His clothes weigh him down with gold and silver, and dazzle the eyes with their brilliance."[3]

Rich as Peter was, his marriage to Princess Varvara Cherkasskaia catapulted him into the ranks of the world's wealthiest men. The Cherkasskys belonged to the ancient Boyar aristocracy. Some sources claim the family was descended from Egyptian sultans who had come to Russia by way of the Caucasus. Varvara's father, Prince Alexei Cherkassky, was the richest man in Russia in the early eighteenth century. Along with his home in St. Petersburg, the prince kept a residence on Moscow's Nikolsky Street directly across from the Field Marshal's mansion. Count Peter Sheremetev fell in love with the girl next door. Varvara was born on 11 September 1711. She was a beautiful girl—vivacious, smart, sophisticated without being prim, and warmhearted. As an eight-year-old she dazzled visitors to the salons of St. Petersburg with her marvelous dancing, and Peter the Great himself taught her how to shoot a rifle. As a young woman, she was every man's desire.

Varvara and Peter married on 28 January 1743. Her dowry, combined with Peter's wealth, made them the richest couple in all of Russia. Peter and Varvara settled in an enormous St. Petersburg mansion on Millionaia Street that had belonged to Varvara's father (the street was named after the great sums he had spent on his residence). It was next door to the Winter Palace, its windows opening out onto the Neva River. Under its new inhabitants, the house became the scene of many of the capital's most sumptuous balls, masquerades, and fêtes. In Peter, Varvara found her equal, and not just in terms of wealth and lineage, for according to all accounts the marriage was a successful one. The couple shared a love and natural intimacy that only seemed to deepen as the years passed.

Peter's and Varvara's second son arrived healthy and strong, although with a bad case of cradle cap. In early childhood Nicholas picked up intestinal worms that often left him weak and listless and plagued him for the first two decades of his life. Although his mother loved her other children dearly, her baby Nikolasha came to occupy a special place in her heart, and of all the children his name figures most prominently in her letters from these years. Perhaps she saw much of herself in him, for Nikolasha took after his mother both in looks and temperament. Portraits from the period depict a smallish boy with dark hair, rather thin and pale. Part of his mother's doting was an understandable result of his poor health. Varvara and Peter had already lost two children before Nicholas was born—Maria and Alexei, both of whom died in 1747. Terrified of losing a third, Varvara coddled her youngest and could never do enough to see to his health and safety.

In keeping with noble tradition, Nicholas was placed in the "female half" of the household, where he was shamelessly pampered and spoiled. Along with his mother, a small army of wet nurses, nannies, and nursemaids attended to Nicholas and his siblings. The staff-to-child ratio was seven to one. These first years of Nicholas's childhood were largely happy and carefree, despite his poor health. He enjoyed playing with his sister Varvara and was sad when apart from her for any length of time. On visits to Moscow the two liked to push each other around the rooms of the family mansion in a pram or lose themselves for hours playing with the toys their parents showered upon them. The family had a favorite parrot they always took with them on their travels. Nicholas's father gave him several hunting dogs as well, and Nicholas came to share his father's passion for hunting.[4]

It was common for noble sons to be placed under the care and education of men beginning around the age of seven. Nicholas may have made this transition around the time of his elder brother Boris's death in January 1758. Thirteen-year-old Boris had been the apple of his father's eye. He was smart and diligent and showed great promise as the heir to the family title and fortune. After his death, all their hopes were placed on sickly Nikolasha. They worried over him obsessively, which couldn't help but leave traces on his malleable character. Peter saw to directing Nicholas's education. Nicholas's father could be a strict, domineering man, demanding and imperious, and Nicholas grew to fear him, so much so that even as a grown man he would often tremble in his presence. Later in life, Nicholas would exhibit many of his father's traits, especially his quick temper.

An intense, wide-ranging program of study was put together for Nicholas, one that included all the subjects necessary to prepare the scion of a great noble family for life either at court or in the military: religion, languages (Russian, French, and German), world history, the classics, geography, natural history, international commerce, civil administration, mathematics, astronomy, heraldry, engineering, fortifications, and artillery. Nicholas read the works of the German historian Samuel von Pufendorf, the French naturalist Georges-Louis Leclerc, Comte de Buffon, and the Swedish botanist Carolus Linnaeus. He received the polish required of a nobleman: there were lessons in the fine arts (painting, sculpture, architecture), mythology, allegory, drawing, dancing, fencing, and riding. He was taught estate management and administration. All of this learning was encompassed within the spirit of the Enlightenment and required numerous instructors under the supervision of Nicholas's French tutor, Villeneuve, and later one Monsieur de Woesian. It was around this time that Nicholas acquired a taste for music and was given lessons on the violin and clavichord.[5]

Like all young noblemen, Nicholas was entered into state service at an absurdly young age: in 1759, the eight-year-old child was made a sergeant in the prestigious Preobrazhensky Life-Guards Regiment. In 1765, he was promoted to lieutenant, and three years later, shortly after his seventeenth birthday (on 9 July), Catherine appointed Nicholas one of her gentlemen-of-the-bedchamber.

Winter was spent in the home on Millionaia, summer at the nearby Fountain House, and autumn at the family estate in Markovo. Peter enjoyed visiting several of his other estates with the family, especially Meshcherinovo and Kuskovo. Late in the summer of 1763, the family journeyed to their estate of Voshchazhnikovo in Yaroslav province. Had anyone told them that five years later a serf girl would be born here who would become a famous opera singer, Nicholas's wife, and the mother to the family heir he would have been held for a madman. Even now it doesn't quite seem possible.

When in St. Petersburg, Nicholas spent a good deal of time with his friend Grand Duke Paul, Catherine the Great's pug-nosed son and heir to the throne. Around the time of her coup in 1762, Catherine selected Nicholas along with a handful of other boys from trusted, prominent families as her son's playmates. It appears that the grand duke liked Nicholas most of all, and together with Prince Alexander Kurakin the boys formed a tight-knit troika, amusing themselves with card games, chess, badminton, cup-and-ball, forfeits, and hide-and-seek. Once the boys were seen dancing like Cossacks about the Winter Palace, their happy shrieks echoing through the long corridors.

Nicholas and Paul both loved the theater and acting, and together they put on productions. On 20 September 1764, Paul organized a masquerade in his palace apartments for his friends in honor of his birthday. The boys dressed up as members of the Ottoman court, a sort of eighteenth-century Russian version of cowboys and Indians. The grand duke was the Sultan, and Nicholas got to be the Grand Vizier. Their other young friends were attired as Janissaries, pashas, and eunuchs.[6] In October 1765, Paul and Nicholas put on a puppet show for Catherine and her suite. The empress was most taken with the performance, and she invited Nicholas to stay for dinner. Once when the grand duke fell ill and couldn't perform in the mythical ballet *Acis and Galatea* staged by young chevaliers and maids of honor, Nicholas stepped in for him as Hymen, dancing before the court for several performances. When they weren't staging their own productions, Paul and Nicholas enjoyed watching plays in the palace theater.[7]

On 1 February 1765, Catherine, her courtiers, and members of the foreign diplomatic corps were invited to the Sheremetev home to watch a production of Philippe Néricault Destouches's comedy *The Married Philosopher*. This was the first theatrical production staged by Count Sheremetev. Theater was becoming all the rage among the Russian elite. It is hard now to appreciate its popularity and the influence it exerted in Russian society in the second half of the eighteenth century. One would have to imagine combining Hollywood movies, television, and popular music to arrive at some rough contemporary equivalent.

The actors that evening included the count's children, Anna, Varvara, and Nicholas. Nicholas played the role of the servant girl Finette. The Sheremetev children were joined on stage by other nobles, and three members of the distinguished Chernyshev family lent a hand: Count Zakhar Chernyshev, president of the College of War, collected tickets, his brother Count Ivan, the head of the Russian navy, directed the performance, and Ivan's wife served as an usher. The play, although full of the theatrical clichés of the day, eerily foreshadowed Nicholas's own life with its story of forbidden love and a secret marriage. The empress was so enamored of the performance that she asked Peter to repeat it for her four days later.

Inspired by this initial success, Peter put on several more plays during the next year. On 21 February 1766, he organized three short comedies with a cast of courtiers and distinguished aristocrats and his children. Peter's daughter Anna and the three Chernyshev countesses appeared on stage covered in family jewels said to be worth two million rubles.[8]

These pleasant days came to an end when Nicholas's mother died in October 1766. Her death hit Nicholas hardest of all the children, given his closeness to his mother and his sensitive nature. The family was still in mourning when they were dealt a second blow.

In the spring of 1768, Nicholas's sister Anna died suddenly after contracting smallpox. Anna had been her father's favorite. She was beautiful, elegant, the most exquisite of the young maids of honor at court. Catherine the Great supposedly wanted to marry her to one of the Orlov brothers, but her father had been against a match with a man he considered an upstart. Instead he arranged a marriage to Count Nikita Panin, one of the most powerful men in Russia and his close friend, almost thirty years Anna's senior. The engagement lasted only a few months before she died. The family's grief was compounded by a rumor that Anna had been murdered. It was said that a jealous woman determined to become Panin's wife had killed Anna by secretly placing tobacco infected with smallpox in her snuffbox.

Devastated by the loss of the two people he loved most, Peter retired from state service at the end of July, intent on leaving St. Petersburg and its painful memories for his estate of Kuskovo outside Moscow. The old count had miraculously survived the intrigues of court life for over half a century, but these sudden, unforeseen deaths broke him and sent him into self-imposed exile.

The deaths also seem to have worsened relations between Nicholas and Peter. Instead of following his grief-stricken father and his sister Varvara to Kuskovo, Nicholas chose to remain in the capital. Having no family in St. Petersburg to keep an eye on his impressionable eighteen-year-old son, Peter began to consider other options for guarding Nicholas from the city's many temptations. He worried about the direction his son's life was taking as Nicholas began moving among a group of aristocratic rakes. A contemporary portrait of Nicholas suffused with a decadent sensuality conveys the dissipation into which he fell during this period.

After consulting with Count Panin, Peter decided the best course of action was to get Nicholas out of the capital and send him on an extended grand tour of western Europe.

TWO

The Blacksmith's Daughter

Like so much of her life, Praskovia's birth remains obscure. Her grave-stone states that she was born on 20 July 1768, but no records can confirm this date. Several locations have been proposed as the place of her birth, the most likely being the estate of Voshchazhnikovo in the province of Yaroslav.[1]

The province lies some hundred miles northeast of Moscow. The land forms an extensive plain, tilting slightly to the southeast and gouged in places by ravines and hollows. The black earth of central Russia gives way here to a dark-gray soil. In the eighteenth century the province was covered with dense forests of pine and spruce and birch teeming with elk, bears, wolves, and lynxes and echoing with the calls of woodpeckers, snowy owls, and willow grouse. The Volga River enters the province from the southwest, flows northward for a ways, and then turns abruptly to the south on its path to the Caspian Sea, cutting a large pie-shaped slice out of the province's southern half.

In this wedge midway between the provincial capital of Yaroslavl and the ancient town of Rostov the Great was the estate of Voshchazhnikovo. It had belonged to the Sheremetevs since 1706, when Peter the Great gave it to the Field Marshal in recognition for his having crushed a re-bellion in the southern outpost of Astrakhan the previous year. The Field Marshal and later his son Peter visited Voshchazhnikovo often, seeking solace from the pressures of court life and hunting in the estate's forests and meadows.

In the second half of the eighteenth century Voshchazhnikovo was one of the larger Sheremetev estates. It comprised dozens of villages, some made up of just a few households and others, like Voshchazhnikovo, the largest village and source of the estate's name, encompassing more than a hundred. Some serfs grew rye and spring wheat on small fields cleared among the forests. Some engaged in trade. Others worked in one of the estate's manufactories—tanning leather, making candles, boiling soap, and weaving napkins and tablecloths—or at the Uslavtsevo stud farm, famous for the beautiful horses that pulled the count's carriages through the streets of St. Petersburg. It was a hardscrabble existence; still, the peasants of Voshchazhnikovo lived better than most Russian serfs, thanks in part to the relatively modest demands of their masters.

On the day of Praskovia's birth, the village midwife was called to the hut of the local blacksmith, whose wife had gone into labor. Following folk custom, she would have made sure not to close the gate or door upon entering and would have told the father-to-be to open all of the windows wide: she had to be sure there were no obstacles blocking the baby's way into the world. Next, she sat down alongside the smith's young wife, who was moaning and drenched in sweat, and began rubbing her belly with potions and intoning various folk spells and prayers. They all prayed for an easy birth but were ready to resort to other, more extreme measures if need be: knotted string could be untied to release the vital forces, and the mother could be carried to the bathhouse for a good steam or, if all else failed, hung by her wrists from the rafters.

Praskovia was the couple's first child. Her father, Ivan Stepanovich, was thirty, give or take a couple of years. He had a pale complexion, gray eyes, thick light-brown hair, and a nose too long for his face. The thumb on his right hand protruded at an unnatural angle (the result of a work-related injury, no doubt). According to some accounts, he had a slight hunchback, possibly from the early stages of Pott's disease, a tuberculosis of the spine. Ivan was known by three surnames—two, Kuznetsov and Kovalyov, based on his occupation (both being Russian equivalents of Smith) and one, Gorbunov (from *gorbun*, or hunchback), possibly based on his physical deformity. Praskovia's mother, Varvara Borisova, was eight years his junior and the daughter of a serf who had worked in one of the Sheremetevs' palaces.

Varvara gave birth to a healthy baby girl. They named her Praskovia, from the Greek *paraskeuē*, "Friday," and Paraskeva, the common form for the Orthodox saint martyred in the first century after Christ. Most of her life, however, she would be known simply as Parasha. In Russian folklore, Praskovia was the patron saint of the fields and cattle. The peasants would decorate her icons with ribbons and flowers and sweet-smelling grasses on church holidays and pray to her to cure them of toothaches, fevers, and hallucinations brought on by the devil. According to the *Life of St. Paraskeva,* she was the firstborn child of pious parents who for years had prayed and fasted and sacrificed in the hope of being blessed with a child. Ivan and Varvara may well have had this story in mind when they chose Praskovia's name, for until her birth they had been childless for two years — a long time in the world of the Russian peasant. Her christening took place within three days, a serf named Anna Andreeva (still living in the estate parish of Uslavtsevo in the early nineteenth century) being chosen as her godmother.

Yet Praskovia's birth was not an occasion for outright celebration. High infant mortality taught the peasants not to make too much over the birth of a child, and in this patriarchal world parents were disappointed if their firstborn was a girl. Ivan knew he could expect a good beating at the hands of the other men in the village, as was the custom for those who fathered a girl first.

Ivan Kovalyov was the son of two Sheremetev serfs.[2] His father, Stepan Kuznetsov, had been a blacksmith who served for a time in Field Marshal Sheremetev's Fountain House in St. Petersburg. Stepan and his wife, Yelena, had six children, of whom Praskovia's father was the second eldest. Little Ivan learned to be a blacksmith at his father's side. The family lived in one of the Sheremetev homes in Moscow and at the estate of Meshcherinovo until Stepan's death in 1764, after which they were sent back to the Yaroslav province. Ivan's mother died in 1765, and the following year he married eighteen-year-old Varvara. Praskovia was born two years later, and four more children followed at three-year intervals: Afanasy (in 1771), Matryona (1774), Nicholas (1777), and Michael (1780). A fifth, Ivan Ivanovich, was born in 1788. By then, Praskovia had left the family and was starring on the Sheremetev stage.

Praskovia spent her first years, however, on the back of a wooden cart in her mother's arms, bouncing along dusty back roads from one Sheremetev estate to another. As Ivan's skill as a smith grew, he was shuttled about with his family among Voshchazhnikovo and Yukhotsk in Yaroslav province, Pavlovo, a large metalworking center near Nizhnii Novgorod, and Konstantinovka, which lay southeast of Moscow. This peripatetic life went on until, several years later, word of Ivan's talent reached the count's administration in Moscow. He was ordered to Kuskovo, then undergoing a major reconstruction that required the best craftsmen and skilled laborers from all the Sheremetev lands.

In the eighteenth century, travelers heading to the east departed from Moscow via the Vladimir Road. After passing the Rogozhsky gate, they left the city behind and made their way through a patchwork of kitchen-gardens and small stands of apple trees and currant bushes. Beyond these plots, the Vladimir Road entered a dense forest of fragrant pine and spruce that was home to several magnificent country estates. The grandest of them all, situated on a level piece of ground near the intersection of the Vladimir and Kolomensky roads, some seven versts from Moscow, was the Sheremetev estate of Kuskovo.

Kuskovo had belonged to the Sheremetev family since the beginning of the sixteenth century. Nicholas's father had spent much time here as a boy, and after his marriage to Varvara had made it their main summer residence. They were both drawn to the natural beauty of the area. The land was heavily wooded and dotted with ponds that cooled the sultry summer air. Intensive work began on the estate in the early 1750s, when Peter ordered his managers to collect two kopecks from every serf on his lands to pay for renovations. Although major work was completed by the late 1770s, the building and rebuilding at Kuskovo never really stopped until Nicholas and Praskovia left for Ostankino in the 1790s.

The view from the steps of the Big House, as the manor was called, opened out onto a broad man-made lake that had taken hundreds of serfs more than four years to dig. In the eighteenth century, the lake was home to the count's private navy, consisting of a full-scale six-gun battleship, a Chinese junk, a barge, a launch boat, and numerous oared vessels. An allée stretched off the right side of the lake through the woods, exposing a set of ruins meant to be the former home of a seaside dweller; to the left another allée cut through a leafy grove leading to an expansive zoological garden, home to hundreds of deer, Siberian wolves, American pigs, and other rare creatures. A field had been cleared in the center of the garden so that the count could hunt in a "controlled environment." His master huntsman, whippers-in, and scores of hounds lived nearby in the neo-Gothic hunters' house.

On the other side of the Big House, spread out over seventy acres—nearly the size of the tsars' park at Tsarskoe Selo outside St. Petersburg—was the most elaborate, richly constructed, and aesthetically pleasing pleasure garden in Russia. There was a French garden whose parterre—four rectangular lawns lined by tall, tightly planted lime trees—led to an orangerie filled with exotic fruit plants and a spacious Vauxhall for entertaining. Laurel-hedged allées beckoned visitors to follies, temples, gazebos, and pavilions scattered about the garden. There was a Dutch House, fittingly situated on a small canal and surrounded by tulips. Inside were blue and white Delft tiles and dark wood; an upstairs gallery included works by Rembrandt, Van Dyke, and other Flemish masters. Near the Dutch House was the Pagodenburg, a Chinese-style structure crammed with Asian porcelain and figurines, and facing this a building housing two picture galleries that displayed the family's collection of old masters. There was a hermitage for intimate parties, an Italian palazzo, and a grotto filled with swirling, richly tactile mosaics of bright shells imported from the Adriatic Sea. The far side of the French garden was home to the amusement park, the so-called games' alley, complete with carousel, swings, skittle alley, fortuna (a form of lawn bowling), and a course for *jeu de mail,* a forerunner of croquet.

Beyond the orangerie lay La Solitude, a large English garden (the name notwithstanding) that was Count Peter's retreat. Amid the shady groves and meadows, streams, ponds, and artificial waterfalls, he built a modest house where he could find respite from the demands of estate management and entertaining. Peter gave free rein to his fancy here: La Solitude had a "philosopher's hut" with books and a bust of Diogenes, caves with lions and dragons of crystal and rare stone, a "Capuchin's refuge," a "temple of silence," and a gallery containing the portraits of over one hundred Russian and European crowned heads.

The estate as a whole was worked by one thousand serfs, including a staff of almost two hundred that kept the Big House and the other buildings in proper order. At the head of this army was Alexei Agapov, the count's scrupulous steward.

In 1775, a cart bearing Ivan and Varvara Kovalyov and their three children arrived at Kuskovo. They were settled in the Old Quarter, a large area near the fish pond and the farmyards where most Kuskovo serfs lived. Just beyond the Old Quarter in the direction of the Big House a series of outbuildings housed the estate managers and their families, the count's dozens of footmen, his gardeners and carpenters and painters, his beaters, and the sailors and oarsmen of his navy. In the opposite direction, near the edge of the estate, were the stables and barns and brew house and the smithy where Praskovia's father was to work.

Ivan's and Varvara's new home wasn't large, yet a surviving inventory hints at a degree of domestic comfort rare among Russian serfs.[3] A large clay stove anchored one corner of the main room. It was used for cooking and heating, but its broad, tiled top doubled, in the Russian manner, as a sleeping surface during the long cold winters. Opposite was the so-called beautiful corner, a feature of every Russian peasant home, where the family displayed its icons. Here Praskovia and her parents and siblings would gather to pray before images kept in a glass-front case: the Mother of God and Savior (to bless the Kovalyovs' marriage), John the Baptist and the Great Martyr Varvara (the couple's patron saints), the Kazan Mother of God, and the Holy Mother of All-Lamenting Joys. This last icon took on special significance for Praskovia for reasons that remain mysterious, and she worshiped it throughout her life. About the icon case hung crudely framed biblical scenes and a wax relief of Peter the Great on horseback. A modest cupboard in another corner held the family's best dishes (two teapots, a few cups and plates), a saltcellar, and a tea chest. Low benches ran along the walls, and a heavy wood table where the family took its meals occupied the center of the room.

By the time Praskovia arrived at Kuskovo, around the age of seven, she had been helping with the household work for several years already. In the mornings she would tend to Afanasy and Matryona while her mother stoked the stove and warmed the breakfast kasha. She then led the family's two cows out of the yard to the pasture near the woods, returning for them in the early evening. Back home there was always work to be done. She had to feed the chickens, weed the garden, pick apples and gooseberries, chop cabbage, bake bread, tidy the house, and wash the clothes—all while keeping an eye on her two younger siblings. There was no thought of her receiving any formal education.

In the patriarchal world of the peasantry, the male head of the household held near-absolute power over his wife and children—perhaps most hideously exemplified by *snokhachestvo,* the practice that allowed peasant fathers to take their sons' wives for their sexual pleasure. Labor, not love, bound the peasant family together. Women, judging by folk sayings, were chiefly necessary for the work they contributed. "A hen is not a bird; a woman is not a person," claimed one peasant adage. This is not to say that women weren't valued—just no more so than the family horse.

The Kovalyov family fit this standard, although the atmosphere in their home was tenser and darker than in most. Ivan had a weakness for the bottle, and when he drank he apparently became violent and beat Varvara. This must have been especially hard on Praskovia, who was old enough to understand what was happening yet too little to do anything about it. Varvara suffered from poor health, and the frequent pregnancies and beatings meant she was often too weak to work. Despite her youth, Praskovia was forced to take over for her. Ivan's drinking got him in trouble with the estate managers: his name appears in lists of serfs punished for "carelessness and drunkenness."[4] During these early years at Kuskovo, it appears that his binges were neither as frequent nor as debilitating as they became later, and he was still able to work. Within a year or so of the family's arrival, Ivan was promoted to master blacksmith.

In the rare hours when she wasn't working, little Praskovia would escape with the other youngsters into the surrounding forests and meadows, running barefoot through the tall grass, playing games, and telling stories. At times she would make for the Big Road, which cut through the estate on the way from Moscow to the village of Kosino. Ever since pagan times Kosino and its lakes were said to harbor mystical powers. The lame and sick would journey from miles around to be cured by the waters of the Holy Lake or the miracle-working icon of St. Nicholas, which had been found floating on the surface of the White Lake a century earlier. The pilgrims would stop, tired and hungry, at the Old Quarter and be given food, drink, and a place to spend the night. Praskovia and the other serfs would gather around these holy wanderers to listen to their songs and prayers and wonder at their stories of miraculous healings taking place in the nearby lakes and forests.[5]

This Russian folk religiosity appears to have shaped Praskovia's young character in a powerful way. It became the source of the deep Christian faith that gave her seemingly infinite reserves of strength and love, upon which she would draw so heavily years later as the star of the Sheremetev stage and as Nicholas's lover. At the time, however, there was nothing to suggest that Praskovia's life would be any different from her mother's or the lives of generations before her. Her world would extend no farther than the hut and the field, it seemed, revolving around familiar drudgeries of physical labor and child rearing.

THREE

Grand Tour

With twenty thousand rubles in his pocket, nineteen-year-old Nicholas left Petersburg on his grand tour in the autumn of 1770, accompanied by his tutor Monsieur de Woesian. They reached Berlin by November, and there, another tutor, Monsieur de Sacken, replaced Woesian. The following month Nicholas reached Leiden, where his boyhood friend Prince Alexander Kurakin was waiting for him.[1] The two young Russians enrolled at the university, and for the next year they studied law, modern languages, mathematics, and history. In September 1771 they left for England. The channel crossing from Calais to Dover was miserable; the weather was foul and the sea was choppy. Alexander spent most of the eleven-hour passage throwing up in the captain's cabin.

By the end of October they had arrived in London, where they stayed just long enough to catch the races at nearby Epsom before setting off on a trip through the English countryside. They visited Windsor and the universities at Cambridge and Oxford and toured the manufactories at Leeds, Manchester, and Birmingham. They were received at the duke of Devonshire's home at Chatsworth and at the duke and duchess of Kingston's Thoresby Hall in Nottinghamshire. The latter couple's relaxed hospitality charmed them; they were particularly taken with what they called the duchess's "fine manner"—ironic, considering she had scandalized English society years earlier by appearing at a masquerade ball half-naked and attired as Iphigenia. During their return to London they stopped at Bath and saw its famous pump house. Back in the metropolis, Nicholas and Alexander visited the Tower, the British Museum, and the hospital at Bedlam. Then they made time for an execution at Newgate Prison.

Their lure through all of these travels, though, lay not in England but back on the Continent. To visit Paris was every educated Russian's dream; Parisian culture shaped the upper classes' concept of taste and refinement. In early March 1772, Nicholas and Alexander left London for Paris.

Together with a small group of expatriates that gathered at the home of Nikita and Alexandra Demidov on the Rue Jacob in St. Germain, Nicholas and Alexander threw themselves into exploring the French capital. They visited the Louvre and the Tuilleries, observed military exercises at the Bois de Boulogne, and viewed the king's collection of paintings at the Luxembourg Palace. They dropped by the studios of the sculptor Jean-Baptiste Pigalle, the master watchmaker Monsieur Brille, and the Swedish portraitist Alexander Roslin. Nicholas sat for Roslin, who depicted him luxuriating in youthful, aristocratic pride.

Nicholas and Alexander met some of the great minds of the Enlightenment, including Denis Diderot, and mingled at the literary and artistic salon of Madame Geoffrin. With the help of a handy local guide—*The Code, or the New Regulation concerning the Places of Prostitution in the City of Paris*—they also made the acquaintance of women of a different class. Nicholas and Alexander consulted this text along with such related must-reads as *Sex without Childbirth, or Pleasure without Pain* and *The Art of Meeting Women, with an Appendix on Adultery.*[2]

Still, loftier society beckoned. In April they made their first trip to Versailles and were presented to King Louis XV, the dauphin, and the rest of the royal family. Nicholas and Alexander were invited back two more times—once on the day of Pentecost for a ceremony of the knights of the Order of the Holy Spirit, followed by lunch and a tour of the gardens and Petit Trianon.

Impressive as these experiences were, nothing could compare with the theater, which was unlike anything the young men had seen before. Nicholas's encounter with the Parisian stage marked a turning point in his life: it awoke what was to become his great passion. Although Nicholas wrote no letters during his travels, Alexander, who shared his fascination, did. "We went to see the Grand Opéra," Alexander wrote to Grand Duke Paul. "The tumult of my senses, caused by the beauty of the spectacle, told me that I had been wrong to permit such a powerful impression to be made on my soul on the first exposure. The style of the scenery, the precision of the machinery, the gracefulness of the dances, the decency and good order observed by the spectators—all this enchanted me."[3]

Nicholas and Alexander frequented the city's main theaters— l'Opéra, the Comédie-Française, and the Comédie-Italienne. The quality of the performances amazed them, and they became avid devotees of the city's theatrical stars. *Opéra-comique* was all the rage in Paris at the time. The best of these were staged at the Comédie-Italienne in the Hôtel de Bourgogne, where every night a packed house wildly applauded the works of André-Modeste Grétry, Pierre-Alexandre Monsigny, and François-André Philidor, the reigning masters of comic opera. It was at the Comédie-Italienne that Nicholas and Alexander saw Grétry's *Lucile,* his most popular opera of the decade, starring the remarkable Madame La Ruette; they were equally in awe of the theater's other stars: Carlino Bertinazzi, famous for his catlike suppleness and spontaneity in his role as Harlequin, the tenor Jean-Baptiste Clairval, and Joseph Caillot, the leading baritone, whose acting was praised by Garrick himself. Then, in April 1772, the two young men attended the most-staged comic opera of the decade, Monsigny's *The Deserter,* starring Marie-Jeanne Trial. Nicholas would later produce both operas at his theater.

At the Comédie-Française they marveled at the great Lekain, famous for his wild, hideous expressions, and at Mademoiselle Dumesnil, the celebrated tragedian. Nicholas met a cellist with the opera's orchestra, Monsieur Hyvart, with whom he began taking lessons. Hyvart would later come to play an important role as Nicholas's chief theatrical agent in Paris.

The theater was more than mere entertainment for the two men. Like many of their contemporaries, they ascribed to it an irresistible transformative quality. "What better means is there to correct the vices of the heart or to perfect the faculties of the spirit than to frequent these schools of good taste and good mores?" Alexander wrote after one of their theater outings.[4] Much of opéra-comique's allure for Nicholas, Alexander, and other theatergoers came from its capacity to bring Enlightenment social ideals onto the stage in a direct, dramatic, and convincing manner.

Opéra-comique has been disparaged as *larmoyant,* or lachrymose. This description is not incorrect, but it misses the larger point, namely, that the stories told in these operas reflect the era's preoccupation with sentiment and feeling. They belong to the age of sensibility. As the librettist Barnabé Farmian de Rosoi noted, the goal of opéra-comique was to provoke not merriment, à la *opera buffa,* but "intense feeling."[5] Feeling, in Rosoi's estimation, would be the tool for destroying class differences. "By following the idea of Shakespeare while correcting his faults," he wrote, "we could create a Theatre of History; a school where the son of a peer and the son of an artisan sitting side by side might learn to judge men . . . to recognize true virtues in all classes and from all ages."[6] Librettists and composers sought to speak to the heart and to arouse sympathy between spectator and performer. By leading the audience to identify with the emotions of a character onstage, they hoped to bring them into connection with the universal nature of feelings that united all humanity in a common fellowship.

What was new about these operas was the type of people the audience was meant to sympathize with—not kings and queens, but everyday people, even the humblest peasant. This was a radical notion in eighteenth-century Europe, and opéra-comique's potentially subversive message did not escape the authorities. Of Grétry's opera *Silvain,* based on a tale by Jean-François Marmontel dealing with peasants' rights, the diplomat and critic Friedrich Melchior Grimm wrote, "They are deeply convinced at court and in the great world that such subjects are deliberately treated by the philosophes to spread their dangerous opinions about the equality of all men and on the prejudice of birth." *Silvain* was hugely successful in Paris and abroad, Russia included.[7] Marmontel had been a protégé of Voltaire, and his tales, imbued with the spirit of the Enlightenment, inspired many opéras-comiques that shifted the focus away from title and rank toward men's and women's shared humanity, toward what Marmontel called the "sacred names of friend, father, lover, spouse, son, mother."[8]

Nicholas's encounter with opéra-comique proved fateful, though its effect on him was not instantly pronounced. The seed it planted in him lay dormant for many years before a Russian serf brought it to life.

While in Paris Nicholas fell ill from the intestinal worm that had troubled him since childhood. Alexander wrote home that Nicholas was often tormented with pain and suffered attacks.[9] Several doctors had prescribed medicine to flush the worm from his body, yet Nicholas balked, fearing the cure might be worse than the disease. His poor health was impinging on the men's socializing and became a source of tension. Alexander's patience wore thin, and he began to find it hard to sympathize; he hadn't come all this way to play nursemaid. Nicholas eventually agreed to treatment, which rid him of the worm but left his gut a raw mess. For weeks he was too weak to go out; the trauma left him with shattered nerves.

Yet by late March 1773 Nicholas was feeling better, and he and Alexander set out for home. He grew stronger along the way, thanks to a strict diet, lots of fresh air, and vigorous riding. He was sleeping well again, his appetite had returned, and the depression caused by his illness was lifting.

After nearly three years abroad, Nicholas and Alexander arrived back in St. Petersburg on 3 June 1773 on a ship from Riga, Latvia. A racehorse and five trunks crammed with haberdashery, musical scores, and books arrived separately. The next day Nicholas dined with Catherine the Great to tell her of his adventures, and that same month Nicholas celebrated his twenty-second birthday.

Nicholas soon returned to Moscow to visit his father. He couldn't stay long, however, since he was expected back at court. Peter didn't want to see Nicholas leave him and return to court after so many years apart; he worried his son would fall back into the same crowd that had occasioned the grand tour. Peter relented only after Prince Kurakin's grandfather promised to keep a close watch on Nicholas.[10]

By September, Nicholas was back in service at court. His duties were far from onerous, so he spent a good amount of time in the company of other rich and idle youths in the capital. There were balls, masquerades, lavish meals at the Winter Palace, and amateur theatricals in which Nicholas took part along with the grand duke, Prince Kurakin, and other aristocrats. Nicholas spent the summer months at Tsarskoe Selo, the tsars' palace outside the capital. He was regularly invited to join the empress's intimate circle. In late May 1776 he was included in a small party that visited Prince Grigory Orlov at his estate of Gatchina; the following month he was one of nine courtiers who accompanied Catherine for a ride in two carriages up and down the dusty Slaviansky Road near Tsarskoe Selo.

Nicholas spent all of 1775 in Moscow, where Catherine and the court had gone to celebrate the Treaty of Kuchuk-Kainardji, which ratified Russia's victory in the Russo-Turkish war of 1768–74. He joined other courtiers on horseback to accompany Catherine's triumphant entrance into the ancient capital on 25 January and then spent the next nine months in a whirl of balls, concerts, ceremonies, and royal processions. On 21 March, Nicholas and his family received Catherine and a small suite of chevaliers and maids of honor at Kuskovo; they dined in the orangerie to the sound of French horns and clarinets. Catherine enjoyed herself and stayed for several hours before returning to Moscow that evening.

The Sheremetevs were such marvelous hosts that Catherine returned several times. On Saturday, 22 August, she visited Peter at Kuskovo for a day of entertainments that ended with a short opera performed out-of-doors in one of the park's allées by a group of professional French actors hired for the occasion. There were also visits to the Sheremetev mansion in Moscow off Red Square and to the family's estates of Markovo and Meshcherinovo.

Yet the story of Nicholas during these years depicts an impressionable young man with too much money, too little supervision, and no direction in life. The few surviving descriptions of him do not paint a flattering picture.

"It is generally believed that Monsieur de Chérémétief is an honest young man, that is to say, he has no vices," wrote the Chevalier de Corberon, secretary to the French ambassador in 1776. "I do not share that opinion. He is a Russian without *esprit*, whose travels didn't educate, whose riches don't bring happiness, and who will never know how to enjoy himself. He is by nature distrustful, which is the hallmark of petty souls and weak spirits; he doesn't know how to either love or hate; he lacks understanding of his own feelings, and his affections fall by preference to accommodating flatterers and his servants. In his manners and appearance one notices certain irreconcilable differences. His clothes, carriages, and servants are all of a brilliant ostentation, yet he makes little impression himself, and in such way sins against the order of his own home."

Corberon later added to this description: "I just learned from a Russian that this Chérémétief I just spoke of is a mediocre man who's gotten into the habit of preferring a French harlot, whom he supports and doesn't take out, to good company. Another person told me that he was the richest fellow in all of Europe, but also the most villainous."[11] The stories of reckless womanizing appear to have been true. Even Nicholas's own doctor wrote that he "devoted himself to a lot of women, though he happily escaped the perils that come with such intimate relations." By "perils" the doctor meant venereal disease, which Nicholas did contract and admitted to his friend Prince Kurakin.[12]

Toward the end of his life Nicholas recalled these years of folly in a letter to his son: "It is of course difficult amid the abundant blessings of Fate to protect oneself against the immoderate misuse of them; . . . Feasts, all manner of entertainments and magnificence will of course draw toward you a great many acquaintances and friends ready to take pleasure in these things; their unctuous compliments and insincere expressions of friendship will lead you to the greatest excesses."[13]

That Nicholas was something of a rake in his youth is neither terribly unusual nor revealing. More significant is Corberon's reference to Nicholas's "preference to accommodating flatterers and his servants." To noblemen like Corberon such an attitude was both unimaginable and inexcusable. Servants were, after all, people of a lower sort; their job was to serve, not to socialize with their betters. Even as a young man, however, Nicholas began demonstrating different notions about such things, seeing servants—at least some—as people in their own right. It's intriguing to wonder how he came by such ideas. Some might be explained by his education and the influence of European experiences like the opéra-comique, and some by a youthful rebellion that enjoyed shocking good society. But Nicholas also harbored a feeling of superiority, fed by his name and wealth, that inspired him to act above the social norms of his contemporaries. It was this pose of hauteur toward fellow nobles that caused men without Nicholas's resources, such as Corberon, to seethe.

Whatever its sources, Nicholas's willingness to shun "good society" for his servants would become decisive a decade later when one servant in particular attracted his attention. Other Russian nobles might have found themselves drawn to Praskovia, given her undeniable charms, yet it took someone of a special makeup such as Nicholas to see in her not just an outlet for sexual desire but a woman worthy of his respect, love, and name.

Yet that was still in the future. At this young age, Nicholas showed scant concern for doing the right thing—and this ambivalence extended to marriage. By now his friends were settling down. Grand Duke Paul had already married twice—first in 1773 and then again three years later after his wife died in childbirth. In 1774, a fellow dandy from his circle, Count Alexei Razumovsky, reluctantly married Nicholas's sister, Varvara. Their marriage would prove a disaster. Rumor claimed that Nicholas was considering marrying a distant cousin, Yelena Sergeevna Sheremeteva, but could not commit. The affair seems to have caused Yelena considerable suffering: she never married and subsequently turned away from society to join Moscow's Rozhdestvensky Convent. "Sheremetev doesn't want to marry anyone, and he's doing the right thing," Princess Kurakina wrote to her grandson from Moscow in 1774. "Better he let the brides come looking for him." Her daughter, Princess Agrafena Alexandrovna, wrote that same year, "Sheremetev, to his credit, is not about to change his mind; he insists he has no intention of marrying."[14]

Nicholas showed as little interest in making a career at court as he did in marrying. Although Catherine had promoted him to the rank of chamberlain in 1775, the distinction did nothing to motivate Nicholas to seek higher honor. Instead he requested a six-month leave of absence and in 1776 left the empress's court for the so-called young court of the grand duke and duchess. This change also failed to motivate him. He had grown bored with his life and was ready for something new. For centuries every generation of Sheremetevs had served the rulers of Russia, out of both necessity and a sense of duty. But in 1762 Tsar Peter III abolished obligatory state service for the nobility, letting nobles choose for themselves whether they wished to serve. Most continued to do so, but Nicholas decided he had had enough and quit. He would be the first Sheremetev to decide for himself the course of his own life.

In October 1777, Nicholas attended one last party at Prince Potemkin's Petersburg palace. Soon thereafter he bid farewell to the empress and his friends and set out on the road to Moscow.

FOUR

The Big House

The Kovalyovs had not been at Kuskovo a year when Praskovia was taken from her family and moved into the Big House. Her parents must have been concerned: serfs gave up their children only reluctantly, and losing Praskovia meant losing the labor of their eldest child, an important member of the household. It also meant placing her safety and well-being in the hands of strangers and relinquishing their power to protect her. From now on Praskovia would live at the complete mercy of their masters, subject to their every whim and their unknown ways. She was only eight years old.

What must have gone through Praskovia's head that fateful day the overseer came to take her from her family and lead her across the estate to the Big House? Fear must have gripped her heart. Her life would never be the same. How could she have known that from then on she would live in two worlds, that of the serfs and that of the masters, and never be truly at home in either?

The narrow rear stairs of the Big House led up to the second floor, more an entresol with a low ceiling and windows placed close to the floor. An elderly princess, Martha Dolgorukaia, lived in one of the rooms along the main hall. Dolgorukaia was Peter Sheremetev's niece, although she was several years his senior; her father had been Peter's much older half brother. The princess, widowed half a century earlier, had been taken in by Peter's family and never left. She followed her nephew when he departed St. Petersburg for Kuskovo and became an honored and much-beloved member of the extended Sheremetev household.

Now Praskovia was to be her servant. She was to stay by the princess's side, attend to her needs, be mindful and obedient. It is a mystery how Praskovia was chosen. Peter had decided to find a handmaiden for the aged princess, but it doesn't seem he had Praskovia specifically in mind. Perhaps her recruitment was mere chance; or perhaps the pretty little girl had come to the attention of Alexei Agapov, and he had recommended her to Peter. It seems unlikely that her developing voice had anything to do with her being taken into the Big House.[1]

In any case, Princess Dolgorukaia was pleased with Praskovia, who displayed a maturity beyond her years. Years later Nicholas would write that even as a young girl Praskovia had shown signs of "a bright mind, a modest demeanor, and a character and physical appearance that were nothing but attractive." The princess, he noted, "gave special care to the cultivation of her morals and manners; as this girl grew she showed ever greater talents and this, in turn, strengthened Princess Martha's affinity, care, and love for her. For this reason, Count Peter Borisovich Sheremetev began to pay special attention to and show favor toward this ward."[2]

Princess Dolgorukaia shared the floor with several others, and in the months that followed these fellow residents populated Praskovia's new life. One of them was a teenage girl with sparkling black eyes and an impish smile. Anna Nikolaevna, or Annushka, as she was best known, was an ethnic Kalmyk, derived from Mongols who had settled along the southern reaches of the Volga River in the early seventeenth century. She had been adopted by the Sheremetevs along with her sister, Catherine, several years earlier, when "native peoples" were something of a fashion at court. By 1775 Catherine had moved out to live with a family friend and only Annushka remained. She loved her adopted family, and they loved her. (She would later name her two children Peter and Varvara, after her Russian parents.)[3]

When Praskovia arrived at the Big House, Annushka lived in two cozy, crimson-colored rooms overlooking the kitchen wing and the estate's baroque church. Praskovia must have looked up to her. One can imagine her visiting Annushka in her room, listening attentively to the girl's stories about her life with the Sheremetevs. The stories would have introduced her to Nicholas. (It's unlikely that Praskovia herself saw

Nicholas until late 1775 or early the following year, when he often visited Kuskovo.) From Annushka's room Praskovia could point out her family's hut in the Old Quarter.[4]

Among the Big House servants, Praskovia met Tatiana Shlykova, a girl who would become not just a friend and fellow star of the Sheremetev stage, but her one true companion for the rest of her life. Tatiana was the daughter of two serfs, Vasily, keeper of the count's armory, and Yelena, a trusted maid of the late Countess Varvara. She had been born in or around Moscow in 1773 and came to live in the Big House before 1778.

Near the end of her long life, Tatiana loved to recount her early days with Praskovia to Count Sergei Sheremetev, Praskovia's grandson. She told Sergei that she herself had not been a beauty, but this was either modesty or bad memory. Her portrait shows a beguiling young woman; a mischievous glint in her eyes hints at her delight in pranks and practical jokes. Sergei wrote that when talking of those bygone days Tatiana always spoke in the first-person plural, meaning "Praskovia and I," as if their lives had been one. Before training for the stage filled their days, the girls had had lots of time to play in the halls of the Big House and explore the gardens and surrounding woods.[5]

Like the rest of the estate, the Big House was a place of exotic wonder, especially for a peasant girl like Praskovia. Next to Annushka's rooms was the *Kunstkammer,* or cabinet of curiosities. One can see the girls, their young eyes wide with amazement, exploring this collection of weird and wonderful things gathered from the far corners of the earth—a fossilized frog, a piece of human skull, part of a Babylonian mummy, a preserved hairy tarantula, and lifeless sea creatures floating in murky jars.[6] Elsewhere in the entresol was the count's *Kriegskammer.* This was where Tatiana's father worked, keeping an eye on the large collection of swords and shields, pikes and chain mail, muskets and carbines from across Europe and Asia. One of the count's most prized objects was the saddle of King Charles XII of Sweden, which Peter the Great had presented to the Field Marshal after the Battle of Poltava.

Downstairs the girls explored the enfilade of ceremonial rooms. This complex of sumptuously appointed halls and suites had only recently been completed from plans sent by the noted Parisian architect Charles De Wailly. In the gallery hung works by Peter Paul Rubens, Raphael, and Correggio. Flemish tapestries adorned the walls of the reception room, and busts of Voltaire, Jean-Jacques Rousseau, and Benjamin Franklin watched over the darkly paneled library. There was a room for billiards and another for cards, a divan room for intimate conversations, and a spacious formal dining room. Nearby were the state bedroom and the white hall (or hall of mirrors) which, while not as large as Versailles's, was almost as impressive. The interiors were covered in silks, brocades, and damasks; glittering chandeliers hung from the ceilings; gilt sparkled on the walls. To little Praskovia, seeing it for the first time, it must have looked like something from a fairy tale.

Tatiana recalled some of the famous personages who visited Kuskovo when she and Praskovia were children. In the spring of 1780, Joseph II of Austria toured the estate with Prince Grigory Potemkin. Tatiana later said that she and Praskovia had run into the garden and hidden behind a hedge to spy on the Holy Roman Emperor as he examined the grounds. One can see the girls suppressing their laughter when the emperor lost his balance and, to the dismay of Potemkin and Count Peter, nearly fell headlong into the lake in front of the Big House.[7] Once they witnessed old Count Kirill Razumovsky, grand hetman of Little Russia and brother of Empress Elizabeth's morganatic husband, riding a gentle nag into Kuskovo from his neighboring estate of Perovo, an outlandish pair of green goggles strapped on to shield his eyes from the summer glare.[8]

Tatiana had fond memories of Peter. In her reminiscences he appears as a much livelier, friendlier, and more relaxed man than his son. The count enjoyed playing games with Tatiana, Praskovia, and the other children in the house, and he would spoil them with gifts. When they were ill, he fussed over them and brought medicinal powders.[9]

Yet life for the girls in the Big House wasn't all fun and games. When not attending to Princess Dolgorukaia, Praskovia was being taught to read and write—part of the nobles' effort to expurgate her peasant roots and mold her into a respectable young maiden versed in the habits of polite society. Sometimes the discipline was painful, as when Praskovia and Tatiana were forced into iron hoops and corsets to straighten their posture. They received instruction on the proper use of hairpins and powder and rouge, on the application of *les mouches* (or fashionable moles), on the wearing of farthingales, on the correct way to hold one's purse, and on proper table manners. So amazed was the princess by Praskovia's progress that she dubbed her "my little noble girl."[10]

All of this must have seemed strange, confusing, and at times even frightening to Praskovia. Tatiana's memories of her childhood with Praskovia recalled at the end of her life are suffused with the warm glow of time that has erased all the bad experiences of these years. These memories bear no trace of the sadness Praskovia must have felt at being taken from her family, however difficult life had been with them, of the anxious disorientation upon moving into the Big House, or of the fear bred by an utterly imperceptible future.

FIVE

First Meeting

In the early years of the nineteenth century the serfs at Kuskovo liked to sing a song that told of Nicholas's and Praskovia's first meeting. Late one evening while driving the cows home from the wood, Praskovia sees the master riding from the hunt with his dogs. Catching up with her, Nicholas asks in a friendly voice, "Hi there, pretty girl, what village are you from?" To which Praskovia replies, "I am your lordship's peasant." Smitten with the young lass, Nicholas informs her, "Tho' born a peasant, tomorrow you're to become a lady!" Frightened, Praskovia runs home and asks her friends what she should do. They, however, only laugh at her naïveté: "He can do whatever he wants," they tell Praskovia, "and he's sure to do as he pleases!"[1]

From Kuskovo the song spread to the other Sheremetev estates and then eventually to all of peasant Russia. The mezzo-soprano Elizabeth Sandunova, famed for her renditions of folk songs, learned the verse from the Kuskovo serfs and helped to popularize it among the beau monde in the early years of the nineteenth century. Sandunova had been one of Praskovia's voice teachers, and she liked to tell her audiences that the song they were about to hear told the true story of her famous pupil's first encounter with Count Sheremetev.

Praskovia's folk song makes for a romantic story. The truth of their first meeting, however, was assuredly less dramatic. Nicholas and Praskovia may have met for the first time in 1775 or 1776, when Nicholas was in Moscow and at Kuskovo. More likely, however, little Praskovia knew her young master by sight but was not presented to him. If they did meet it left no impression on Nicholas, for he never recalled such an encounter. She was, after all, only seven or eight years old, while he was in his midtwenties. Just as it was theater that would become the lifelong bond between them, so it was theater that brought them together.

Although Nicholas's father had kept a serf choir and orchestra even before retiring to Moscow, it wasn't until the mid-1770s that he thought about establishing his own theater. The play Peter staged for Catherine during her visit of 1775 with hired actors may have been the impulse behind its origins. His choir and orchestra were adequate for putting on masquerades, entertaining at balls, and accompanying simple dramatic performances, but they were not capable of staging more complex theatricals, much less opera.

Kuskovo was by now already a popular destination for Muscovites seeking diversion. Around this time Peter began running advertisements in the *Moscow Gazette* inviting the city's residents to attend festivals at Kuskovo every Sunday and Thursday during the summer.[2] They came by the thousands, on foot, on horseback, and in carriages to play games, to admire the gardens and palace, to hear music, to eat, drink, dance, and watch the fireworks. Kuskovo became Muscovites' favorite playground. But magnificent as the estate was, Peter wanted to do more for his guests and decided to start a theater. "So as to adequately show his respect for the bonds of friendship with his visitors, my late father decided to establish a small theater," Nicholas wrote many years later, "to which end the existence of his choir was a considerable help. The most capable of the domestics were chosen and taught to act, and then small plays were put on. In time the harmless fun of this and the good successes gave rise to the thought of increasing the number of actors. To this end, girls whose families served in the house were chosen along with guests who had been living with us for a long time."[3]

Vasily Voroblevsky, the son of Kuskovo's serf estate manager, was put in charge of organizing a theater company. Peter had long admired Voroblevsky for his intelligence and natural talent and had sent him as a boy to study in Europe. A gentle man of unlimited energy, Voroblevsky, now in his midforties, became Peter's factotum, overseeing his library, personal archive, art collection, and Kunstkammer. He even served as the family versifier and in-house man of letters. As early as 1775, Peter had Voroblevsky translating French comedies into Russian. Voroblevsky selected about a dozen serfs from among the children of the serf administrators and house serfs in Moscow and Kuskovo for the troupe. Among the most promising were two pairs of siblings, Stepan and Stepanida Degtiarev and Timothy and Tatiana Bedenkova.

The first theater at Kuskovo had been built in the early 1760s. The outdoor, or green, theater, as it was called, sat just off the parterre near the Italian pavilion. It was constructed of earthen mounds, trees, shrubs, and flowering plants. A raised semicircle of turf formed the stage and was situated so that the evening sun lit up the actors' faces; the wings were spruce shrubs trimmed into a coppice, and the backdrop was wood painted green to resemble leafy trees. Tight lines of birch trees framed the stage and produced surprisingly good acoustics. Projecting upward in front of the stage and orchestra pit was an amphitheater, also of sod mounds, contoured into three hillocks. The green theater was small and obviously of use only a few months out of the year, and so a makeshift theater was set up in the Big House. The count built another theater at his Moscow residence on Nikolsky Street, a sprawling tangle of a place in China Town appropriately known as the Chinese House. Begun in 1776, it formed a two-story wing attached to the mansion that could seat a hundred persons but lacked a hold or other features for staging large productions.

At first, the productions were put on only irregularly, typically in connection with a family or church holiday. The repertoire was limited to a few plays, chiefly light French comedies in Voroblevsky's translations or those of the Russian playwright Alexander Sumarokov. Peter took pleasure in his creation, yet it was but one of the many aspects of his magnificent life that attracted his restless attention. He enjoyed dabbling in theater and considered it a requirement of any self-respecting aristocrat, but it remained a hobby, nothing more.

This was not to be the case for Nicholas, however. Unlike his father, Nicholas had grown up with theater. He had been acting from an early age and had been swept away by the theaters of Paris. Theater was becoming a passion. And so when his son returned in the autumn of 1777, Peter, concerned about where Nicholas's life was heading and seeing that he was casting about for something to occupy his time beyond hunting and consorting with women, he decided to place the direction of the theater in his son's hands.

Nicholas threw himself into his new role as the family impresario. First, he sought out the best instructors. To train his dancers, Nicholas hired the Italian Francesco Morelli. Morelli had arrived in Russia to dance at court in 1768 and from the mid-1770s had taught at Moscow University. He began working with Nicholas's dancers as well and eventually moved into the Sheremetev household. Other Italians were engaged as voice instructors, and some Germans were selected to work with the orchestra. Nicholas sent a group of boys to St. Petersburg to train under the capital's leading musicians, but in addition oversaw much of the musicians' training himself while taking part in the lessons. He participated as well in the troupe's acting lessons, which consisted of the still-dominant classical style of gestures taught by Russian actors and actresses.

Nicholas also decided he needed more performers, and another group of house serfs was selected. Among them was Praskovia. By now someone in the household had noticed Praskovia's "inclination to dance and her superlative voice," as Nicholas wrote later.[4] Perhaps it was Princess Dolgorukaia who first took note of how beautifully Praskovia sang; perhaps it was Peter or Nicholas himself; or possibly Annushka or Tatiana had told someone about their friend's musical gifts. Whoever it was, Praskovia was taken to see Nicholas and presented as a candidate for his theater. He was twenty-six, she was nine. Nicholas had no doubt seen her before about the Big House. He inspected her face, her posture, the way she walked; it was a requirement that all the girls in the troupe be pleasing to the eye. She probably had to sing for him to prove the quality of her young voice. Nicholas was satisfied. He informed her of the plans to enlarge the theater and told her that her role in the household was about to change. Henceforth in addition to seeing after the princess she would become a member of the troupe and given voice lessons. He would be one of her teachers and would be keeping an eye on her progress.

How did Praskovia react to the news? Was she confused, fearful, excited? What did she even know about theater or opera? Did she have any idea what was being asked of her? Perhaps Praskovia had accompanied Princess Dolgorukaia to one of the early productions at Kuskovo. It must have seemed wondrously strange to her, like so much in the Big House. Whatever her reaction, it was not her place to question her master's son, but simply to acknowledge his words and do as he said. If he wanted her to be a servant, she would be a servant; if he wanted her to be a singer, she would be a singer. That's all there was to it.

Nicholas set to work building a permanent indoor theater at Kuskovo. This structure, which would later become known as the old theater, was begun in 1777 beyond the French garden in La Solitude between the maze and the Seventh-Hour Meadow (so named since after seven o'clock in the evening one could stroll here free of the sun's intense summer rays). It took two years to construct. Like the Moscow theater, it was built in the then-popular Italian style, with a deep, oval-shaped seating hall filled with fourteen benches covered in dark red cloth. There was a small enclosure for the orchestra and dressing rooms in back for the actors and actresses. There were eight sets of decorations. It was a rather modest affair.

In addition to preparing his actors, musicians, and dancers, building the theater, and preparing costumes and sets, Nicholas had to procure librettos and scores. He and his father established contacts with some foreign booksellers and musicians in St. Petersburg. Most important among them was the Czech Johann Massner, a violinist, seller of bowstring and sheet music, and occasional musician at the St. Petersburg court. When Massner wasn't able to get his hands on enough printed copies of a work, he employed a small army of copyists to scribble out the necessary number of duplicates.

In 1778, Peter instructed his Petersburg steward Peter Alexandrov to acquire copies of Alessandro Fridzeri's opera buffa *The Bronze Shoes, or the German Cobbler*, intended for the premier of the Sheremetev theater. Massner's copiers were set to work, but the going was slow. An impatient Peter wrote Alexandrov on 8 November with instructions for Massner: "Try to see to it that the opera is copied out sooner and send me with each post whatever is ready for I need it." Massner's men picked up their speed, but this meant more errors, which forced him to later write Alexandrov to tell Massner that the copies he'd received were full of mistakes. On 15 November, the count wrote to Alexandrov again: "Don't tarry to send me the opera, and try to get them to finish what's left as quickly as possible and send it to me with the first post."[5]

By the end of 1778, all the preparations had been made. "My theater is ready," Peter wrote Alexandrov from Moscow on 20 December, "and we've had two rehearsals and Sunday is to be the opera and comedy and given all the work on this I haven't written you for so long."[6]

But something apparently went wrong at the last minute and the premier was postponed. The Sheremetev theater finally opened with a performance of *The Bronze Shoes* on 11 January 1779 in the Chinese House theater. Nothing is known about how the first night went. The opera, based on a vapid story of a cobbler too blind to his wife's charms to tell her feet apart from another's, quickly fell out of the repertoire, suggesting the first night was less than a resounding success.

SIX

Praskovia's Debut

Praskovia didn't perform that night. It's possible that she was there in the wings, watching and learning. The thrill of the evening must have filled her with nervous excitement, just as it did the rest of the troupe, and Nicholas and his father. Praskovia spent that winter and spring in Moscow rehearsing and waiting. Nicholas put on a second work, *The Painter in Love with his Model,* by the Italian master of opera buffa, Egidio Duni, on 7 February. In late May, the Sheremetev household packed up and left for Kuskovo. There, on 28 June, the company performed Desbrosses' comedy *The Two Cousins* in honor of Nicholas's golden birthday.

The next day had been set for the premier of Grétry's *Friendship Put to the Test,* which Nicholas had selected "for its elegant and pleasing music."[1] Based on one of Marmontel's *Moral Tales,* the opera is a story of the struggle between duty and love. Nelson, a member of the British Parliament, falls in love with Corali, a young Indian girl entrusted to his care by his friend Blandfort. A ship's captain, Blandfort had saved Corali during an attack by his fellow British soldiers during the Seven Years' War that left her Brahmin father dead. His budding love for Corali leads Nelson to despair, torn between his affection for his charge and his sense of duty and friendship for Blandfort, now away at sea. Corali divines Nelson's feelings and confesses her own for him, adding that she had always looked upon Blandfort as a father, not a lover, and that he had always impressed upon her the importance of being free to marry whomever she wished.

Nelson tries to flee London for the country when Blandfort suddenly returns. Blandfort implores his friend to postpone his departure, for he is on his way now to fetch the notary for his wedding to Corali. Overwhelmed, Nelson retreats to his study, grabs a pistol, and prepares to take his own life when he is restrained by Corali and his sister, Lady Juliette. Blandfort comes back with the notary and learns the truth after Corali breaks down and confesses. Blandfort, informed of Nelson and Corali's mutual love, blesses their union and even has the notary sign over all his property to his happy friends in the event he is killed in the war.

Friendship Put to the Test reflected opéra-comique's preoccupation with affairs of the heart, and particularly the question of marriage, a question that Nicholas and Praskovia would struggle with themselves for many years and that would come to dominate the plays and operas Nicholas chose for his theater. The plots, so common in the era of the Enlightenment, invariably revolved around the complications arising from the obstacles of caste and estate and, in this instance, race and culture that society placed before true love.

Stepanida Degtiareva played the role of Corali and Tatiana Bedenkova that of Lady Juliette; two gifted young tenors, Grigory Kokhanovsky (as Nelson) and Andrei Novikov (as Blandfort), made their debuts. The playbill listed another new performer that day: "Praskovia Ivanovna Gorbunova" in the role of Hubert, Lady Juliette's chambermaid.

Praskovia made her first appearance at the beginning of act 1, scene 5. It was an inauspicious debut, consisting of six words addressed to Corali while walking, without pause (so the stage directions), across the stage: "Ma'am, your singing instructor has arrived." Her biggest part came in act 2, scene 2 when Corali, having learned Nelson has decided to leave for the country, prepares to return to India:

CORALI: A ship is leaving this evening for Madrid. Embrace me, ah, you will never see me again.
HUBERT: What are you planning on doing?
CORALI: To leave forever this terrible land where it is forbidden to love, to speak the truth . . . Please, don't tell a soul . . . Leave me . . . Farewell . . .

HUBERT: (*Upset, leaving.*) Poor Corali! I must tell Julie of this, for it would be dangerous for me to keep quiet.[2]

There were two more appearances, both without lines, and that was it. It was a modest role, to be sure, but fitting for a girl a month shy of her eleventh birthday and one that left a strong impression. After a year of lessons and training and watching the others perform, of no doubt impatiently waiting for her opportunity to join them but vaguely aware of a nervous light-headedness that intensified as the hour of her debut approached, Praskovia had now felt the rush of adrenaline that came with performing on stage. As she joined hands with the rest of the cast at the front of the stage to take her bow and the audience's warm applause filled her ears, Praskovia couldn't help but feel a surge of pride. This had been one of the biggest days of her young life.

Impressed as they were by the undeniable skill and budding professionalism of Nicholas's theater, the audience was taken aback by what they saw that day in the playbill. Instead of listing his serf performers by the familiar form of their given names—Masha, Pasha, and the like, as was the norm—Nicholas had supplied their full names, including their patronymics, the second name taken from one's father.[3] This was most unusual and in the eyes of his peers amounted to a suspicious breech of etiquette. It elevated their status and lent them a degree of social recognition, indeed respect, that few if any noblemen would have considered warranted or advisable, and it suggested odd notions about the proper attitude toward serfs that lurked in their host's head.

Praskovia's talent must have been considerable, for a little over a year after her debut Nicholas chose her to sing the lead of Belinda in Antonio Sacchini's *The Colony* even though she was only twelve years old. The decision may have been forced on Nicholas. Around this time Tatiana Bedenkova fell ill, possibly with tuberculosis, and his other leading lady, Stepanida, was apparently sick as well. Nicholas could have canceled further performances until he had time to train some of his more mature performers, yet he took a risk by handing the part to Praskovia, a sign of his confidence in her abilities. Recalling these years, Nicholas wrote, "One of the girls was blessed with natural abilities and shined with greater promise than all the others; the best experts were invited to teach her, and these pleasant experiences quickly gave rise to the hope that with time they would produce great success."[4]

Throughout the late summer and fall of 1780, Praskovia rehearsed intensely with Voroblevsky, Nicholas, and the rest of the cast. Sacchini's music was melodic and moving and filled with dramatic and difficult arias. No one could be certain her young voice was ready for such a technically demanding part, or that a girl of her age could make audiences believe that she was a full-grown woman in the grip of a passionate love.

It was dark when a crush of sleighs and carriages, their passengers wrapped in heavy furs against the cold, pulled into the courtyard of the Chinese House in the early evening hours of 5 November 1780. Liveried footmen briskly opened the conveyances' gilded doors, and noblemen and their ladies in their damask and silk and lace spilled out into a blast of frigid air and hurried toward the warmth and soft light beckoning through the mansion's windows. They were greeted by their host, Peter, and shown to the theater.

Backstage, Praskovia was getting into costume and applying her makeup. Next to her sat another young actress, Anna Buianova, about to make her debut. One can imagine the air of nervous anticipation that filled the room and feel the nauseating butterflies fluttering about in their stomachs. Adding to the tension, Peter had a last-minute surprise for the two singers. They would no longer perform under their real names, but as the gems of his theater: Anna was to be "the Emerald" and Praskovia, "the Pearl." The girls must have been stunned and scared to think their performances might not measure up to such precious names. In time other gems were added: Arina "the Sapphire" Kalmykova, Fekla "the Turquoise" Uruzova, Avdotia "the Amethyst" Kochedykova, Arina "the Crystal" Sitova. Peter did not forget the men. There was Kuzma "the Cornelian" Deulin, Nicholas "the Marble" Serov, Andrei "the Flint" Zhukov, Roman "the Coral" Peshnikov, and the somewhat out-of-place Ivan "the Hopeful" Voshchin.

After the guests had exchanged greetings and taken their seats and the bright house lights had been doused, the curtain rose to reveal a recently settled island. A road cuts through a dense forest, at the end of which stands a tent. In the distance, a bit of the sea can be discerned. On their way across the Atlantic Ocean to the island of Martinique, a group of colonists has been caught in a violent storm, their ships became separated and eventually washed up on the shores of a deserted island. Two pairs of lovers—Fontalb and Belinda, Blaise and Marina (in Voroblevsky's Russian translation)—lose each other in the mayhem. Fontalb, the newly chosen governor of the colony, proposes marriage to the beautiful peasant Marina after learning, falsely, that Belinda has betrayed him by marrying another. When Belinda hears the news, she is distraught and flees the island in a small boat, hoping to drown in a storm brewing at sea.

Fontalb learns the truth of Belinda's innocence and rushes to save her. Reunited, the truth revealed, Fontalb and Belinda warmly embrace, forgive each other, and promise to marry. Blaise must now forgive Marina, and she assures him that it was he she loved all along. As the curtain falls, harmony has been restored.

The opera was a success, and Praskovia's performance as Belinda showed that Nicholas's confidence in her had not been misplaced. Despite her age and inexperience, despite the fact that the role of Belinda demanded of Praskovia the expression of emotions that she was herself still only dimly aware, despite the immaturity of her voice, which was years away from attaining its full beauty and range, the audience had found her believable.

But her success was owing to more than just her voice. Praskovia was a gifted actress as well. Perhaps because of the harsh realities in the Kovalyov home and the need to grow up quickly after moving to the Big House, she had a precocious maturity that made her appear older than her years and great depths of sympathy that permitted her to identify completely with the characters she played. Although important for any dramatic performance, these qualities were especially important in Enlightenment opéra-comique, which aimed to create a harmony of feeling between performer and spectator. The emotions displayed on the stage were intended to strike a chord of recognition in the members of the audience and so move them to a realization of a shared humanity. The guiltlessly suffering heroine, virtuous, true, self-sacrificing, and dutiful, swept away by the passions of first love, as exemplified by Belinda, was a stock figure in these operas, and they became Praskovia's *emploi*. Throughout her career she would revisit this role over and over again. It was a role that later mirrored the one she played off the stage as well.

SEVEN

Early Success

Praskovia did not have long to savor her debut. Within days she and the other performers were busy rehearsing the next opera. Ever since he had heard Monsigny's *The Deserter* during his stay in Paris, Nicholas had been enthralled by its triumphant yet deeply moving music, suffused with the early roots of romanticism. *The Deserter* was wildly popular, and all of Europe was swept away by its musical charms.[1] The craze also gripped Russia. The opera had premiered at court in 1775 and been performed at Moscow's Petrovsky Theater four years later. Nicholas was the first to produce it in Russian on 7 February 1781.

The stage is set to depict a French army camp near the border with Flanders. The young soldier Alexis has been granted leave to visit his fiancée, the farmer's daughter Louise. Upon his return he sees Louise about to marry her cousin Bertrand. Distraught, Alexis runs away and is arrested and sentenced to death as a deserter. When she learns of Alexis's impending execution, Louise, who had been forced to play this cruel joke on her beloved by the wicked archduchess, vows to save him. Louise stops at nothing to win an audience with the king (conveniently passing through the area at the time), tells him of this injustice, and convinces him to pardon Alexis. Louise rushes to deliver the king's amnesty, arriving just as the soldiers are about to shoot Alexis.[2] Monsigny's music heightens the passions of the story. Expressive and direct, it rises and falls in cascading waves of crescendos, evoking the shifting emotional states of the protagonists. The overture was especially moving and struck a chord with operagoers.

Praskovia and the serf tenor Grigory Kokhanovsky sang the leads. Andrei Novikov played the role of a judge, and Stepan Degtiarev that of Bertrand. Anna the Emerald also performed, as did Arina the Sapphire. Arina was the sister of Peter Kalmykov, the orchestra's future assistant Kapellmeister and Praskovia's brother-in-law.

It was at this performance that Johann-Heinrich Facius most likely made his first appearance. Facius had been born in Bonn, where as a young man he became an accomplished cellist and contrabassist and frequented the home of the city's most famous musical son, Ludwig van Beethoven. In 1780, he moved to Moscow and the next year joined Nicholas's orchestra, playing alongside his serfs for 1,225 rubles a year. Nicholas appointed Facius first cello and second violin and asked him to conduct during the performances. He and Nicholas hit it off well, and Facius was permitted to take his meals at the count's table. He remained with the orchestra until Nicholas shut down his theater following Praskovia's retirement. After Facius's death, Nicholas provided his widow with a yearly pension of 500 rubles.

The Deserter was another success for the Sheremetev theater. Despite her age (she was only twelve years old) and limited experience, Praskovia again pulled off the role of Louise in a convincing manner. In the final scene, she races, shoes in her hands, her dark curls waving in wild streaks behind her, to deliver the joyous news to Alexis, almost certain she is too late. Bursting into the jail and disbelieving her eyes, she collapses in her beloved's arms, saying, "Alexis, you . . ." before passing out from shock. The curtain fell to cries of "Fora! Fora! Bravo! Bravo!" and loud applause. Some in the audience tossed coin-filled purses onto the stage to show their approval, an act that would be repeated over and over during her career.[3]

News of the Sheremetev theater had by now spread throughout Moscow and beyond. In early 1781, the dramatist Vasily Kolychev wrote to Peter of his amazement with his theater: "Two years ago, upon departing for St. Petersburg, I left Your Excellency's theater in its infancy; but having recently returned to Moscow, I saw it much grown up since then."[4]

So impressed was Kolychev that he wrote a "pastoral opera," with music selected from several French opéras-comiques, especially for the Sheremetev theater titled *Futile Jealousy, or the Kuskovo Boatman*, which debuted that same summer at the outdoor theater. Kuskovo was both the venue and the setting for the opera: the stage was decorated to depict a smaller version of the estate where the work was being presented. The libretto praised the count's hospitality and taste and wealth as if he were a king. Praises were sung to the wonders of Kuskovo, including the theater: "Liza, let's go to Kuskovo," says the shepherd Likandr to his beloved. "Let's see how they amuse themselves there—Maybe we'll be lucky enough to look through the windows of that building they call a theater—I've heard said they depict boyars and shepherds in love there."[5]

Despite the local color, *Futile Jealousy* is the usual fare of *paysannerie*. The shepherdesses Aniuta and Liza love Lubim and Likandr (played, respectively, by Praskovia, Anna, Grigory, and Andrei) yet doubt their fidelity. Likewise the two shepherds suspect their beloveds have been cheating. Their mutual suspicions upend the couples' plans to attend one of the fabled fêtes at Kuskovo. Praskovia once more played the role of the fair maiden wrongly accused. She suffers stoically Lubim's hurtful words and accusations, refusing to give up hope that their love can be saved. Despite the pain in her heart, Aniuta places her friend's welfare first and manages to reconcile Liza and Likandr, and they, in turn, help Lubim to see the error of his thinking. The lovers are reunited and harmony is restored.

On 28 June, Nicholas celebrated his thirtieth birthday. No longer a young man by the standards of the time, Nicholas's reluctance to marry and the details of his rather mysterious private life were becoming the source of gossip and speculation. On 2 November 1781, Prince Alexei Kurakin wrote his brother Alexander that Nicholas was "delighted to be near Mlle Chérémeteff who, it is said, is very likely to be married to him." Whether the Sheremeteva in question was Yelena, the previous object of his affection, or her sister, Martha, as some believed, isn't clear. Either way, the talk of marriage came to nothing. That same year Princess Yelena Viazemskaia, a distant relation of Nicholas's and the wife of Procurator-General Prince Alexander Viazemsky, tried to arrange a match between Nicholas and one of her daughters, without success.[6]

It is one of the curious things about Nicholas that with the exception of his Sheremetev cousins he does not appear to have been drawn to women of his own class. It wasn't that Nicholas was indifferent to the opposite sex; far from it—Nicholas never could go for long without a woman. But the women he found most appealing tended to be his own serfs.

One of his mistresses was apparently a Kuskovo serf by the name of Anna Ivanovna. On 2 June 1780, Anna gave birth to a son. A year later Nicholas took the boy to him as his "ward," the term Russian nobles favored for their illegitimate children. He was given the name Ivan Yaki-mov. Nicholas loved Vaniusha, as he always called him, dearly and doted on the sickly little boy. After his death in 1804, Nicholas recalled that "he was never not by my side; on short and long trips, on visits and at home, on the briefest walks in silence, he always accompanied me."[7] As a young boy Ivan showed artistic talent. He was a gifted drawer and dancer, later appearing on his father's stage as Cupid. Nicholas later commissioned a ballet in his name—*Vaniushin*—in which Ivan starred.

Anna wasn't the only serf Nicholas found himself attracted to. Legend has it that Nicholas had numerous mistresses among his serf actresses. A spectator of a Sheremetev performance observed, "It goes without saying that the actresses and the ballerinas are practically the same as the bench on which the count sits while watching the performances, . . . that is, his property, and so must they also please him in another way in those instances when one of them strikes his fancy and he drops his handkerchief at her feet."[8] These words gave birth to the story, no doubt apocryphal, that after rehearsals Nicholas would casually drop his handkerchief at the feet of the one who caught his eye for the moment and then come for it, and a bit more, that night. This is, of course, the stuff of romance novels; nevertheless, Nicholas was far from chaste and was not above exercising his *droit du seigneur*.

The actress Tatiana Bedenkova appears to have been his first mistress from the troupe. Decades after Nicholas's death an elderly Tatiana Shly-kova recalled a serf mistress with the same name as she who had died of consumption in her arms in the early 1780s. She refused to tell Nicholas's inquisitive grandson any more than that, likely out of respect for Pra-skovia. Bedenkova may have been the mother of Nicholas's second illegitimate child, Alexandra Remeteva, born 7 April 1782, whom Nicholas called Aleksasha.[9]

There were three other Remetev children at Kuskovo: Anastasia, Yakov, and Margarita. They were the illegitimate children of Nicholas's father, born to him after he left St. Petersburg. As was common among the nobility, Peter gave these children part of his last name—all but the first syllable—to acknowledge the blood relation without going so far as to recognize them as full members of the family. Their mother was apparently a serf by the name of Alyona Stepanovna. Aleksasha and the other Remetevs lived in a modest house in La Solitude with a small number of servants, Alyona, and Peter, who had ceded the Big House to Nicholas.

Praskovia remained with her friend Tatiana in the Big House. She may have still been under the supervision of Princess Dolgorukaia, though that seems unlikely since the princess would have been over eighty years old and had most likely died by now. Summers were the happiest time for Praskovia, months when she could be near her family in the Old Quarter. Since she had left home two more children had appeared—Nicholas, around 1777, and Michael, in 1780. Although rehearsals left her little free time, Praskovia managed to escape for brief visits to see her mother and father and play with her young brothers. Her feelings of estrangement from her family had been eased after her younger sister, Matryona, had also been taken into the Big House to be trained alongside her. Matryona debuted in the role of a shepherdess in the Russian comic opera *Misfortune from a Coach* around 1780.

Praskovia's parents had to have been amazed by their daughter's transformation. They had given her up a simple peasant girl, and after a few years she came back to them more like a child of the nobility. She wore expensive clothes, she walked and talked with a new manner, she could read and write and was learning foreign languages; she had become an actress and singer of considerable promise, and she moved in worlds about which they hadn't the slightest understanding or experience. Yet despite all this, Praskovia appears never to have turned her back on her family or looked down on them. She loved and cared for them, and later, when her place alongside Nicholas became relatively secure, she used her influence to make their lives easier. Praskovia had left the peasant world behind, but it seems she never forgot where she came from.

The rest of the summer of 1781 and on into the next was a busy time in the life of the troupe. In addition to *Futile Jealousy*, they rehearsed and staged four new operas, two comedies, and a short musical by the name of *The Kuskovo Nymph*. The first of the operas, Nicolas-Jean Le Froid de Méreaux's *Laurette*, debuted late in 1781 in Moscow with Praskovia in the title role.

Like so many of the era's opéras-comiques, *Laurette* is a tale of forbidden love, although with a twist. Count Liuzzi has fallen in love with Loretta (as the heroine became in Voroblevsky's translation), and his life has turned upside down. But there's a problem: Loretta is a peasant, the daughter of a retired soldier, Vasily. The count's friend, Marquis Klantz, advises him to leave in order to forget her, for there's no way they can ever be together. Meanwhile, Vasily is busy trying to find a suitable match for his beloved only child. He has set his sights on Kolen, a poor yet honest peasant. Loretta, however, loves the count, not Kolen. She tells her father that Kolen is crude and simple, while acknowledging that she is ready to submit to her father's will. Loretta is the personification of goodness, and "virtue radiates from all her features."

Count Liuzzi confesses his love to Loretta and implores her to overlook the great social distance separating them: "Oh, be calm, Loretta. Love has made you my equal. And does it recognize any difference between us? . . . My noble status, my titles, my wealth—I lay them all at your feet, but say it, Loretta, make me happy, tell me you love me." Loretta is stunned and doesn't know how to reply, except to say that the villagers are sure to be jealous and to think the worst when they hear of the count's affection for her.[10]

Realizing the danger toward which the count is heading, the marquis tries once more to convince his friend to flee. In a pleading aria he sings, "Passionate love is a dangerous thing!/For those whose hearts it burns there'll be many troubles./He doesn't know what he's doing./My count has lost himself./He doesn't recognize inequality,/He's going to marry a peasant,/And he thinks of no one else."[11]

Count Liuzzi realizes his friend is right and begs Loretta to leave the village immediately and elope without bothering to tell her father. He tells her his family is forcing him to make an "advantageous" marriage to a woman of a good family whom he doesn't love. He is convinced Loretta's father would never agree to their marrying, so there's no point in asking for his blessing. But he assures Loretta that he will see to it Vasily is well cared for. Time is running out. They must act now or it will be too late and they may never see each other again.

Vasily overhears these words and rushes to save his daughter. Before the count can explain, Vasily accuses him of trying to buy his daughter and of destroying her reputation. The count pleads his case before Vasily and eventually wears him down, convincing him that his love for Loretta is true. At this point Vasily divulges the family secret about which even Loretta knows nothing: he too is a nobleman and was once a wealthy and proud officer in the army. Yet after losing all his money and status, he had felt it necessary to hide the family's noble status in order to protect Loretta from grief and embarrassment. Loretta and the count are overjoyed. They can now marry without cause for shame. The curtain falls to universal rejoicing in the village and the manor.[12]

In the autumn of 1782, Peter was elected marshal of the Moscow provincial nobility, and Nicholas was chosen one of the ten district marshals. The delegation departed Moscow at the end of November for a round of meetings and receptions in the capital, where they arrived on 7 December. Four days later they were presented to the empress in the Winter Palace. This was Peter's first time back in St. Petersburg since leaving for Kuskovo fourteen years earlier. If he had any fond memories of his decades spent there, he kept them to himself, and his letters home are filled with disdain for the "vanity" of the court and the capital. It didn't help the count's mood that a bitter cold had descended on the city, plunging temperatures to minus thirty-one degrees Fahrenheit.[13]

Only two things gave the count pleasure. One was seeing Catherine the Great again and being granted entrée to her private apartments. Here Peter, Catherine, Alexander Lanskoy (her current favorite), and a handful of the empress's intimates would sit up till late in the evening playing cards, chatting, and reminiscing about the old days to the sound of sneezes and sniffles (Catherine and Lanskoy had come down with nasty colds). The other pleasure was the newly unveiled equestrian statue of Peter the Great—immortalized in Alexander Pushkin's *The Bronze Horseman*—by Etienne Falconet. So impressed was the count that he had his coachmen drive him past it on every possible occasion.

The delegation remained in St. Petersburg until early January 1783.

The end of its visit was celebrated by a feast at Prince Grigory Potemkin's. In keeping with Potemkin's grand style, the food was served on richly gilded plates and in such massive quantities that Peter complained Potemkin "stuffs us like pigs being readied for slaughter" and griped of an awful stomachache. After a month in the capital he was more than ready to leave for home.[14]

Nicholas said goodbye to his father and stayed on until the middle of the month so he could attend a ball given by Grand Duke Paul. Nicholas had been having a much better time than his father, although his thoughts were often with the girls back home, one in particular. "Annushka," he wrote to Anna Kalmychka, "my dearest, hello! Please pass on my compliments to the princess and sweet little Parasha."[15]

EIGHT

Serf Diva, Serf Mistress

The nature of Nicholas's feelings for "sweet little Parasha" is difficult to establish, although it seems clear that by now his interest in her was moving beyond the purely theatrical. After her death, Nicholas described in a letter to their son those first sparks of love that took flame during these years:

> Blessed with a quick mind, a humble manner, and attractive spiritual qualities, she drew my special attention and care; I saw to her education and as yet not aware of the stirrings beginning in my soul, I chiefly thought about preparing her for the theater. Her natural talent for music and her superlative voice amazed the many friends who attended the performances at our home. Such fruits, I might say, of my own labors, accompanied at first by the innocent attentions I gave this pupil, could not help but make a special impression on my feelings. My affection for her began to become clear to me, although by my disposition I had never been a philanderer who seeks dissipation for my pleasure. The strict rules of family life laid down in olden days have always been my guide; no debauched woman could ever ensnare me, and even the mere thought of becoming a prisoner of seductive passion produced in me disdain that has protected me from contamination. The path of honest constancy has always been the goal toward

which I have strived. What is more, the one creature upon whom my eyes always fed, igniting the spark of tender love, found its way into the depths of my heart, creating a spiritual union for all time.[1]

There is a good deal of wishful thinking, self-delusion, and exhortative moralizing in these lines. In this same letter he admits to his youthful "lost days" that led him to "violate the purity of God's laws."[2] When Prince Alexander Kurakin once complained of "inflammation" in a particularly sensitive area of the body, Nicholas gave him a knowing reply. "Believe me, my dear friend," he wrote, "you didn't get this from your horse. Try to limit your amorous encounters, for they are the sole cause of your discomfort. Trust me as a doctor who can judge such matters both by my own experience and knowledge."[3]

Praskovia was still just fourteen years old when Nicholas returned from St. Petersburg. It is possible that Nicholas is being honest when he writes that his attentions for her were still innocent, although it is impossible to say for certain. In a short history of Praskovia's life composed after her death, Nicholas, writing in the third person, suggests that she had become his mistress even earlier. The many long hours spent in rehearsal made him aware of Praskovia's unusual talent and character. It wasn't long before he found himself drawn to her:

His Excellency Count Nicholas Petrovich Sheremetev, . . . who had a special inclination to this delicate talent and had been a witness to the growing successes of this attractive charge in her still flowering youth, often enjoyed the pleasure of studying music with her himself, lending taste and style to her abilities as well as the further perfection of her talent. These frequent exercises led him over time to a fuller appreciation for her excellent spiritual gifts and moral qualities with which Countess Praskovia Ivanovna had been blessed. The spark of their tender love grew, and their spiritual attachment to each other became eternal! They were never apart, during which time this loyal wife, devoted with all her emotions, forever living with one will, with one desire, and with passionate commitment to her husband, and this, combined with their having grown accustomed to each other over twenty years, was the sole reason she gained the respect that led him to raise her up to the highest rung of worldly happiness.[4]

By "highest rung" Nicholas meant marriage, which implies that their relationship might have begun as early as 1781, when Praskovia was thirteen years old. Much depends on what Nicholas meant by "accustomed." Did their being around each other every day extend beyond rehearsing and music making to include something more? Offensive though the notion is to our sensitivities, it would not have been in the eighteenth century. In *The Parting, or the Hunters' Departure from Kuskovo,* an opera composed for the Sheremetev theater in 1785, Anna the Emerald sings to her teenage niece, played by Praskovia, "at fifteen it's time to begin to love and to live."[5]

If Nicholas had indeed added Praskovia to his favorites as early as 1781, he kept it quiet. The earliest evidence of Nicholas's attraction doesn't come until early May 1784, when, in excited if somewhat veiled terms, he wrote to his friend Kurakin to tell him of his infatuation with "le petit nez musical," the little musical nose, his code name for Praskovia.[6]

Whatever the exact nature of their relationship, Nicholas clearly had his eye on Praskovia by now. As the rising star of his theater and the growing object of his attention, Praskovia began spending more time with Nicholas, not only together with the troupe, but alone. Nicholas worked with Praskovia on her various roles, rehearsing her parts and offering instruction on her acting. Nicholas supervised her lessons on the clavichord and fortepiano. Praskovia's education went well beyond music, and Nicholas made sure she received instruction in religion, history, literature, and Italian and French from Signor Ignatio Torelli.

Kuskovo's immense library (nearly twenty thousand volumes) included the major works on architecture, astronomy, geography, the classics, history, theology, natural history, physics, philosophy, and belles lettres. Here were the writings of the French philosophes—Voltaire, Montesquieu, Diderot, and Rousseau. There were books by Corneille, Fontaine, Molière, Cervantes, Milton, and Pope. There were French translations of Henry Fielding's *Joseph Andrews* and *Tom Jones,* Laurence Sterne's *A Sentimental Journey,* and Samuel Richardson's *Pamela.* There was a collection of erotica kept separately under lock and key that included books with alluring titles like *Venus in the Cloister, or The Nun in*

Her Chemise (with illustrations) and *The Sensual Life between the Capuchin Friars and the Nuns* and a number of bucolic genre prints of shepherds and shepherdesses, hunters and fishermen that, when one slid an inconspicuous lever, transformed themselves to reveal their subjects arranged in lewd poses.

Books from the library, with the likely exception of the pornographic items, formed part of Praskovia's education. Nicholas also lent her works on theater and music to read as well as instruction manuals on singing and acting. Praskovia's introduction to the writings of St. Dmitry of Rostov, which became her chief source of spiritual comfort in later years, may have taken place about this time. The hours spent reading, like the time spent on stage, allowed Praskovia to escape to another world where she could forget she was a serf and imagine herself to be someone else, if only for a while. These hours of escape were only temporary, and their brevity, combined with the beauty of the worlds they hinted at, highlighted her lack of freedom.

Friendship provided comfort. Tatiana took lessons alongside Praskovia, and together they practiced French and Italian and read literature. By the age of fourteen Tatiana had become a good drawer and woodcarver, and, although she had a wonderful voice, Tatiana's talent as a dancer was most evident, and she was given intensive dance lessons.

Within weeks of writing Kurakin about "le petit nez musical" in the spring of 1784 Nicholas fell ill. He began bleeding heavily from his posterior, and the doctors had to be called to Kuskovo. They blamed his ailment on the unusually hot and dry weather and suggested this was also the reason they were unable to stop the bleeding. At first Nicholas kept his spirits up, but after several months passed and he continued to suffer from bleeding and severe pain despite the doctors' best efforts, he grew weak and downcast.

Nicholas's health problems had begun the year before upon his return from St. Petersburg. Since the grand tour Nicholas had enjoyed relatively good health and an active life, "abundant with pleasure," to quote his physician.[7] And then suddenly he was hit by prolonged bouts of constipation and what appeared to be hemorrhoids. He tried to soothe the pain himself with cocoa butter, but this brought little relief. Red puffy sores broke out over much of his body, and he succumbed to a "bilious fever," perhaps an attack of gallstones causing bloating, nausea, and intense abdominal pains.[8] Nicholas eventually recovered, but he was a changed man. He became withdrawn and moody, subject to depression, and he increasingly sought out solitude. He began poring over medical texts in his free time to gain insight into his condition. His physicians made a diagnosis of "hypochondriac anxiety" and noted signs of "melancholy," eighteenth-century terminology for what we would today call depression, which had afflicted others in the Sheremetev family. For the rest of his life Nicholas would suffer from a range of debilitating and painful maladies—catarrhs, convulsions, carbuncles, boils, unexplained rashes and stomach cramps (possibly signs of porphyria). The treatments (bloodletting, leeches, ice baths, poultices, herbal pills and powders, laxatives) left him listless and weak. One long bloodletting caused Nicholas to lose consciousness for over thirty minutes. The periods of good health were few, and when he was well Nicholas couldn't stop obsessing about his health.

Nonetheless, Nicholas continued to work on the theater, and the mid-1780s marked the beginning of its most active period. Nicholas gave himself over completely to making the company the best in Russia. Between 1784 and 1788, the Sheremetev theater staged over forty different productions: eighteen opéras-comiques, eight comedies, fourteen ballets, and two lyric dramas or grand operas. Of these, well over half were presented only on the Sheremetev stage and nowhere else in Russia.

A key figure in the life of the theater during these years was Monsieur Hyvart, Nicholas's friend from his Paris visit. Nicholas realized Russia lacked the resources to develop his theater as he wished and wrote to Hyvart asking him to become his homme d'affaires for all things theatrical. Hyvart was flattered by the offer and devoted himself wholeheartedly to his new work. No request of the count's was too trivial for Hyvart, no task too demanding. Their correspondence, which lasted nearly two decades, opens a window onto Nicholas's theater mania—his obsessive desire to have the newest works before anyone else in Russia, his fascination with the smallest details of costume and makeup and props, his nearly fanatical preoccupation with the latest developments in theater construction and machinery for achieving the most realistic special effects.

Once or twice a year Hyvart packed up large wooden crates with Nicholas's orders. The crates were sent by barge down the Seine River to

Rouen, where they were placed on ships heading out to sea at Le Havre and from there on to St. Petersburg. In the winter when the river was frozen, the crates went overland by carriage to Lübeck and from there by ship.

Hyvart sent copies of dozens of operas and plays, often in various editions to reflect minor changes; he sent the music for unpublished vaudevilles, romances, and arias, for symphonies, chamber works, and sacred oratorios; he sent scores and descriptions for ballets, even those that had not yet been performed, manuals on the latest Italian techniques of vocal instruction, prints and drawings depicting the native dress of exotic peoples to help with costume designs, costumed dolls, plans and cross-sectional depictions of Paris's main theaters, and a large model theater complete with miniature working machinery; he sent the finest violin, bass, and harp strings from Naples, rose garlands of cambric for the leading ladies, ostrich, heron, and kite bird feathers in all hues, Parisian silk stockings, semiprecious stones, and costume jewelry; he sent two hundred jars of liquid pomade of various scents (rose, jasmine, heliotrope, tuberose, vanilla) from Provence to perfume the actresses, hundreds of pounds of powder, two dozen tortoise-shell combs, yards and yards of black hair ribbon, three hundred toothbrushes, and even a pair of tight-fitting gloves and a face covering of black gauze for operas with Moors. By the late 1790s, Nicholas had acquired over five thousand costumes, one thousand pairs of shoes, and an equal number of headdresses.[9]

Hyvart fed Nicholas's hunger for the very latest. Like any passionate collector, Nicholas had to have what couldn't be had. When Hyvart got his hands on an ariette from Grétry's *Richard the Lion-Hearted* for Nicholas without the composer's knowledge, he wrote, "Grétry would fly into a rage if he knew someone else in Paris other than he had a copy of this!"[10] In 1787, he secretly made a copy of an aria for Nicholas from Antonio Salieri's *Tarar,* which had just gone into rehearsals. After searching for three months for a copy of the libretto to Christoph Willibald Gluck's *Alceste,* Hyvart finally went to see the great composer himself, who gave him his own dog-eared, heavily marked copy, which Hyvart, overflowing with self-approbation, forwarded to Nicholas. All of this endeared Hyvart to Nicholas and made him feel as if he were part of the Parisian theater scene.

Hyvart did more than act as Nicholas's Parisian buyer. He also kept him informed of the most recent developments in the world of opera. Although opéra-comique was as frequently performed as during Nicholas's grand tour, lyric tragedy had grown in popularity, as best exemplified by the work of the reformer Gluck and his epigoni. These new operas required much more complicated staging and special effects, larger theaters, more advanced theatrical machinery, and more accomplished singers and musicians. Nicholas was the first in Russia to receive librettos and scores of Gluck's new operas, and they swept him off his feet. He was especially drawn to Gluck's *Alceste* and *Iphigénie en Tauride*. But the opera he admired most was Salieri's *Les Danaïdes*. "The music is so beautiful," Nicholas wrote Hyvart, "I've fallen utterly in love with it."[11]

Salieri's opera had everything about the new style that moved him: large, intricate stagings, all manner of spectacular special effects (thunder, lightning, floods, castles that collapsed in walls of flames), numerous set changes, and an intensely dramatic plot. Nicholas wrote to Hyvart seeking precise details about the staging, but Hyvart replied that the new operas required much larger stages than Nicholas had at Kuskovo and Moscow and so it wouldn't be possible to perform them. Undeterred, Nicholas sent plans of his theaters to Hyvart instructing him to hire artists and set designers in Paris to construct scaled-down models and sets that would work in his theaters. Throughout 1785 and 1786 Nicholas obsessed over the opera and the complexities involved in producing it. He hounded Hyvart for more models and specific details on how the special effects were to be done in a convincing manner. Nicholas initially wanted to stage the opera in September 1786, and then that autumn pushed it back to July of the following year. Despite the great time, money, and work devoted to *Les Danaïdes,* it never did appear on the Sheremetev stage.

As the months dragged on and the difficulties surrounding the production of Salieri's opera grew, Nicholas realized he would have to build a bigger theater if he wanted to produce the new operas. In the summer of 1785, he wrote Hyvart of his plan to commission a new theater. There was no one in Russia with the knowledge of the latest designs, so he placed the work in Hyvart's hands. Hyvart was soon sending Nicholas plans and precise models for the special effects machinery—the "thunder device" guaranteed "to instill ineffable terror" in the audience and "la gloire" capable of whisking actors up into the air and off into the wings.[12] By the end of the year work on the new theater at Kuskovo had begun. The plans included a radical new idea: building a parterre that could be raised after performances to the level of the stage, thus transforming the theater into an expansive ballroom. Nicholas did eventually build such a theater, but not for another ten years, and not at Kuskovo, but Ostankino.

As work got under way at Kuskovo Nicholas decided to continue staging smaller operas better suited to his theater. Hyvart sent him the latest successes from the Parisian stage — *The Beautiful Arsene* and *Aline, Queen of Golconde* by Monsigny, *The Comic Duel* by Giovanni Paisiello, and Grétry's *Lucile* and *The Marriage of the Samnites,* the last of which would be his company's greatest opera and Praskovia's most famous role.

This period saw an intensive effort to expand the troupe's dance repertoire and improve its corps de ballet. Previously ballets had figured solely as divertissements between opera acts. Although this continued, Nicholas, as part of his effort to mimic as accurately as possible the practices of the Parisian theater, pushed the creation of full balletic works. Nicholas knew ballet, having danced as a child at court and being acquainted with the work of the great choreographic innovator Jean-Georges Noverre. In 1786, Charles Le Picq, a student of Noverre, arrived in Russia, and Nicholas sent Tatiana Shlykova and Yelena Kazakova to St. Petersburg to study under him. Two years later he hired the respected Italian Giuseppe Salomoni, another follower of Noverre, as his troupe's ballet master.

Again, Hyvart recommended the most popular ballets to Nicholas, many of which were based on the day's opéras-comiques. Nicholas staged Noverre's *Annette and Lubin,* from the eponymous opera, starring Tatiana, and *Ninette at Court* by the other great choreographer of the day, Maximilien Gardel, based on Duni's opéra-comique of the same name. Nicholas also commissioned new works specifically for his dancers, including *Mavrin,* named after his dancer Mavra "the Turquoise" Uruzova, and ballets on mythological (*Cupid with a Garland, Cupid with a String, Thyrsus*) and national (the Spanish, the Dutch, the Turkish Ballets) themes.

By 1790, Nicholas's ballet was among the finest in Russia. His dancers introduced the latest balletic works from France and surpassed in this genre the ballets of both the court in St. Petersburg and Moscow's Petrovsky Theater. Such supremacy would continue throughout the next decade, during which Nicholas's corps de ballet would play a central role in bringing to Russia the latest developments in choreography and particularly the new school of Noverre, staging pathbreaking pieces such as his tragic *ballet d'action Medea* ten years before the Petrovsky Theater, and encouraging Diderot's notions of dance as an independent art form.

These years were the most productive of Praskovia's career, filled with never-ending rehearsals, performances, and the demands of learning new roles. Between 1784 and 1786, she appeared in six operas: *The Three Farmers* by Nicolas Dezéde, *L'infante de Zamora* by Paisiello, *The Parting, or the Hunters' Departure from Kuskovo*, a comic opera written for the Sheremetev theater, Grétry's *The Marriage of the Samnites*, and *The Beautiful Arsene* and *Aline, Queen of Golconde* by Monsigny.

Seven other operas and comedies premiered on the Sheremetev stage during these years. The names of the performers are not known, but it seems likely that Praskovia sang in some, if not all, of them. Some of Praskovia's sheet music for a few of these operas, bound in soft marbled covers, has survived. An unknown hand has marked in the score for *The Beautiful Arsene* the parts for "Parasha," "Arina" (the Sapphire Kalmykova), "Andrei" (Novikov), and "Anushka" (Anna the Emerald Buianova).[13] The music for Monsigny's *Rose and Colas* has instructions penned in specifically for Praskovia ("Parasha, sing this vaudeville 3 times") and minor changes to her arias to tailor them to her voice. The music for Joseph Haydn's *Stabat Mater* has also survived, with notes to Praskovia and a few others.[14] These old pages even offer clues to how Praskovia talked. The music for Nicolas-Marie Delayrac's *Nina* is marked in places for Praskovia to drop the broad unstressed "o" of her youthful Yaroslav accent for the more common sounding "a" (*kagda* for *kogda*, *gavari* for *govori*) and to soften her hard "ch" (*shto* for *chto*, *kaneshno* for *konechno*).[15]

So far Praskovia had played the part of innocent peasant girls and soubrettes, ubiquitous examples of sentimental female virtue that were easy for her to identify with and did not demand a great stretch of her acting. This changed with her appearance in *L'infante* in 1784. For the first time Praskovia played the part of a queen, the ruler of Zamora. At the age of sixteen, she had to transform herself into a character unlike anyone she had encountered in her life and to convey royal pride and a regal bearing, and this before audiences who had an idea how monarchs behaved from personal experience. Nicholas must have helped Praskovia acquire the proper mannerisms and habits of speech in the rehearsals. Seated on a gilded throne and resplendent in a crimson satin gown, a brocaded cloak, and an elaborate headdress tufted with enormous ostrich feathers, Praskovia captured all the power and splendor of the exotic queen. The audience was thrilled, and *L'infante* was another resounding success.

Having proved herself, Praskovia was given ever more demanding roles—the rebellious Amazon Eliane in *The Marriage of the Samnites*, the mysterious ruler of the Indian land Golconde, the tormented Arsene abandoned in a magical garden beyond the clouds. Word of the quality of the Sheremetev theater grew with Praskovia's increasing range, maturity, and professionalism, and Nicholas viewed his rising star with ever greater pride and pleasure. Praskovia's soprano had developed into a subtle instrument of great color and beauty, possessing amazing range, emotion, and power, to which years of classical Italian training added precision and clarity. She had become the troupe's diva.

In the spring of 1786, Nicholas was appointed to the Fifth Department of the Senate, a branch of the state administration devoted to judicial matters. The office held little interest for him, and he gave it little time or thought. Theater remained his passion, although no longer his only one.

About this time Nicholas became the subject of renewed talk in certain noble circles. The precise nature of this talk has been lost, but comments were made about "slander" and damage to Nicholas's "honor" as a nobleman. Princess Yelena Viazemskaia wrote to Peter of the gossip, telling him that he would be wise to keep a closer eye on his son, whose ways were placing the Sheremetev family in an unflattering light.[16]

Princess Viazemskaia was apparently still upset about her failure to arrange a match between Nicholas and her daughter and was also angered by Nicholas's behavior toward his cousin Yelena Sheremeteva. It is possible that after giving up all hope for her daughter, the busybody Viazemskaia had given herself the task of reconciling her wayward great-nephew and his cousin. To that end, she tried to enlist the support of his father by scaring Peter with talk of family dishonor. It's likely that the dishonor to which Yelena was referring was Nicholas's relationship with Praskovia.

In the two years since he had written Alexander Kurakin of "le petit

nez musical," Nicholas and Praskovia had become lovers. Exactly when
and how this happened will most probably never be known. Nicholas had
watched Praskovia grow from a little girl into a woman during the mid-
1780s. She was physically attractive, if not a great beauty, with auburn
hair, dark, expressive eyes, a pale complexion, and a slight, almost fragile
build suggesting vulnerability that belied a steely inner strength.

It is not hard to imagine why Nicholas fell in love. Praskovia's gifts
as a performer and her artistic nature, her profound spiritual depth, her
intelligence, combined with her beguiling appearance, made her difficult
to resist. Nicholas and Praskovia were together nearly every day, often
for hours at a time in rehearsals with the troupe or after hours, just the
two of them, perfecting difficult passages. Watching her play the part of
innocent maidens emerging into adulthood, still only dimly aware of the
new feelings inside them, and listening to Praskovia sing arias about the
love in her heart, Nicholas became aware of his own feelings. The musician in him was awed by, and perhaps a touch envious of, her superior
talent. She placed him in the shadows, and he thrilled at being near such
a natural performer. There was an element of self-love as well. Nicholas
had discovered this great talent, untrained and wild, and fashioned it into
something refined. Praskovia was his creation, the Galatea to his Pyg-
malion. He shared in her successes and basked in her applause. Nicholas
had made her who she was, and he would have her as he had had his other
serf mistresses.

It seems unlikely that the first time Nicholas took Praskovia to his
bed he had any idea how profound a hold on him his desire would take,
or where it would lead. Nicholas later wrote, "I had the most tender, the
most passionate feelings for her. Yet I examined my heart—was it overwhelmed merely by passionate desire, or did it see past her beauty to her
other agreeable qualities? Seeing that my heart longed for more than love
and friendship, more than mere physical pleasure, for a long time I observed the character and qualities of my heart's desire and found in her a
mind adorned with virtue, sincerity, a true love for humanity, constancy,
fidelity, and an unshakable faith in God. These qualities captured me
more than her beauty, for they are more powerful than all external charms
and much rarer."[17]

Whether this was true at the time or only a later reinterpretation,
Nicholas saw his falling in love with Praskovia as a life-altering moment

when, through Praskovia's example, he was saved from the vanity, pride, and vice of his life and was reborn in virtue. "Voluptuous love, innocence's poison, the destroyer of physical and spiritual health whose shameful amusements usher in temptation and repentance—all these pleasures changed in my eyes," Nicholas confessed. "Steadfast, sincere, tender love drove from my heart shameful love, for which I am grateful to my departed wife—in a word, I turned toward virtue."[18]

In trying to fathom the nature of their relationship, it is ultimately impossible to get beyond the sentimentalist language in which Nicholas cast it. In everything he wrote, Praskovia is the personification of maidenly virtue that saves the debauched aristocrat, redirecting his life toward higher ends. This is how Nicholas chose to remember his love.

What about her feelings? Did she share his desire and freely return his love? Praskovia had grown up in Nicholas's shadow as one of his father's serfs, a piece of property. She had been a child when they met and had seen Nicholas take other serfs to his bed over the years. It must have seemed strange and frightening when she became the object of his attention. She wondered if she were to be just another in a series of affairs or whether Nicholas's feelings for her were indeed different, as he no doubt professed. Whatever her reservations, it doesn't seem possible Praskovia could have resisted Nicholas's advances. To do so would have been to risk incurring his anger. The ways in which he could punish her for refusing him must have seemed infinite.

Given the power Nicholas had over Praskovia, it is tempting to assume that she had no choice but to submit to him. What's more, Nicholas had a temper. Even some in his own family admitted that Nicholas could be "proud and hot-tempered" and "impulsive."[19] In light of his family's wealth, power, and social standing, it is quite understandable that Nicholas was accustomed to getting his way. But even if Praskovia felt she had to give herself to Nicholas, this does not necessarily mean she found him unappealing. He was undeniably handsome, cultured, and worldly. There was a sensitive, tender side to him. Nicholas never belonged to that class of masters who took sadistic pleasure in abusing their serfs. He was generous and something of an eccentric dreamer. He was not the type to use physical force but relied on charm to woo his lovers. It is not hard to imagine Praskovia being flattered by his attention and going half-willingly to his bed.

There were other considerations as well. Becoming the master's mistress could bring a serf and her family certain advantages—more pay, extra food, a better place to live, reduced work, gifts, and preferential treatment in general. Becoming Nicholas's lover would enhance Praskovia's position in the troupe as well. This had been the case with Anna "The Emerald." Before shifting his attention to Praskovia, Nicholas appears to have had a brief affair with the pretty Anna, indulging her with money and expensive clothes. Praskovia and Anna were used to being rivals in their stage roles, but one can imagine Praskovia would have been apprehensive about taking the rivalry offstage into real life, where the repercussions could be great.

At the same time, however, Praskovia had little chance to meet and fall in love with anyone else. The performers lived in isolation from the rest of the serfs and from each other; the males and females were housed in separate wings and prohibited from casual, unsupervised socializing. The thought of falling in love with any of the uneducated men working the estate was by now out of the question. Praskovia had stopped being a peasant years ago; although a serf, given her upbringing, work, and the cultural milieu in which she lived, she now belonged more to the world of the aristocracy than to that of the peasantry. She shared Nicholas's life in significant ways, notably his passion for music and theater. She was indebted to him for her training and her career. He had shown great confidence in her even before it was perhaps warranted and given Praskovia everything possible to develop her talent. He had made her who she was, and she was grateful.

All these things must have gone through Praskovia's head and kept her up nights as she debated just what to do about Nicholas's advances. Tatiana and her sister Matryona were there to listen and offer advice. In the end, Praskovia relented.

We shall likely never know Praskovia's feelings for Nicholas. An overlooked document in the archives does offer one clue, albeit small and inconclusive. In a draft of the short history of her life quoted earlier, Nicholas wrote that Praskovia's "spiritual goodness expressed itself first of all in her love of God, her strict devotion to her faith, her loyalty to her husband, and her aid to the suffering." After writing this, Nicholas read it over and decided it was not quite right. He picked up his quill and crossed out "loyalty to her husband," replacing it with "loyalty to matrimony."[20] Perhaps it was a meaningless edit, a mere stylistic change. Or perhaps this new language more accurately reflected the nature of Praskovia's feelings. Maybe Nicholas was admitting that Praskovia had never loved him the way he had loved her and that what had been most important to Praskovia was the sacrament of marriage, not her feelings for her husband. Perhaps.

NINE

Entertaining Catherine

In the autumn of 1786, Nicholas and his father began preparing for Catherine the Great's visit to Kuskovo, planned for the following summer. The empress would be passing through Moscow on her return from a lengthy tour through southern Russia and the Crimea organized by Prince Potemkin, the trip that became the source for the fabled stories of the "Potemkin villages." It had been eleven years since they last hosted Catherine, and they wanted to make certain everything was ready to assure this visit would surpass anything she had experienced before. No expense was too great, no detail too insignificant. On 17 May 1787, Peter wrote to his St. Petersburg steward, "I am particularly busy making preparations for the upcoming visit and am building quite a lot. . . . The money is flowing like water."[1]

Nicholas wrote Hyvart repeatedly to request items for the theater and to seek his advice on what opera to perform. Nicholas was having trouble deciding among Salieri's *Les Danaïdes* or *Tarar*, Grétry's *Richard the Lion-Hearted*, Gluck's *Iphigénie en Tauride* or *Alceste*. On 12 September 1786, Hyvart sent off an enormous crate weighing nearly three hundred pounds and filled with decorations, scores, lyrics, sketches, set designs, props, and costumed dolls for the reception. With regret Hyvart informed Nicholas the next month that the crate arrived in Le Havre two days late for the ship bound directly for St. Petersburg; the next one, *Winged Mercury*, was sailing first to Hamburg, which would mean a considerable delay.[2]

A vexed Nicholas now realized he would have to stage an opera that was already in the company's repertoire. His father had been pushing for *The Novgorodian Hero Boeslavich,* written by the empress herself. In January, he wrote to Alexandrov in St. Petersburg instructing him to acquire from the director of the Imperial Theaters not only the score, but precise details of the sets and costumes in the hope of staging at Kuskovo an exact copy of the version performed at court.[3] The tug-of-war between father and son went on for months, practically up to the day of Catherine's visit.

Catherine arrived at the village of Kolomenskoe outside Moscow on the evening of 23 June. The next day Nicholas and other Moscow nobles dined with the empress at her palace, where she regaled her guests with tales of her trip. On the twenty-seventh Catherine made her ceremonial entrance into the ancient capital and the following day celebrated the twenty-fifth anniversary of her accession to the throne. Both Nicholas and Peter were there to congratulate her in the throne hall of the governor-general's house.

The morning of Wednesday, 30 June, was cloudy and cool. Moscow was abuzz with talk of the fête planned for that day at Kuskovo. Crowds began clogging the roads heading out of the city by early afternoon. Around five o'clock in the afternoon a richly appointed phaeton left the governor-general's house carrying Catherine (refreshed after a short postprandial rest), her favorite Alexander Dmitriev-Mamonov, Ivan Shuvalov (the aged lover of the late Empress Elizabeth), the Austrian and French ambassadors Count Ludwig Cobenzl and Count Louis-Philippe de Ségur, respectively, the noted adventurer Prince de Ligne, and two of the empress's ladies. Numerous carriages bearing the rest of her court followed in their dusty wake.

The clouds had burned off by now, and the day had turned hot and sticky, the thermometer pushing into the mideighties. As the carriages approached Kuskovo they began to pass under arches and triumphal gateways constructed for the occasion, and trumpeters announced the empress's progress. Peter, Nicholas, and other members of the family were waiting for Catherine on the edge of the estate next to a massive faux marble arch surrounded by large Seville orange and lemon trees heavy with colorful fruit.[4] Catherine ordered her driver to stop and permitted Peter and Nicholas to approach and kiss her hand. Peter joined the empress, and they set off. As they neared the Big House the small private navy, afloat in the man-made lake and festooned with bright flags twisting lazily in the muggy air, greeted their arrival with the firing of cannons and guns. As the phaeton slowed to a stop in the drive, young maidens in white dresses with colorful garlands on their heads appeared and sprinkled a path of bright flower petals to the front door.

Peter showed Catherine and his guests into the Big House, where they rested, took refreshments, and briefly toured the staterooms before heading out into the garden toward the theater. Meanwhile, inside the theater the stagehands were checking that everything was ready for the performance, and the orchestra tuned up under the direction of Herr Facius. Backstage, Praskovia was getting into costume and waiting for her makeup and hairdressing with the other actresses and dancers, while busy attendants rushed about. The singers ran through scales and practiced some of the more difficult passages from the night's opera; the muffled shuffling of feet and shutting of doors could be heard from another dressing room overhead, as other performers rushed excitedly through their preparations for the performance.

That evening marked the opening of Kuskovo's new theater that Nicholas had begun two years earlier. He had razed the existing structure on the Seventh-Hour Meadow and written to Hyvart requesting plans from France. Sketches, designs, architectural drawings, and models flew back and forth between Moscow and Paris as Hyvart tried to meet Nicholas's exacting demands. Nicholas not only wanted something bigger and grander, he wanted something that would be able to accomplish various dramatic special effects. He was adamant about being able to stage floods with realistic waves and crashing thunder.

Hyvart promised Nicholas he would have a theater on par with the best in Paris. He hired Charles de Wailly, who had done work for Kuskovo before. De Wailly was one of the architects of the king's opera at Versailles and had become of late the architect of choice for theaters. Hyvart also contracted the head machinist at the Versailles opera. Together they came up with a design nearly identical to the king's theater. The new theater at Kuskovo was twice the size of the previous one, with seating for 150, and it was unequaled in Russia in terms of architecture, design, and technical capabilities. The construction was overseen by the serf architect Alexei Mironov.

The interior was sumptuously finished with finely carved fretwork and moldings and Corinthian columns—all richly gilded—that glowed against the pale blue walls.[5] The loges were covered in velveteen, the benches in a dark red cloth. The count's box could seat twelve. An ornate gilt chair had been especially built for Catherine. A massive crystal chandelier and girandoles along the walls bathed the theater in warm light.

Nicholas had not overlooked the dressing rooms, which were outfitted with style and comfort. The walls in the actresses' room were covered with pink paper decorated with delicate flowers and birds. There were several birch chairs with cane backs; six canvas screens with green floral designs provided a bit of privacy for the women as they changed in and out of their costumes. One screen off in the corner hid a leather-seated chamber pot. On one wall two smallish windows let in air and light; on another hung two heavy, full-length gilt mirrors before which the women could fix their hair, makeup, and costumes. The men's room was much the same with one notable difference: it had no lock on the door. The Sheremetevs, like other noble impresarios, were always careful to control access to their female performers.

The atmosphere in the dressing rooms that evening was thick with nervous anticipation. Everyone in the troupe knew great expense, effort, and time had gone into preparing for Catherine's visit, and they were well aware how important it was to Peter and Nicholas that they give the performances of their lives. Praskovia sensed this would be the biggest night of her professional life. Ten of the count's valets and footmen were posted in the loges and gallery with instructions to extinguish the candles upon his signal. All the doors and theater machinery had been greased in advanced to assure there were no unpleasant squeaks.[6]

For the night's performance Nicholas and Peter had agreed upon Grétry's *The Marriage of the Samnites*. The opera had debuted on the Sheremetev stage nearly two years earlier and was becoming one of Praskovia's best roles. Grétry came upon the idea for his opera from an eponymous story in Marmontel's *Moral Tales*. He composed an opera based on the tale in the late 1760s that bombed in Paris, but which he then radically revised with a new libretto and premiered in 1776. Although this second version did not fare much better than the first in Paris, it was quite popular in the provinces and abroad, and parts of the score made their way into Mozart's piano variations.

Set in Italy in the fourth century BC, *The Marriage of the Samnites* is one of the few neoclassical opéras-comiques. Typical of opéra-comique, it takes up matters of love, personal freedom, and obligation to family and society, yet at the same time embraces history. Although he would be guillotined as a royalist supporter during the French Revolution, the librettist, Barnabé Farmian de Rosoi, considered himself a philosophe and the theater a laboratory for destroying class hierarchy and celebrating the fellowship of man. In fact, Rosoi was rare in that he even wanted to tear down the wall between men and women, and in his hands Marmontel's tale became an attack on patriarchy.

The Samnites were a warlike people of the Abruzzi who for nearly a century waged a doomed struggle against the Roman expansion that left southern Italy ravaged. In Marmontel's tale Samnium is a place that prizes heroic virtue above all else, where duty to family and the state is paramount. Courting is done only with the eyes; men secretly convey their choice of bride to their parents, and it belongs to the young women to obey.

After Catherine and her hosts had taken their seats and the house had quieted down, Facius raised his arm, and the orchestra launched into the overture. To convey the Samnites' commitment to valor, the patria, and a noble simplicity, Grétry gave his music a martial implementation and coloring and an ordered restraint unusual for the composer. He included horns and trumpets, almost unheard of in opéra-comique, and timpani to create a military atmosphere.

The curtain rises on a picturesque grove. In the distance a town is visible. Two Samnite warriors enter hand in hand: Agathis (sung by Grigory Kokhanovsky) and his orphaned friend Parmenon (Andrei Novikov). The day when young men choose a bride is approaching, but according to the laws of Samnium they cannot reveal to each other the name of their beloved. Fearful that they may be rivals in matters of love, Agathis and Parmenon sing a duet expressing their unbreakable friendship.

High above the stage the serf machinist Fyodor Priakhin carefully orchestrated the lowering of decorations from the rafters, transforming the scene into a village square as the stage filled with Samnite soldiers, maidens, their mothers, and old men. The performers were resplendent in their costumes of imported fabric. The warriors wore grayish cuirasses, tunics, and flesh-colored capes. To give them a more muscular appearance, padding had been stuffed around their shoulders and chest beneath their costumes. The village men wore stylized Roman attire—short-sleeved violet tunics with loose belts over white satin pants. The young Samnite women were dressed in white chemises of satin and crêpe decorated with light gauze and pink flowers. Their hair was adorned with beads and paste jewels, and on their feet they wore taffeta boots laced with ribbon.

The crowd gathers around the chief, who tells them the enemy is at the gates. Before marching off into battle, the warriors reveal their hearts with furtive glances: Parmenon looks toward Eliane, played by Praskovia, and Agathis toward Céphalide, played by Anna the Emerald.

The second act opens in the same grove with Euphémie, Céphalide's mother, surrounded by a group of Samnite maidens. They have covered themselves with flowers in anticipation of their weddings upon the men's return. The youngest of them, radiating "enchanting innocence," is played by Praskovia's friend Tatiana, now performing as the Garnet. At this point Eliane steps on stage and sends the action off into an entirely unexpected direction. Marmontel's Eliane had been a cipher, yet Rosoi has created a strong female character, a dissenter unwilling to accept the male-given laws of the state that reduce women to a purely passive role. Praskovia mesmerized the audience with an incredibly long and technically demanding obbligato recitative and aria. Her gorgeous soprano leaping from high a″ to low e′, from high g″ to low d′, Praskovia swings wildly between fear over Parmenon's safety and her initial feelings of helplessness. Grétry had composed new music for Eliane for this revised version of his opera, including ten arias, and it was stunningly difficult, full of roulades and trills and grace notes requiring virtuoso control.

Céphalide and the other maidens reject Eliane's criticisms of Samnium and try to talk her out of taking any drastic action. Yet she resists being mollified, refusing to be just an object of men's desires and proclaiming her intent to throw off society's "yoke," which denies her the freedom afforded men. "No, better let God speak," she sings, "for when the state does not consult my heart can I consider myself free? . . . What weapons can we use against our tormenters when they have all the power! . . . I want to be a wife, but not the victim of the law's whim. Can the woman who scorns death live in humiliation?! If my hand is not afraid to bear arms or to brave death, what man has the right to forestall my choice?" Eliane grabs a sword and rushes from the stage to join the soldiers, knowing that her fate is to perish on the field of battle. Cries of "rebel" and "outlaw" follow after her.[7]

The Samnite warriors are welcomed home in act 3 with a victory parade. The chief informs the people that three fighters have distinguished themselves through their heroism—Parmenon for saving a friend's life and taking a Roman standard; Agathis for tending to his wounded father and then leading his men to victory; and a third, unknown warrior for saving the general's life.

Agathis and Parmenon now make known the names of their beloveds, and while they are relieved to learn they are not the same, Parmenon and the others are overcome with fear upon realizing that Eliane has vanished. Suddenly, a golden chariot appears bearing a mysterious warrior. He is dressed unlike the others in a billowy blouse of white crêpe trimmed with silk lace, a blue and gold bodice, and a long, flowing orange satin cape flecked with tiger prints. On the warrior's head rests a large spiked helmet sprouting white and gray ostrich feathers. In his hands, he holds a gold sword and bejeweled shield. Diamonds and other precious stones cover his costume.

The arrival of this unknown figure elicits consternation. Only gradually is he revealed to be Eliane, and in a long aria punctuated by blaring trumpets and thunderous timpani she recounts her exploits on the battlefield. Eliane is pardoned and united with Parmenon as the two express their eternal love in a lengthy duet. In a closing choral sequence, they all reaffirm their duty to Samnium and pledge to live in peace and harmony. Racing strings and a final crashing of timpani mark the opera's joyous conclusion.

Catherine and the rest of the audience burst into applause. One can almost feel the wave of euphoria mixed with exhausted relief that must have washed over Praskovia. The performance had been a brilliant success, and the months of preparation had not been wasted. Standing before the house, she felt a sense of her own power. For hours she had held the Russian empress and the elite of society in her hands. She had been able to make them forget she was a serf and believe the illusion depicted on stage. In their mind she was Eliane. She had convinced them of the reality of her words, had moved them to share her feelings, had dominated their senses with her glorious singing, the beauty of her movements, and the expressiveness of her eyes. Such moments were the most precious in Praskovia's life, when for a brief while she could lose herself in the magic of performance, that place where masters and serfs and the ugly realities of Russian society slipped from her consciousness and she was alone in her head, cognizant of nothing more than her breathing, the sound of her voice, and the beauty of the music.

After a final curtsy Praskovia returned to the dressing room to fading applause as the corps de ballet took the stage. When the evening's entertainment concluded, the valets quietly opened the theater doors and strode into the parterre, their flickering candelabras casting muted shadows along the walls.

Although not a music lover, Catherine was deeply moved by the opera. It was not simply the quality of the acting and singing, the richness of the costumes and staging that so impressed her. The story itself no doubt touched something inside the empress. This tale of a headstrong young woman who refused to quietly accept the place society had prepared for her and instead risked everything to fight for what she considered rightfully hers showed parallels to Catherine's own life. In donning a soldier's uniform and racing to meet her fate, Eliane acted in a way that echoed Catherine's coup nearly twenty-five years to the day earlier, when she had traded her dress for an officer's uniform of the Preobrazhensky Guards, mounted her steed, and ridden off to seize the Russian throne from her husband.

Catherine told Peter and Nicholas that it was the most magnificent performance she had ever seen.[8] And then she did something most unusual: she asked to meet Praskovia and Tatiana. A valet was sent running backstage to tell them the empress desired their presence. Praskovia and Tatiana were brought to the empress, who praised their performances and spoke to them briefly. To Tatiana, she gave several gold coins. The Garnet never forgot the experience and loved to recall it well into old age, a dim reflection of that day's excitement radiating from her cloudy eyes.[9] Nicholas was immensely happy with how the opera and ballet had been received and especially to see the empress express her pleasure to Praskovia in person.

Count Ségur had been impressed by the entertainment as well, but he admitted to a feeling of displeasure with what he had seen. "Notwithstanding my little taste for fêtes," he wrote in his memoirs, "I shall not pass over in silence that which was given to the Empress by the count Scheremeteff, at one of his estates outside Moscow."

> We found the road brilliantly illuminated. The Count's immense park was decorated with transparencies composed of all colors and exquisitely designed. A grand Russian opera was performed on a very noble theatre; and all who understood the story, pronounced it very interesting and well written. I could only judge of the music and the ballets; the one astonished me by its harmonious melody; the others by the richness of costume, the grace of the female, and the lightness and activity of the male dancers.
>
> But what appeared to me almost inconceivable was that the poet, and the musical authors of the opera, the architect who had built the house, the painter who had decorated it, the actors and actresses of the piece, and the male and female dancers in the ballets, as well as the musicians in the orchestra, were all slaves of Count Scheremeteff.
>
> This nobleman, one of the richest in Russia, had caused them to be educated with the greatest care; they were indebted to him for their acquirements; why were they not also indebted to him for their freedom? To enlighten those whom we still hold in slavery, is to inform them of their misfortune.[10]

The heat of the day had subsided and the burning sun was now but a faint glow in the sky as Peter escorted Catherine back into the brightly illuminated gardens. Torches burned along the canals and waterways, and flames arose from two obelisks across the lake from the Big House. Lights from the battleship and galleys were reflected in the water, and members of the count's choir sang folk songs from gondolas rowed about on the lake by oarsmen in traditional Russian costume. Peter and his guests returned to the Big House and played cards until supper was served at eleven o'clock. The table, set for fifty-seven persons, was covered with gold and silver and precious stones. The sardonic Count Ségur was amazed by the richness before him: "The supper was at least as sumptuous as the entertainment; I never saw more gold and silver vases, more porcelain, alabaster and porphyry. But, what will appear most incredible, is that the immense crystals which covered the table for a hundred persons, were ornamented and enriched with fine and precious stones of all kinds and colors, and of great value. Thus the Russian nobles, so lately civilized, imitated already the Roman patricians in an extreme of grandeur, which was too quickly followed by its decline, and more than one Lucullus was to be found in Moscow."[11]

Catherine offered the first toast of the evening to her gracious host, and Peter then bid his guests to drink to the health of the empress. When they raised their glasses, cannons roared and the horns and strings of the orchestra played. It was going on one in the morning when Catherine thanked her host and his family and departed for Moscow. As her phaeton pulled away from the house, the cannons fired and the orchestra struck up a final time. Lanterns and barrels of burning tar lighted the road back to the city. Thunder rumbled overhead in the dark sky.

The next day Peter and Nicholas dined with Catherine in Moscow. The events of the previous day were no doubt fondly recalled. Catherine had been most pleased with the fête, and Praskovia had made quite an impression on her. The details of the empress's conversations with her guests were not recorded, but it's tempting to think Catherine asked Peter and Nicholas about Praskovia, about her background, her training, her character, and their plans for her.

Even though Catherine had congratulated Praskovia and praised Sheremetev father and son for their accomplishments, she felt this wasn't enough, that she wanted to do more. She spent a good deal of 2 July selecting a gift for Praskovia, eventually settling on a diamond ring worth 350 rubles. On the third she gave the entire troupe a thousand gold coins. Catherine had always been generous with her gifts, but to give presents to serfs was most uncommon and a rare sign of royal approval.[12] That same day Catherine and her suite left Moscow for St. Petersburg. Catherine and Peter parted unaware that they would never see each other again. In a year and a half the old count would be dead.

The success of the Kuskovo celebration stayed fresh in everyone's mind for months, and talk of it spread far. On 5 November, Nicholas wrote to Hyvart, "You have heard talk of our fête. It is all true, everything went exceedingly well, and Her Majesty said with her usual kindness that it was the most magnificent and pleasing performance she has ever seen."[13]

TEN

The Sheremetevs and Their Serfs

Velikolépno, "magnificent," was the word most often used to describe how the Sheremetevs lived. Their palaces were magnificent, their collections of art were magnificent, their parties were magnificent, everything about their way of life was magnificent. "This count lived, as they say, in the Russian manner, in other words, most magnificently," observed Nicholas Kotov, a Moscow merchant, of Peter. "He lived magnificently, owned a perfectly magnificent carriage, and the exquisite estate of Kuskovo. He loved everything that was magnificent."[1]

The Sheremetev servants wore livery of rich velvet embroidered with gold thread. The horses that pulled their carriages sported tassels of silver and gold. Nicholas's saddles were imported from England, as were his billiard tables, his porter, and his hunting dogs. The dogs were fed choice cuts of beef brought to Russia on ships from Hamburg. His ham Nicholas preferred to import from Westphalia. The Malaga for his table had to be "the oldest that can be found."[2] Nicholas purchased his clothing, his pomade, powder, even his tobacco, razors, and teeth cleaner from Paris. So fine was the quality of his fabrics that upon Nicholas's death bolts of his flannel were purchased by Tsar Alexander I for his personal use. Nicholas's chef, Olivier, was a Frenchman, as was his hairdresser, a man by the name of Rousseau.

The Sheremetevs lived less like noblemen and more like petty kings. His serfs addressed Nicholas as "Your Highness, Our Lord and Master";

his and his father's birthdays were treated as national holidays on the family's lands, days when none of the serfs were obligated to work. Hussars guarded their estates. Aping the tsars' court, the Sheremetev household had its own wine cup bearer and coffee cup bearer, and the pages wore special livery with the count's cipher. The Big House at Kuskovo had a state bedroom decorated in the French style, complete with a *lit de parade* inspired by the one built for King Louis XIV in the Mercury Salon at Versailles. In La Solitude Peter built his own *hameau,* or little hamlet, modeled after that of Marie Antoinette. He created here for himself a Cockaigne, complete with sham huts in which he settled some carefully selected serfs and ordered them to play the part of carefree peasants. Not for nothing was Kuskovo referred to as "the Russian Versailles."[3]

The magnificence of the Sheremetevs was made possible by the forced labor of hundreds of thousands of Russian serfs.

Russia in the eighteenth century was overwhelmingly rural and overwhelmingly peasant. In 1795, the population of the Russian Empire was approximately thirty-seven million. The vast majority of the population was made up of serfs, who lived on land owned by nobles, and peasants, who lived on crown or state lands. There were about 360,000 male nobles, most of whom owned fewer than 60 serfs. Only 1½ percent of all nobles owned more than 1,000 serfs. When he died in 1809, Nicholas owned 210,000. This was nearly the size of the population of St. Petersburg or Moscow. By contrast, on the eve of the U.S. Civil War only one slave owner had more than 1,000 slaves. The Sheremetevs owned estates in seventeen provinces totaling more than two million acres, almost three times the size of the state of Rhode Island.[4] They were among the richest private landowners in the world.

By the second half of the eighteenth century Russian serfdom had become a form of slavery. Although serfs were considered legal persons, their master's control over their lives was nearly total. They were subject to the almost complete jurisdiction of their masters. Serfs could not enter contracts, marry, or move without their master's permission. Serfs were bought and sold, as individuals or in groups, with or without land. The *St. Petersburg* and *Moscow Gazette* carried advertisements for serfs alongside horses, houses, women's hats, and writing paper. Nobles could not execute their serfs but could inflict punishment guaranteed to result in death. Serfs had little recourse; attempts to petition their masters over what they felt to be unfair treatment typically resulted in reprisals.

Like black slaves in the United States, serfs in Russia were perceived by their owners as being inherently different, a people apart, their shared religion and ethnicity notwithstanding. Serfs were believed to be lazy and childlike, requiring constant supervision. A steward at Kuskovo wrote to Peter in 1763 that the serfs chosen to work in his home "are incapable of looking, speaking, and walking, they are like wild savages," good for nothing but "hard labor."[5] Sentimentalist literature at the close of the century would begin to poke holes in this belief, but for most nobles it wasn't until well into the nineteenth century that they could imagine that "beneath the peasant's sheepskin coat was a human soul."[6]

Despite the similarities, serfdom never sank to the brutalizing and utterly dehumanizing level of slavery in the Americas, which deserves its reputation as the most horrific system of bondage in human history. Russian serfs were, after all, not aliens in a foreign land, and tradition played a role in mitigating exploitation. More important, serfs were spared the oppressive presence of their masters because most were absentee owners. This afforded the serfs a greater degree of independence in their daily lives than that of American slaves.

Peter and then Nicholas after his father's death in 1788 administered their landholdings from a home office in Moscow run by a staff of 126, all of them Sheremetev serfs. The office was in communication with every estate, and each of these had in turn its own administration under the direction of a steward in whose hands rested all local power. Under him were village elders, tax collectors, peasant police, forest wardens, sentries, and clergymen (the Sheremetevs administered the 130 churches on their lands, paying the priests' salaries). This vast administration totaled over 1,500 persons.

Nobles expropriated the labor of their serfs in two ways, either through corvée, a set number of days' work on the master's land (typically three per week), or quitrent, a direct payment to the master in cash or kind. Almost all the Sheremetev lands operated according to quitrent. In 1765, the obligation was 2 rubles yearly per "soul," as adult male serfs were called; by 1798, it had risen to 5; on some estates it was as high as 9. Nicholas's income from his serfs that year exceeded 630,000 rubles, a fantastic sum. Magnificence wasn't cheap, however, and expenditures usually exceeded income. Both Peter and Nicholas ran into serious cash flow problems and were forced to borrow money every year. By 1800, Nicholas was spending almost a third of his yearly income on servicing his debt.[7]

A sliding scale of punishment ensured compliance with the master's will. On the Sheremetev lands, first offenses resulted in fines. Serfs guilty of repeated infractions were placed under guard and fed bread and water for several days. More serious offenders were sent to dig canals or break rocks. Corporal punishment was left for extreme cases. Drunkenness, leaving the estate without permission, stealing, fighting, resisting authority, all were cause for being locked up in irons or beaten with sticks, whips, cudgels, or the knout. Beatings were carried out in front of the entire village to instill fear and submission. Serfs who found it impossible to change their behavior were sent off to the army (a virtual death sentence in the eighteenth century) or to distant estates known as Sheremetev Siberia.

Serf unrest was rare on the Sheremetev estates, and when it did occur it was usually due not to the actions of the master, but to those of his local stewards, some of whom were crooked and tried to squeeze a bit extra out of the serfs for their own pockets. Peter and Nicholas dealt with these wayward stewards swiftly and harshly. The Sheremetevs treated their serfs more humanely than most owners, a fact borne out by the testimony of contemporaries and the relative prosperity of their serfs. Some of their serfs even became wealthy themselves through trade and manufacturing.

So rich were the Sheremetevs that a few of their serfs had serfs. The most famous of these was Yefim Grachev, a serf in Ivanovo who started his own calico-printing manufactory. As his business grew he turned to Nicholas to request permission to purchase serfs as workers from another nobleman. Nicholas granted his request, but only if the new serfs were registered in his name. By 1795, Grachev owned a large factory, eighty-two hundred acres of land, and twenty-eight hundred male and female serfs. Grachev became so wealthy he was able to present his master with a large emerald ring encrusted with diamonds and lent him money when he was short of cash. He had more assets than most Russian noblemen. But Grachev remained a serf, and he could do nothing with his property, or with his life, without Nicholas's permission. Grachev was one of the few serfs Nicholas allowed to purchase his freedom. It cost him dearly: 135,000 rubles, his factory, all his land, and all his serfs.[8]

Having rich serfs added to the Sheremetevs' magnificence. When one millionaire serf approached Nicholas requesting to buy his way out of bondage, he replied, "Keep your money. I receive greater recognition in owning a person like you than in an extra million rubles."[9] Nicholas liked to show off his wealthy serfs. He once invited the French chargé d'affaires to dine at the home of a serf merchant. The Frenchman was amazed to be served an exquisite meal on silver plate and fine china from Saxony.

"A great many of the serf merchants belonging to the Sheremetevs are millionaires," wrote another foreign visitor. "He takes an arrogant pride in owning such slaves, and he never raises their annual quitrent to reflect their wealth. Yet should any of them get the idea of buying their freedom, the count steadfastly refuses their requests, even if they lay half their wealth at his feet. Exceedingly rare are the instances when he has acquiesced and gone against his strict rules, which form part of a special family code."[10] The reluctance to sell serfs was more than a Sheremetev family principle, however. In those days wealth in Russia was measured not in money or land, but in serfs.

There was a separate category of serfs that did not work the master's land or pay him quitrent. These were the *dvorovye liudi*, the household serfs, taken from the fields to serve in their lord's urban palaces and country estates. Wealthy noblemen maintained huge numbers of domestics, up to six times the number of their European peers. Foreigners were as struck by theses armies of servants as they were by the Sheremetevs' serf millionaires. On a visit to Russia in the early years of the nineteenth century, the English painter and traveler Robert Ker Porter observed with disbelief that the mansions were "filled with vassals, or servants, both male and female, who line the halls, passages, and entrances of the rooms in splendid liveries. In almost every antechamber some of these domestics are placed, ready to obey the commands of their lord or his guest; and continually your ears are saluted with the theatrical call of 'Who waits?' when two or three run in at the same instant, as promptly as I ever saw the gentlemen-in-waiting answer the like summons from the boards of Drury-Lane or Covent-Garden."[11]

As one would expect, the Sheremetevs outdid everyone in this regard. In 1802, Nicholas had 1,082 domestics serving in his main properties. Of these, some 300 were employed in seeing to his personal needs.

Household serfs worked as butlers, footmen, valets, maids, seamstresses, laundresses, nannies, cooks, nurses, gardeners, postilions, cleaners, bakers, and watchmen. At Kuskovo they served in the navy and tended to the animals in the zoological garden. The position of the household serfs was ambiguous. Since they did not farm or engage in trade, they relied entirely on their masters to pay them a salary and provide food and shelter. They lived cut off from the mass of serfs and were resented by them since the household serfs were seen as living off their labor just like the master. More domestics meant fewer serfs sharing the obligations to the lord. Within the ranks of the household serfs there developed a group that became known as the serf intelligentsia, to which Praskovia belonged. This included the musicians, composers, artists, dancers, actors, and architects trained by their masters to give them aesthetic pleasure.

Living alongside the master and mistress provided opportunities to develop personal relationships that could bring real material and emotional benefits. Honest, caring bonds of affection between master and serf did exist. Many household serfs felt themselves superior to the poor folk slogging away in the fields. But such intimacy also exposed household serfs to their masters' whims; they lacked the day-to-day independence afforded by the hundreds of miles that lay between the lord and his serfs in the village. Household serfs had little defense against insult and abuse; attractive girls and boys made for easy prey. In the homes of aristocrats like the Sheremetevs, where the number of domestics had less to do with need than with the desire to impress, idleness bred boredom and lethargy.

The life of the house serf was not necessarily an enviable one. "Ah, you stupid peasants," a popular song proclaimed, "live a while with us! There's surely nothing worse in the world than a house serf's life!"[12]

ELEVEN

The Old Count's Death

Count Peter Sheremetev died after a brief illness in Moscow early on the afternoon of 30 November 1788. He was seventy-five years old. His passing was accorded all the pomp and solemn observance typically reserved for royalty. The *Moscow Gazette* gave the story substantial coverage, and its pages were filled with verses of lament.[1] He was buried on 9 December in Moscow's Novospassky Monastery. Present at the burial were Nicholas and Varvara, the Remetev children, hundreds of household staff, and the entire choir. Praskovia was most likely among the attendees. Despite the bitter cold weather, tens of thousands came out to witness the procession. Father Platon, metropolitan of Moscow and a close friend of the family, read the eulogy.[2]

Nicholas was devastated by his father's death. Insomnia gripped him for weeks, and his father's majordomo observed that he was in a "pitiful way."[3] Although they had never been close, still, Peter's death left Nicholas feeling lost. Until his death Peter had continued to manage the extensive Sheremetev landholdings, a demanding, time-consuming job. This all now fell to Nicholas, who lacked the temperament and talent for it. He viewed the role of landowner as a headache, and with time it showed. Although Nicholas made repeated attempts to keep order in his economy, management of the estates and of his personal finances became more disordered with each passing year.

As his father's sole heir, Nicholas became one of the richest men in the world. This gave him almost unlimited financial freedom to devote to his theater; no longer would he have to ask his father for money. But with his inheritance came problems as well. The largest of them was known as the affair of the claimants.

The story begins in the reign of Peter the Great. In 1714, Tsar Peter issued the Law of Single Inheritance, which did away with centuries of partible inheritance in favor of unigeniture. Russian noblemen were now forbidden from dividing their land among their children and were required to will it all to a single heir. The goal was to create a hereditary class of noble landowners in the west European tradition. The timing had been perfect for Nicholas's father. In 1719, the Field Marshal died, and all his lands and serfs passed to his son Peter.

The Russian nobility (Peter excluded) chafed under the Petrine inheritance law and connived under his successors to have it repealed, which they succeeded in doing under Empress Anna Ioannovna in 1731. Shortly thereafter, a group of the Field Marshal's relations petitioned the empress to overturn his will. They were led by Count Michael Sergeevich Sheremetev, the Field Marshal's great-great grandson via his first wife, and by Michael Petrovich Saltykov, Count Peter Sheremetev's uncle.

Around these two gathered a bitter group from several branches of the family, including Prince Ivan Mikhailovich Dolgoruky. Dolgoruky (nicknamed the Balcony for his protruding chin) was the grandson of Peter's sister Natalia, who had been exiled to Siberia with her husband (later executed) in 1730. Throughout his life Ivan cultivated an intense hatred of his great uncle and, after his death, of his son, Nicholas.[4] Dolgoruky was a close relation of Princess Martha Dolgorukaia, Praskovia's mistress. Prince Dolgoruky knew Praskovia, and she became another of his targets in his campaign against the Sheremetevs.

Empress Anna turned down the claimants' initial petition, but they were not deterred and carried on their fight for the next half century. They directed their efforts at both the crown and Peter, hounding him to hand over most of his inheritance up until his last days. Between 1787 and 1788, Peter wrote over 260 letters and directives to his secretaries on the matter. Throughout their lives, Peter and Nicholas helped several of the claimants with annual gifts of money. This generosity, which the claimants not only readily accepted but had great need of, was salt to the wounds and served to intensify their sense of having been wronged. Catherine the Great was apprised of the family feud more than once before ultimately endorsing the Senate's decision in 1792 against the claimants. Even this did not put the matter to rest. The claimants continued pressing Nicholas for money, and usually he paid them. He kept on giving Michael Sergeevich money and serfs until 1799, when he wrote him an irate letter telling him this was the final payment and to henceforth leave him and his future heirs in peace.[5] Animosity toward Nicholas coursed through the veins of his extended family into the next century.

The affair of the claimants seems to have influenced Nicholas's and Praskovia's relationship. One wonders whether a factor in his decision to marry Praskovia was a desire to ensure that his estate would go either to his widow or to any offspring and would not fall into the hands of his ungrateful relatives. After they married, Praskovia gave some of the claimants expensive jewelry from her own collection, perhaps as an attempt to calm the waters. It is hard to imagine they would have accepted such gifts from a former serf without a sense of indignation. And after their son Dmitry was born, both Nicholas and Praskovia feared for his safety. The claimants were considered to be among the little boy's foes.

With his father's passing Nicholas retreated one step further from society. Although he continued his (desultory) work in the Senate, made inspections of his estates in the Yaroslav and Vladimir provinces, and could be seen riding to the hunt with a few neighbors on the lands surrounding Kuskovo and Markovo, he seldom appeared in the smart homes. The friends of his youth had gone their separate ways, and he wasn't close to his sister Varvara or his many cousins. Nicholas could count only three true friends at the time: Prince Alexander Kurakin, Prince Andrei Shcherbatov, and Vasily Sergeevich Sheremetev, his cousin. Only Shcherbatov lived in Moscow, however, and he was married and preoccupied with his own family affairs.

Part of Nicholas's withdrawal can be explained by the unpleasantness of his relatives, whether seeking money or trying to find him a bride, part by the tendency of the fabulously wealthy to seclude themselves from the world, and part by Nicholas's personality. The ill health that had given encouragement to his hypochondria and melancholy pushed Nicholas deeper into protracted spells of dreamy introspection. He grew increasingly introverted and found the gallant sociability of the age, of which his father had been a shining exemplar, a burden. Nicholas's prickly sensitivity made him quick to perceive insults, even where none existed.

To society, Nicholas's penchant for solitude was a reflection of more disturbing changes. In early 1789, Nicholas issued a series of orders aimed at improving the lives of his serfs. They would henceforth be permitted to petition him directly, either in writing or in person. The practice of sending uncooperative serfs off to the army as punishment was to be stopped (a policy that would be rescinded later). The schools, hospitals, and almshouses on his lands were to be put in proper order, and more were to be built. Changes such as these did not sit well with many of Nicholas's fellow serf owners. Neither did the way he often behaved toward members of his social group. It was noted that Nicholas acted as if he preferred the company of his serf musicians to that of his guests and how after performances he would immediately retire to his room without so much as a goodbye. "The head of our clan is quite a scoundrel," growled his cousin Anna Semyonovna Sheremeteva.[6]

Nicholas's affair with Praskovia magnified his image as a scoundrel. The family knew about Nicholas's serf mistress, as she had been his lover for a few years now, and they weren't pleased. True, his father had taken a mistress at Kuskovo and lived with her as his common-law wife, but that was acceptable seeing as how he had already been properly married and raised his legitimate children. The situation with Nicholas was a different matter.

It isn't clear where Praskovia was living by the late 1780s. She may have moved out of the Big House at Kuskovo into the actresses' wing in the early 1780s; it seems more likely, however, given her earlier position with Princess Dolgorukaia, her valued place in the troupe, and Nicholas's keen interest in her, first professionally and later personally, that she never left. Nicholas's rooms, located on the first floor overlooking the French garden, served as the site for their assignations. His small bedroom, decorated with fine satin, silks, and taffeta in soft reds and greens, offered them a refuge. The thick cloth covering the floor softened their footsteps. Nicholas's bed was tucked inside a niche behind a heavy curtain.[7] Here, in the dark, Praskovia and Nicholas could forget for a just a while that they were serf and master and lose themselves as lovers.

The Big House was crowded with domestics and relatives and friends of his late father who had come to visit and never left. Nicholas found it awkward living under their disapproving eyes and hearing their whispered gossip as he made his way through the palace. Catty noble ladies visiting the estate liked to approach Praskovia and ask with spiteful glee, "Do tell us, where's the smithy? Do you know the blacksmith? Does he have any children?"[8] So in early 1790, Nicholas decided to move out and set up a home for the two of them. He chose the former washery, a small, one-story wooden building near the theater that he converted into a number of comfortable yet modest apartments. They each had their own suite of rooms on either end of the house, complete with separate entrances. Praskovia's comprised five rooms. Light from two large windows spilled into her bedroom. The walls were covered with French floral paper and held a mirror and paintings of shepherdesses in gilt oval frames. A ruffled chintz curtain opened to reveal a niche with a bench, small table, bed, and nightstand. The furniture was mostly birch or pine, as were the floors. Icons hung in all her rooms, including an image of the Prophet Ilia, Praskovia's birth saint.

A door behind the niche led to an empty room, which opened to Nicholas's suite. His rooms, six in all, were equally modest and furnished in the same manner. Praskovia and Nicholas took their meals in the dining room, the one common area, under an image of the Lord and surrounded by walls covered with little shepherds and hunters with their dogs. They ate Nicholas's favorite dish, venison with radishes and huckleberry preserves, off yellow faience, and when it was cold they lit a fire in the marble fireplace. A room for servants was next to the dining room.[9]

The move to the old washery marked a new phase in their lives. Although Nicholas had had mistresses before, he had never set up house with any of them. Now it became clear to everyone in the Big House, to the troupe, and to the serfs on the estate that Praskovia was not just the latest of the master's favorites. Nicholas had raised her to a higher state, but this did not mean Praskovia's place was an easy one. By protecting Praskovia from the petty indignities that confronted her in the Big House, Nicholas had isolated her from her friends. Tatiana and her sister were free to visit, but for the most part Praskovia now lived cut off from the larger life of the estate. She mingled with the other performers and instructors at rehearsals and performances but then returned alone to her apartments. The only other path she trod was to the estate church and back. It was a quiet life. Her grandson later wrote that Praskovia's life from now on became "difficult" and "lonely."[10] "At times I'm sad, yet I don't even know myself why." Praskovia spoke these words as Milovida (Nice-Looking) in *The Parting, or the Hunters' Departure from Kuskovo.*[11] They must have resonated with her heart.

Praskovia's memory among the serfs at Kuskovo was held in reverence well into the next century. No one could remember her abusing her position as Nicholas's mistress or taking advantage of it to harm any of the other serfs. Rather, she sought to use her closeness to Nicholas to help others in need. Still, her place alongside Nicholas produced envy and ill will in the hearts of many serfs.

When Nicholas was at the estate, they would spend the evening together. He was fond of accompanying her on the cello, joined by Tatiana, who would turn the pages of the sheet music for him. Or they would sit quietly, Praskovia working on some needlework while Nicholas read from his favorite writer, Marcus Aurelius, or from Dr. Tissot's medical treatises.[12] Their home was nice and comfortable, but to Praskovia it was a golden cage. In the coming years the cages would become increasingly ornate but no less confining.

Interlude
Serf Theater

About the time Count Peter Sheremetev began the theater at Kuskovo, many of his noble peers were building theaters of their own at their urban palaces and country estates across Russia. Serf theater is a fascinating chapter in the history of the Russian dramatic arts, simultaneously alluring and repellent, magnificent and squalid, and shot through with the paradoxes, injustices, and cruelties of a society in which millions of men, women, and children labored to provide a life of luxury and leisure for the noble elite. Few art forms have ever displayed so nakedly the inequities of wealth, power, and status that made their existence possible.

That serf theater arose at all is an unlikely coincidence of circumstances that came together at the just the right moment and held together just long enough to give it life. At its most basic, serf theater required two things: time and wealth. The former came with emancipation from state service under Tsar Peter III in 1762. The nobility suddenly had time on their hands, and some began casting about in search of a new purpose in life. The reigns of Peter's successors—Catherine the Great, Paul I, and Alexander I—were a period of unprecedented power and prestige, the so-called Golden Age of the Russian nobility. Never before and never again would the nobility so utterly dominate Russian society or have at its disposal wealth of such fantastic proportions. Wealth in Russia was measured in terms of serfs. And serfs, noblemen discovered, could be made to sing, act, and dance as well as to plow, sow, and harvest.

Serf theater traces its origins back to the court of Empress Elizabeth. It was here that the aristocracy acquired its taste for theater. Mimicking court fashion, the richest grandees, like Count Sheremetev, began putting on small productions in their palaces performed by their fellow aristocrats, their wives, and children. When these emancipated noblemen started leaving St. Petersburg for Moscow and the provinces, they no longer wanted to perform for each other, but to have others perform for them. They dreamed of playing tsar on their estates no matter how far-fetched the limited resources of most of them made this appear. As for the richest aristocrats—the Sheremetevs, Stroganovs, and Golitsyns, the Yusupovs and Razumovskys—the dream could be made reality since they truly did live like kings and queens on their estates, where they set out to create a facsimile of the tsars' court.

Traditional notions of hospitality also played a role. It was de rigueur for wealthy noblemen to keep open house, and as the century progressed it became increasingly common, even expected, for hosts not only to feed and lodge their armies of guests, but to entertain them with banquets, balls, illuminations, and, eventually, theatrical performances. Such openhandedness fueled a competition among the wealthiest noblemen to outdo each other with the extremes of their largess and the extravagance of their entertainments. No self-respecting nobleman dared opt out because his family's honor came to require that he keep an orchestra or theater, no matter how modest, to amuse his guests. One contemporary recalled, "There was not a single wealthy landowner's house where an orchestra did not make a din, where a choir did not sing, and where a stage was not erected."[1] The necessity of keeping up with the Sheremetevs ruined many noblemen of not inconsiderable means.

Serf theater flourished between 1770 and 1820, when some 2,000 serf actors, actresses, dancers, musicians, and set designers worked in more than 170 theaters. About a third of the theaters were found on rural estates, some in remote provinces far from any urban centers, although the majority operated in Russia's two capitals. The greatest concentration was in and around Moscow. All but a dozen or so of these would not warrant the name theater by today's standards. They were typically makeshift affairs of the sort set up by Count Gavriil Wolkenstein in an empty hall of his manor house and consisting of no more than a swath of blue canvas for a proscenium, a striped cloth tacked to the ceiling for a curtain, and a large trestle table for a stage. Most theaters were intended for the private entertainment of their owners and guests, although in some provincial towns they operated as quasi-public theaters.

Only a handful of noblemen were wealthy enough to take dozens of their serfs away from productive labor and devote them solely to theatrical work. More common was the situation at the estate of Prince Alexander Suvorov, the fabled Russian military commander. Although well-off, Suvorov couldn't afford to have his serfs rehearsing and acting all day long, and so he simply added to their already considerable duties. Along with overseeing the estate, his majordomo was now forced to conduct the orchestra and train a small number of serfs to act and sing; the new thespians were now expected to perform on stage as well as cook, clean, and wait table as before.

The best theaters, like Nicholas's, set up well-run schools that provided as good a theatrical training as one might find anywhere in Russia. Some nobles hired professional performers from the Imperial Theater and the Petrovsky, Moscow's largest public theater, to train their students. At his estate near Shklov, Semyon Zorich, a former lover of Catherine the Great, invited European stars on their way to St. Petersburg to stay with him and rehearse with his troupe. A few serfs were sent even to study under virtuosi in Italy and Germany. Serfs were at times put to work in the manor house as domestics to observe the manners of their masters as part of their training. Prince Nicholas Shakhovskoi had his actresses serve as maids to his wife so they could see firsthand how noblewomen walked, talked, and sipped their tea. When they were preparing Alexander Griboedov's classic *Woe from Wit,* he escorted his serfs to several balls at Moscow's Noble Assembly to observe the nuances of polite society. Masters like Shakhovskoi no doubt derived a snobbish pleasure from playing Henry Higgins to all their Eliza Doolittles.

The lack of professionalism of most serf theaters, combined with the eccentric personalities of many of their owners and their serfs' understandable resistance to the entire enterprise, produced some undeniably humorous results. Vasily Gladkov, usually deep in his cups during shows at his Penza theater, liked to deliver a running commentary on his troupe's performance in full voice, much to the annoyance of the other spectators and the embarrassment of the performers. From his loge Court Chamberlain Rzhevsky would dance along to the steps of his ballerinas. The old crank liked to wave his arms about wildly and shout, "Aniuta, higher, jump higher! Grushenka, arms, arms! You, dancing the part of Amura, simply beautiful! And all you others, *cosí, cosí!*"[2]

Prince Alexander Suvorov had a serf by the name of Nikita who performed on his stage. Accounts state that he was quite talented, although this seems hard to believe. Apparently, Nikita had been taught the basics of reading, but his teacher never found the time to give him a lesson on punctuation. On stage Nikita would race through his lines as fast as he could, pausing only to catch his breath. This went on for a time until an exasperated Suvorov wrote his majordomo that he really must set aside some time to instruct Nikita in commas, questions marks, full stops, and exclamation points.

Incomprehensibility undermined the performances in other theaters. Prince Ivan Dolgoruky witnessed a bizarre production of Molière's *Le Bourgeois gentilhomme* in Poltava that sounds like some early theater of the absurd. "No two actors were speaking the same dialect," Dolgoruky observed, "some Russian, some Circassian, some Ukrainian, some Polish. A regular Tower of Babel! No unanimity in attention: as soon as one spoke, another, turning aside, whispered over his lines so he wouldn't forget what came next."[3]

The greatest nineteenth-century serf actor, Michael Shchepkin, described a riotous scene from a staging of *Don Juan* he witnessed in Kharkov in 1816. The play required a device to lower a Fury from above onto the stage, and the deity was then supposed to whisk Don Juan away. Yet as the Fury was being lowered on a rope, she began to spin around and around out of control. By the time she finally landed on the stage she'd made twenty revolutions and was so dizzy she could barely stand, let alone find Don Juan. As she stumbled around, Don Juan yelled in her direction, "Over here, you heathen, over here!" Once the Fury finally found Don Juan she was far too disoriented to hook him to her harness, and the two began fumbling about to howls of laughter and cries of "Bravo! Bravo!" As the curtain was hastily lowered the audience was left with a scene of an enraged Don Juan pulling the Fury's hair.[4]

The director of Ivan Shepelev's theater in Vladimir had trouble keeping his serf choir sober. A large bass by the name of Abram was the worst offender. He had to be locked in a closet offstage before performances to make sure he wouldn't get drunk; the director could always hear him in there begging for a drink to calm his nerves. Once when the director opened the closet he found Abram had escaped through an unlocked window. Abram, dressed in his costume of medieval armor, had made straight for the nearest tavern, telling himself he'd stay for just one drink. When the men in the tavern caught sight of this knight-errant inexplicably transported from the court of King Arthur to dusty rural Russia, they refused to let him go, buying him round after round. By the time Abram staggered out the door he was too drunk to make it home. They found him the next morning asleep in a ditch, muddy and hung over but still in costume.[5]

The repertoire of most serf theaters mirrored that of the Sheremetevs, comprising chiefly French and, to a lesser extent, Italian works. Opéra-comique and bourgeois drama were the most popular. Tragedy was performed only rarely, the assumption being that serfs were incapable of summoning from their simple souls the requisite depth of sentiment. (Of course, the sad irony is that serf actors were often much better able to grasp the ideas and emotions expressed in these works than their masters.) In the eighteenth century, a few impresarios, Sheremetev among them, championed works by Russian composers. In the next century the repertoire of native works grew, and so serf theater can thus be called the cradle of the great Russian theatrical tradition.

The repertoire, if somewhat behind the theatrical fashions of the moment in Paris or Vienna, reflected prevailing European tastes, although when transplanted to Russia the works were perceived with significant differences. Not only were these operas and plays foreign, and so tinged with the allure of the exotic, but the social contexts in which they were staged differed as well. In the capitals of Europe, theater was a large, professional institution supported by the crown and increasingly by a sizeable theatergoing public; the beginnings of contemporary theatrical life can easily be discerned. In Russia, however, theater was still an almost exclusively private enterprise run by the court and aristocracy and free of any pressures of the marketplace.

Noble impresarios possessed absolute power over their performers, and it was the nature of this serf–master relationship that lent a distinctive *frisson* of excitement to the enterprise. Although all theater requires transformation, for the nobleman the experience was enhanced by the knowledge that he could turn his serfs into whatever he desired—kings, queens, grandees, or naïve shepherdesses—and just as quickly turn them back into chattel. This power beguiled not only the master, but his guests as well. Martha Wilmot, an Irish visitor to Russia in the early nineteenth century, wrote during her stay at Princess Dashkova's estate of Troitskoe, "We have a little Theatre here, and our labourours, our cooks, our footmen, and *femmes de chambre* turn into Princes, Princesses, Shepherds and Shepherdesses &c. &c. and perform with a degree of spirit that is astonishing. 'Tis droll enough to be attended at Supper by the Herd of the piece who has been strutting before your Eyes in Gilded robes &c. &c. for half the Evening."[6]

This does not mean, however, there weren't moments of subversive pleasure. Serfs, in their roles as clever servants, were permitted to say things on stage they never could in real life. This did not go unnoticed. "A servant, for example, says such witty and pointed words to his master," commented one worried observer, "that no serf in any home would ever dare say; maids do the same thing in the theater, and these are the characters who get the most laughs in the comedy."[7]

If the serfs found it difficult to fully get inside their roles as idealized shepherds and shepherdesses, there were stock characters that must have struck a chord, most notably the omnipresent lecherous master forcing himself on some poor servant girl. And one wonders what the performers in August von Kotzebue's *The Negro Slaves* (1796), staged at Gladkov's Penza theater, must have been thinking as they sang, "We pitiful Slaves are drowning in our own bitter tears! Come, dear Brother Death! Oh, come and free us!"[8]

Serf actors suffered from a unique double stigma of being both slaves and performers. As in the West, where for centuries stage performers had been perceived as social outsiders, so, too, in Russia actors, because they were considered to make their living by dissembling and deception, were viewed with disdain and suspicion by polite society. They were thought to be dissolute and, especially in the case of women, immodest, unworthy of respect, and lacking virtue. Being beyond the bounds of social propriety conferred upon these women the dangerous glamour of the outsider that adheres to groups on society's margins. This enhanced the perception of the theater as a place of lubricious pleasures, a perception that was especially true of serf theater, where the actresses were even more beyond the pale, even more vulnerable and available.

Like all serfs, serf performers were bought, sold, and given away as presents, just like any other piece of property. Advertisements such as these from the *Moscow Gazette* in 1797 were common: "For sale: 3 horses, 2 bay stallions each 4 years old, and also a 3 year old grayish-brown gelding of English stock. In this same house also for sale is a musician who plays the bassoon and is learning to sing (bass), reads and writes very well. 15 years old. For sale: a housemaid, 16 years old, with a nice voice, sings quite skillfully, and so with this advertisement the owner informs all theater lovers that this girl could well perform theatrical roles, and then clean and prepare good food for the table."[9]

In 1805, a noblewoman from Tambov sold her entire serf choir and orchestra, including their instruments, music, and family members totaling ninety-eight men, women, and children, for thirty-seven thousand rubles. In the second half of the eighteenth century, Prince Grigory Potemkin purchased Count Kirill Razumovsky's serf orchestra for forty thousand rubles, and Prince Shakhovskoi's troupe of nearly one hundred was auctioned off after his death in 1827 for over one hundred thousand rubles. A good male musician could fetch fifteen hundred rubles; an actress, as much as five thousand. Count Kamensky tried to buy Michael Shchepkin for twelve thousand rubles.

Playbills never included a "G"—for *gospodin* or *gospozha*, mister or miss—before the names of serf performers. Neither did they list their last names; to do so would have been to accord them undue respect. Instead, actors and actresses were referred to only by their nicknames—Feklusha, Marfushka, Sashka, Grishka, and the like. Shchepkin recalled a visit the professional actress Pelageia Lukova made in 1805 to the home of his master, Count Wolkenstein, in the provincial town of Kursk. Among the more enlightened noblemen of the town, Wolkenstein received Lukova in his drawing room, where he showed her to a seat and served her coffee and cakes. Shchepkin observed that in those days it was unheard of for an actress—any actress, let alone a serf actress—to be received in such a way in the homes of the provincial nobility. The memoirist Philip Vigel was deeply offended when he dined at the home of Paul Yesipov, a small landowner in Kazan, and his host permitted his serf actresses to sit at the same table with them.[10]

A Frenchman by the name of Passenans who was visiting Russia in the late eighteenth century heard the tragic tale of a serf violinist sent to train in Italy. When he returned, his master was so impressed with his playing he had him perform a difficult concerto by Giovanni Battista Viotti, a prominent composer and the greatest virtuoso of the day. The man's artistry awed his master's guests, and so he ordered him to play it again, and again, and again. When, after three hours of uninterrupted playing, the poor man asked for a brief rest, his master replied angrily, "You will play, and if you dare not to, then I shall remind you that you are my slave and shall have you beaten with the rod." The man ran to the kitchen, grabbed a butcher knife, and in a fit of hopeless desperation chopped off his left index finger. "Cursed by the talent that cannot free me from slavery!" were his supposed words.[11]

On rare occasions serfs fought back. Field Marshal Count Michael Kamensky sent two of his serfs to Leipzig to study music around 1810. They returned not only excellent musicians, but also with new ideas about freedom and universal human dignity. At first the count treated them with a certain respect. Yet after a minor incident, he ordered them whipped in front of all the serfs on his estate. Outraged and consumed by a desire for vengeance, the two later crept into the count's bedchamber one night. They reproached him for taking them from the world God had chosen for them, educating and enlightening them as free men, only to return them to slavery. They set upon him with their axes and hacked him to pieces. The two men fled the estate but soon gave themselves in. They were sentenced to three hundred lashes with the knout, dying well before the final blow had been inflicted.

Some serfs lodged complaints with the authorities, to no purpose; some ran away; some tried to drink themselves into oblivion; and some sought escape through suicide. Still more hardened their souls as a way of distancing themselves from their plight and so denying their masters the pleasure of watching them suffer. Liubov Onisimovna, the aged heroine of Nicholas Leskov's nineteenth-century novella *The Toupee Artist: A*

Graveyard Tale, which deals with the cruelties of serf theater, recalls how she and the rest of her fellow actors and actresses "had all become like stone, we had been trained in fear, and in torment, and so our hearts had become incapable of feeling." Perhaps this is what Prince Dolgoruky was sensing when he saw a group of serf actors performing as if they were "breathing automata."[12]

The history of serf theater is filled with stories of sadistic cruelty that stagger the imagination. A visitor to the actors' wing of Prince Shakhovskoi's theater told of being shown into a room where he found a young man standing in a *rogatka,* a heavy metal collar lined with sharp spikes. The slightest movement caused intense suffering, and the man's face was lined with pain and exhaustion. "What is this?" the visitor gasped. "Oh, I ordered him punished a little," the prince calmly replied, "so that he plays the role of King Oedipus a bit better next time. I'm having him stand like this for a few hours. His performance is sure to improve."

In the next room the visitor came upon a man chained by the neck to a chair in such a manner that he couldn't move. "This here's Seryozha, one of my fiddlers," Shakhovskoi explained, "he played out of tune the other day, and so I've had to punish him." The prince also kept a whip hanging in the wings that he himself would use on the actors when they made mistakes.[13]

Prince Dolgoruky wondered after visiting Shakhovskoi's theater, "What sort of theatrical gifts can one expect to find from a slave who can be lashed and chained to a stool for no reason but arbitrary cruelty? His crowd of actors, which there are many of, perform exactly like an ox with a heavy load being driven on by a Circassian with a switch."[14]

Curses and blows and lashes of the whip were dealt out with regularity and for the most absurd reasons. Gladkov was known to run on to the stage during performances and start beating his actors when they made mistakes. A spectator called his performers "pathetic figures, whose whole demeanor spoke of thrashings . . . you could sometimes see the bruises through their rouge and powder."[15] No theater could compare for horror and ruthless violence with that of Count Sergei Kamensky, son of the Field Marshal Kamensky axed to death by his musicians. Kamensky was a sadist. He would jot down in a little book his actors' slightest mistakes and then go back stage and whip them during intermission. Their screams could be heard over the conversations of the spectators. The plays tended to take longer to perform than at other theaters since the actors needed extra time between acts to bandage their wounds.

"Oh! keep us clear of gentry! Look out for trouble every day with them. And may we be spared the worst of all—the Master's temper and the Master's love." These oft-quoted lines from Griboedov's *Woe from Wit* speak to the other danger that threatened serf actresses. Love, however, is definitely not the right word here. The feelings Nicholas had for Praskovia were rare, possibly unique. *Lust* is the word that best describes what has been called the "erotic bondage" of serf theater.[16]

The promise of living out erotic fantasies played an undeniable role in serf theater's popularity. It did not take long for nobles to realize that the pleasure they received from their actresses need not be limited to the merely aesthetic but could include those of an earthier nature as well. Of course, masters' preying on their servants is an old story. What made this different were the forms these predatory instincts took on, reflecting in revealing ways the culture and mentality of the Russian nobility.

The same tradition of noble hospitality that helped to give rise to serf theater also served to extend the idea of what it meant to entertain one's guests. Serf actresses occasionally doubled as hostesses, waiting on the master's guests at table and in the bedroom. General Ismailov tried to outdo his peers with his hospitality by giving each male visitor to his estate one of his serf girls for the length of his stay. Another nobleman set up his own "Isle of Love" inhabited by dozens of compliant nymphs. Some estates were decorated for parties with living statues of naked women on pedestals striking classical poses; on many stages the ballerinas danced in see-through gowns. Prince Nicholas Yusupov treated his guests to orgies that Moscow society euphemistically called "gallant escapades."[17] As soon as the prince dropped his cane, all his dancers would shed their costumes and dance naked.[18]

Some masters chose not to share their actresses with others, keeping them locked up when not on stage. There was an element of make-believe in this, a whiff of the exotic East. The master played the role of an Ottoman sultan, the actresses' wing became his harem, and the actresses, his odalisques. No one took this fantasy further than Ivan Shepelev. He had his private apartments done up in the Turkish style and went about in nothing but Oriental robes. He hired a director for his orchestra, yet reserved for himself the right to work with the women's choir.

In *Journey to Little Russia*, a book that reads like a nineteenth-century precursor to a guidebook for the modern sex tourist, Prince Peter Shalikov describes with quivering excitement his visit to an estate near the village of Buda. Shalikov and the other male guests were entertained at this "island of charms" by "young Terpsichorean nymphs" and "captivating creatures" from their host's corps de ballet. Shalikov was especially taken by the prima ballerina dressed as a gypsy: "Imagine one of the Graces, with black hair, black eyes, the most pleasing smile on the most perfectly formed rose-colored lips, in a dress of scarlet cassimere; and along with this, imagine the lively expressiveness of a Gypsy dance. . . . I thought I was in Athens in the Temple of Pleasure." Throughout his narrative Shalikov inverts the true order of things. The serf dancers are his masters, he is their prisoner, a defenseless captive to their irresistible charms. Only the gypsy, he sighs, can "set him free." After her dance, this goddess descends from the stage, approaches Shalikov, and "comforts and helps a poor, pitiful me . . . gives me everything." The orgy went on for days—in the theater, in the gallery, and in a pavilion tucked away in the estate park.[19]

Confronted with the plight of serf actors, one might think, if only they had been free their lives would have been different, so much easier and less degrading. In fact, the lives of all actors, serf and free alike, were remarkably similar. Most professional actors in Russia during this period started out as orphans in foundling homes, where, from around the middle of the eighteenth century, they were given acting lessons and then farmed out for more training (often for a price) either directly to the imperial theaters or to a theater school. All of them were at the mercy of the authorities—first, the men in charge of the foundling homes, then the masters at the theater schools, and finally the theater directors themselves—who controlled every aspect of their personal and professional lives. Actresses could not marry without their permission, nor could they quit the stage unless they first purchased their retirement for an exorbitant sum (that is, paid their own ransom), which few actresses could ever afford. Performers who disobeyed were beaten with rods or, in extreme cases, sent off to the army for a life sentence. In 1816, a female dancer in the Imperial Theater was arrested simply for refusing to perform in an opera. Punishments like these were common well into the 1840s, after serf theater had largely disappeared.

Professional actors had no legal recourse; the law began and ended with the theater director. Most actresses learned early in life that their bodies were their greatest asset. The pretty (and lucky) ones found wealthy patrons to supplement their meager incomes, lavish them with expensive gifts, and, when necessary, intercede on their behalf with the manager. Sex was commonly traded with the managers for all manner of favors, from better roles or costumes to a pay increase or a reprieve from punishment. Karl Knipper, head of St. Petersburg's German theater, reportedly forced every one of his new actresses to have sex with him before her debut; after that, he would pimp them out after every performance. Some of the theater schools functioned as brothels, forcing girls as young as twelve into prostitution. And it wasn't just the girls; young boys were also sold for sex.[20]

Although these tales of depravity, degradation, and sadism were real and common, one ought not allow them to obscure serf theater's important legacy. More than a diverting pastime for the nobility, serf theater laid the foundations for the great flowering of Russian theatrical life in the nineteenth century. Even its harshest critics begrudgingly admit that the best serf theaters, such as the Sheremetevs', rivaled the great theaters of Europe and provided a crucial stimulus to theatrical development in Russia. In a country with no significant middle class, only wealthy noblemen had the resources to build and maintain theaters. They brought the theatrical arts to the provinces for the first time, introducing the best of European and Russian music, singing, and dancing. Thanks to serf theaters, a theater public was born, one whose ranks soon spread beyond the aristocracy to embrace the gentry as a whole, civil servants, merchants, and tradesmen. These classes began to seek out a more national repertoire and helped generate a truly Russian theater culture.

Before the rise of serf theaters, acting had been the domain of imported Europeans. Noble impresarios found native talent and nurtured it, creating the first generation of Russian thespians. Some serfs took to the stage, and not all of them acted merely out of compulsion. There were instances even of serfs organizing their own theaters, although these were typically shut down for operating without their masters' permission.

Many serf performers were extremely gifted, later going on to distinguished careers in public theaters and the Imperial Theater in the nineteenth century. Shchepkin's performances in *Woe from Wit* and Nikolai Gogol's *The Inspector General* helped to make them classics. Ivan Turgenev was so impressed with Shchepkin that he began writing plays for him. Shchepkin's style of acting, which stressed naturalness and simplicity, inspired the renowned Konstantin Stanislavsky. Indeed, one of Shchepkin's last students, Glikeria Fyodotova, gave the young Stanislavsky some of his first acting lessons, and the core of Stanislavsky's ideas on method acting is rooted in those first elaborated by Shchepkin.

The origins of Stanislavsky's method might be traced back even further, all the way to Praskovia. Shchepkin's father is thought to have seen the Sheremetev theater perform at Kuskovo. It is possible that his tales of the Pearl inspired his son Michael to take to the stage.[21]

Napoleon's invasion in 1812 dealt the first blow to serf theater. When the Grand Armée retreated, it left the Russian countryside in ruin. The nobility took on massive debts to rebuild their ravaged estates and burned-out palaces, making theater more of a luxury than it had been for the previous generation. Some sons of the noble impresarios could no longer afford the opulent lifestyle of their parents. Some no longer cared to. By the late 1820s, serf theater was seen by many as old-fashioned and vaguely distasteful, just as the previous generation had reacted against their fathers' fondness for dwarves and blackamoors. The party had moved on.

Capturing the atmosphere of this bygone world, Alexander Pushkin wrote, "The estates around Moscow are all empty and woeful: the sound of horns no longer rings in the groves at Svirlov and Ostankino; lampions and colored lanterns don't light the English paths, now overgrown with grass, and where once myrtle and wild orange trees grew. The palace theater has stood empty since the final performance of some French comedy. The wings are dusty, and there's mold and rot. The nobleman's house falls into ruin."[22]

II

OSTANKINO

Quiet, comforting, peaceful Ostankino, its soothing groves of pine and lime trees perfume the air with their luxurious fan and cool the sultry midday hours. . . . This pleasant place breathes of a particular freshness, a green emerald near Moscow's ancient white walls, a calm little spot where one can find respite from the bustling noise.

—ANDREI MURAVYOV, *The Russian Fivaida of the North*

TWELVE

"*I intend to build . . .*"

I intend to build a theater at Ostankino," Nicholas wrote his steward Agapov on 13 February 1790. That same day he issued an order to his home office appropriating twelve thousand rubles for the construction of the theater and new palace at his estate north of Moscow.[1] This order marked the beginning of what was to become the major building project of Nicholas's life. Nicholas intended Ostankino to be the greatest theater-palace in Russia and the perfect showcase for Praskovia and his theater. It would stand as a monument to Nicholas's wealth and taste and the glory of the Sheremetev family. It took nearly a decade to build, at monumental cost. When it was finally finished in 1798, Nicholas was millions of rubles in debt, Praskovia had retired from the stage, and the Sheremetev troupe had given its last performance.

After his father died Nicholas embarked on a manic building spree. In July 1789, he ordered the reconstruction of the old theater in Moscow; that autumn he began remodeling the theater at Kuskovo. Then, in August 1790, he began building a brand new theater at the estate of Markovo and later one at his dacha Champêtre outside St. Petersburg.

All of these projects were secondary to what Nicholas was planning to erect in Moscow. His idea was for a giant Palace of the Arts to be built on the site of the Chinese House. The palace, referred to as Une Grande et Belle Maison, was conceived as a unified architectural complex comprising two parts: a suite of private apartments for daily living and another of public rooms large enough to accommodate a thousand visitors. The private half would include rehearsal space, wardrobe, and storerooms, living quarters for as many as 250 actors and musicians, and the count's apartments. The public rooms would include painting and sculpture galleries, a Kunstkammer, a hall for scientific experiments, a cabinet of natural history, a library, and an arsenal. This enfilade would double as a grand foyer to a theater big enough for four hundred.

There was nothing like it in Russia, and the plans alone sent the count's acquaintances into paroxysms of amazement. "Such a grandiose, expansive, and magnificent work," wrote Count Julius Litta, "will create such an impressive sight and will at the same time combine the pleasing with the useful. There will be nothing comparable to it in Russia. It will inspire the best artists in Italy and will unleash a competition to design buildings, and their art will be erected here in the North."[2]

Nicholas commissioned plans from the leading architects in Russia— Ivan Starov, Yelizvoi Nazarov, Giacomo Quarenghi, and Francesco Camporesi. When they failed to capture his vision, he hired architects in Italy, France, and Sweden. He purchased the architectural plans for the fifteen largest theaters in Europe for use in designing a theater that would excel them all. Nicholas insisted on the best acoustics, on scenes that could be changed instantly, and a moveable parterre that could quickly be raised to the level of the stage, thus transforming the theater into a large ballroom. He instructed his architects that it was to look like nothing ever built before—his Palace of the Arts would outshine "the Coliseum in Rome and the theater at Herculaneum."[3]

These projects did not put a stop to the troupe's performances. During Shrovetide, Praskovia and the company performed *The Marriage of the Samnites* in the Chinese House in Moscow. The performance was a big success, and Nicholas rewarded the troupe with a gift of two hundred rubles.[4] A performance and fireworks display were given at Kuskovo on 2 August. In September, Praskovia debuted in Nicolas Marie Dalayrac's wildly popular sentimental drama *Nina, or The Girl Mad Through Love.* Around this time Nicholas also staged Voltaire's *Nanine, or Prejudice Defeated.*

Shortly after *Nina* premiered on the Sheremetev stage, Nicholas received word of a production being performed by a troupe of noble amateurs in St. Petersburg that was causing a great stir. When members of this group arrived in Moscow at the beginning of 1791, Nicholas asked Prince Ivan Dolgoruky if they wouldn't perform for his own serf actors. An eccentric, temperamental figure and sworn enemy of the Sheremetevs, Dolgoruky was ruled by three passions: poetry, women, and the theater. He ran his own modest serf theater for a time but was best known as an amateur thespian whose mania for the stage extended to all aspects of his life. He liked to go about Moscow in colorful costumes he'd worn onstage and couldn't perform in a play without seducing one of the actresses, much to the chagrin of his long-suffering wife, Yevgenia Smirna, a talented performer as well.

No matter how great his animus for Nicholas, Dolgoruky's vanity couldn't say no, and for the next several weeks, the prince, his wife, and other members of his family rehearsed for Nicholas and Praskovia, who sat in the parterre watching and perhaps silently critiquing Yevgenia's performance. Many years later Dolgoruky left an account of this experience (or, more accurately, his wishful remembrance of it) that oozes with the envy many nobles felt toward Nicholas, the hatred the claimants harbored for him, and the beau monde's disdain for Praskovia:

Count Nicholas Petrovich Sheremetev was a base, miserly, vainglorious, and in all ways empty man. A true satrap, nothing more. He loved opera, and his people performed it for him, which his father started. An inherited taste! When my first wife and I arrived in Moscow on leave from Petersburg, it was in the winter time, after my wife had successfully performed *Nina* there, the count wanted us to perform it for him so that his favorite singer (and lover) Parasha, whom he later married, could observe her and copy her artistry. (Parasha still had a long way to go to perfect her roles. Where there's a will, there's a way.) He kept after us to do him this favor; the old man wanted to see how my wife acted, and this was the only opportunity. Wishing to please him, we decided to grant the count this indulgence and all gathered to perform *Nina* at his theater. But so that we could be our own complete masters of this business and to do away with the slightest suspicion that we were doing this out of some slavish wish to amuse this Croesus, we set the following conditions with him, namely, that we shall give the roles ourselves to whom we wish, that we shall not use any of the persons he proposes, and that two-thirds of the tickets will be for us, one-third for him, but he could not give out a one without our knowledge.

And so, having in this manner maintained for ourselves complete control over his theater, we began rehearsals, during which he directed the orchestra himself seated at the fortepiano. Our troupe consisted of our family; my wife performed, my younger sister, I, Rukin, and Yakovlev. The choir comprised the count's singers. . . . On the last day before Lent we performed our opera, and even though there was an enormous ball for Potemkin at the Noble Assembly, and even though that ball was the last winter gathering for the nobility, the count's theater, which seated as many as 150 spectators, was full of the city's best people. Not one seat was empty, and the count himself directed the music. The opera was a big success, and everyone was delighted with my wife . . . and I must admit it was very difficult for me to put on a comedy at the count's theater, for I felt nothing but loathing and scorn for him his entire life.[5]

Prince Potemkin did indeed pass through Moscow in early February 1791 on his way to the capital. He was returning from his army headquarters at Jassy in the south to confer with the empress on the war against the Ottoman Turks and to take the measure of her new lover, Platon Zubov. For weeks Moscow had been a whirl of activity in anticipation of Potemkin's arrival.

Potemkin was a friend to the Sheremetevs, and Nicholas wanted to publicly acknowledge this fact with a large entertainment. On 8 February, a grand concert was given for Potemkin in the Petrovsky Theater to honor the recent Russian victory over the Turks at Ismail. The music was by Giuseppe Sarti, the noted Italian composer and Potemkin's Kapellmeister, and the musicians and chorus were mostly Nicholas's. It isn't known whether Praskovia and the other stars performed that night, although her sister, Matryona, apparently did. Nicholas was most pleased with her performance and gave her a raise of seven rubles. In early August, Potemkin returned to Moscow on his way back to the south, and Nicholas hosted him at Kuskovo. The prince, as famous for his conquests in the bedroom

as for those on the battlefield, was taken with the dancing of the beguiling Tatiana. He asked Nicholas if he might meet her afterward, which
he did and presented her with an expensive kerchief.[6] This was to be the
last meeting between Nicholas and Potemkin.

Nicholas had recently recovered from the first serious recurrence of
his illness in several years. He was confined to bed for much of June and
July with what he described as bilious fever; he would begin to recover
after weeks of rest, only to be laid low again with rectal bleeding, fever,
paroxysms, and exhaustion. Never one to suffer in silence, he wrote to
Prince Andrei Shcherbatov in St. Petersburg, asking him to make sure
everyone at court was informed of his illness.[7]

That autumn of 1791 while still at Kuskovo Nicholas received word of
his cousin Vasily Sheremetev's wedding. The match had caused a commo-
tion in Petersburg, for although Vasily's bride, Tatiana Marchenko, was
a noble, society considered her a rube (she was from Poltava), unworthy
of the Sheremetev name and entrée to the finer homes. The upholders of
aristocratic society saw the marriage as evidence of the collapse of traditional norms. "Society has been so utterly ruined," moaned one snob upon
hearing of Vasily's wedding, "that our descendants may well choose their
brides from Kamchatka."[8]

Vasily confided in Nicholas and found in him a sympathetic friend.
Nicholas supported Vasily's decision to marry for love and told him he
had been right not to let society choose a bride for him. The controversy
brought the men closer; they realized they saw matters of the heart in
similar ways and began to entrust each other with their secrets. Vasily was
one of the few people Nicholas told of his feelings for Praskovia. Their
intimacy extended to include Praskovia and Tatiana, and although they
were rarely together, through their letters the couples gave each other
the warmth, friendship, and understanding they could find little of elsewhere.

There were others close to Nicholas with intimations of Praskovia's
special place. Earlier that summer, Prince Dmitry Trubetskoy, a relative
on Nicholas's mother's side, wrote a warm letter expressing his wish to
visit Nicholas and "the 'countess'" at Kuskovo.[9] The choice of words is
vague and intriguing. It might be a reference to Nicholas's sister, Varvara,
although she and Nicholas were no longer close and rarely spent time
together. Perhaps it is a playful and knowing reference to Praskovia. If so,

that would suggest that, to some, Nicholas and Praskovia had become a true couple, even if they had to keep it a secret. And perhaps the idea of marriage first occurred to them at this time, if only dimly, a decade before it became a reality. But before Nicholas could convince himself to marry Praskovia, he first had to overcome his prejudices about noble birth.

It is something of a paradox that as he fell deeper in love with a serf, Nicholas was becoming more conservative in his social views. Now a man of forty, Nicholas was no longer the young maverick described by Marie-Daniel Bourrée Corberon in his journal. True, he held himself apart from noble society much of the time, but his thinking about the hierarchies upon which Russian society rested was increasingly falling into line with that of his peers. Once when Nicholas learned that his clothes were being washed in the same kettle with those of his domestics, he flew into rage, ordering this stopped at once.[10] The world was filled with kings and queens, nobles, commoners, and serfs; these differences were sanctioned by God and were to be recognized. If Nicholas couldn't conceive of dirty clothes mingling, it was a long way to taking Praskovia for his wife.

By late summer 1791, things were looking up for Nicholas. He had fêted Prince Potemkin, and the news of his entertainment had reached the empress. After months of poor health he was feeling well again, and he had set up a household with Praskovia that afforded a degree of calm and privacy. But the most exciting thing still lay ahead—Catherine had accepted his invitation to be his guest in Moscow before year's end.

The empress had last visited the Sheremetevs in the summer of 1787 at Kuskovo. The reception had been a huge success, yet all the accolades had gone to his father. Now it was Nicholas's turn to host Catherine, and he intended to outdo Count Peter. Nicholas was most excited about an opera he had commissioned for the occasion from Hyvart the previous year. Hyvart had written in December 1790 that he had found a "very talented, although second-tier, poet to compose a large opera in three acts with recitatives according to the wishes of Your Excellency, in which the rare services and incomparable virtues of the Empress will be praised. This opera will depict the visit of the Sovereign Empress to the home of Your Excellency."[11] He promised to send the opera to Nicholas the moment it was ready.

On 27 March 1791, Hyvart wrote that things were almost ready:

The libretto for the grand opera, including the choruses and dances, as you ordered has just been finished. I am only awaiting the drawings of the decorations and costumes, which are not quite ready, before sending it to you. The opera is called *Tomyris—Queen of the Massagetai*. It is a heroic opera in three acts. This composition, being by its nature a serious and political work, is beyond comparison with the opéra-comique *The Marriage of the Samnites*. . . .

The four main dramatis personae are Her Imperial Majesty, in the guise of Queen Tomyris; Their Imperial Highnesses the Grand Duke and Duchess under the names of Fyodor and Pentazilei; and Your Excellency, under the name of Governor Bartses. Permit me to say that I already feel some of the pleasure that you are experiencing knowing that Her Majesty may well visit you once again this year and will see the premier of *Tomyris*.

The decorations and costumes will be as luxurious as one might expect from the costume of a Scythian.[12]

Three weeks later Hyvart sent the score, libretto, set drawings, and costume sketches.

In his history, Herodotus tells the story of Tomyris, queen of the Massagetai, who slayed Cyrus, founder of the Persian Empire, on the river Araxes in 530 BC. The Massagetai were considered a Scythian race. They were a fierce, warring people who, so Herodotus writes, practiced human sacrifice and cannibalism on the elder members of the tribe (these elements were probably left out of the opera). When Cyrus threatened to attack the Massagetai, Tomyris warned that if he did not turn back, she would give him his fill of blood. In the ensuing battle, Tomyris's son was killed (another awkward moment for the librettist) along with the greater part of the Persian army. Tomyris kept her vow. She had Cyrus's head brought to her, dipped it in a skin filled with blood, and spoke: "Thus I make good my threat, and give you your fill of blood." The scene was recalled in sculpture and painting, most memorably by Peter Paul Rubens. Later versions of the story talk about how Tomyris went on to expand her kingdom to the shores of the Black Sea, which fit well with Catherine's war against the Ottoman Turks and Russia's expansion into these same lands.

Nicholas was jittery with anticipation about the approaching fête. As a small sample of what awaited her, Nicholas sent Catherine a gift of several crates filled with fresh produce (cherries, apricots, pears, cucumbers, asparagus) from his orangerie at Kuskovo. The Sheremetevs had been famous for decades for their lavish hospitality. Nicholas was about to show the world that everything up until now had been no more than a foretaste of even more magnificent pleasures.

THIRTEEN

Farewell to Kuskovo

On 5 October 1791, Prince Potemkin died unexpectedly in Bessarabia. His death devastated Catherine and threw the court into turmoil. The reception Nicholas had been preparing for the empress was canceled. The collapse of his plan sent Nicholas into a depression and marked a turning point in his life. He began to cut his connections with Kuskovo and to focus his energies increasingly on Ostankino and the Palace of the Arts.

As a kind of farewell to Kuskovo, Nicholas organized a grand festival on 1 August 1792. The fête signaled both Nicholas's adherence to the older Kuskovo traditions of his father and his breaking away from this glorious past. It was a beautiful clear day, and by noon thousands of simple folk had arrived at the estate to feast on fruit and ice cream, tea, punch, and wine laid out on large tables in front of the Big House. The invited guests were treated to lunch in the white hall while the orchestra played and a chorus performed Italian arias. Following the meal Nicholas bid the guests to the balcony to enjoy a view of dozens of serfs dressed in colorful costumes parading about pretending to be engaged in lively conversation. It was a scene worthy of "Rembrandt's brush," one participant noted.[1]

The party moved on to the outdoor theater—their path flanked by two rows of serfs doing traditional Russian dances—to see Monsigny's *Rose and Colas* and Grétry's *The Talking Picture*. The common folk were permitted to watch as well. Later, Marc-Antoine Désaugiers's short opera *The Two Sylphs* was performed for the noblemen and women in the wooden theater. No playbills have survived from that day, and so while it cannot be said for certain that Praskovia performed, it seems likely she did. One guest wrote that the female lead "amazed everyone with the purity and beauty of her voice."[2] This must have been Praskovia. At least one more opera would be performed again at the estate, but it isn't known whether Praskovia performed in it. It is possible this was her swan song at Kuskovo.

Although it was now late, the fête went on for several more hours with dancing, fireworks and illuminations, supper, and music in the park by the horn orchestra. No one wanted to leave, and when the sun arose the next morning many weary revelers were still trodding the road back to Moscow. Although it did not compensate for the failed celebration intended for Catherine, the fact that everyone in the city talked of nothing for days but the "magnificence" of his party, which surpassed anything done by his father, offered Nicholas a measure of consolation.[3]

Nicholas and Praskovia left Kuskovo the following month for the estate at Markovo, where Nicholas liked to spend some time every autumn. He fell ill again and suffered from catarrhs and insomnia. Dr. Frese prescribed bloodlettings and leeches, which Nicholas resisted since they induced in him frightful fainting spells.

While at Markovo Nicholas received a letter from Vasily Sergeevich Sheremetev urging him to come to St. Petersburg. Nicholas replied that he was not against visiting although he had no desire to move there permanently. The idea of a trip to the capital had been on his mind for some time. He wished to see Catherine and check his credit with Platon Zubov, now the most powerful man in Russia following Potemkin's death. Yet he hesitated; he was worried how he would be received and feared being snubbed. Vasily tried to lure him with the possibility of being presented an order, possibly that of St. Alexander Nevsky, the third highest state order, of which there was talk at court. The idea tempted Nicholas, but the risk of making the trip and then being denied the honor frightened him. This would give rise to all sort of talk that he wished to avoid. His first inclination was not to take any chances and to remain in his "nest"—unnoticed and undisturbed.[4]

Vasily also wrote that it was time for him to seriously consider getting married. Nicholas replied, "Your friendly insistence that I marry and your thoughts on the subject are fair; but you can easily see that this is such a thing that one cannot compel even oneself to do. I shall say that I have every intention of marrying and that my mind tells me of the necessity of this; but since I have yet to come to a final decision, so I am unable to go through with it. God's will and the proper time, determined by the Creator, are also necessary; then everything will happen quickly of its own accord."

In a postscript Nicholas asked Vasily to destroy his letter after reading it and apologized for not having written the letter himself, but dictating it to a "trusted person." This trusted person was Praskovia.[5]

The exchange between Nicholas and Vasily raises several questions for which there are no clear answers. Was Nicholas now actually considering marrying Praskovia? Had the two of them discussed the matter? And if they had, why hadn't Nicholas thought to free Praskovia? Nicholas's love for Praskovia had grown deeper over the past several years, and Vasily was one of the few people he trusted with his feelings. But had he dared tell even him the true extent of his affection for Praskovia? It seems unlikely that Vasily would have been urging Nicholas to marry Praskovia at the same time he was trying to get him to come to St. Petersburg and test the waters. Marrying his serf would have ruined Nicholas at court and ended any hope of an order or any further benevolence from the empress.

So Vasily must have had someone else in mind; unfortunately, his letter has been lost, and so we don't know whether he named anyone in particular. Perhaps it was meant as a general piece of advice. One hopes so, for otherwise the hurt that writing these lines would have caused Praskovia would have been enormous. As it was, any talk of Nicholas's marrying must have been difficult for her. It is hard to imagine they had come to an understanding about marrying in 1792. Praskovia must have known it was her lot to be Nicholas's mistress and that he was bound to marry someone of his class, even if in the tender moments they shared he told her otherwise.

Later that autumn, Nicholas overcame his trepidation and decided to make the trip to St. Petersburg. First, however, he had to put things in order. Construction had begun in January 1792 at Ostankino and by May the theater was taking shape. That spring the architect Camporesi presented a plan for the entire palace-theater complex. Nicholas, however, was not pleased with the pace, and so in October he sent his serf architect, Alexei Mironov, and his head scene-shifter, Fyodor Priakhin, there to take over and speed up the work. On the eighteenth he dispatched Agapov as well with instructions to force everyone to work harder and faster and to send Nicholas regular reports on the progress. The men began to work on Sundays and holidays from five in the morning until ten at night by the dim glow of candlelight. Nicholas surrounded the project with secrecy. He sent orders that no outsiders were to be permitted near the palace and even prohibited any of his relatives from coming on the property. He had the main bridge onto the grounds torn down. Six Hussars patrolled the estate's perimeter day and night and a tall fence was built to shield the work from view. Overseer Siziakov was instructed to lock the doors to the theater and permit only workmen inside; he was to keep the keys on his person, entrusting them to no one.[6] Going back on his earlier decision, Nicholas threatened that anyone failing these orders would be handed over to the army.

In November, Nicholas turned his attention to another of his Moscow properties, a hospital to care for the poor, old, and infirm near the Sukharev Tower. Nicholas had laid the cornerstone for the building on 28 June, his forty-first birthday, and now ordered that it was to begin accepting up to fifty needy persons. This was the beginning of what was to become known as the Sheremetev Almshouse, which over the next two centuries would offer aid and comfort to millions of people and would become a shrine to Praskovia's memory.

Nicholas, Praskovia, and dozens of the extended household and staff, along with several of the best performers and musicians, arrived in St. Petersburg toward the end of December. Nicholas made his first appearance at court on 9 January 1793, attending a comedy at the Hermitage Theater and a ball in the Winter Palace. Whatever concerns he had about his favor with Catherine were put to rest, and although he did not receive the order (this wouldn't happen for several years), the empress on several occasions did invite Nicholas to dine with her and a small number of intimates in her private apartments, a clear sign of Catherine's pleasure.

Zubov received him politely, if not effusively, and let it be known he bore Nicholas no ill will.

As he had expected, Nicholas's visit unleashed a torrent of gossip. There was talk that he had come to win a post at court and had no intention of returning to Moscow. And there was talk he was planning to marry. In early April, Count Vladimir Orlov wrote Nicholas from Moscow, "There have been rumors here recently that many distinguished personages in your parts wish to enter into marriage, and they include you in their number, and it's said a Petersburg beauty has managed to win your heart." Nicholas answered, "To this I shall report to Your Excellency that my heart still does not feel conquered, and there's little hope of this until such time that the obligations of honesty and faith determine."[7]

It is intriguing to wonder whether this mysterious "Petersburg beauty" had any connection to Vasily's letter from the previous autumn. The name of this particular lady has been lost, but there must have been many beauties with their sights on Nicholas. Although he was no longer young, he was not unpleasant looking and was still the richest bachelor in Russia. The rumors must have been difficult for Praskovia to hear, not that she had to confront them. She remained at home, not accompanying Nicholas on his social outings, where the air was thick with marital intrigue.

This was Praskovia's first visit to the capital. Like the other performers, she had no opportunity to explore St. Petersburg. What she saw from her carriage window, however, would have filled her with wonder and surprise, for here was a city unlike any she had seen before, with its canals, its long, straight avenues, its gilded spires, and its ornate palaces. As in Moscow, most of Praskovia's day was spent rehearsing. It appears she gave at least one concert during their stay. In a letter from April to Major Alexander Kuchetsky, who had married Nicholas's half sister Anastasia Remeteva the previous spring, Nicholas makes reference to a concert at which Praskovia performed the day before. "They praised her to the sky," he wrote. "You cannot hear such singing here."[8]

In May, Nicholas followed the court to the tsars' summer residence at Tsarskoe Selo before returning with Praskovia and the others to Moscow in late June 1792. Buoyed by his warm reception at court, Nicholas began making plans to return as soon as possible. Staying just long enough to check up on the work at Ostankino—now in the hands of the architects Ivan Starov and Vincenso Brenna—and his Palace of the Arts (the building materials were being stockpiled), he and Praskovia left Moscow in the heat and dust of late August.

Preparations for the trip were made with great secrecy. In July, Nicholas wrote to his steward in the capital not to tell anyone but Prince Andrei Shcherbatov of his pending arrival; negotiations on renting a home were to be done "in silence." The reason for the secrecy had to do with the fact that he wanted to keep his living arrangements private. Nicholas communicated to his steward that the home should be big enough to accommodate his large staff, yet have discrete rooms in it for "a husband and wife and their four maids." If necessary, it would be fine to find space for this pair in a separate home close by, as long as it is quite comfortable. Nicholas and Praskovia couldn't stay at the Fountain House, which was rented out until October 1794, or at the dacha outside the city at Champêtre on the Peterhof road, which Nicholas had made available for the Turkish ambassador.[9] On 11 September, Nicholas was once more at court. The next month he was one of three invited to dine with the empress in the Winter Palace. His credit was indeed on the rise.

On his name day in November, Nicholas received a present of caviar and cake in the post from Prince Ivan Alexeevich Dolgoruky, the son of Princess Martha Dolgorukaia. He included a brief letter with best wishes to Nicholas along with a playful reprimand: "I have also enclosed three cakes for Praskovia Ivanovna, and I ask Your Excellency to promise to give them to her and not to eat them yourself, as you did last year."[10]

From St. Petersburg Nicholas directed the work at Ostankino. Detailed instructions and long lists of questions were dispatched almost daily throughout the first three months of 1794. As always, Nicholas attended to the last detail: Did the furniture arrive yet from Petersburg and did it suffer any damage from dampness or mice? where are the profile drawings of the main theater and the Egyptian pavilion from Ostankino? how many statues are there and what kind of condition are they in? has a new sculptor been hired and at what pay? is enough wood being cut down for Ostankino at Zhulebinskaia Grove? is the stove for the theater's reception room being constructed precisely according to the drawing I sent?[11]

As the weeks passed Nicholas became ever more agitated by the slow pace and pushed them to work faster. He never made it clear why the palace had to be built in such a hurry, but it seems he had decided to make Ostankino his new home and was intent on moving in as soon as possible. He no longer wanted to live at Kuskovo, filled as it was with so many memories. Kuskovo was bound with his father's name, and Nicholas wanted to strike out on his own, to create a name for himself as a patron of the arts and grand seigneur.

And then there was the matter of Praskovia. The serfs at Kuskovo knew her story, and Ostankino offered Nicholas and Praskovia the opportunity to start afresh, to make a break from their past and leave behind all the gossip and cruel talk that followed them there. At Ostankino they would live quietly, unobserved and undisturbed, except for performance days, when Praskovia would be able to display her talent on the finest stage in Russia. One more thing was eating at Nicholas. This was Praskovia's family. Having them nearby was a constant reminder of Praskovia's peasant origins, a fact Nicholas didn't care to recall. Taking Praskovia away from Kuskovo would make it easier for him to forget that she was not to the manner born. It would also make it harder for her family to interfere in their lives. Seeing Praskovia living with the master and hearing the talk of the other serfs, they were certain to get ideas about improving their own lot that he didn't care to encourage. Better to be out of sight, and so out of mind.

All of these things fed Nicholas's dream of a new life for the two of them at Ostankino, and it became an obsession that couldn't be realized fast enough.

From St. Petersburg he complained to his overseers at Ostankino. "Stop writing me these incompetent reports, for my patience truly is running out," he scrawled at the bottom of one directive. He worried they were slacking: "About Mironov—check to see whether he's sick and sketching the plans, because he's ruled by laziness and stubbornness. . . . I've noticed that without me there people have gotten lazy; so I advise you to be more diligent and keep a close watch on everything." And he began to suspect his orders were being ignored and that Mironov was hiding things from him and was up to "something suspicious." He threatened Agapov and Modest Balagaev that he was on to their "intrigues" and would eventually catch them out and punish them.[12]

The expense was getting out of control. In 1792 alone, Nicholas had spent over eighty thousand rubles just on Ostankino, not to mention his other building projects. He pushed his stewards to find ways to cut costs, either by haggling for better prices, reusing old materials, or finding cheaper replacements. In late February, he ordered a full accounting of all expenditures, down to the last kopeck, for the previous year on his theater, Kuskovo, Ostankino, the Palace of the Arts, and other estates. In March, Nicholas ordered his office to draw up a statement of all his outstanding debts, "not overlooking the smallest one."[13] On the fourteenth of the month, he ordered all work stopped on the Moscow almshouse to save some money. Days later he ordered a halt to all other building projects except Ostankino. Although it wasn't mentioned by name, this probably included the Palace of the Arts, which was never to be realized. It wasn't enough to cut back on spending; Nicholas was desperately short of cash. He missed the due date on a ten-thousand-ruble loan owed his sister Varvara and had to ask her for an extension. He borrowed one hundred thousand rubles from the State Bank in Petersburg at 5 percent, seventeen hundred rubles from his ballet master Cianfanelli, and twenty thousand from a Voshchazhnikovo serf by the name of Semyon Barin. At the same time Nicholas began increasing the quitrent on his estates. Between 1765 and 1798, the dues increased nearly threefold on most estates and as much as eight and a half times on some.[14]

Nicholas and Praskovia remained in St. Petersburg throughout the spring of 1794. Nicholas was now attending court infrequently, having instead to tend to work in the Senate's Land Survey Department, much to his displeasure. He was working so much there that he began to worry in April he might have to move permanently to the capital against his wishes. This was a lonely time for Praskovia. On 3 February, Tatiana, several of the other dancers, and Cianfanelli and his wife were sent back to Moscow on twelve sledges accompanied by soldiers of the Preobrazhensky Regiment. To help keep Praskovia occupied Nicholas arranged for the court harpist Jean-Baptiste Cardon to come to the house and give her lessons.

On 17 May, Nicholas wrote Zubov to request leave from the Senate until January 1795 so that he might return to Moscow and put his affairs

Plate 1. Countess Praskovia Ivanovna Sheremeteva. For a long time it was believed Nicholas had commissioned this portrait around the time of their wedding, although it was most likely painted only after Praskovia's death as part of Nicholas's efforts to commemorate his late wife. (N. I. Argunov, 1803–04. © Kuskovo Estate Museum)

Plate 2. Senator, Actual Privy Counselor, and Chief Chamberlain
of His Imperial Majesty's Court Count Nicholas Petrovich Sheremetev
depicted in the regalia of the Order of Malta in 1801, the year of
his marriage to Praskovia. (John Atkinson, 1801.
© Kuskovo Estate Museum)

Plate 3. Praskovia "the Pearl" Kovalyova as Eliane in Grétry's
The Marriage of the Samnites at the height of her career around 1790.
(Johann Bardou [?]. © Kuskovo Estate Museum)

Plate 4. Prima ballerina Tatiana "the Garnet" Shlykova in 1789. Praskovia's closest friend, Tatiana took her knowledge of Praskovia's and Nicholas's intimate affairs with her to the grave. (N. I. Argunov. © Kuskovo Estate Museum)

Plate 5. Countess Praskovia Sheremeteva in the early 1800s. After their wedding, Nicholas showered Praskovia with jewels. (N. I. Argunov [Tonci-?]. Oil on canvas. 71.5 × 58 cm. © The State Hermitage Museum)

Plate 6. A tender portrait of Praskovia by an unknown artist, painted most likely during her pregnancy with Dmitry. (Unknown artist, 1802–03. Courtesy Ostankino Estate Museum)

Plate 7. Nicholas in his ceremonial court uniform as chief chamberlain from around the time of his wedding. (N. I. Argunov. Oil on canvas. 85 × 68 cm. © The State Hermitage Museum)

Plate 8. Posthumous portrait of Praskovia pregnant with Dmitry.
The deathly pallor of Praskovia's face belies the new life inside her
waiting to be born, while the strange bust of Nicholas that appears to
have come inexplicably to life adds to the scene's macabre atmosphere.
(N. I. Argunov, 1803. © Kuskovo Estate Museum)

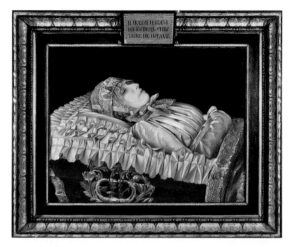

Plate 9. Praskovia's deathbed portrait. The text at the top is her most beloved Bible passage, Psalm 118, verse 18—"The Lord hath punished me severely, but He hath not given me over to death." (N. I. Argunov, 1803. Courtesy Ostankino Estate Museum)

Plate 10. Praskovia's and Nicholas's son, Dmitry, as a little boy. (T. Vodo, 1804. Courtesy Ostankino Estate Museum)

Plate 11. Posthumous portrait of Nicholas commissioned by Nicholas's friend Alexei Malinovsky to hang in the great hall of the Sheremetev Almshouse, which is visible in the background. A bust of Tsar Alexander I looks on at right. (Vladimir Borovikovsky, 1818–19. © 2006, State Russian Museum, St. Petersburg)

in order before moving to St. Petersburg for good. Later that month, Catherine granted his request.

Nicholas and Praskovia returned to Moscow around the beginning of July; he immediately rode out to Ostankino to inspect the work. That summer Nicholas shuttled back and forth between Kuskovo, Ostankino, Moscow, and Markovo. As he put it, he was forced to "run about like a messenger." All the while, he didn't neglect the theater. On 5 August, Nicholas raced from Ostankino to Kuskovo, where the next day an opera was to be performed.[15]

With the end of his leave approaching, Nicholas wrote Zubov and other powerful men at court in late November to ask for an extension until June 1795, which the empress agreed to. Nicholas had suffered another painful attack of his anal fistula that autumn; Dr. Frese resorted to attaching leeches to his posterior, which brought some relief, but Nicholas still felt too weak to travel. The main reason for his request, however, was the poor condition of the Fountain House, which Nicholas planned to remodel after his tenant moved out in October. He told Zubov that he wished to return to the capital only after his primary residence was suitable for habitation. The work was entrusted to Starov. Plans included replacing the old wooden floor in the entrance hall and main staircase with stone, adding fresh stucco to all the walls and ceilings, and putting in new oak floors on the second floor. The master bedroom was to be completely remodeled in a more sumptuous manner, with a new floor, doors, and stove, marble windowsills, and fresh wallpaper.

In his instructions to Starov, Nicholas made one unusual request—he wanted thick felt affixed to all the bedroom walls and doors facing the main staircase so that "not the slightest sound" could be heard in the hall.[16] Nicholas was not about to let nosy servants eavesdrop on his private life with Praskovia, on their intimate conversations, and the sounds of their lovemaking.

FOURTEEN

Ostankino's Premier

Nicholas and Praskovia finally moved to Ostankino in the summer of 1795. The paint was still drying on the walls and there was more work to be done, but the palace was close enough to completion for them to settle in. Nicholas's leave was to end soon, and they would be forced to return almost immediately to the capital. Desperate to stay, he once more wrote Platon Zubov to intercede on his behalf with Catherine, and once more she agreed to a six-month extension. At least for now, they could relax and get to know their new home.

Ostankino lay several versts north of Moscow just beyond Marina's Grove, once a favorite place with bandits and thieves. The palace sat in quiet solitude, surrounded by lakes, rivers, and woods. From the upper story one could just make out through a cut made in the woods the gold cupola of the Ivan the Great bell tower in the Kremlin; when the bells tolled, their faint echo could be heard all the way out in Ostankino.

The area around Ostankino was believed to have a cursed past. In pagan times witches and sorcerers were said to have been buried here in richly jeweled garments. Their remains were watched over by a mysterious old woman who warned anyone against disturbing the ground. Legend had it that several of the owners of the land had refused to heed her and had come to bad ends. In the nineteenth century, villagers told the story that this old creature had warned Nicholas from digging there too, but he hadn't listened and paid for this with the death of Praskovia.

Nicholas and Praskovia did not live in the main palace, which was meant for entertaining, but in a small wing called the Old Home off the courtyard near the Church of the Life-Giving Trinity.[1] The rooms possessed the same simplicity of their quarters in the Kuskovo park. Nicholas had his own bedroom with a large mahogany bed, stove, and red-tile fireplace, a study, and library. A narrow chamber with icons of Nicholas the Miracle Worker and St. Dmitry of Rostov provided a place for prayer. The bright song of canaries carried throughout the house from a cage that hung outside Nicholas's bedroom.

Praskovia's room was off the dining room and adjacent to a large room for Tatiana and a few of the other actresses. The walls and ceiling were painted light blue; the plain wood floor was covered with a black rug with yellow and red flowers and a red border. She had two birch chairs painted white and green with striped cushions, a large mahogany trunk, a small bench covered in green fabric, two nightstands, a table with a toilette mirror and kit, two small alabaster candleholders, and a bronze desk clock. Thin curtains parted to reveal glass doors opening onto a private garden. In the spring the sweet smell of lilac filled her rooms.

Prints and paintings covered her walls. There were two portraits of Catherine the Great, one of Nicholas, and a panoramic depiction of the death of Prince Potemkin. There was her own portrait as Eliane from *The Marriage of the Samnites,* painted just a few years earlier. But mostly there were sentimental depictions of loving families — a woman in a white dress holding a small girl by the hand; a man and woman, arm in arm, looking down at a baby boy nestled between them; a woman working at a spinning wheel under the loving gaze of her husband. The scenes were standard eighteenth-century images, yet in them Praskovia possibly saw something worth more to her than her fame as a singer and all the Sheremetev riches. They represented the unattainable, a simple, happy domestic life that Praskovia longed for. Here men and women were lovers, husbands and wives, mothers and fathers, not masters and serfs. They offered Praskovia a vision of a world she longed to join but never would.

No matter how much they differed from her own family life, the images could not have helped but make Praskovia think of her parents and siblings back at Kuskovo. She was grateful to have Matryona with her, but she did not forget the others. Praskovia did what she could to help them, and Nicholas was not deaf to her entreaties. That same year Nicholas increased her father's salary from fifteen to fifty rubles, clearly not because his work had improved (he descended further into alcoholism with each year), but as a favor to Praskovia. This was added to the ten rubles he was already paying her mother, who had to look after seven-year-old Ivan Ivanovich. Her brother Michael had been apprenticed to a dressmaker three years earlier and was now living with a women's tailor by the name of Linbe in Moscow. Nicholas provided for his clothing, salary, and living expenses too. Her brother Nicholas had also been taken from Kuskovo and was being trained by a foreign master to be a violinist in the count's orchestra.[2]

Nicholas also kept an eye on Praskovia's godmother back in Voshchazhnikovo. That spring the local deacon had moved into Anna Andreeva's house and Nicholas wrote the estate manager to make sure he wasn't bothering her and was being of use about the cottage. If the deacon was causing any trouble, he wanted to know about it and wanted him punished straightaway.[3]

It was a consolation to Praskovia to know that her relationship with Nicholas could make her family's life easier, and his willingness to help communicated to her both the depth of his love and the goodness in his heart. In April of that year, Nicholas renewed work on the hospital at Sukharev Tower, possibly after discussing the matter with Praskovia, who was deeply committed to the charity.

No sooner had she settled in at the Old Home than Praskovia was busy rehearsing for the debut at Ostankino. Every morning she would cross the courtyard to the palace, the fine gravel crunching softly underfoot, and wend her way through its gilded corridors to the theater, where she would spend her days. Despite having grown up surrounded by the splendor of the Big House at Kuskovo, Praskovia had never seen something so grand.

Ostankino palace was not a private home, but a spectacular theater attached to a series of ornate halls and pavilions filled with art and antiquities. As had been the plan for the Palace of the Arts, the theater at Ostankino was the focal point of the ensemble from which the rest of the palace radiated outward. The glory of Ostankino was its theater. It was one of the largest in Europe, equal to that of the Swedish Royal Drotningholm built for Gustav III and Paris's Théâtre de l'Odeon. The elegant horseshoe-shaped hall seated 250. The palette was warm and bright, with pinks, bluish-greens, silver, and gold. A giant retractable chandelier hung from the ceiling, and the wings were lit by 150 candles in holders with special reflectors of the latest design from Paris. The acoustics were superb.

The theater had been outfitted with the most modern machinery. The space above the stage was divided in two sections. The first section was crisscrossed by a web of twelve interconnected bridges. The forwardmost was the "captain's bridge." It sat twenty-two feet above the stage and afforded clear views of the stage and seats and access to *le paradis* (the balcony) and a staircase leading to the actors' loges just offstage. From his perch on the captain's bridge, the machinist Priakhin directed the complex scene changes and special effects with a whistle, using long and short peeps and pauses to send his instructions to the twenty-six stagehands. The second section off to one side was the "machine gallery." Two massive wooden wheels were rolled along the floor of a large, hollow cylinder above the proscenium to create the sound of thunder. There was a narrow shaft fitted with metal flaps arranged in a checkerboard pattern running down an interior wall to the hold below the theater. This was the rain machine. The slow pouring of sand into the top produced the sound of gentle rain; pieces of small shot created the sound of heavy rain; large wooden balls cascading down the shaft produced thunder. There was a wind machine and a device to mimic floods. Either side of the proscenium was fitted with a hidden system of ropes and pulleys that could whisk actors off the stage and into the heavens, the so-called *la gloire* device. Three large wooden drums in the hold below the stage were turned to create the impression of large armies on the march.

As had been planned for the Palace of the Arts, the theater could be transformed into a large ballroom in less than an hour by raising the parterre and enclosing the stage with dummy walls and columns of papier-mâché and a ceiling of painted canvas.

The premier was set for 22 July 1795. There was still work to be done on the palace, but Nicholas's impatience got the better of him, and he simply couldn't wait any longer to show it off. The opera was *Zelmira and Smelon, or the Capture of Ismail,* Osip Kozlovsky's lyric tragedy based on a libretto by Count Paul Potemkin, a general, writer, and cousin of the late great prince. Nicholas had originally planned on performing Antonio Sacchini's *Renaud,* based on the Italian poet Torquato Tasso's epic poem *Jerusalem Delivered* (1580), and had already ordered the necessary costumes and sets, practiced his stage-shifters in the complicated and quick scene changes and special effects, and put the troupe through rehearsals. But then Nicholas changed his mind.

During the years of planning and construction Nicholas came to see Ostankino as more than just his palace and an expression of his person. Rather, it took on a larger, national significance in his mind. Ostankino expressed a "supreme" act "worthy of amazement" from all.[4] It was a sign of Nicholas's service to the Russian state, a fulfillment of his patriotic duty to the nation. He decided that *Renaud,* which told the story of the First Crusade, was too foreign for such an occasion; he considered *Tomyris,* but it didn't seem right without Catherine present.

Nicholas was enthralled by Turkish themes at the time and sought an opera that brought this together with recent political and military events. It's possible that Nicholas commissioned the work, which reads like a translation of *Renaud* into a contemporary Russian context, from Count Potemkin. Kozlovsky, an epigone of Gluck and the composer of works trumpeting Russia's victories on the battlefield, was the ideal choice for expressing the dramatic heroism of Potemkin's story, a fanciful account of the bloody capture of the Turkish fortress of Ismail in 1790. General Alexander Suvorov's stunning victory had been a turning point in the Second Russo-Turkish War and unleashed a boom of patriotic fervor. To add to the solemnity of the occasion, Nicholas invited veterans of the siege to the premier.

Hundreds of guests began arriving for the premier late in the afternoon. For years Muscovites had heard about the new palace Nicholas was building at Ostankino, but no one had ever seen it. They couldn't wait to get inside and see for themselves what Nicholas had built at such great cost and under such unheard-of secrecy. None of the guests that day recorded their reactions, but they must have been as awestruck by what they saw as later visitors to Ostankino were.

"One of the servants led us through all the rooms," wrote a foreign guest in the early years of the nineteenth century. "I saw there such treasures that even an Indian Moghul doesn't possess: gold, mirrors, paintings, statues, vases, jeweled fabrics shimmered all about. I saw it all in passing, moving from one object to the next. It appeared to me as if the place were magical, the marble seemed to be alive. . . . What luxury! What magnificence!"[5]

Such wonderment was typical. "The estate of Count Sheremetev . . . is called Ostankino, and he has a palace, the interior splendour of which exceeds anything I ever saw of the kind," wrote a German traveler.[6] A bewitched Philip Vigel sighed, "No one surpassed Count Sheremetev's magnificence. . . . The luxurious décor of his home appeared to be the work of magic."[7]

After viewing the palace, the guests were shown into the theater. *Zelmira* opens to a scene of the Russian forces gathered below the sheer walls of the fortress of Ismail on the lower reaches of the Danube River. The hero, the Russian officer Smelon (Courageous in English) performed by Peter Smagin, is in love with Zelmira, the daughter of the commander of Ismail (sung by Praskovia), who offers Zelmira's hand in marriage if Smelon will call off the siege. In the struggle between love and duty the latter wins; Smelon renounces his heart, and the Russian troops seize the fortress. Yet so impressed is the commander by Smelon's bravery, he gives Zelmira to him anyway.

The opera met Nicholas's demands, both as a glorification of Russian military power and as a work of art, with its rapid scene changes, large cast requiring as many as seventy performers together onstage, and spectacular effects culminating in the walls of the fortress tumbling down in a mighty crash amid bright flashes of light and explosions produced by lycopodium powder. The horror of the battle scenes was contrasted by moments of tender love between Zelmira and Smelon.

The performance was a triumphant success and inspired an anonymous versifier to praise the opera's power to make "the Victors weep!"[8] As his guests left, Nicholas basked in their compliments. After years of work he had finally achieved his goals. He now had a theater large enough to stage the grand operas of the Gluck school. He had a talented and excellently trained troupe of actors, singers, and dancers and an outstanding orchestra. He had developed an extensive repertoire of the latest, most popular operas, ballets, and plays. He had amassed an enormous collection of costumes, props, sets, and stage designs. And he had established his theater as the finest personal theater in all Russia. Nicholas's theater was the subject of talk across Russia and as far away as London.[9] So successful had the Sheremetev theater become that Michael Maddox, the impresario of the Petrovsky Theater, Moscow's largest public theater, lodged a complaint with the city authorities, claiming it was stealing his audience and running him out of business.

Little did anyone suspect that that night was to be the theater's final premier and the beginning of the end of Praskovia's career.

Zelmira was performed a second time on 26 August, after which Nicholas and Praskovia left Ostankino to visit some of the other estates around Moscow. Before he left, Nicholas ordered more work done on the palace. The first two fêtes had shown that a vestibule and upper foyer had to be added to comfortably accommodate all the guests. Laborers and craftsmen immediately set to work; walls came down, new ones went up, parquet floors were laid, ceilings painted, furniture ordered, statues, paintings, vases, and sculptures purchased. Despite Nicholas's insistence that the work be finished quickly, repairs would drag on until the spring of 1797.

While away, Nicholas wrote the overseer to have everything ready for their return at the end of September. The stoves were to be lit to drive the chill from the air. "Put in double frames on the windows," he ordered, "caulk and putty the cracks in the walls and floor. Also, don't forget to plug all the mouse holes, and do what you can so there aren't so many of them. Bring in some cats to get rid of the mice if necessary. Check for holes in my small rooms, and check Parasha's and the girls' rooms as well and stuff any holes with wadding. Put in a double-pane window in Parasha's room, and raise the floorboards if needed so there's no draft and her room is nice and warm."[10]

They remained at Ostankino that autumn just long enough for Nicholas to inspect the work on the palace and attend to a few theater matters. He had a fresh layer of gold gilt applied to Praskovia's chariot from *The Marriage of the Samnites;* he increased the salary of many of the singers and doubled that of all the dancers (from six to twelve rubles) and those of the chaperones.

Nicholas and Praskovia next visited Markovo and Meshcherinovo in October, where he sacked several overseers accused of stealing and extorting bribes from the serfs, before heading for Kuskovo at the end of the month. The weather had turned bad to match Nicholas's mood following the visits to his estates. To make matters worse, he was laid low with illness. His fistula had flared up and was causing him anguish. The bleeding wouldn't stop, and he was afflicted with "cold spasms" that gave him headaches and made it difficult for him to breathe. He was bedridden almost the entire month of December.[11] Praskovia stayed by Nicholas and did what she could to comfort him.

Nicholas was in the middle of a letter to Prince Andrei Shcherbatov ("The bleeding, which has gone on now for long, is frequent and considerable, is ruining my body, and my spirit as well, and has rendered my frail constitution quite weak") when the doctors arrived and prepared to apply a Spanish fly. All this depressed Nicholas and gave him little cause for hope. "It appears the blind are leading the blind," he concluded.[12]

It was a sad end to what had otherwise been a spectacular year.

FIFTEEN

Training the Troupe

In the early years of the theater Nicholas had been able to find enough performers from among the house serfs on the estate at Kuskovo and other nearby estates. Over time, however, he was forced to make broader searches and periodic levies of young serfs between the ages of nine and thirteen from distant lands. The favored place was the Sheremetevs' southern estates in Ukraine, especially Borisovka and Alexeevka.

Serfs didn't wish to hand over their children to the overseer to be sent off to their master's home for use in his theater. Some tried to hide their children; others bought off the overseer with bribes. Facing resistance, Nicholas sent the serf musician Fyodor Smagin to Borisovka in 1790 with orders "to select for my home theater orphaned girls who are literate and whose faces and bodies are not deformed in any way."[1] Orphans were desirable since they had no parents to get in the way. Smagin and others sent to the estates were told to go out into the fields and attend church services and listen for promising young voices. Nicholas had chosen Smagin because he was tough and less apt to give in to the overseers' excuses.

The locals closed ranks when Smagin arrived and did their best to subvert his mission. They became wary about singing in the open and continued to bribe the estate administration. Sometimes the overseer gathered the requested number of boys and girls and sent them to Moscow regardless of the quality of their voices simply to meet the quota.

Boys who failed their vocal tests in Moscow were sent back home; girls who couldn't sing but were pretty were kept to be used as actresses. Smagin reported the difficulties he was facing. Nicholas responded by giving him a pay raise and improving the benefits for recruits—fifty rubles yearly salary, extra money to cover room, board, and clothing, and freeing their families of all taxes. In 1795, Nicholas offered two hundred rubles to the "best bass or tenor among my Little Russian serfs who expresses his desire and ability to join my choir."[2]

Nicholas eventually put Smagin in charge of a music school in Borisovka. This school and a second in Alexeevka became feeders, preparing dozens of children for the main musical academy at Kuskovo. Nicholas ran the most professional theatrical school of all the noble impresarios. Indeed, his school might rightly be considered one of the finest in Russia, free or serf. By 1791, the number of students had grown to over thirty. Several of the instructors were themselves serfs. The sexton Peter Naumov taught reading and writing; the serf architect Mironov taught mathematics; Stepan Degtiarev taught singing; and Fyodor Riabinin, literature. The program of study also included history, geography, catechism, and moral philosophy. Students studied under specialists in their given fields, be it music, singing, or acting. Nicholas also trained serfs to be set builders, carpenters, stagehands, tailors, seamstresses, and hairdressers, all assigned just to the theater. Nicholas even trained serfs to be instrument makers. One of these serfs, Ivan Batov, the "Russian Stradivarius," rose to become one of the greatest makers of stringed instruments in all of Russia. Tsar Alexander I once paid two thousand rubles for a Batov violin.

For singers and actors instruction in a foreign language was required. In 1789, Signori Torelli and Babarini were hired to teach Italian and French and give singing lessons. The following year Nicholas hired Vincenzo Alippi, a tenor he had brought to Russia from Parma to work with his troupe. An irascible character, Alippi lasted less than a year. He was prone to loud shouting at Nicholas's table, stomping his feet and ranting how he'd been lured to work for the count under false pretenses. He had expected to perform for Nicholas and his friends, not teach serfs. Nicholas typically sat quietly during these rants—interpreted for him by the other Italians on his staff—and tried to answer his complaints. Finally, the household awoke one morning to find Alippi gone, having fled Moscow for St. Petersburg, where he joined up with an opera buffa troupe newly arrived from his homeland.

Girls were afforded special attention in order to transform unsophisticated peasants into polished ladies, fluent in French and Italian as well as in the manners of polite society. To that end, Nicholas hired two Frenchwomen, Madams Chevalier and Douvre, as governesses who also taught comportment and manners.

Performers who displayed promising talent took lessons from the stars of the Russian stage. Nicholas sent his actor Vasily Zhukov to St. Petersburg to work with Ivan Dmitrievsky, one of the fathers of the Russian theater. Dmitrievsky instructed Zhukov in acting, singing, violin, and clavichord.[3] Around the same time three actors took lessons in St. Petersburg from Sila Sandunov of the Imperial stage. A brilliant comedic actor, Sandunov's *emploi* was that of the clever, witty servant. Sandunov worked with Andrei Chukhnov and Fyodor Kiriushchenkov, also gifted comedians, in the role of buffa, and Ilia Ptishnikov in that of the lover. When Sandunov visited Moscow, Nicholas hired him on a short-term basis to rehearse with his troupe. Sandunov's wife, the actress Elizabeth, taught Avdotia Beliaeva. Nicholas also engaged the young Vasily Pomerantsev, one of the finest actors of his generation, praised by the writer Nicholas Karamzin as "the Russian Garrick." Pomerantsev, Yakov Shusherin, and Peter Plavilshchikov, a popular actor of the Imperial stage and Maddox's Petrovsky Theater, all worked for Nicholas. Nicholas also rented a loge at the Petrovsky and took his performers to watch and learn from the performances there.

Dance instructors were almost exclusively foreigners. The first had been Francesco Morelli, employed for several years beginning in 1779. Although Morelli was lured away by the Petrovsky Theater, he had nothing but respect for Nicholas. Years later, after the death of his first wife, he married the daughter of one of Nicholas's servants and moved back to Ostankino. He was still there in 1813, when he wrote requesting a position as an overseer on the Ostankino estate, claiming he single-handedly saved the palace from Napoleon's forces. Morelli's first wife, Angelica Caselli, had danced at court with her husband before leaving to teach for Nicholas. Caselli stayed on with the count even after her husband had moved to the Petrovsky Theater.

Nicholas replaced Morelli with Giuseppe Salomoni. Maddox had brought Salomoni de Viena, as he was known throughout Europe following a glorious engagement in the Austrian capital, to Moscow for the Petrovsky. In 1788, Salomoni, a choreographer as well as a dancer, staged his own ballet, *The Honest Thief*, at Kuskovo, and two years later Nicholas engaged him as an instructor.

In 1791, Nicholas hired one more Italian dance master, Antonio Cianfanelli, who had been the number two dancer at court since his arrival from Florence in 1785. He turned down a contract extension from the empress in 1791 to join Nicholas's theater: the count offered to pay him more. Cianfanelli arrived with his wife, Caterina Coppini, the prima ballerina at court.[4]

Nicholas was immensely satisfied with Cianfanelli and his work. When he fell ill, Nicholas provided him the best medical attention and ordered one of his footmen to stay with him at all times. He left Antonio and Caterina alone with Tatiana Shlykova in St. Petersburg for several months and permitted the three of them to travel in his carriage back to Moscow in February 1794. When Cianfanelli and his wife left for Italy in the summer of 1795, Nicholas gave them a promissory note worth eleven thousand rubles and a gift of one thousand for the journey. They were replaced by Pietro Pinucci, dance master at the Petrovsky, and then by Alessandro Guglielmi, a dancer at the Imperial court theater.

The greatest of all dancers working with the Sheremetev troupe was the Frenchman Charles Le Picq. Catherine the Great herself brought him to her court in 1786 after a spectacular career across Europe. Nicholas sent his two best ballerinas—Tatiana and Mavria "the Turquoise" Uruzova—to St. Petersburg to study with Le Picq. What most drew Nicholas to Le Picq was that he had been a star pupil of Jean-Georges Noverre, the creator of modern ballet. Nicholas was fascinated by Noverre's reforms, which had turned dance from a stiff, artificial interlude between opera acts into a true art form full of emotion and drama, and he wanted to be the first in Russia to show off the new *ballet d'action*. So profound was Nicholas's passion for Noverre that years later he sent the aged master a gift of two hundred rubles via Le Picq's widow. His dedication to the ballet paid off, and by the mid-1790s the Sheremetev dance troupe was second only to that of the Imperial Ballet.

For the orchestra Nicholas favored Germans, first among them Johann-Heinrich Facius. In 1789, another German by the name of Feyer joined the orchestra as first violinist and served alongside Facius as one of its directors. A few other free musicians played at times in the orchestra—a German oboist by the name of Wenzel Mai and a pianist named Meier. A handful more Germans were hired on as occasional music teachers, and in the spring of 1793 Nicholas tried to negotiate the hire of a few musicians from Vienna. All told, eleven foreigners performed in the Sheremetev orchestra, along with a few free Russian musicians.

The Germans Facius and Feyer were in charge of the orchestra. In their absence, three talented serfs took over: Assistant Kapellmeister Peter Kalmykov, a first violinist, pianist, and expert in instruments, entrusted by Nicholas with purchasing his pianos and clavichords; second violin Ivan Volodomirov, in charge of rehearsals; and the composer and former singer Stepan Degtiarev.

Degtiarev was the standout. He had been the orchestra's first director and conductor, but as time went on he increasingly devoted his energies to musical arrangements, composing, and serving as choirmaster. Degtiarev and his sister Stepanida had been taken from the estate of Borisovka as children to sing in the choir. He received some of his earliest music lessons from the composers Giovanni Rutini and Giuseppe Sarti. Considered one of the founders of Russian classical music, he composed over his long life nearly sixty concertos, numerous songs, and several large oratorios—the first ever by a Russian composer. His greatest work, *Minin and Pozharsky*, composed during Russia's war with Napoleon, was revived during World War II to inspire Russians in the struggle against Nazi Germany.

The foreign masters formed the top layer of instructors. Below them was a group of the best serf actors, dancers, singers, and musicians to lead the daily rehearsals, usually under the supervision of Vasily Voroblevsky or the actor Nicholas Kiriushchenkov. The singers did scales and solfeggio almost daily or rehearsed selections from operas.[5] Each orchestra member was assigned pupils—as many as five—and expected to bring them up to the level of the other musicians. The pupils typically did not get to select their instrument but were assigned one by Nicholas or Peter Petrov. If the young musician proved unable to make progress, he could petition to switch to another instrument.

Nicholas put together the rehearsal schedule. "See to it the musicians, first: practice their horns from nine to eleven in the morning; second: from eleven to twelve all are to memorize their parts in their rooms; third: from two until five all masters are to work with their pupils; fourth: if the musicians cannot play their horns due to illness, then rehearse the music from one of the operas."[6] He instructed overseers to keep a strict eye on all rehearsals. "You are to keep a close watch over all the actors in my theater," he wrote, "so that they all rehearse with the necessary dedication their roles for all the operas and comedies and display exemplary zeal. Should anyone be seen to be negligent or careless in the fulfillment of his duties, then you are to report this to me."[7] He had his stewards collect for him weekly reports from every teacher.[8] Nicholas followed the progress of his troupe while away, and at times grew angry at what he considered the slow pace and lack of zeal on the part of some of the teachers and his stewards. On 13 January 1793, Nicholas wrote from St. Petersburg to Petrov in Moscow,

> I am extremely surprised that during my absence the instruction of my actors and actresses has been going quite slowly and that some of the instructors, such as Maria Siniavskaia, Pomerantsev, and Shusherin, come by only rarely and so only the slowest progress has been made. Yet as I was convinced of their good disposition toward me, so I had hoped to see much greater progress in the instruction of my actors and others. . . . I think that were I there three weeks would not go by without instruction, and to be honest one is obliged to do behind one's back what one has promised to do to one's face. If they really wanted to do it, they would find the time. And so it is clear they do not care to do me a good service, which I am quite sorry to see.[9]

When not preparing for a performance, the dancers were required to rehearse only three times a week. Nicholas wrote Petrov that more than this was superfluous and "there's no reason to work them hard if it's not necessary."[10] Nicholas always attended the final rehearsals before any major production. He was adamant about making sure everything was just right and refused to accept any invitations or guests during the buildup to a performance.

For the first ten years or so of her career, before she left the other performers to live and travel with Nicholas, Praskovia followed the same schedule as everyone else. Her days were routine and monotonous. As it became clear she was to be the prima donna of the troupe, Nicholas made sure Praskovia received the best possible instruction.

Siniavskaia was the leading lady at the Petrovsky, famous for her roles as the virtuous, long-suffering heroine imbued with great feeling and an unshakable sense of duty. She came to work for Nicholas in 1790 and taught Praskovia and the other females in the troupe for the next eight years. Siniavskaia, together with Anna Pomerantseva, Vasily's wife, worked intensively with Praskovia. They helped her to improve her acting, developing her mastery of the new sentimental style favored in the 1790s, which stressed the cultivation and expression of concrete personal feelings, of individualism, and the exploration of the individual's subjective emotional world.

Another influential teacher was Elizabeth Sandunova, an opera diva of enormous talent. Her warm soprano, with its breathtaking range of almost three octaves, enthralled audiences. Her repertoire extended to over two hundred roles, and although equally at home in French, Italian, or Russian compositions, she made her greatest mark in Italian works. Sandunova was also a brilliant actress; she loved playing women of different nationalities and spent long hours perfecting her accent, hand gestures, body movements, and the smallest details of her costume to make her characters believable. A beautiful woman with dark eyes and hair and a graceful figure, Sandunova became the object of desire of many powerful men, most notoriously Count Alexander Bezborodko, Catherine the Great's lecherous advisor. Bezborodko stalked her and tried to stop her marrying the actor Sila Sandunov. Only the intervention of the empress saved her from the rapacious Bezborodko.

It is intriguing to wonder how much of her experiences on- and offstage Sandunova shared with Praskovia. In the rehearsal breaks did she tell her of the difficult life that faced free actresses? Did Praskovia dare to wonder how she might fare on her own? The thought was ridiculous; the Sheremetevs didn't free their serfs. But even if Nicholas did, what would it mean? How would she survive? Could she fend for herself?

Sandunova's story and those of other actresses made it impossible for Praskovia to fantasize about an easy, uncomplicated life beyond the cloistered world in which she found herself. The many broken lives were a caution to serfs who might think they could survive as free artists. Praskovia was not free, but she had everything she might hope for to develop her talent. What's more, she was well cared for, was treated with respect, and lived better than many nobles. And Nicholas loved her. It would have been unimaginable to ask for anything more.

SIXTEEN

Life in the Troupe

The men and women in Nicholas's troupe lived much better than the serfs in other theaters and were treated more humanely. They were kept separate from the other serfs and cut off from the outside world in a series of wings attached to Nicholas's urban palaces. At Kuskovo and Ostankino the performers and musicians were housed in a few buildings beyond the administration wings. The buildings were not crude barracks, but well built, comfortable structures with bright white columns and plenty of windows. The group of actresses installed in the Old Home near Praskovia's apartments at Ostankino enjoyed a commodious main room with two stoves, bright yellow wallpaper, mahogany furniture, a clavichord, a wall-mounted thermometer, and even a cage for a pet canary.[1]

The troupe also had good clothing and food, better than those of domestic serfs, let alone the mass of peasants. All the men were issued camisoles and pants of Spanish cloth; the women had dresses, skirts, and blouses. They all received fine hats and well-made leather shoes and heavy fur coats for winter. Members of the orchestra wore uniforms for performances and special everyday tailcoats that distinguished them from the rest of the troupe. When they needed new clothes, the performers did not feel constrained in telling Nicholas. In the autumn of 1797, the male dancers and musicians petitioned Nicholas for new winter coats and hats, and he immediately granted their request, adding that hats and coats be purchased for all the singers too.

The leading actresses had clothes of the latest style and the finest materials. Nicholas gave them gifts of money, too, so that they might order finery from the Moscow haberdashers. Nicholas once purchased a dress for Anna the Emerald worth 200 rubles—the annual salary of a low-level noble official. Nicholas ordered fancy outfits from the best tailors for his actresses and ballerinas; the eleven hairdressers on his staff kept them beautifully coiffed. He bought them jewelry and ordered colorful powders and pomades, ribbons and bows and fine silk stockings from Paris; they performed perfumed in scents imported from Provençe. Every woman in the troupe was given a separate clothing allowance. In 1789, Praskovia received 80 rubles; Anna, 60; Tatiana, 50; Praskovia's sister Matryona, 30. In 1799, Nicholas gave Praskovia a shoe allowance of 100 rubles a year, plus an additional 560 rubles for her purse. The men received an allowance as well, though considerably less.

Along with the food, clothing, and shelter Nicholas provided in kind, he also gave his performers supplementary cash payments and a salary, unusual among noble impresarios. Members of the choir earned 35 kopecks, in silver, a month; the male lead, 1 ruble. The top male actors received between 12 and 17 rubles per year, which was little compared with the salaries of the top females. In 1797, Praskovia was paid 50 rubles a year; Anna, the next highest, 30; Tatiana, 25.

In all, Nicholas spent nearly 1,000 rubles a year on salaries alone, not counting the money expended on clothing and food and housing and the same expenses for his hundreds of other domestics. So well did Nicholas pay Praskovia and a handful of the leading actresses that in 1785 his estate administration turned to them for a loan of 433 rubles and 22 kopecks (most of it from Praskovia and Anna) to ease a temporary liquidity problem. The money was paid back in full eleven years later, plus 592 rubles and 64 kopecks in interest. Five serf actresses had, in effect, more than doubled their money in ten years by playing, willy-nilly, moneylender to the richest man in Russia![2]

Performers were assigned one of six grades of food rations. At the bottom was the "lower ration," which was the same given the lowest rank of house serfs. Next came the "footman's ration" for the hundreds of the count's lackeys, footmen, and servants. The "junior dancers' ration" was the third level, followed by the "upper ration." A small number were admitted to the "kitchen table," where all the waiters and servers ate, and a handful or so received the top ration, that is, the food served Nicholas at the "Master's table."

Like everything else connected with his theater, Nicholas oversaw the details of the troupe's diet, down to the last spoonful of tea. "Give the girl comedians for dinner," Nicholas wrote his steward in 1796, outlining the food requirements for the upper ration, "1 soup, 1 roast meat with gravy, 1 milk porridge; for supper: soup, roast meat with gravy, milk porridge à la maître d'hôtel, 1 fancy bread, 1 piece of white bread (made from sifted flour). For all those with this same ration, they can go to the kitchen once daily for 1 extra piece of fancy bread. The actresses Fekla and Mavra Biriuzova are to be given 1½ zolotniks of black tea and 12 zolotniks of sugar a day. The actor Nicholas Kiriushenkov and dancer Vasily Vorobyov are each to receive 1 zolotnik of black tea a day. The singers Ivan Nikolaenkov and Grigory Kokhanovsky, each 1½ zolotniks of black tea and 12 zolotniks of sugar for both every day."[3] They regularly received carp and cabbage and cucumbers soaked in brine. For Praskovia and a few others there was white bread brought in daily from the French baker in Moscow. When Nicholas felt their rations weren't enough, he would order extra cabbage and butter.

Nicholas kept strict discipline over the troupe and was especially careful of leaving the men and women together unsupervised. Men and women, children and adults all lived in separate quarters under the watchful eye of overseers, stewards, duennas, and governesses. The actors' and actresses' dressing rooms at Kuskovo and Ostankino were purposely placed on opposite sides of the theater. The frequent travels between Kuskovo, Moscow, and Ostankino afforded opportunities for casual interaction, but Nicholas was careful to convey the women separately or with adequate oversight. Females were taken in separate carriages to their rehearsals, and when Nicholas once learned that his serfs Fyodor Travin and Avdotia Beliaeva had ridden together to a lesson with Sila Sandunov he flew into a rage, requiring Sandunov to assure him that nothing untoward had happened.

Alexei Agapov was in charge at Ostankino. Directly beneath him were several overseers and "commandants" who had authority over all the serfs on the estate, including the troupe. Two or more overseers looked over the male and female halves of the troupe, always of the same sex. They in turn had two helpers and several young boys beneath them whose official job was to tend to the performers' daily needs, but also acted as spies to collect information on the goings-on in the actors' wings. All the musicians and dancers were required to appear before Assistant Kapell-meister Kalmykov every morning and evening for roll call.

Nicholas was vigilant about controlling access to the women in his troupe. The duennas did their best to keep them out of trouble and away from the men. At times the actresses were forbidden from leaving the estate, except to attend church. Not surprisingly, they managed to get around the rules. When Nicholas would find out, he tried to increase the surveillance. On 25 December 1796, he wrote to Petrov complaining of the lax oversight, especially by the governess Arina Antonova. He ordered everyone to be much more vigilant, not to allow any men, even their brothers, in to see them or else they would all be punished; the over-seers would lose their pay and be exiled to distant estates. Antonova was a weak link, and Nicholas repeatedly had to reprimand her carelessness.

Nicholas's order to Vasily Voroblevsky before leaving on a journey in the spring of 1790 gives a good idea of how things were to be run:

During my trip from Moscow to my distant villages you are to keep watch over the girls and singers, dancers and musicians left behind and act in accordance with the following paragraphs.

The many girls who have been left under the supervision of the woman Catherine Sysoeva are to be moved from down-stairs to the upstairs rooms, and you are to inform yourself daily whether they are all well and everything is in order, and now and then go to their rooms yourself and check that the quarters are clean, and have your wife go check on their condition from time to time. Lock the downstairs door so that there's no way in to the girls, and make sure nothing's unlocked upstairs.

Have Ustinia, Domna, Akulina, Uliana, and Smagin prac-tice their music with Signor Solci on the usual days, and watch to see they practice well and the time isn't wasted. Have Stepan Degtiarev rehearse with the other girls who've already started learning the music; should there be any laziness, negligence, or resistance in their music studies, then they are to be punished by being forced to kneel and put on bread and water, and report to me the slightest incident. . . .

All the singers are entrusted to your care together with bass Grigory Mamontov. Tell them that it is my will that without your permission no one is to dare leave the courtyard for whatever reason; rather, they must come to you first every time. Order Kokhanovsky and Yampolsky to appear before you twice a day—every noon and evening—to report on their condition.

On nice days, warm ones, that is, when they are not rehearsing, the girls can be let out for walks on the side streets under the supervision of their chaperones. . . .

You are to keep a close watch on all these people to see that none of the men, be they singers, actors, dancers, or musicians, ever leave the house to go anywhere without asking you for permission, and to make certain the house is kept quiet and peaceful. Should someone go out without asking you first, then he is to be punished, depending on the infraction, and you are to write to me about it. Their overseer Bykov is to report to you every morning, and if you don't have time to check that everyone is present in the house, then you may send Bykov, or a footman if necessary. . . .

You are to report to me, and I expect the honest truth, twice weekly on the behavior of everyone entrusted to you and on the progress in his musical studies.

You are to read my orders before a gathering of the entire troupe and tell them again that no one is to violate my orders. Be assured that no offense against my will shall go unpunished.[4]

Discipline was ensured through a range of punishments. The most common were a reduction in rations or a cut in pay. Vasily Vorobyov, Nicholas's principal dancer, was always getting in trouble for his drinking and sleeping around. Once he came down with "a disgraceful disease" (that is, syphilis) days before a big performance and couldn't dance. Nicholas reduced his salary from a hundred rubles to four until he was well enough to return to the stage; another time he was demoted from the upper to the lower ration for "bad behavior." Yet Nicholas often showed generosity even in his punishments. In September 1795, Vorobyov was deprived of his pay for "debauchery"; but instead of keeping the money, Nicholas gave it to Vorobyov's parents. Years later, after the theater had closed and Vorobyov succumbed to ill health, Nicholas did not forget him and made sure he was cared for and given the necessary treatment.[5]

In 1796, Nicholas ordered all the men in the troupe denied their coffee and tea rations. When bassoonist Nikita Chupakhin was caught stealing, he was ordered to work in the stables. More serious offenses were punished by forced manual labor of the worst sort—digging ditches, dredging ponds and canals—or banishment to a distant estate. Female performers received the mildest punishments, typically being forced to kneel or placed on a ration of bread and water.

Unlike most impresarios, Nicholas was generally loath to use corporal punishment. He dealt harshly with Kuzma the Cornelian for yelling at and hitting his fellow dancers during rehearsals and told him it was not to happen again. Part of Nicholas's reaction can be explained by his not wanting his performers beating each other. He told Sandunov, on the other hand, it was appropriate for him to use the birch rod on the performers if they misbehaved.

Punishment wasn't merely about stopping thieves, slackers, and curfew breakers. It sent a message to anyone who might be contemplating disobedience of whatever sort. It reminded them, should they forget, who was in charge. And this was particularly important among serf performers, men and women who knew a good deal more about the world than most serfs, who had been exposed to Enlightenment notions of human equality, and who might think the words they sang on their master's stage about the hollowness of noble birth and its privileges might have meaning after the curtain fell. An educated slave, Nicholas knew, was a dangerous thing.

Nicholas cared about the troupe's well-being, even if mostly because it represented an enormous investment and without it the theater couldn't go on. When he was away, Nicholas received regular reports on everyone's health, down to the least sniffle, and always wanted to know what was being done for them. He ordered his overseers to make sure they "were kept clean, that they washed their hands and face every morning, before lunch and dinner, that they were taken to the baths once a week, that they were all free of scabs or rashes, and that their clothes were clean."[6] When he learned in the autumn of 1797 that many of the dancers had fallen ill (fevers, diarrhea, coughs and colds, rheumatism, gumboil were the usual problems), he issued an order to his steward to improve their living conditions: "The female dancers are often ill, and quite a few of them. Check to see that their rooms are decent and they have enough room and move them into better quarters. Check their food as well; if it is bad and not enough, then let me know and add buckwheat and butter or cabbage to everyone's ration you can so that they all have a good dinner. . . . Check on them occasionally to see that they are living in a proper fashion; order the overseers not to be lazy and to do their job, taking good care of everyone and ensuring everyone's health and honor is preserved."[7]

Illness was common, just as it was for everyone in the eighteenth century, whether noble or serf. Scurvy was a danger, laying up actors and actresses for months at a time. Nicholas responded to outbreaks by increasing the butter and cabbage rations. Consumptive diseases, pneumonia and tuberculosis, claimed several of the troupe's performers, not just Praskovia.

The actors and actresses, singers, dancers, and musicians were an elite within an elite. If the hundreds of house serfs that served in Nicholas's homes saw themselves as a cut above the poor ignorant peasants, then the theater troupe was a rung higher still. They formed a quasi-aristocracy among the hundreds of thousands of Sheremetev serfs. Their privileged status bred envy among the other serfs; keeping the troupe isolated from the other serfs was a way of keeping interaction and thus the chances for conflict to a minimum.

If materially richer, their lives were in some ways harder than that of other serfs. They had considerably less control over their daily lives than did the peasants in the village, and their education made them painfully conscious of the fact. Their days ran according to a rigid schedule set by Nicholas; he decided nearly everything in their lives. The master's pleasure determined the quality of one's food, dress, salary, and living arrangements. Each performer's place within the hierarchy of the troupe was immediately and unavoidably evident by what she wore, by where she slept, by the strength of her cup of tea, by the color of her bread. Nicholas liked to give gifts to his favorites of the day—a lavish gemstone for Anna, for example, extra butter for another, or a day off from rehearsing for the dancer who had been particularly impressive at the last performance. This fostered competition for Nicholas's favor; gossip, innuendo, flattery, and backstabbing were among the weapons for getting ahead.

This placed Praskovia in a difficult position. The entire troupe knew she had influence with Nicholas, even if they did not know all the details of their relationship. Praskovia did offer her opinions on matters of household management, and Nicholas did, at least at times, listen. He mentioned in one letter that he had appointed Agapov his head steward at the suggestion of Praskovia. Some serfs sought to get on with her in the hope this would improve their own situation; others wanted nothing to do with a master's mistress. In both cases, attitudes toward Praskovia drew from her place alongside Nicholas. It was inescapable. Everything depended on the will of the master.

SEVENTEEN

To St. Petersburg

Nicholas and Praskovia had been at Ostankino less than a year when a letter arrived from St. Petersburg in late March 1796. The empress was calling Nicholas back to the capital to serve in the Senate. He felt he had little choice but to obey, and in May they packed up and left Ostankino. With that, Nicholas's dream of a quiet life with Praskovia at their new home came to an end. Nicholas later looked back on this with sadness. "Having adorned my estate of Ostankino," he wrote "and presented it to spectators as something enchanting, I thought that having achieved a great feat worthy of wonder and received by the public with delight, in which my knowledge and taste were evident, I would enjoy my creation in peace forever."[1] As the carriages pulled out of the courtyard and the palace slipped from view, no one in their party had any idea just how much their lives, and the country's, were to change in the coming months.

Traveling with them was a five-month-old baby girl named Tatiana Orlova. Her parents were said to be Kuskovo serfs, although shortly after birth she was apparently taken from them and made Praskovia's ward. Taniusha, as she came to be known, lived with Praskovia until the latter's death in 1803.

She remained in the Sheremetev household and was raised alongside Praskovia's son, Dmitry, by Tatiana Shlykova and Yelena Kazakova, a former actress and Dmitry's nanny. Although a serf, Taniusha was given an excellent education; she was taught to read and write in Russian as well as French and took lessons on the fortepiano. In his will of 1804, Nicholas left Taniusha a dowry of thirty thousand rubles to be paid whether or not she married. Her surrogate parents showered her with expensive jewelry, gold and precious stones, and they dressed her in clothes of imported fabric. Around her neck hung a gold medallion with a portrait of Nicholas on one side and a braided locket of his hair on the other.

Like so much in Praskovia's life, Taniusha is a mystery. Was she really the daughter of serfs, as the large file on her in the Sheremetev archive claims? And if so, why was she taken from her parents, both of whom were still at Kuskovo well into the nineteenth century? Praskovia knew the pain of being separated from one's parents at a young age to be raised by strangers. So why would she now subject this little girl to that life? Or is it possible that Taniusha was Praskovia's and Nicholas's own child, and the story of her parentage had been a fabrication? This might explain why Taniusha was with Praskovia apparently from birth as well as why she was given such a respected place in the household after Praskovia's death and the lavish and intimate gifts. If Taniusha was indeed Praskovia's daughter, then she would have been several months pregnant at the time of her premier in *Zelmira* in 1795. Her pregnancy would have been apparent by then, although the right costume could have hidden her rounding belly.

Taniusha most likely wasn't Praskovia's child. If she had been, Nicholas almost certainly would have freed her at some point in his life, which he never did, and recognized his blood ties to her by giving her the Remeteva name. And it doesn't seem possible that a man other than Nicholas could have been the father of any child of Praskovia's.[2]

The mystery surrounding Taniusha raises another question: why hadn't Praskovia and Nicholas had any children by now? They had been lovers for a decade or more. We know from the fact that Praskovia did give birth to a child by Nicholas seven years later that both were physically capable of conceiving. Given the limited birth control options in the eighteenth century, it seems unlikely that Praskovia never got pregnant during these years. And if she did, what ever became of the baby? Perhaps she miscarried or it died soon after birth. But if a child had died early, it seems some record of it would have survived in the Sheremetev archive. Or perhaps she had pregnancies that were terminated. Praskovia was, after all, the star of the company, and motherhood would have been a distraction from her career. Since at least the ancient Greeks herbal abortifacients like wild carrot, nutmeg, pennyroyal, mugwort, and cantharides (the toxic agent from the crushed blister beetle or Spanish fly) had been widely used, despite their extreme toxicity and danger to women's health.

It is intriguing to wonder whether Nicholas ever had the doctors use these herbs on Praskovia. Might they have played a role in her later poor health? We will never know. We do know that an anguished sense of sinfulness tormented Praskovia throughout much of this period. A dead child may have been part of the cause.

Since the Fountain House was still undergoing renovations in the spring of 1796, another house had been rented for Nicholas, Praskovia, and the rest of the household. Shortly after their arrival, Praskovia's brother Mikhail left Moscow to join them. Nicholas stayed just long enough to see to it that everything was unpacked and everyone settled in before departing for Tsarskoe Selo.

As always, Nicholas's arrival occasioned talk of marriage. But this time the source was one to cause everyone to listen. One evening that summer, Catherine the Great turned to Countess Varvara Golovina, one of her ladies, saying, "Do you know that I am very much concerned about settling my granddaughter Alexandra. I am thinking of marrying her to Count Sheremetev." Golovina was not surprised by her words, replying, "So I have heard, Madame, but it is said that his family objects."[3] Catherine was amused by the countess's reply and asked why anyone would object to marrying her granddaughter. Was the count in love with someone else, Catherine possibly wondered, and if so, who? If Golovina knew about Praskovia, she most certainly didn't breathe a word about her to the empress. Both Countess Golovina and Nicholas attended a ball with Catherine at Tsarskoe Selo on 1 June. It's possible that Golovina, or Catherine even, told Nicholas of their exchange that night. The countess's words make it clear that the empress had discussed this plan with others, and sooner or later Nicholas would hear about it.

Nicholas and Grand Duchess Alexandra, Grand Duke Paul's eldest daughter, would have made an odd couple. Alexandra was only thirteen years old at the time; Nicholas was forty-five. Even in eighteenth-century Russia, such an age difference between husband and wife was striking, but not unheard of. In 1777, for example, the forty-three-year-old Prince Grigory Orlov married his fifteen-year-old cousin Catherine Zinovieva. Society was outraged by the marriage, not, however, over the age difference, but because of their close blood relationship. More than the age difference, the fact that Nicholas's and Alexandra's father had been boyhood friends must have made the idea of such a marriage distasteful to both men.

Yet Catherine had her reasons. She still remembered the late Count Sheremetev fondly, and her estimation of Nicholas had improved considerably during the past few years. She liked having smart, cultured men around her who added to the luster of her court, and she didn't much like or understand his preference for Moscow. Marriage to Alexandra would bring him back to St. Petersburg permanently; the timing of Catherine's letter to Nicholas would suggest her calling him back to the Senate that spring had something to do with matchmaking. Catherine also possibly hoped the marriage might rekindle the relationship between Nicholas and her son, for the two men had grown steadily apart since the mid-1770s, when Nicholas left state service for Kuskovo. She had grown increasingly worried about the band of Prussophiles that comprised Paul's company at his Gatchina estate and his murky connections to the Freemasons. Nicholas belonged to neither of these groups and might counter their baneful influence.

It isn't known whether Catherine ever discussed her plan with Nicholas. It would have placed him in a difficult position. There was no way he could have told the empress he couldn't marry Alexandra since he was in love with one of his serfs. The fact that Catherine had heard Praskovia perform at Kuskovo nine years earlier and been so impressed that she asked to meet her after the performance would have made no difference. He must have tried to deflect her comments, just as he had previous attempts to marry him to one society woman or another, with a casual shrug of the shoulders and the repeated insistence that he would marry when God determined the time was right. Talk of this potential bride, however, refused to be so easily dismissed, and it seems to have become more than Nicholas could bear, causing him to absent himself from court in late June 1796.

Talk of Catherine's matchmaking would not have been pleasant for Nicholas's extended family either. They had by now convinced themselves that Nicholas would never marry and were already counting on their share of the inheritance. Of course, Nicholas's marriage into the royal family would create advantages that might possibly flow to them, but these could not compete with the tantalizing promise of riches so close within reach.

On the morning of 5 November, Catherine collapsed while attending to her toilet in the Winter Palace. Her chamberlain discovered the empress's hulking body lying awkwardly on the floor unconscious, and with the help of several valets he managed to drag her back to her bedroom and lay her upon a mattress on the floor. Catherine's face was a deep crimson; wet gurgling sounds bubbled up from her throat. The doctors were summoned. Throughout the day and on into the next the court waited anxiously for news. The empress died late in the evening of 6 November, never having regained consciousness. She was sixty-seven and had ruled Russia for nearly four decades.

Years later Tatiana Shlykova said that Nicholas had seen Catherine playing cards days before her death and been struck by how her face was "like a dark night."[4] Tatiana's words have the ring of something she imagined once having been told. Nicholas didn't attend court from the end of June until Catherine's death; he may not have even been in the capital, but with Praskovia in Moscow.

That autumn was a difficult time for Praskovia. On 19 October, Agapov wrote to Nicholas that Praskovia's mother had fallen ill at Kuskovo with "an obstruction of the stomach and vomiting." Praskovia possibly left Nicholas to be by her side. For the next month, Agapov continued to inform Nicholas regularly of Varvara's poor health: "1 November, Varvara is still ill with obstruction, though she feels a bit better and is no longer vomiting; 19 November, day twenty-sixth of her illness, her obstruction continues, the vomiting has stopped, and she claims to feel better; 21 November, day twenty-eight of her illness, no change." Nicholas wrote Agapov to bring Varvara to Moscow and have his physician Dr. Frese care for her. He stressed that this was of the greatest importance and that they were to do everything possible for her. Agapov's next report was on 1 December: "Varvara is still beset by an obstruction, no improvement." This was the last mention of Varvara.[5]

It isn't clear where Praskovia was when she learned of her mother's death. Nicholas, it seems, was back in St. Petersburg by late October after a visit to Moscow. We don't know whether he took Praskovia with him.

Grand Duke Paul and Grand Duchess Maria Fyodorovna arrived at the Winter Palace on the night of 5 November. The halls were crowded with courtiers and officials. An atmosphere of nervous anticipation hung in the air, as one long and proud reign drew to a close and a new, uncertain one waited to begin. Paul, Maria Fyodorovna, and their sons entered Catherine's dimly lit bedroom. They knelt beside her, kissing her hands and praying over her body throughout the night.

Nicholas left no account of his actions during these momentous two days, but he most likely heard of Catherine's collapse on the fifth and went to the palace that same day. It was probably with some hesitation that he climbed into his carriage for the short ride from the Fountain House. Nicholas was torn between his sense of duty and respect for Catherine, which told him he should be present at this tragic moment, and his apprehension over what Paul's reign held in store for him.

Nicholas's fears were confirmed when he saw Paul on the sixth. Although Catherine was still alive and thus Russia's rightful ruler, Paul had presumptuously fired the chief marshal of her court, Prince Bariatinsky, and ordered him to leave the Winter Palace immediately. The impression at court was that Paul considered Bariatinsky partially responsible for his father's murder thirty-four years earlier. He then appointed Nicholas in his place. The stunning announcement put Nicholas in a dangerous position. To accept the appointment was to commit treason, to refuse it was to court the wrath of the man who was about to ascend the throne. It didn't take long for Nicholas to realize that the only choice was to accept.[6] His life as a private man was over.

EIGHTEEN

Tsar Paul

The reign of Paul I was the most difficult period in Nicholas's and Praskovia's lives. For the next four and half years they would be beholden to the whim of an unstable tsar. From the first days of his reign, Paul's suspicious character was apparent. He was impulsive, erratic, and sickeningly touchy about respect for his person. He set everyone on edge. "One could never be certain of his good graces," observed one contemporary. "In a word—whether by chance or by forethought—a single shadow of suspicion was sufficient to replace recently granted charities with persecution. Those in greatest favor quaked at the thought that tomorrow they might be removed from court and exiled to distant places. Such was the atmosphere in the country throughout his entire reign."[1] Nicholas would have plenty of opportunities to learn this himself.

As the chief marshal of the imperial court, Nicholas became the tsar's majordomo. It was an enormous responsibility, one that would have been difficult under the most understanding of monarchs and was practically fatal under Paul. Nicholas was in charge of every aspect of court life, from arranging grand ceremonies to checking the temperature of the tsar's food, from managing the court finances to making sure there was always enough seltzer water on the tables. A once proud aristocrat was now forced to spend his days trying to locate missing tableware for the imperial family, buying the tsar's candy, hiring a woman to look after the undergarments of the late empress, checking all the ladies' hairdos to make sure no one was sporting an *à la guillotine,* firing the wet nurse of little Grand Duke Nicholas, the future emperor, and so on.[2]

Nicholas had to spend every day at court, where he took most of his meals with the emperor and empress. He joined them and a few intimates in the evenings to play cards and listen to chamber music. They typically met in the tsar's corner office or in the light-blue salon on the second floor of the Winter Palace that opened onto Palace Square. From here Nicholas could look out in the direction of the Fountain House and wish he were there with Praskovia. As early as January 1797 he sent a letter to the tsar requesting permission to give up his post because of poor health and be assigned the less taxing position of chief chamberlain.[3] His request was denied.

At first Nicholas enjoyed the emperor's favor. On 1 February, Paul awarded Nicholas the Order of St. Andrew, the highest imperial order. On the afternoon of the thirteenth Nicholas hosted the tsar and his family at his home and treated them to a concert at which Praskovia sang and played the harp. Days later he wrote with excitement to his Moscow steward instructing him to get Ostankino ready to receive the emperor during the upcoming coronation festivities. "Everything must be ready by Holy Week," he wrote. "I plan on leaving here in about five days. It would be a pity if you aren't ready and so made it impossible for me to receive my dear guest, who visited me here the day before yesterday. He was wonderfully kind and very gay; he stayed for the concert and praised Parasha and even gave her a ring. In a word, his kindnesses are beyond count."[4]

The tsar obviously knew that Praskovia was Nicholas's mistress, and this did not express itself negatively in his feelings for his old friend (Paul had his own mistresses, though they weren't serfs), but the tsar had little insight into the nature of their relationship. Nicholas was likely cautious about what he told Paul and wouldn't have confided in him the depth of his love for Praskovia. He could never be sure how the tsar might react and was apprehensive that what Paul looked on with approval one day, he might the next consider abhorrent and beneath the dignity of a man of Nicholas's class and of his chief marshal.

Nicholas saw the tsar again on the afternoon of 26 February at the ceremonial laying of the cornerstone for the new St. Michael's Palace, halfway between the Winter Palace and Fountain House, which was to be Paul's new residence, the place where four years later he would be murdered.

Back at Ostankino, the men were working seven days a week in extreme cold (the thermometer had dropped to minus thirty degrees Fahrenheit) and heavy snows to get everything ready for the coronation festivities. The snow was so deep they couldn't get the trees felled at Zhulebinskaia Grove to Ostankino for the new wing. An entire shipment of glass from St. Petersburg arrived in February smashed to pieces from the poor roads.[5]

In the first days of March, the imperial court packed up and set out for Moscow and the coronation. The weather was cold, and the travelers wrapped themselves in furs as their sledges raced across the snow toward the ancient capital. Nicholas, Praskovia, Tatiana, and Margarita Remeteva rode together, arriving in Moscow on the morning of 8 March. The tsar arrived a week later, stopping at the Petrovsky Palace outside the city, where he remained until early April for his ceremonial entrance. The coronation took place to the peeling of bells on a clear and cool Easter Sunday, 5 April, in the Kremlin.

As the chief marshal, Nicholas played a prominent role in the coronation ceremonies. Part of the proceedings was the presentation of gifts. In keeping with tsarist tradition, Tsar Paul handed out hundreds of awards to the court and noble elite. Shockingly, however, he gave Nicholas nothing.[6] The reasons are unclear, but it can only have been interpreted as a sign of Paul's displeasure. Nicholas must have viewed it as a terrible public humiliation. It did not bode well for the tsar's visit to Ostankino, planned for later that month.

By now the nightingales had returned to the park at Ostankino, and the oaks and pines swayed in the spring winds, leaving only the giant Siberian cedars stiff and erect. On Saturday, 25 April, Nicholas and Praskovia rode out early in the morning to Ostankino to receive the tsar. Paul, however, was in no hurry, choosing to spend the morning in the Kremlin. Finally, at 2:45 in the afternoon, accompanied by his mistress Catherine Nelidova and three others, Paul climbed into his phaeton for the ride to Ostankino. It was after four by the time they arrived. Nicholas was waiting for them in the courtyard. The reception he had been preparing for months and so looked forward to was an utter failure. Paul made a quick tour of the palace, exchanged a few pleasantries with his host, and then hastily returned to the Kremlin. His visit lasted only a few hours. Nicholas was crushed by the cold treatment, especially after having been so publicly snubbed at the coronation. He had to swallow his pride, however, and was back serving at the Kremlin the next day.

Days later a letter from Prince Andrei Shcherbatov in St. Petersburg arrived filled with gossip from the capital and the hope that the tsar had granted Nicholas's wish to be made chief chamberlain. The prince's letter began, "Given the rumor in town I expect to be able to congratulate you with the title of Chief Chamberlain. The city here has also already married you several times, and so I plan on seeing you upon Your Excellency's return with the countess, which would make me extremely happy."[7]

The letter didn't help Nicholas's mood, but he had little time to dwell on its contents since he was busy overseeing plans for a large fête at Ostankino scheduled for 7 May. The guest list included the cream of aristocratic society and great names of Russia's noble past—the Golitsyns, Dolgorukys, and Trubetskoys, the Kurakins, Yusupovs, and Cherkasskys, the Saltykovs and Naryshkins. Two of Catherine the Great's former lovers were to be there (Alexander Vasilchikov and Count Alexander Dmitriev-Mamonov) as well as Nicholas's former flame Yelena Sergeevna Sheremeteva. The ambassadors of Austria, Prussia, Great Britain, Venice, Naples, Spain, and Portugal were all invited. The guest of honor was Stanislaw August Poniatowski, another of Catherine's lovers and the last king of Poland. Paul had deigned not to remain in Moscow for the celebration and returned to Gatchina.

After the humiliating failures of the previous months, Nicholas was desperate to prove himself, and he did. The entertainment featuring a presentation of *The Marriage of the Samnites* was a great success, prompting a member of King Poniatowski's suite to write that "the King had never seen someone better at giving parties."[8]

Another guest, the statesman Jacob Sievers, wrote to his daughters in glowing terms of the party:

> I must tell you of the house of Count Sheremetew, who the day before yesterday gave a party for the King of Poland and a select public of 500 persons. No reigning duke in Germany and only a few archdukes have anything that can compare. It is a palace fit for a King situated on level ground with no water, save a small

pond. Everything on the ground level sparkles with gold, marble, statues, vases. One would believe there couldn't possibly be any more. Then one ascends to the main level and is astonished to find more splendor equally befitting a king, a large and beautiful theater, and a troupe of actors, dancers, and musicians — all of them the gentleman's own property. The plunder of the Sabines has been given to the Russians. As one wanders the halls for an hour in wonderment, the theater transforms itself into a dance hall. I danced the Polonaise, twice.[9]

Among the partygoers that evening was a Russian dandy in his early twenties. As he strode about the halls, listened to the opera, feasted on the food and drink, and overheard the gasps of amazement uttered by the other guests, he was filled with a barely contained excitement. This was Count Peter Razumovsky, Nicholas's nephew, who had come to the party along with his two sisters and his estranged parents. Peter and his brother, Kirill, were the heirs to their uncle's fortune unless he should marry and have children, the likelihood of which seemed to fade with each passing year. It was now simply a matter of time before Ostankino and everything else of their uncle's would be theirs. Given Nicholas's poor health, Peter believed the day might not be far off.

The fête that night was the culmination of Nicholas's dreams and ambitions. Everything he had worked for for nearly two decades came together in a virtuosic blend of art and antiquities, music, song, and dance, food and wine and gracious hospitality. It had outshone the debut of 1795 — Ostankino looked even more impressive, the opera was more inspiring, the guests more distinguished. Nicholas's triumph was also his swan song. That night marked the last time Praskovia sang and the last time an opera was performed by the Sheremetev theater.

Praskovia had fallen ill that year. It isn't known precisely when, but it seems she was not well that spring in Moscow. Nicholas had her examined by his serf medic Gavrila Krasnopolsky and then by Dr. Frese. Frese prescribed purgatives — chicory syrup and rhubarb in a glass of cold tamarind water, magnesium sulfate and a tincture of liquefied rhubarb — to clean her bowels. He bled Praskovia, applied plasters of stinky Spanish fly, and had her soak in baths of warm mare's milk.

The nature of Praskovia's illness, like the efficacy of Dr. Frese's treatments, is unknown. In the nineteenth century the story arose that she suffered from chronic tuberculosis. This might be true, but considering the disease was not defined until decades after her death and the descriptions of her condition are scanty, it cannot be held for certain. Praskovia was unquestionably hit by some sort of consumptive illness that damaged her lungs, possibly pneumonia, and that proved resistant to the doctors' best efforts. It didn't kill her, although she would come close to dying several times, but it did destroy her health, making it impossible for her to sing. That spring Praskovia's career came to an abrupt end. She was three months shy of her twenty-ninth birthday.

On 10 May, a late snowstorm hit Moscow. Two days later, just before leaving for St. Petersburg, Nicholas increased the pay and food allotment of Praskovia's brother Afanasy, who had married that spring. Praskovia stayed behind for several days, most likely because she was not well enough to travel. Nicholas was already late getting back to court. Several days after his departure, Agapov informed Nicholas that "Praskovia Ivanovna and the other girls left to join Your Excellency in Petersburg on Monday the morning of the 18th, and I have instructed Terekhov and Gorshov to drive carefully the entire route and with all caution." A second set of carriages set out two days later bearing Tatiana's mother, Praskovia's brother Nicholas, and several other actresses and female dancers.[10] Most of the troupe and the best musicians soon followed. Despite Praskovia's poor health, Nicholas hoped to stage works in St. Petersburg until he could return to Ostankino. The daily rehearsals at Ostankino came to an end.

Praskovia arrived in Petersburg toward the end of the month, and she had only a day or two together with Nicholas before he had to leave to join the court at Gatchina on 28 May. They rarely saw each other for the next two months, during which time the court shuttled back and forth between Gatchina, Pavlovsk, and Peterhof. The emperor had decided Pavlovsk would be his primary summer residence, not Tsarskoe Selo, where his mother had summered. Nicholas found he couldn't bear the quarters assigned him at Pavlovsk and wanted a place where he could be with Praskovia, so he purchased the dacha of his former dance master Charles Le Picq at Pavlovsk for seventeen thousand rubles.[11]

Having Praskovia with him was a comfort given the tense situation Nicholas was facing at court. Shortly after the coronation, the privilege of reporting in person to the emperor had been taken away from him, which was deeply humiliating. To make matters worse, several of the courtiers were engaged in intrigues against him in hopes of taking his position. Late that summer his health broke under the stress. Nicholas returned to the Fountain House in early September with Praskovia and thought seriously about retiring. In September, he bared his soul in a letter to Prince Alexander Kurakin bemoaning the back-stabbing atmosphere at court. He admitted that he had never been able to stand this aspect of court life and it was becoming ever more intolerable. The tsar had closed his doors to Nicholas, who now had to go through intermediaries. "His Majesty's way of thinking is becoming increasingly unknown to me," he wrote, "even more so than it was when I first took up my position."[12] In early September, Nicholas requested to be relieved of his position.[13] Paul again denied his request, and by 10 October Nicholas was back at Gatchina.

Praskovia remained at the Fountain House. Tatiana, little Taniusha, her sister Matryona, and several of the other actresses were there to keep her company. She sat for the French artist Charles de Chamisso, who painted a miniature of her for Nicholas. The awful cold heralding the onset of the capital's notorious winters damaged her fragile health, and she often complained of headaches and vague pains and could barely eat.

News from home didn't help her spirits either. On 15 September, Nicholas had written Agapov asking to have Praskovia's father moved back to Ostankino, where he had lived for a time, and to keep an eye on him to ensure he behaved himself. Ivan had probably been moved from Ostankino back to Kuskovo during the coronation festivities to prevent any embarrassing scenes. At Kuskovo, a serf widow by the name of Avdotia Manbetova had been assigned to live in with him. She had turned out to be as unreliable and troublesome as her charge, which caused all sorts of problems, and had to be removed as his caretaker.

Nicholas returned to the Fountain House on 6 November, when the court moved to the Winter Palace for the winter. The final months of the year were unusually cold and snowy in the capital. On Friday, 25 December, Nicholas attended church services with the tsar in the Winter Palace, followed by a dinner for fourteen. But his mind was at home with Praskovia, who lay desperately sick in bed. That evening, after sitting with Praskovia and discussing her condition with Krasnopolsky, he wrote an anguished letter to Dr. Frese in Moscow:

Monsieur,

Having so much proof of your sincere friendship, and your honest disposition toward me, and knowing always to appreciate your talent and knowledge, I cannot hide from you, as a friend, the deplorable state of the poor Mademoiselle Praskovia's health. To give you a full history of the dire beginning and progress of her illness up until now, I add here another document, by which you can see the progression of her illness and the manner in which we are treating it. But despite all the help we are receiving here, we truly feel the lack of your sound advice, and the absence of a dear friend, for which we find no replacement. Being in a most critical situation, I decided to turn to you for help. Tell us what to do and please do not withhold your advice from us.

What should we do today? After all of the cures that you have learned of by now from the attached note, the doctors decided on hot milk baths. But we don't want to make any decision without your approval, and that's why I have sent an express courier who should return right away, and I dare to hope that your personal help and advice, even in your absence, will be enough to bring some relief. And it will be much more useful than the treatments that have been prescribed up until now. In the hope of receiving your response as soon as possible, for which I will wait impatiently, I remain as always, with sentiments of the utmost respect and consideration, &tc., &tc. . . .

Count Nicholas Sheremetev

25 December 1797

Along with this letter Nicholas enclosed a lengthy "Note," composed the day before, detailing Praskovia's illness and treatment:

Since the time that you healed us, my dear Monsieur, nothing remarkable has happened concerning the health of the poor Mademoiselle Praskovia, other than that since then she has had headaches almost daily and some pain in her limbs. After the warm season passed, her face was covered with pimples that she was careful to wash with certain waters and this cleaned her face perfectly. Instead of lessening as I thought they would, her headaches have continued, and she has a buzzing in her ears; from time to time she has head colds, and since the month of October she has had a severe headache every day, no desire to eat, and vague pains throughout her entire body, except the chest and shoulders which don't show any sign of pain. She has said, nonetheless, that she feels a vague coldness in her chest, sometimes a light pressure there too, and mild vertigo, very often with a cold. And she said that there was something that she didn't know how to explain which moved inside her chest like a piece of matter that had been blocking the chest.

From time to time she has a slight cough. We saw that as not very important, but Gavrila [Krasnopolsky] now tells me that earlier he found the cough to be very bad and it showed heat; I had always been dissuaded from bleeding her, but after speaking with Dr. Rogerson [Dr. John Rogerson, physician to Catherine the Great] I decided to bleed her in the end. That is what we did in the month of November and we took out very little blood, no more than two teaspoons at first. The day after having bled her, her feet began to hurt and her hands were hot, which we did not consider serious. She didn't lie down, and one day she stayed at church to her disadvantage, for this did harm to her poor chest and half of her back; her skin became hot and all of a sudden she felt a pain at night in her shoulder and then another shooting pain, first on one side, then the other. The pain was the sign of an attack in her chest. It began on her left side, resulting in a cough and painful breathing. I first ordered an application of *les mouches cantarides,* and that was done. I then left for the court; Mademoiselle Praskovia did not expect the pain to be serious, and after feeling the pain caused by the fly, she unfortunately decided to remove it in my absence, and the next day her illness increased rather severely, so that we didn't know, that is to say not I, but the others, including Doctor Rogerson, whether they should bleed her or apply the fly. It was my opinion that the fly was most necessary, but since we all agreed that the patient had been bled only a little we resolved to bleed her, ten days after the first bleeding. That is what we did. The first and the second bleeding were full of matter, especially the second. Between the first bleeding and the second, she had a fever and chills, the second bleeding had no effect. We watched her daily, and I was worried about the treatments that caused her to cough up a lot of yellow matter, and the pain was the same.

The fly on her shoulder caused a lot of matter to come up and made her breathing very difficult and even very painful, but once the pain subsided her shoulder felt better after a few days. After that the pain eased considerably, and after a few days the illness in her shoulder passed, but one night there was a terrible accident when a candle at her bedside set fire to the boy sleeping in her room.

She was constipated for four days, and so Monsieur Rogerson and Doctor Rogger ordered purgative pills; but instead of these pills I had her take three spoons of the liquid decoction that you had always used to purge her. She was purged once and rendered a lot of white matter. But the same evening the pain in her chest and shoulder became stronger than before and the pain passed from one to the other, her breathing became very difficult and even more painful and I applied the fly very firmly for the second time. The fly worked for two days, and her linen shirts and all her bedding were wet with perspiration. She was very relieved, but she still had pain in the front and the back when she breathed. The pain, however, was not severe, though her skin became red and full of pimples like her face. She began to sleep much better, and her appetite improved as well, but she was still constipated. We gave her pills, for which you will see the recipe. Twice while going to her dresser she felt the same pain, and so I applied the fly once more.

Cantarides had a beneficial effect, but the pain, although bearable, remained about the same; at times it became stronger and at times weaker. Her cough never goes away; it is not very strong and is dry, and she has not been spitting up anything. Her pulse is sometimes weak, sometimes strong, but always irregular. Her urine is almost always good and at night red and with some sediment. Her blood itself appears very good, as are her eyes, but she has no appetite, interrupted sleep and many troubles with her limbs. I ordered she be given a hot milk bath.

24 December 1797[14]

Nicholas sealed the letters and gave them to a special courier to take to Dr. Frese in Moscow. There was nothing more to do but wait and hope for the best. On the last day of the year, a depressed Nicholas confided to Prince Urusov, "Let me be honest with you in saying that it is with a heavy heart I meet the New Year."[15]

Interlude
Serf Actress Stories

I t is not surprising that Praskovia left behind no diary or reminiscences, for no serf actress ever wrote her memoirs. A few actresses, however, did tell their stories to others who wrote them down. Perhaps the best known of these accounts is Alexander Herzen's "The Thieving Magpie."

Herzen wrote his tale in 1846. It was inspired by the tragic story he had been told by Michael Shchepkin about a serf actress named Kuzmina Vorobyova. Kuzmina had belonged to the Kazan landowner Paul Yesipov. Like Praskovia, she was a brilliant performer and singer, had been taught foreign languages—French, German, and Italian—and given a fine musical education. Yesipov had intended to free Kuzmina but died of a stroke before the emancipation papers had been completed. To cover his debts, Yesipov's heirs sold the entire serf theater to Count Sergei Kamensky in 1815 for three hundred thousand rubles.

Shchepkin once heard Kuzmina sing at Kamensky's theater in Oryol and was astounded by her voice. "I barely heard her words," Shchepkin recalled, "but I did hear her voice. 'Good Lord!' I thought, 'how can such sounds issue from such a young breast?' They are not contrived or founded on solfeggio but actually suffer as the result of some dreadful experience."[1]

Shchepkin, called simply "a famous artist" in Herzen's story, felt he had to meet this young woman and learn her secret. After the performance he approached Kamensky (Prince Skalinsky in "The Thieving

Magpie"), who gave him a pass to visit Kuzmina in the actresses' wing at noon the next day. Shchepkin arrived at the appointed hour and after showing his pass to two guards—one posted outside the actresses' wing, another inside—was admitted into a modest room. Before him stood a beautiful woman with sad eyes who proceeded to tell him her story.

I want to tell you about myself. I must get everything off my chest. It's possible I shall die before ever meeting another fellow artist such as yourself. Perhaps you will laugh—no, that was stupid of me to say, you won't laugh. You are too much of a human being to do that, it's more likely you'll take me for mad. Indeed, what sort of woman throws herself with such frankness on someone she doesn't know? But then, I do know you, I saw you perform once on the stage—you are an artist.

My story is not long, it's very short, I won't bore you. If for no other reason, listen to it in light of the pleasure I gave you playing the role of Aneta.

I haven't been here long with this troupe. Earlier I was in a different provincial theater, much smaller, much more poorly outfitted, but I was happy there, perhaps because I was young, carefree, exceedingly stupid, and I lived without thinking about life. I so gave myself over to my love of art that I paid no attention to anything else around me. Increasingly, I believed the notion, one that I believe you may already be aware of, that I had been called to the stage. My own conscience told me that I was an actress. I studied my art without interruption; I cultivated my modest talents, and with joy saw how I surmounted challenge after challenge. Our master was a good, simple, and honest man. He respected me, appreciated my talent, gave me the opportunity to study French, took me with him to Italy and Paris. I was still quite young, in experience if not years, and thought that I was bound to my guardian by some special bonds of duty. If only he'd had one more year! Oh, what might have been . . . He died suddenly, and we spent the next six weeks in a dismal fear. Men came, they examined his things, but the manumission papers he had written out for us disappeared, or perhaps they had never existed, or perhaps he simply never got around to it, and simply told us he had, out of politeness. The news stunned us. While we were still sobbing and wondering what to do, we were sold at a public auction and the Prince bought the entire troupe. He received us well, put us up nicely, as you see, and even paid us. But this one was not like our former master, humane and indulgent. It wasn't long before he made it extremely clear to us the immense difference between him and his harem girls appointed for his pleasure. He was accustomed to servility. It was hard on us, very hard, still there were moments of joy. I was well taken care of thanks to my talent, and I was still able to lose myself in my art and forget the world around me.

I began to notice that the Prince took special interest in me. I understood what was behind his attentiveness, and guarded myself. The Prince was not used to anyone from his troupe saying no to him. I pretended that I didn't understand a thing, and he began to express his intentions more directly. Late one evening, having returned from a performance, I was reading aloud from a new translation of the German tragedy *Kabale und Liebe* [Friedrich Schiller's 1784 bourgeois tragedy]. You no doubt know it. It is filled with so much that touches the soul, so much indignation, so many reproaches, and proof of the absurdities of life. Reading it, you feel as if you know the story, as if it's all happened to you somehow . . . And so, I was reading *Kabale und Liebe* and was fully under its spell, carried away by it and inspired when someone suddenly said, "Wonderful, wonderful!" and placed his hand on my exposed shoulder. Frightened, I sprang to the wall. It was the Prince.

"What is it you wish, Your Excellency?" I asked, my voice shaking with rage and indignation. "I am a weak woman, as you just saw, but I assure you that I can also be a strong woman."

"I ask for nothing," the Prince replied, trying to adopt a charming expression, "could one ask anything of such eyes: it is they who have the power to make requests."

I looked him straight in the eyes, and this confused him. He was waiting for some sort of answer. But he quickly recovered, approached me and said: "Ne faites donc pas la prude, don't play the fool, don't look at me so, others would take this for a great honor." He grabbed me by the arm, but I pulled it free.

"Prince," I said, "you can send me off to a remote village, but even the weakest animal has certain rights that cannot be taken away from him, at least while he is alive. Go to the others, make them happy, if you have indeed succeeded in educating them of such things."

"Mais elle est charmante!" the Prince replied. "How well this rage suits her! But enough with this role."

"Prince," I said dryly, "what is it you want in my room at such an hour?"

"Well, let's go to my room then," he answered. "I don't receive my guests so rudely, and am indeed much friendlier than you." And then he gave his eyes a sugary tender look. At that moment the old man was most loathsome, with those quivering lips, and that expression . . . that repulsive expression.

"Give me your hand, Prince," I said, "and come over here."

He didn't suspect a thing and gave me his hand. I led him to my mirror, showed him his own face, and asked:

"And you think I'm going to give myself to that ridiculous old man, to that bald womanizer?" And I laughed.

The Prince blanched with rage. He pulled his hand away and probably would've hit me in the face if he'd been more in control of himself. Instead, he merely swore at me and yelled as he left:

"I'll teach you to forget your place! How dare you say that to me! You're no actress, no, you're nothing but my serf wench!"

I slammed the door behind him and threw onto the floor the knife I'd mindlessly picked up while reading, and then slipped up my sleeve just in case.

You can well understand how I felt, how I spent that night. I don't want to tell you all the insults and petty unpleasantries that began for me from that very day. They took from me the best roles, they tormented me with a never-ending series of roles for which I had no talent, all the Prince's men started treating me rudely; they stopped giving me good costumes. I don't want to tell you all this, for it may seem to speak in the Prince's favor. He could've treated me quite differently; after all, he could've inflicted other, harsher forms of punishment on me. No, he did it all with a certain delicacy, he mocked me with this persecution. But worst of all were these last words of the Prince. They cut into my head, and into my heart, and gangrene set in around them. I couldn't escape them, I couldn't forget them . . . I've been in a fever ever since, sleep offers no respite, towards evening my head burns, yet I wake up in the morning in chills. I'm ill now when I make my entrance onto the stage, in some sort of feverish state, and the audience still applauds me even though they don't understand my acting. Ever since I've been playing the same role and can't play any others, but the spectators don't suspect a thing. My talent is fading . . . And so, it's all over, my talent and my life . . . I feel I've only another year or two to live, then they can write the Prince's words on my grave.

And with that, Shchepkin noted, she stopped. He was at a loss for what to say to comfort her, and they sat there for a time in silence before Shchepkin excused himself and left.

Herzen made up the rest of Kuzmina's sad tale. The prince places her under virtual house arrest, yet to prove that ultimate control over her body rests with her, Kuzmina gets herself pregnant. Still, she feels her situation is helpless. Two months after giving birth, she dies of consumption.

Stories like Kuzmina's were not unheard of, yet Herzen's depiction betrays signs of melodrama suggesting he embellished Shchepkin's story to make it a more effective weapon in the struggle against serfdom. The inclusion of consumption, a tragic death following childbirth, and a passing reference to Kuzmina's possible "secret marriage" unavoidably call to mind Praskovia's life story as another source of literary inspiration and the extent to which Herzen shaped his story for dramatic effect.

Most serf actresses were spared Kuzmina's fate. At least one even looked upon her life and career fondly. The nineteenth-century actress Catherine Piunova-Shmidgof recalled the stories she had been told as a girl by her grandmother, Nastasia Piunova, a serf actress of Prince

Nicholas Shakhovskoi. Her reminiscences are particularly striking since they contradict the common view of the prince as a beast.

"They took me from the village still in my bast shoes," Nastasia told her granddaughter. "I was then ten years old. They washed me up, dressed me, and put me in the girls' wing." She told Catherine how they were all kept under lock and key in the actresses' wing and were never let out of sight of the various "aunties" appointed to watch over them. The females were taught how to read but not how to write, lest they be tempted to enter into a correspondence with any of the men in the troupe, or an admirer from the audience. They were permitted to learn to write only after they married, which the prince himself arranged when they reached the age of twenty-five. He would call in all the male performers and ask whether any of them found so-and-so appealing. If any did, he set the date, provided a dowry, gave away the bride, and blessed the couple. As a wedding present, he increased their salary.[2]

"Plays were staged at the prince's theater," Nastasia remembered, "in this manner: the prince would not decide on a play at the beginning of rehearsals; rather, everything would be decided at one of the last rehearsals when he would express his will: 'Let it be,' or, 'It is not to be.' . . . It happened that we would be learning some play, struggling, really struggling with it, but for whatever reason the prince didn't like it . . . He would get up, wave his hand, take a pinch of tobacco from his gold snuffbox, and say—'Don't care for it!' . . . And so we'd begin preparing a different play.

"The prince knew all his actors and actresses by their names and had the habit of 'giving' each one a nickname appropriate to his age and position. The prince hated crude female names, and since all his actresses had come from the villages so there were, of course, some Akulkis and Matryoshkis. It happened that new girls would be brought in, dressed, and taken to be presented to the prince. Their names would be announced, and if the prince found a name crude, so he would give a new one right then and there."

The very thing happened to the old lady. The prince had given her the name Zoia. His wife, however, objected, suggesting that Nastasia was more fitting. The prince agreed, and Zoia was thrown out for Nastasia.

Nastasia did not think of her master as cruel. True, there were times when he lost his temper at some of the male performers and would hurl his snuffbox at them, but these incidents did not stand out. Nor did she recall him forcing himself on any of his serfs. "Of course, there were actors and actresses the prince favored, but he never had any 'female favorites' in the usual sense—for the prince was an ideal husband and father, as well as a true Christian."

Shakhovskoi enjoyed treating the members of his troupe to surprises. "Sometimes in the fall they would bring a cart filled with grapes from his Orangerie, and he would order his men to hang them on the lime-trees in his garden. Once this operation had been finished, he would order the bell rung and then all the girls were brought into the garden. He would be seated in a chair with wheels and two valets would push him up and down the allées. The whole time the old man was shouting: 'Well, girls, the grapes are ripe, so go pick them!'"

In 1853, many years after the prince's death, Nastasia and the other serfs had to leave the manor house, which had fallen into disrepair. The move hit her hard. This was where she had spent most of her life, had married, raised her only child, and seen him marry and begin his own family. Towards the end of her life she liked to go back to look at her "little nest" with her granddaughter. Here she would tell Catherine the stories of her life. Gazing upon the old actresses' wing she was reminded of how much more comfortably they had lived than in the small apartment she now shared with her son and his family. Nastasia was there when the crumbling manor was eventually demolished. The old woman dropped to the ground, sobbing uncontrollably. She was dealt a second blow that year when the theater burned down.

Nastasia died in 1875 at the age of eighty-nine. Listening to her stories makes one take pause before assuming that life for serf performers was nothing but misery. Yet, one wonders to what extent the passing of time had colored her memories, blotting out the worst experiences and infusing the rest with a warm glow. She had liked to tell Catherine that she and several hundred other serfs had been given their freedom upon the prince's death according to his wish. In truth, it appears they were freed only after his heirs had sold them to a new master to pay off the prince's debts.

We shall never know what stories passed among Praskovia and the other women in Nicholas's troupe before rehearsals in their dressing room. How many tragic Kuzminas were there whose stories are now lost to us but whose pitiful lives must have filled other performers with empathy and a sense of relief that they had somehow been spared serf theater's worst cruelties?

III

THE FOUNTAIN HOUSE

I believe I see her waiting shadow

Wandering about this place.

I approach! But soon this cherished image

Brings me back to my grief

And flees, never to return.

—Inscription on Nicholas's monument to

Praskovia in the Fountain House garden

NINETEEN

Freedom

Praskovia convalesced throughout the first months of 1798. It isn't known whether Dr. Frese's prescriptions, whatever they may have been, were responsible for saving her life or whether she recovered on her own. It wasn't until springtime that Praskovia had regained most of her strength. The attack had scared her and Nicholas and placed in doubt whether she would ever sing again. Her lungs had suffered and appeared to have been damaged beyond repair.

She remained throughout her convalescence at the Fountain House with Tatiana, Anna the Emerald, Arina the Sapphire, her sister, and Taniusha. The days were quiet and uneventful. She spent much of her time in the palace chapel praying and attending services, or she would read or do needlework. Two of her handicraft pieces have survived—one of a bouquet of flowers, the other of two griffins. When she was feeling well enough and the weather permitted, Praskovia would go out for rides through the snowy streets in her sledge, warmed beneath a bearskin throw. When Nicholas was home, they would sit together before the fire. Sometimes she would play the harp or piano, and Nicholas would accompany her on the cello.

In 1712, Peter the Great granted Field Marshal Sheremetev a piece of marshy land beyond the city limits on the banks of the Yerik River and ordered him to build a house on it. This he did, and the new house became the Sheremetevs' summer home. Peter Sheremetev tore down the house in the 1750s, replacing it with a large palace with extensive gardens. It became known as the Fountain House after the Fontanka (Fountain) River, the Yerik's new name, whose waters fed the fountains in the Summer Garden. After Peter left the capital for Kuskovo, the Fountain House was let out to a series of renters and over time it fell into disrepair until Nicholas began major renovations in 1795. By the time he had finished, Nicholas had created a stately ochre-colored palace that, while of more modest scale, was worthy of comparison with his other homes. A foreigner characterized it as "the magnificence of Asia guided by the taste of Europe, filled with everything that art could offer in the way of diamonds, gems, and curiosities."[1]

Nicholas's intent in remodeling was twofold: first, to strip the house of the now old-fashioned midcentury decor of the last renovation and give it a fresher, more up-to-date look, and second, to create a set of secret apartments for him and Praskovia. It wasn't enough to simply divide the home into public and private spaces, as was typically done; Nicholas, true to his penchant for secrecy, wanted to have a refuge into which they could retreat and where their actions would be unobserved. This was not easy to do considering that more than three hundred domestics lived in the Fountain House.

The left wing of the new second floor of the Fountain House contained an enfilade of sumptuous rooms and galleries for entertaining. The right wing formed the family half. It could be reached only by way of a narrow covered walkway built onto the exterior of the house that led from Nicholas's winter bedroom to Praskovia's apartments. The first of these was the spacious red "Turkish" room that looked out onto the Fontanka. From here a door led to a small anteroom and bedroom facing the garden in the rear of the house. These chambers were quite small with high ceilings and tall, narrow windows that rattled in the biting winter wind. The rooms faced north, and so were dark and cold much of the year. During the long winter months, lamps had to be used nearly around the clock. To keep warm Praskovia bundled up in heavy brocaded dresses, spencers of rich satin, and snug caps. The anteroom held a mahogany cabinet containing five icons of the Virgin and Russian saints. Here and in a side chapel added between the main chapel and her rooms, Praskovia would pray for hours at a time. Nicholas's summer bedroom and the chapel of

St. Varvara the Great Martyr completed the family half. A back staircase beyond the chapel afforded discreet access to the ground floor and garden.

In the garden, surrounded by apple and cherry trees, Nicholas erected a commodious pavilion. The structure was solidly built, complete with a stove to make it habitable in the winter; in the summer months, light, cool air and the faint singing of the girls next door at the Catherine Institute filtered in through a series of round windows. The pavilion became one of Praskovia's favorite places at the Fountain House. She enjoyed working in the garden, in whose lush stillness she could forget that she was in St. Petersburg. Praskovia never did take to the capital and seems to have longed for Kuskovo, wanting to be near her family and those places filled with memories of her childhood.

In April 1798, Nicholas, citing poor health, twice requested permission to retire, and both times Paul refused, saying he wished to "keep you near me."[2] Nicholas was at Pavlovsk, having arrived around the middle of the month with Praskovia and several others of the household, when the tsar turned down his second request. Praskovia, together with Tatiana, kept out of sight at the dacha purchased the previous year. They spent much of their time planting lime trees around the house and gathering mushrooms. They took great pleasure in finding the best ones, choosing not to pick them right away but admiring their beauty for several minutes before putting them in their baskets. In the evenings when Nicholas was free they would eat oysters, washing them down with porter. Afterward Tatiana would take out her snuffbox and enjoy a pinch of her beloved fine-cut French tobacco.[3] One day an English fortepiano arrived at the dacha from St. Petersburg. Nicholas had bought it as a gift for Praskovia. There were other presents that spring—diamond earrings, gemstones, expensive trinkets.

Nicholas had been giving a lot of thought to their future and by summer had convinced himself that he and Praskovia were, someday, to be married. He confided this to his cousin Nicholas Vladimirovich Sheremetev, who, in a letter of 1 July, replied, "I am certain, my dear Sir, that your words and protestations are truthful, and so I still flatter myself with the hope that in the days of my old age I shall have the pleasure of seeing you together with your wife, whom God has given you."[4]

Decisive in Nicholas's decision was seeing how terribly Praskovia was suffering. He knew that the hours she spent in prayer were vain attempts to expiate for the sinful nature of her ménage with Nicholas. The writings of St. Dmitry of Rostov especially moved her. One of his works, a lament of sorts called "A Prayer of Confession to God, Being a Useful Beginning to Everyday Salvation," became her vade mecum. She copied it down in her own hand and kept it with her at all times:

Find a secluded place where you will be alone, and sit thinking about your life, calling to mind all the sins that you have committed, whether confessed or not, and having recalled all the sighs from the depths of your heart and breast, cry, kneel, and lift your mind above the earth to the throne of God surrounded by His cherubs and seraphs. See there with your mind's eye God on His throne up high, and glorify the One seated there, fall to His merciful feet and with fear tell him this—

Most Benevolent God, Source of all that is Good, Creator of unlimited Mercy and my Savior, Thou who knowest my innermost secrets and tests my heart, I confess my sins and bring to Thy all-seeing eye and to the ears of all Thy angels and archangels my wantonness, having sinned, my Lord and Creator . . .

O Merciful Healer, Lord, cover these sores and ulcers of mine, these are my deeds and my nakedness; O Lord of everlasting patience, with these deeds I have saddened, enraged, and irritated Thy goodness; with this I have defiled Thy image, offended Thy Holy Host, chased away my guardian angel; with this I have flouted Thy precious blood which was shed for me, taking it for nothing; with this I have destroyed the beauty of the soul, stripped myself of Thy goodness and created a den of thieves, a dwelling place for devils and passions; with this I have corrupted Thy church which was bought by Thy blood, and fouled all my body, creating lecherous bonds, fouling my soul as well as my thoughts, which are clever, proud, secular, and lecherous, and which I have encouraged and found sweet pleasure in for the sake of the Devil and the grief of the Angels. My soul has died, it lies in a coffin, beyond feeling and resting under a stone of hardness. . . .

I, the damned, the sea of unsurpassed loathsomeness, the bottomless abyss of all that is unclean, the doer of all filth and evil, I, in the sickness of my heart, resort and lean on Thee, the All-Merciful and All-Generous God, crying with repentance, having sinned before the Heavens and Thee; sinning in my un-lawfulness I was a transgressor of Thy commands; having sinned as none had ever sinned before, I am not worthy to look and see the Heavenly heights . . .

I am an abyss of sins, and I throw myself into the abyss of Thy mercy; My God, I implore Thee, edify me, edify me for the true repentance and bring to her senses the unfeeling one, for Thou received the repentance of many repenting sinners. . . . As I did before work for the flattering Satan so shall I work even more for Thee, my Lord and God, Jesus Christ, during all my days, if He gives His goodness to help me.[5]

Nicholas knew the pain he was causing Praskovia, but his fear and indecision kept him from acting. He wavered, and his inability to act caused him considerable guilt. No longer the young rake, he came to share in Praskovia's spiritual suffering. About this time Nicholas wrote to Father Amfilokhy of Rostov, asking him to remember Nicholas in his prayers "since I have great need of this."[6] In his heart he considered Praskovia his wife, although no one else saw her as such. And so they both waited. Her position was unenviable. As her place alongside Nicholas solidified, so did the envy, jealousy, and spite of many of the other serfs as well as the ill will of Nicholas's family and noble society. The fact that Praskovia never took advantage of her place, never lorded it over the other serfs or put on airs, only made the hatred stronger.

In the middle of October 1798, shortly after returning with the court to St. Petersburg, Nicholas was struck by excruciating pain caused by his fistula and unable to rise from his bed. The doctors were summoned, but none of the past remedies (solutions of magnesium, aluminum, and iron sulphate, tartrates of potash, and cold water baths) offered any relief. After ten days of watching Nicholas suffer, they decided the only option was to operate. It was a dangerous procedure, and they couldn't guarantee Nicholas it would be successful or that he would even survive. On 24

October, Drs. Bloch and Lakhman rolled Nicholas over on his stomach, exposed his posterior, and then set to work cutting out as much of the fistula as they could reach with their sharpened scalpels. Nicholas's hideous wails filled the room.

The operation was a success. The bleeding stopped, and the pain slowly subsided. A delirious Nicholas rewarded the doctors with gifts of several thousand rubles. He gave all the house serfs in Petersburg and Moscow an extra year of their salaries as an expression of his gratitude to God and in recognition of their concern for his health. The tsar visited Nicholas the day after the operation. He sat with Nicholas for awhile before returning to the Winter Palace, retiring to his private apartments alone.[7] Later that day Nicholas, revived by the tsar's display of concern, wrote his sister of the past days' events: "It is difficult, if not impossible, to describe. My home was beside itself, it was hard to look anyone in the face. They cut me six times. Faith in God is never in vain, and throughout this agonizing experience the Almighty gave me comfort—for Our Sovereign deigned to show great concern for my illness; twice every day he sent someone to inquire after me and then finally today he deigned to please me with his visit. He sat at my bedside. Although I am quite weak, my grateful heart has lost nothing. The Emperor held my hand, embraced me, and congratulated me on the successful outcome. I covered myself with tears of joy and kissed his hand. The Empress is also very saddened by my illness, and inquires every day."[8]

After seeing Nicholas in such a pitiful state, the emperor relieved him as chief marshal, appointing him chief chamberlain. Nicholas was grateful. In his new role he would still have to serve at court but with fewer duties and fewer bureaucratic headaches. By the middle of November, Nicholas was out of bed and well enough to leave the house for short walks. His mood had greatly improved as well. He wrote to a cousin of his miraculous surgery and recovery, about how the experience had given him renewed vigor and optimism and how the tsar had shown him genuine kindness. As always, though, Nicholas's newfound favor with the tsar was to be brief.

Since his operation Nicholas couldn't get a horrifying thought out of his head: what would have happened to Praskovia had he not survived? As long as he was alive, she was safe. But what would happen to her upon his death? Would she be safe under his heirs? Might they seek to take revenge against her? Clearly, she was in a dangerous position, and he had to do something to protect her. Nicholas knew the only thing to do was to free her; a self-reproachful inner voice must have chided him for having been so late in coming to this decision. On 15 December, he drafted a document granting Praskovia her freedom and sent it to the St. Petersburg Provincial Chamber of Justice and Punishment, Second Department. They were no longer serf and master. Praskovia, now thirty years old, was a free woman.

Or so they thought. As the emancipation letter worked its way through the bureaucracy, a punctilious official noticed that Nicholas had paid a processing fee of only thirty kopecks, even though Regulation no. 532 on domestic serfs clearly stated that the processing fee for emancipation was sixty kopecks. Thirty kopecks stood between Praskovia and freedom. Officials of the Provincial Chamber took the matter into consideration for several days before deciding that in light of Count Sheremetev's distinguished name and unimpeachable reputation they would process his request with full confidence that he would pay the remainder in a prompt fashion.[9] Finally, on 29 December, Praskovia gained her freedom.

TWENTY

The Curtain Falls

O n the morning of 16 December 1798, a brilliantly appointed carriage attended by four coachmen and postilions and an equal number of footmen attired in livery of red and black velveteen, their sable collars turned up against the cold, drove out of the Fountain House courtyard. Inside sat Nicholas. He was on his way to the Winter Palace to begin his duties as chief chamberlain after an absence from court of two months. Nicholas would remain in this position for several years. His new office required attending to the tsar—serving his food and drink, pushing in his chair at mealtime, introducing important personages, assisting him as he conducted affairs of state in the throne room, carrying his train during processions.

The position was a double-edged sword. Although Nicholas was called on to perform less work as chief chamberlain than as chief marshal, he had to spend nearly all his time in Paul's presence, which required extreme patience and self-control, as he would find out. In January 1799, Nicholas replied to Vasily Sheremetev's congratulatory letter with a weary sigh, bemoaning the fact that his new post did not afford him "that pleasant peace that you are now enjoying living with your happy family. It still remains for me to await that day when God will bless me with such a life, and then I shall begin to enjoy true happiness."[1]

It wasn't, of course, entirely up to God, but Nicholas found in such reasoning an excuse for not taking the risk of going through with his plan to marry Praskovia. They were both still getting used to the fact that she was no longer a serf. The change had little impact on how either of them led their daily lives, especially since her emancipation had been kept secret. No doubt Tatiana knew and Praskovia's sister as well, but not many more. Nicholas most likely shared the news with his cousin Vasily and possibly one or two others. The rest of the household serfs, Nicholas's family, and society at large were entirely in the dark. But did those around them notice something different in how they interacted? Did Praskovia's sorrowful mood lift just a bit, did her mien exude a greater air of confidence, did she show a newfound self-possession? She was free. And yet that didn't change her dependence on Nicholas for everything. There was no thought of starting her own life, of establishing her independence; there were no opportunities for someone in her position to do anything of the sort. The Sheremetev household was the only world she had ever known; it was her life. What's more, Nicholas loved her, and she knew this. Even if her feelings for him could not match his, she loved him too, in her way.

The spring and summer of 1799 saw another hectic round of remodeling at the Fountain House. Nicholas was never content to leave his homes as they were. He had all the floors ripped up and replaced with beautiful parquet taken from the nearby Tauride Palace of the late Prince Potemkin. Hammering and sawing and dust filled the home, forcing Praskovia and Nicholas to escape to the garden pavilion. Later they moved with the court to Pavlovsk and Peterhof, where Nicholas had found a dacha to rent for Praskovia. In July, they visited the family estate at Voznesenskoe on the west bank of the Neva River south of the city.

With its groves of birch, fir, and maple, Voznesenskoe lay in a picturesque setting, and Nicholas loved to come out here with Praskovia and Tatiana. When she was well enough, Praskovia enjoyed bathing in the cool waters of the Neva. The quiet of Voznesenskoe helped Nicholas forget a new annoyance in his life—his nephews Peter and Kirill Razumovsky. Around this time their mother began hounding Nicholas with worried letters describing her sons' dire straits and imploring him to help. This would go on, sadly, for years and became a source of frustration and worry for the entire extended family.

Varvara and Count Alexei Razumovsky had four children, two boys and two girls, during their difficult marriage. Alexei was intelligent and gifted, a fervent freethinking Freemason, although repressively arrogant and cruel, especially toward members of his family. He was the eldest son of Kirill Grigorievich Razumovsky, the brother of Empress Elizabeth's favorite (Count Alexei Grigorievich Razumovsky). He could scarcely tolerate his awkwardly shy, pious, and admittedly dim wife. Nicholas never felt any warmth for his brother-in-law, in part because of his cruel treatment of his sister, and he not unjustly considered the Razumovskys parvenus, with traces of mud from the Ukrainian village whence they arrived at court in the mid-1700s still visible on their boots.

In 1784, Alexei threw Varvara out of the house, keeping the children for himself. Devastated at the loss of her children, Varvara moved into a new home near Moscow's Lubiansky Square. From then on she lived alone and relied on her brother for everything. Alexei had kept the children merely to spite Varvara and showed little interest in them, leaving them to be raised by Swiss and French governesses, with whom he communicated only in writing. Alexei took a woman by the name of Maria Sobolevskaia as his common-law wife, and together they produced ten children who went by the name Perovsky.

Peter Razumovsky was born in 1775. His governess instilled in him a love of all things French, and this predilection only grew stronger with time. In 1790, Peter was sent abroad to study. He returned five years later an effete Francophile snob, a lover of the arts, an accomplished musician, fencer, and drawer of modest talent. He lacked any desire to serve and was criticized by his father for his laziness and "insouciance." In many ways he resembled his Uncle Nicholas at the same stage in his life, with the important distinction that Peter's father, unlike Nicholas's, was not about to let his son devote his life to the arts. And so Peter reluctantly embarked on a brief, scandal-ridden career in the military before making his way to St. Petersburg. His father wrote him long, exasperated letters pleading with him to straighten up and to stop spending all his time in "such bad company" and ignoring court and the best houses. His greatest concern, however, was his living between "l'avarice et l'extrême prodigalité." Peter's finances were forever in shambles; he was deep in debt, chiefly from gambling, and constantly begging his parents for more money.[2]

Peter's younger brother, Kirill, was the more gifted of the two. Even as a child he amazed everyone with his intellectual abilities and was pushed hard in his studies. Handsome, passionate, and percolating with an energy he could scarcely control, Kirill arrived in the capital in 1796 and, through the intervention of Platon Zubov, was made a gentleman of the bedchamber attached to Grand Duke Constantine. Young Kirill cut quite a figure at court, and he quickly became the star of the city's *jeunesse dorée*. His father worried about Kirill, calling him "a true scapegrace" and "a wicked subject" who spends all his time "in places of debauchery."[3] Alexei wrote Nicholas asking him to watch over him as a surrogate father: "Given his youth, his inexperience, and his empty-headedness, I have adequate reason to fear such a disposition will lead to the worst results."[4]

Nicholas did what he could. He kept Varvara and Alexei apprised of the boys' reprehensible behavior and their complete disregard for the rules of polite society. Again and again he paid their debts—sometimes as high as ten thousand rubles—and helped Kirill become a court chamberlain in October 1799, a favor the younger Razumovsky repaid by spreading malicious rumors about his uncle's unorthodox private life with his serf, rumors that made their way around the St. Petersburg salons. Upon their father's insistence, Peter moved in with Kirill to keep an eye on him, which was like asking the fox to guard the chicken coop. Neither brother saw any reason to rein in their spending or mend their ways for the simple reason that they were well aware that one day Russia's two largest family fortunes would be theirs. On their father's side, they stood to inherit the estate of their late great uncle (the favorite Count Alexei Grigorievich Razumovsky), which had descended to their father; on their mother's side, they stood to inherit the even larger fortune of their Uncle Nicholas, the committed bachelor. Nothing, as far as they knew, could prevent them from becoming the richest men in Russia. The promise of such riches fostered a cavalier attitude toward money and an arrogant belief that the normal standards of behavior did not apply to them. In Peter's case, it also fed fantasies of living a life devoted to the arts and culture just like his uncle. All they had to do was be patient and wait.

If Peter's artistic dreams lay ahead, Nicholas's were coming to a sad end. It was by now undeniably clear that Praskovia would never again perform. Her damaged lungs simply couldn't take in enough air for her to sing. Nicholas had had his doubts for some time and had taken the first steps toward closing the theater as early as April 1798, when he sent an order to have the singers in Moscow put to use as clerks and scribes in the Home Office. A year later he ordered the partial disbanding of the troupe, assigning many of the actors and actresses as domestics in the Fountain House. The use of all the gemstone stage names was to be discontinued. Henceforth, Nicholas instructed, Praskovia was to be called only by her full given name.[5] The Pearl existed no more. In January 1800, the ballet was cut to fourteen dancers. Such was Nicholas's love of the theater that he could bring himself to shut it down only gradually in phases. It was too dear to him to part with all at once. With its demise his life's work ceased, and the undeniable achievements wrought by decades of great planning, effort, and money vanished into the air.

That winter of 1800 the remaining dancers, including Tatiana, were sent back to Moscow to continue rehearsing under Signor Solomoni. It was a sad parting for Praskovia and her friend, although Tatiana wouldn't be away for long and returned a few months later. The former actresses Arina Kalmykova and Fekla Uruzova were assigned to live with Praskovia; eight others, including Anna Buianova (formerly the Emerald), were put in adjacent rooms, and nine more on the ground floor. Most of the actresses and their chaperones were permitted to stay in St. Petersburg to look for husbands, for which purpose Nicholas supplied each with a generous dowry. Earlier that year, Praskovia's sister had married the former Kapellmeister Peter Kalmykov, a wedding ceremony in which Praskovia most likely took part. Nicholas gave Matryona a dowry of one thousand rubles and made her a domestic at the Fountain House.

The family news from Kuskovo that year wasn't good. In late February, a letter arrived from the steward Alexei Biziaev informing that Uncle Maxim, Praskovia's late mother's brother and the estate's assistant head of gardens, had moved in with her father and had been causing trouble. The situation with Praskovia's father had, of course, been difficult for years. In April 1799, Nicholas, apparently acting at Praskovia's request, had tried to solve the old man's problems by moving him from Kuskovo, where the serfs, who all knew of his daughter's place in the master's house, tried to take advantage of him. He ordered that Ivan be given a decent place to live or put up with a kind family who would see to it he was well fed and cared for. Any family willing to do this would be paid an extra five rubles a year. If he wasn't eating well, the overseers were to prepare special food that satisfied him. They were to make certain he kept sober and to report his condition to Nicholas regularly.[6]

But for some reason Ivan returned to Kuskovo, after which his brother-in-law moved in with him and Ivan's son Afanasy. Praskovia now asked Nicholas to have Maxim removed from the house immediately and sent to live with the rest of the estate serfs. No one, she added, was to be permitted to live with her father except Afanasy. The incident is intriguing for a few reasons. First, it suggests that Ivan and Afanasy had been given better quarters than the rest of the serfs at Kuskovo and that they lived in a separate part of the estate, away from the other serfs. Second, in his order to the Home Office, Nicholas wrote that this action was to be taken "upon the request of Praskovia Kovalyova." By now no one in his administration or back at Kuskovo had need of any further identification. Neither apparently did they question her authority to make such requests. Praskovia was not the mistress of the household in the conventional sense, but her authority was recognized, and Nicholas was clear in communicating it.[7]

By the end of 1800, the mood at the Fountain House was gloomy. The closing of the theater affected everyone, not just Nicholas. If being in the troupe had meant long hours of hard work and strict discipline, it nonetheless gave the serfs a sense of purpose and identity and opportunities for creative expression. To most this was surely better than mindlessly copying papers in a dank office or preparing food in the master's kitchen.

The miasmic atmosphere at court invaded the Fountain House as well. As Paul's paranoia grew, so did his distrust of his old friend. He began to suspect Nicholas of trying to poison him, once even refusing to eat his lunch for fear it would be his last. Nicholas remained loyal despite these absurdities and tried to reassure Paul that evildoers at court were merely spreading lies to push them apart. When Paul became jealous of Nicholas for talking too long to a lady who enjoyed the emperor's particular pleasure during a state dinner, he jumped up from his seat and pointing at Nicholas shouted to one of his footmen, "Tell him that I shall pluck him like a chicken!"[8] The following day a shaken Nicholas reported sick.

"From that time on thousands of suspicions began to haunt Paul," one contemporary observed. "For everyone at court there began a life of utter fear, of eternal uncertainty. It was as if an epoch of terror had taken hold."[9] The British ambassador Lord Whitworth concurred. "The fact is, and I speak with regret, that the Emperor is literally not in his senses," Whitworth wrote in a secret communiqué to Whitehall. "This truth had been for many years known to those nearest to him, and I have myself had frequent opportunities of observing it. But since he has come to the throne, his disorder had gradually increased and now manifests itself in such a manner as to fill every one with the most serious alarm. . . . The Emperor's actions are guided by no fixed rules, or principle; every thing is the effect of caprice and of disordered fancy; consequently nothing can be stable."[10]

At the time it seemed as if this epoch of terror would go on forever. Given the tsar's paranoia, Nicholas didn't dare risk incurring his wrath by marrying now. It was a nightmarish situation for Nicholas and Praskovia, and their lives appeared fated to drag on in limbo as they had for the past four years. Deliverance, however, was only months away.

Figure 1. Panoramic view of the Kuskovo estate in the mid-1770s. In the foreground sits the Big House; to the far right, the Italian palazzo, above which can be made out the outdoor theater where Praskovia performed. (Art & Architecture Collection, Miriam and Ira D. Wallach Division of Art, Prints and Photographs, The New York Public Library)

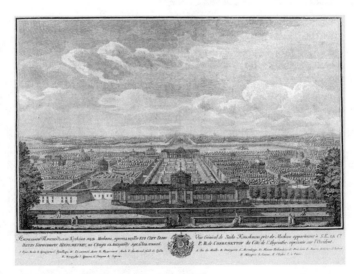

Figure 2. Panoramic view of the Kuskovo estate. The orangerie and games' alley dominate the foreground, while the man-made lake stretches out on the far side of the Big House. (Art & Architecture Collection, Miriam and Ira D. Wallach Division of Art, Prints and Photographs, The New York Public Library)

Figure 3. The white hall at Kuskovo inspired by the Hall of Mirrors at Versailles. The painted ceiling, which celebrates in allegorical fashion the family's patronage of the arts, is titled "Glory to the Sheremetevs." (Photograph by William Brumfield)

Figure 4. Brilliant courtier, grand seigneur, cross-eyed Russian Croesus, Count Peter Sheremetev as painted by his serf artist Ivan Argunov in 1760. (I. P. Argunov, 1760. Courtesy Ostankino Estate Museum)

Figure 5. A rakish Nicholas in 1769 at the age of eighteen. "I was carried away by the desire for sensations," he later recalled of his wild youth, "be they delicate or intoxicating, I craved all that was pleasing and gay." (Nicolas Benjamin Delapierre. © Kuskovo Estate Museum)

Figure 6. Nicholas's sister Countess Varvara Sheremeteva (m. Razumovskaia) in 1769. A simple, devout woman, Varvara lived a life of disappointment and heartbreak, to which her brother's scandalous marriage only added. (Nicolas Benjamin Delapierre. © Kuskovo Estate Museum)

Figure 7. Nicholas's son Ivan
Yakimov dressed as Cupid,
from 1790. (N. I. Argunov.
© 2006, State Russian
Museum, St. Petersburg)

Figure 8. The Ostankino palace in winter.
(Photograph by William Brumfield)

Figure 9. A view of Ostankino with the Church of the Life-Giving Trinity, from the 1820s. The Old Home where Praskovia and Nicholas lived for a time in the mid-1790s is visible to the right of the church. (Courtesy Ostankino Estate Museum)

Figure 10. The theater at Ostankino. Although the theater was built at immense expense to showcase Praskovia's talent, she performed here only a few times before falling ill and retiring in 1797 at the age of twenty-eight. (Photograph by William Brumfield)

Figure 11. The blue salon at Ostankino. "What luxury!
What magnificence!" exclaimed one visitor to the palace. "I saw
there such treasures that even an Indian Moghul doesn't possess."
(Photograph by William Brumfield)

Figure 12. In 1800,
Praskovia sat for the
French miniaturist
Chevalier de Chateau-
bourg. The drawing in
the artist's sketchbook
bears the caption "La
favorita du Comte de
Cheremetov." (© 2006,
State Russian Museum,
St. Petersburg)

p378

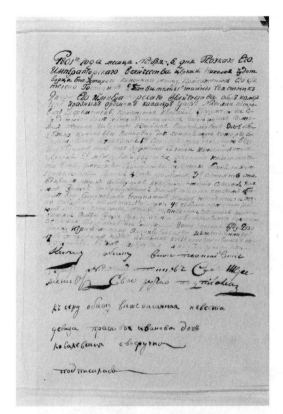

Figure 13. Nicholas's and Praskovia's marriage certificate dated 6 November 1801. The bottom four lines read: "To this warrant the above-mentioned maiden and bride Praskovia Kovalevskaia, the daughter of Ivan, did herself sign." (Courtesy Russian State Historical Archive)

Figure 14. The Fountain House in St. Petersburg as seen from the Fontanka River side. (Photograph by William Brumfield)

Figure 15. The windows to Praskovia's apartments at the Fountain House. The two windows in the second floor's center section mark the room where she gave birth to Dmitry and shortly thereafter died. (Author Photograph)

Figure 16. The sarcophagi of Praskovia, Nicholas, and Dmitry (*r. to l.*) in the Church of St. Lazarus. The large grave beyond Praskovia's is that of Nicholas's grandfather Field Marshal Boris Sheremetev. (Author Photograph)

TWENTY-ONE

The Specter of Death

I n the early hours of 12 March 1801, Tatiana Shlykova was awakened by one of Nicholas's footmen and told to fetch her keys and come to their master's office immediately. She did as she was told and went to Nicholas, finding him before the mirror being attended to by his hairdresser, Rousseau. Nicholas appeared terribly agitated, and his face showed that his thoughts were elsewhere. Tatiana kept the keys to the commode with his jewels, and he told her to open it and pull out everything necessary for his court attire. Tatiana asked Nicholas what was the matter. "The emperor has died of an apoplectic stroke," he stuttered. He was dressing to go to the Winter Palace and present himself to the new emperor.[1]

Nicholas was in shock. He had dined with the emperor and empress, their children, and several officers from the garrison just hours earlier at the St. Michael's Palace. The tsar had been in an unusually genial mood. There was no evidence that night of his usual paranoia, and he reminisced gaily with Nicholas about their youth. All seemed to be enjoying themselves except Paul's son Grand Duke Alexander, who sat glumly starring into his plate. He was the only one at table who knew what was about to happen.

The dinner ended early, and Nicholas rode the few short blocks back to the Fountain House, his carriage buffeted by icy winds, sleet pecking at the glass. Around 11 p.m., a group of drunken officers from the Semyonovsky regiment, accompanied by Count von Pahlen, the city commandant, were quietly admitted to St. Michael's. They made their way up the stairs to the tsar's apartments, overpowered the two Hussar guards, and entered his bedroom. Finding Paul cowering behind a screen, they announced that they were placing him under arrest. When he resisted, the officers set upon him—Nicholas Zubov smashed him in the temple with a heavy snuffbox, one officer pressed a malachite paperweight against his windpipe while another garroted the emperor with a silk scarf. Paul had feared an attempt on his life and had built the St. Michael's as his own safe house. Legend has it he had a secret escape tunnel dug connecting the palace to the Fountain House.[2] Even if there was a tunnel, he never would have made it out alive. In the first hour of the twelfth, the reign of Tsar Paul I came to an end.

The regicide did not occur without presentiments. On 1 March, a sealed letter arrived at the Fountain House for Nicholas. It bore no signs of its address of origin, and the seal did not offer any information as to its author. Nicholas opened it and found inside an anonymous letter addressed to the tsar. The contents of the letter greatly disturbed Nicholas and frightened him at the same time. Unsure what to do, he wrote to Count von Pahlen, describing what had transpired and sending him the suspicious envelope and letter. Just days earlier Nicholas had received a similar letter addressed to the tsar that he had also forwarded to Pahlen. Since the postal service was under Pahlen's jurisdiction, Nicholas thought the count would be the best person to get to the bottom of the mysterious documents. He also asked who should hand the letter over to the tsar: he or the count? Nicholas had lost the authority to present reports to the tsar and thus felt helpless to act without Pahlen's permission.

Both letters have since disappeared, and their contents remain a mystery. But it seems they had something to do with the events of the night of 11/12 March. Perhaps they contained a warning to the tsar.[3] Why Nicholas sent the letter to Pahlen instead of delivering it to the tsar also remains a mystery. Even if he was no longer permitted to report to the tsar, surely this was an exceptional circumstance, one for which the rules could be overlooked. And Pahlen was, after all, one of the conspirators behind the plot to overthrow the tsar in favor of his son Alexander. Is it possible that Nicholas didn't know this? Or was he secretly in favor of the plot as a way out of his intolerable place at court and in his personal life? Did he in fact send the letters to Pahlen precisely so their warning would never reach the tsar? Tatiana said that Nicholas knew of the plot, but he believed Pahlen would protect him.[4]

Pahlen broke the news to Alexander shortly after the deed had been done. Alexander was devastated. He had feared that the plot, which Pahlen had apprised him of, would end in bloodshed but had done nothing to stop it. For a moment he contemplated rejecting the throne, but his wife, Elizabeth, convinced him otherwise. He dressed and left for the Winter Palace to take up the mantle of tsar. The events of that night would haunt him for the rest of his life.

News of the tsar's death sent the residents of the capital out into the streets weeping and crying for joy as if it were Easter. The mood at the Fountain House was more complicated. Nicholas was outraged by the notion of regicide and the lawlessness it implied. Moreover, despite the past several trying years, Nicholas had remained devoted to Paul, both as his sovereign ruler and as his boyhood friend. The beastly end of his life and reign was abhorrent. At the same time, he couldn't help but think that life would be better under Alexander, who was nothing like his father. He was considered a kind, decent young man. It was too early to say how he would act as ruler, but maybe there was finally a reason for Nicholas and Praskovia to have hope for the future.

The specter of death hung over this hope. In January 1800, Nicholas's daughter Alexandra Remeteva died after a brief illness in Moscow at the age of eighteen. Alexandra's death saddened Nicholas and provoked his anger at her governess, whom he held responsible.[5] Praskovia's sister was next. Matryona had become pregnant soon after her marriage and gave birth to a healthy boy in early February 1801. Matryona and Peter named him Nicholas after their master. His birth was the source of much happiness in the Fountain House. Nicholas brought a serf named Martha Yakovleva from his Voronitskaia farmstead to be the boy's wet nurse, and he saw to it Matryona was given a bottle of fresh beer every day. Not long after giving birth, however, Matryona fell ill, most likely with pneumonia. Her condition worsened and the doctors were once more helpless. She died in June of that year. Nicholas gave her a fine burial, made gifts to the poor in her name, and paid for memorial services and prayers in Petersburg and Moscow.[6] The events surrounding her death eerily foreshadowed Praskovia's own fate.

Praskovia, too, fell ill about the same time as her sister. Perhaps one of them gave it to the other. By late May she was in a desperate way, and Nicholas was once more beside himself with worry. On 26 May, he wrote to Nicholas Bem in Moscow, "Let me tell you that I've been indescribably distraught, Parasha is ill with an extreme fever, and after twelve days she is only now feeling slightly better and there's reason for some hope. You can well imagine how I've been. I'm hurrying to her now, it's pointless for you to come, maybe I will soon be visiting you." The last words hint at Nicholas's fear that Praskovia was going to die. Nicholas changed his mind and did summon Dr. Frese from Moscow to attend to Praskovia, having lost all faith in the St. Petersburg doctors.[7] Although he was still officially serving as court chamberlain, Nicholas neglected his duties to remain with Praskovia throughout May and June.

After Matryona's funeral, the two of them left the Fountain House to spend the summer in a house he had rented on the Petersburg Side across the Neva River beyond the Peter and Paul Fortress. They ostensibly went because the air was healthier there, though the real reason was more likely Nicholas's wanting to get Praskovia out of the Fountain House, now filled with horrid memories. Leaving was an attempt to flee the deathly atmosphere that pervaded the palace.

For weeks Praskovia suffered from high fever and spasms. She had drenching night sweats and in the morning would awake exhausted. She could no longer get out of bed. The doctors began a course of mare's milk baths. To make sure they had enough, Nicholas bought a mare that had just foaled and had it brought to the house. To lift Praskovia's spirits, he bought bunches of freshly cut lilacs for her room. Nothing worked, and Praskovia grew weaker.

In the past Praskovia had always done exactly as her doctors had ordered, but now she gave up on their cures. They could help her no more. She placed her fate in God's hands. He would decide whether she was to live or die. She had one of the servant girls read her Scripture, and Praskovia prayed to God, saying that she had made her peace and was prepared to meet her fate. Days passed, and then slowly, miraculously her fever broke, her lungs cleared, and the sweats and spasms subsided. She regained her strength, and by the end of June Praskovia was well again. As she thought about her ordeal, a passage sprang to mind: "The Lord hath punished me severely, but He hath not given me over to death."

Psalm 118, verse 18. She had read these lines many times before, but they now acquired a new meaning. Here was God's message to her. He had indeed punished Praskovia for her sins, yet he had shown mercy. He had forgiven her. Praskovia would utter these words over and over for the rest of her life, making them her personal credo. After she died, Nicholas had them emblazoned on Praskovia's deathbed portrait.[8]

On 28 June, the two of them celebrated Nicholas's fiftieth birthday, and Praskovia's recovery, in their house on the Petersburg Side.

TWENTY-TWO

Coronation

The morning of Friday, 16 August, broke unseasonably cold in St. Petersburg. The sky was clear and calm, and a flurry of activity was under way in the Fountain House. Footmen were struggling as they carried heavy trunks and chests down the stairs and out into the courtyard, packing them into a long line of carriages; grooms were leading the horses out of the stables, fitting their traces, and attaching them to the conveyances. Upstairs, Nicholas and Praskovia were putting on their traveling clothes in preparation for their departure for Moscow and the coronation of the tsar.

Clouds had started to move in and a breeze began to blow by the time everything had been loaded and they pulled out of the Fountain House. As it made its way through the streets of the capital, the lengthy, multicolored procession caused passersby to stop and stare in amazement. Nicholas traveled in a style befitting European crowned heads. He took with him almost half of his domestic staff, nearly 140 individuals, all loaded onto dozens of carriages and carts and wagons drawn by over sixty horses. Along with Praskovia, a few family members, and close friends, their party included dozens of liveried servants, valets, and footmen, several Hussars, coachmen, drivers, and stable boys, blacksmiths, stokers, and saddlers, overseers and personal secretaries. Nicholas even brought with him one of his pastry chefs, his cobbler, his coffee-maker, and two table-setters. Twenty musicians accompanied them as well.

The food wagons were laden with the finest provisions. The wine was Château Lafite and Malaga. There was plenty of beer and seltzer water, Swiss and Parmesan cheeses, imported English mustard, olive oil from Provence, a hundred fresh oranges, as many lemons, homemade cherry and raspberry preserves, candied almonds, two pounds of tea, fifteen pounds of coffee, an entire pood of sugar, five pounds of chocolate, loaves of fresh bread, and cakes. A wagon with Nicholas's wardrobe attended by ten servants had left a few days earlier.

Praskovia and Nicholas each had a retinue. Hers numbered twenty-two persons conveyed by one sumptuously appointed coach, two barouches, and three covered wagons. Riding with Praskovia was Tatiana, Margarita Remeteva, and Taniusha. Nicholas traveled with twenty-five in a convoy of eight vehicles complete with mobile kitchen and two sleeping carriages. Yakov Remetev and Ivan Yakimov shared his carriage. On the penultimate wagon rode Praskovia's brother Nicholas. He now worked as a secretary at Moscow University, having been let go as a violinist in the orchestra, and was returning home after a visit to his sister.[1]

Instead of traveling the main post road to Moscow, they went out of their way to visit the town of Rostov, where St. Dmitry was buried. They had decided to undertake a pilgrimage to make a votive offering to his remains after Praskovia's latest recovery. Rostov was only eighteen miles from Voshchazhnikovo, the village where Praskovia had probably been born and where her godmother, Anna Andreeva, was still living. It's possible Nicholas and Praskovia paid her a visit.

Moscow was bustling by the time they arrived, in late August. For weeks, crowds had been descending on the city. Battalion after battalion of Guards regiments had ridden in on their fine steeds, all the courtiers and aristocrats from St. Petersburg had come with their retainers, and nobles from remote provinces had made the arduous trip to witness the coronation. Families and old friends celebrated happy reunions after years apart. In contrast to the previous coronation four years before, a joyous, exuberant atmosphere filled the air.

The Sheremetev convoy stopped at the Corner House, a sprawling mansion in the heart of the city that traced its origins back to the Field Marshal. Legend had it that he built a small house for himself on the spot in 1703 and that Peter the Great laid the cornerstone. It stood within the shadow of the Kremlin, just up Vozdvizhenka Street from the Kuftafia Tower and directly across from the Krestovozdvizhensky Monastery. The home most recently had belonged to Nicholas's brother-in-law, Count Alexei Razumovsky, who, in the midst of a cash flow crisis, implored Nicholas to buy it from him in 1799 for the exorbitant price of four hundred thousand rubles. In a gesture of kindness, Nicholas had agreed.

A formal staircase ascended to the public rooms on the second floor. From here, the windows looked out onto the red, crenellated walls of the Kremlin. Beyond this enfilade began the private apartments. Nicholas's personal secretary and confidant, Dmitry Malimonov, occupied the first room; next were those set aside for Yakov, Margarita, and Tatiana. Nicholas and Praskovia took the final two rooms. The first of these was furnished as a gentleman's study with mahogany furniture upholstered in green and red morocco. There was a writing desk, a chess table, and a few leather Volterians, big, overstuffed armchairs with high backs. A clock ticked softly on one wall, and in the beautiful corner two icons of St. Dmitry of Rostov gazed down over a collapsible altar bench. The portrait of Praskovia as Eliane from *The Marriage of the Samnites* had been removed from her room at Ostankino and hung here.

A door at the far end opened to the bedroom. The walls were covered in light orange paper with a turquoise border. Off to one side was a large bed and a small mahogany table with a marble top. There was a writing desk, dressing table and mirror, a divan of red morocco, and an altar bench, this one for Praskovia's daily prayers. A single icon of the Virgin Mother of Smolensk hung on the wall. Three windows opened out onto the garden below. This would be Praskovia's and Nicholas's home for the next four months.[2]

Praskovia's days in the Corner House continued much as they had back in St. Petersburg. Although her sister Matryona was gone, she still had Tatiana and Taniusha (she most likely shared Praskovia's room), and Margarita to keep her company, and the four of them spent their days together. Praskovia would do needlework to the sound of the others chatting about the latest gossip and goings-on surrounding the approaching coronation. One of her projects was sewing a gold thread fringe on a few of the valets' livery, for which Nicholas paid her handsomely.[3] Praskovia would play the clavichord for them in the blue Oval Salon, accompanied by the noises from the street below that drifted in through the open balcony door. When it wasn't too hot outside, they sat and read in the garden or went for a ride.

Alexander and Elizabeth arrived in Moscow on Sunday, 8 September. The solemn entry of a new Russian sovereign into the old capital was always an event of momentous political and cultural significance, nearly equal to that of the coronation ceremony itself. At the head of the procession, on horses caparisoned in gold and red, rode members of the Guards regiments, followed by the entire Moscow nobility mounted on horseback in rows of two. They were followed by Alexander himself, then a handsome youth of twenty-three, on a white steed. Elizabeth, tall, fair, and beautiful, a delicate rosebud for a mouth, rode behind in a golden coach drawn by eight grays. Tens of thousands clogged the route to catch a glimpse of the new emperor as he made his way to the Kremlin. The day was warm and sunny and seemed to reflect the feelings of the city's inhabitants.

The coronation took place on the following Sunday. In the early morning hours, heralds rode through the thick fog that had blanketed Moscow the night before proclaiming the glorious news that today a new tsar would be crowned. Hours later, Alexander and Elizabeth, dressed in richly brocaded vestments and escorted by church dignitaries, entered the Kremlin's Uspensky Cathedral and took their places on the imperial thrones. The ancient ceremony, ripe with symbolism and shrouded in a veil of Orthodox mysticism, lasted over five hours. By the time the newly crowned imperial couple exited the cathedral the sun had broken through the fog. As Alexander and Elizabeth made their way out into the sunlight, the large assembly let loose a mighty cry, cannons roared, and the peal of thousands of church bells filled the air. Nicholas participated in the ceremony, serving their royal majesties at the evening banquet and then later at a small gathering with the emperor and empress in the Kremlin's Palace of Facets.

The following weeks witnessed an unending succession of balls, concerts, and parades. Nicholas attended many of these and was invited to intimate dinners with Alexander, Elizabeth, and the Dowager Empress Maria Fyodorovna. Like most Russians, he believed that a man of intelligence, humanity, and goodwill was now ruling Russia. It was as if the country had passed through an interminably long, dark night and emerged into the hopeful light of a new day. Nicholas knew he enjoyed the confidence of the tsar. Alexander showed his pleasure for Nicholas by visiting him three times in October. On the evening of Tuesday, 1 October, Alexander, Elizabeth, and a large group of nobles rode out to Ostankino for a grand ball hosted by Nicholas. Everyone had a marvelous time, and the royal couple didn't leave until three in the morning. Even the empress, exhausted from the ceaseless partying and plagued by migraines, had been impressed.[4]

On Saturday, 5 October, Alexander went for a carriage ride around Moscow and made an unannounced stop at the Corner House for a short visit. Five days later Nicholas threw a ball at the Corner House attended by Alexander and Elizabeth. Again, they stayed until the early hours of the next day. Praskovia was at home for their visits. Was she presented to the tsar and tsaritsa? Did they ask to meet the famous opera singer who had performed years ago for Alexander's grandmother at Kuskovo and about whom they had heard so much? It is likely that they did meet on one of these occasions. One can see Nicholas trying to read the tsar's reaction to Praskovia, hoping to catch a glimpse of his true feelings beneath the polite, public façade. In light of what happened later, Nicholas must have been satisfied with what he saw.

Nicholas threw a final party at Ostankino for several hundred on 13 October. Among the guests was the British ambassador, Lord St. Helens. The next day he gushed about Nicholas's party in a letter to a friend: "The Festivities of our coronation have been extremely brilliant, and that of yesterday evening in particular, which was given by Count Scheremetieff, may be termed an Arabian Nights Entertainment, as in point of splendour and magnificence it equaled and even went beyond what the most fertile imagination could conceive or picture."[5]

St. Helens's estimation seems to have been shared by all, as the splendor of that night is mentioned in more than one memoir of the time. Even the acid-tongued Philip Vigel had to admit that of all the balls and entertainments put on that fall, "no one managed to surpass the magnificence of the most lavish of them all staged by Count Sheremetev. From the city gate known as the Cross all the way to his village of Ostankino, the entire route—some three versts—was brightly lit up. And his luxuriously appointed home that, upon first seeing it years ago, struck us all as a work of magic has lost none of its effect."[6]

Coronation

Although Nicholas and Praskovia couldn't help but be swept up with the rest of Moscow in the excitement of the coronation and the accompanying entertainments, their minds had begun turning to a more personal matter.

TWENTY-THREE

Wedding

By late October 1801, Alexander and the court had left Moscow for St. Petersburg and the crowds had emptied out. Life in the old capital slowly reverted to its usual, quieter rhythms. Except for the inhabitants of the Corner House. To Nicholas and Praskovia the celebrations of the past two months had been a convenient distraction, and now they began preparing for their own private ceremony.

No one knows when Nicholas came to the decision to marry Praskovia. It's conceivable he had already decided when they left St. Petersburg for Moscow in August. Having nearly lost Praskovia that spring had made plain to him just how deeply he loved her. Had she died he would have been haunted by guilt over the fact that he had been too afraid to give her what she, and he, too, so greatly wished for. But if not then, the interaction with Alexander during the coronation festivities, the visits to his homes, and the meeting with Praskovia, if one indeed happened, convinced Nicholas the time to marry had come. There were no more reasons to delay.

There was much to do. A church had to be selected, priests arranged for, witnesses chosen—and all with the utmost secrecy, for although they were ready for this final step, they must have known society wasn't. No aristocrat of Nicholas's standing had ever married his serf, which is what Praskovia was still believed to be, and Nicholas had no desire to cause a scandal. The Sheremetevs' parish church, the Church of Nicholas the

Miracle Worker Near the Old Stone Bridge, located a block away from the Corner House by the Kremlin's Kuftafia Tower, was the logical place. It had been the site of two baptisms late that summer of children born to the count's servants and was the only sanctioned place for Nicholas and Praskovia to wed. But Nicholas was worried about performing the ceremony there for two reasons. First, the church stood completely exposed, surrounded by open spaces, which meant getting in and out unnoticed would be difficult. Second, he was too well known there. If someone were to stumble upon the wedding, Nicholas would be recognized immediately. The Corner House had its own chapel, but for some unknown reason he decided not to use it.

So Nicholas began looking for another church. It didn't take long to find the ideal spot. Set back from any main thoroughfare amid a tangled warren of alleyways once home to the cooks of the Muscovite court stood the Church of St. Simon Stylites. A small jewel of a church dating back to the late seventeenth century, it was out of the way and afforded secrecy and anonymity. Moreover, it was close by—just a short ride up Vozdvizhenka on the far side of the city's old earthen walls.

Helping them with all these arrangements was Father Platon, the metropolitan of Moscow. Platon was an old friend of the family. He had read the eulogy at Peter Sheremetev's funeral, and Nicholas had confided in him about his love for Praskovia. Platon's long, white beard, flowing shoulder-length hair, and fiercely intense eyes gave him the appearance of a fiery Old Testament prophet that belied his generally enlightened outlook. He fully supported Nicholas and Praskovia, and they in turn considered him one of their few friends. He was captivated by Praskovia, and once was so overcome by his feelings for her he threw himself at her feet and kissed her hand. He saw to it that the arrangements were made at both churches and with their respective clergy. For someone of Nicholas's standing, it wasn't hard to bend Church rules.

On 30 October, Nicholas sent an order to his overseer at Kuskovo to prepare the cottage for his arrival, making sure it was cleaned and heated since he was planning on visiting for a day or two at the end of the week.[1] This was the old washery where Nicholas and Praskovia had lived for a time over a decade ago. Now, on the eve of their wedding, they were returning. Praskovia had not been to Kuskovo in years, most likely since the coronation of Paul in 1797. It was a homecoming for her and certainly occasioned a flood of memories. Her father, now sixty-two and in relatively good health despite his drinking, and brother Afanasy were there, and she must have seen them during her brief stay. One wonders what they talked about after so many years apart. Praskovia had a good deal to tell them about her life with Nicholas in St. Petersburg, about how her brother Ivan, now living in the capital, was getting along, and about the birth of Matryona's son earlier in the year followed by her unexpected death.

And then there was the impending wedding. Did Praskovia tell them about that? Was the main purpose for visiting Kuskovo perhaps to break the news to Ivan and ask for his blessing? Perhaps it was only intimated; words may have been spoken to the effect that certain significant changes were about to take place and that Nicholas was making plans to improve their situation. In subsequent months, the behavior of Praskovia's brothers, emboldened by their sister's newfound status, suggests that if she didn't share the secret with them on this visit, she did let them in on it shortly thereafter.

As for Nicholas's family, they were not told, unless this curious note Nicholas sent to his steward Agapov from around this time can be read as bearing the news of his secret: "Upon receiving this note, take it yourself without delay to my sister Countess Varvara Petrovna and ask permission to read this note to her alone, making certain no one else is with you. And once you have read it, do not let it out of your hands, but tear it into pieces and then burn it, so that no one notices what you brought with you. Let me know as soon as you have done this."[2]

The contents of this note remain a mystery.

Prince Alexander Mikhailovich Golitsyn was the head of one of Russia's great noble families, a former ambassador to France and Great Britain, senator and vice chancellor. Golitsyn was a contemporary of Nicholas's late father, and Nicholas had known him since he was a boy. He trusted Golitsyn. He had made him guardian of his sister Varvara's property, had relied on his help to construct the almshouse near the Sukharev Tower, and had used him in the negotiations on the purchase of the Corner House.

For many years Golitsyn had a scrivener in his service by the name of Boris Merkulov, who would come to play an important, if murky, role in Nicholas's and Praskovia's story. In the mid-1790s, Golitsyn no longer required Merkulov's services and lent him out to Count Kirill Grigorievich Razumovsky. Merkulov worked for the count and members of his family, including his son Alexei, Nicholas's brother-in-law, as a legal representative conducting property transactions and other business on their behalf. The precise nature of his work is hard to determine. Merkulov was a factotum and shadowy fixer for the rich and powerful; he was apparently used on delicate matters and knew his way around archives, the law, and the workings of the creaky state bureaucracy. It was because of Merkulov's connections to Golitsyn and Alexei Razumovsky that Nicholas decided to use him in the negotiations concerning the Corner House. Merkulov's once having worked on behalf of Nicholas's cousin Vasily Sergeevich Sheremetev to track down a runaway serf further recommended him to Nicholas.

With Golitsyn's endorsement, Merkulov traveled to St. Petersburg in the summer of 1800 to meet Nicholas and sell his services. Nicholas was impressed and, ignoring the warnings of Alexei Razumovsky, agreed to hire Merkulov to work for him. Razumovsky had lost confidence in Merkulov and wrote Nicholas to watch out for him, as he had "a nasty reputation of knavery and intriguing."[3] Since this information came from his brother-in-law Nicholas didn't give it much credence, though he ought to have.

Merkulov had known for some time that his days working for the Razumovskys were coming to an end, and he looked upon the sale of the Corner House as an opportunity to ingratiate himself with Sheremetev and gain a new and possibly better-paying employer. Indeed, he started working for Nicholas without telling the Razumovskys, even though they were still paying him. Alexei was terribly angry when he found out. But what really threw the Razumovskys into a rage was that Merkulov stole one of their paintings. The work in question was by the popular eighteenth-century Italian portraitist Pompeo Girolamo Batoni. According to the sale contract, the painting was to stay with the Razumovskys, but Merkulov had secretly removed it from the Corner House and delivered it to Prince Golitsyn for safekeeping with the intention of giving it to Nicholas.[4]

L'affaire Batoni was the last straw. Kirill and Alexei wrote back and forth on what to do about Merkulov, denouncing him as that "rogue scrivener," "ne'er-do-well," and "dangerous dirty man." On 27 February 1801, Alexei published a letter in the *Moscow Gazette* notifying the public that Merkulov no longer worked for them and not to accept any letter of representation he might present in the family name.[5]

The purchase of the Corner House completed, Nicholas now had a new mission in mind for Merkulov. It was a secret mission of extreme delicacy involving Praskovia's genealogy.[6] According to certain documents in Nicholas's possession, Praskovia's forefathers had not originally been serfs but were actually Polish nobility. Sometime around 1664 in the reign of Tsar Alexei Mikhailovich, Yakov Semyonovich Kovalevsky was taken prisoner by Russian forces under Prince Yuri Bariatinsky. Kovalevsky told his captors that he was a Polish noble, that he served the Polish king Jan Casimir, and that he had seven villages of serfs near the town of Polotsk. After the Treaty of Andrusovo in 1667 ended the war between Russia and Poland, Alexei Mikhailovich invited all imprisoned foreign nobles to join his service as free men, and Yakov Kovalevsky accepted his offer.

All traces of Yakov Kovalevsky disappear at this point. He and his possible descendants vanish. And then, miraculously, a letter by one Stepan Sergeevich Kovalevsky dated 12 January 1747 and addressed to Count Peter Sheremetev was purportedly discovered among the papers of Nicholas's maternal grandfather. In his letter Stepan Kovalevsky writes to Peter about how he and his father, Sergei Yakovlevich, had long served him and his father as free men, reminding him that his grandfather, Yakov Semyonovich Kovalevsky, had never been "a slave" but was born a Polish nobleman. And so it is with outrage and fear, Stepan writes, that he has learned that the previous year the count's steward, Fyodor Zverev, had placed him on the rolls of the count's serfs and Russified his surname to Kuznetsov. Stepan begs the count to show mercy, to save him from serfdom, to undo this injustice and return to him his "family's noble status — for even without it I shall remain to the death your loyal servant."[7] This Stepan, so the story goes, was Praskovia's grandfather.

The letter was a fake. Stepan had never been a "Kovalevsky," nor was he the wronged descendant of Polish nobility. It was not written in 1747, but much later, probably in 1800 around the time of Merkulov's visit. Who came up with such a tale involving a bogus genealogy and fabricated letters—Merkulov or Nicholas? We shall most likely never know. Nicholas writes at one point that the search for Praskovia's noble rights became Merkulov's self-proclaimed mission and that it began then in 1800 after Nicholas had shown him documents proving the story.[8] Maybe Merkulov had heard about Nicholas's unhappy love affair and came to St. Petersburg to offer him a way out of his situation. Maybe Nicholas called Merkulov to him with the idea of using him in his plan to rewrite Praskovia's family history. Or maybe they came up with it together during their conversations in the Fountain House.

The notion of serfs becoming nobles would have been familiar to both of them. Nicholas had been faced with several cases of his own serfs claiming noble status. In a letter to Prince Alexei Kurakin, Nicholas complained of serfs who had been in his family "since ancient times" coming to him claiming noble status via illegal means. This sort of thing typically happened in Little Russia, and it was not an isolated matter; there were many instances, sometimes involving entire families. In 1796, a serf named Terentei Dolgopolov fled the Sheremetev estate of Mikhailovka south of Oryol with his family and tried to petition the Northern Novgorod Noble Commission for a noble patent. A few years after this, Yefim Beslavov, a deacon from Nicholas's home chapel, fled his master, eventually turning up in Little Russia and pretending to be a nobleman. When he found out about it, Nicholas wrote to Archpriest Silvester and asked him to send this "nobleman" back so he could return him to his "previous condition."[9]

And then there was another world where peasants and nobles traded places with surprising ease and frequency—the theater.

One of the clichés of opéra-comique, indeed of much drama of the era, is that no one and nothing are ever quite what they seem. Queens present themselves as shepherdesses, aristocratic ladies prove to be commoners, vulturine noblemen reveal themselves to be men of rare virtue, and peasant girls are discovered to be of noble lineage. These scenarios were presented over and over again on the Sheremetev stage. In Monsigny's *Aline, Queen of Golconde*, Praskovia played the title role of a peasant girl who becomes an Indian queen and disguises herself as a shepherdess to test her lover; in Grétry's *Lucile*, she sang the part of a noble bride who discovers that she is actually the child of a poor peasant; in

Nicolas Méraux's *Laurette,* she was a peasant girl wooed by a wealthy count intent on running off with her; she resists until her father finally blesses their love, telling them that she, too, is of noble birth, although he felt it necessary to hide this fact given their poverty.

The opera with the clearest resemblance to Praskovia's and Nicholas's situation was Niccolò Piccinni's *The Good Married Girl,* performed at Ku-skovo in 1782. Praskovia played the part of Rosetta, abandoned by her parents and left to be raised by a peasant. Too poor to care for the little girl, the peasant gives Rosetta to the local countess. Rosetta becomes the object of desire of Simonin, the countess's gardener, and of the marquis, the countess's nephew. In her heart Rosetta loves the marquis, but she knows their love can never be, given the social gulf between them. The marquis confesses his love to Rosetta, assuring her that "love will change the decisions of fate and will make us equal."[10] When the countess finds out, she threatens to send Rosetta away for her impudent presumption: "Oh, Rosetta! . . . Is Rosetta permitted to think that she is worthy of the honor of being the wife of the marquis? . . . Now everyone wants a title. Oh, how corrupt is our world!"[11]

Before Rosetta leaves for a convent, a stranger arrives. He tells the marquis that years ago an officer in the army had secretly married a local noble maiden. She became pregnant, but he had to leave suddenly on a mission to America before the child was born. His wife died shortly after giving birth to a daughter, and since the parents didn't know she was married the baby was handed over to a peasant and then taken to be raised in the nearby castle. The marquis tells him that he knows this girl and her name is Rosetta. The man replies that this must be someone else, for this girl's name is Wilhelmina, to which the marquis replies, "Don't worry, my friend, names are easily changed." Rosetta overhears their conversation and is stunned. So do several peasants, who've heard this all before: "A noble father, a noble, who might have been a shepherd. Hah, hah, hah! Why the countess has an entire village of such gentlemen."[12]

Rosetta is reunited with her father, and he blesses her wish to marry the marquis, as does the countess upon learning the truth of her noble origins. As if by a miracle, the lovers are united to cries of joy all around.

It all seemed so neat and easy and logical, and Nicholas perhaps thought that if it could work on the stage, why not in real life?

The plan was to send Boris Merkulov to White Russia—formerly part of Poland—in advance of the wedding to obtain proof of Praskovia's noble lineage. These western lands of the Russian Empire were a hotbed of such illicit transactions. The Polish nobility had long been much larger proportionally than the other European noble classes, and it had never had any official heraldry books (until 1850), thus making it difficult to tell who was and who was not a noble. Polish nobles were often willing to sell noble patents, typically those of their children who had died young, and there were a great many forgers producing Polish noble certificates. One of them, noted for the believability of his bogus documents, would wear the documents in his boots until they took on a convincing yellow patina and the smell of antiquity. For enough money, anyone could acquire Polish nobility.[13]

Helping Nicholas and Merkulov was Alexei Malinovsky, a friend of Nicholas, a minor dramatist, translator, and historian. Most important, Malinovsky was the head of the Moscow archive of the College of Foreign Affairs. This archive contained information on prisoners of war, and it was here, most likely with Malinovsky's assistance, that a suitable forefather in the person of Yakov Kovalevsky was found. His noble status, disappearance from the historical record, and surname that both echoed "Kovalyov" and was the Polish equivalent of "Kuznetsov" made him an ideal candidate. Armed with the forged family tree, Merkulov was nearly ready to undertake his commission.

Next, in October 1801, Praskovia signed a letter of representation to Merkulov attesting to the fact that she was the descendant of Polish nobles by the name of Kovalevsky and authorizing him to go to White Russia and obtain the necessary documentary proof of her heritage from the local noble assembly and with this proof petition the Russian Department of Heraldry for a noble patent. That same month, before Merkulov left Moscow, Nicholas sent Merkulov two emancipation letters—one for Praskovia's father and one for her brother Afanasy—that he had just signed and witnessed in the Moscow District Court and asked him to have the two men placed in the lists of the Moscow merchantry. Then Nicholas drafted a document freeing Praskovia's brother Nicholas Kovalyov. The paperwork took some time, and the final documents for the entire family, including Praskovia's brothers Ivan and Michael, her in-laws, nieces, and nephews, were not completed and submitted until December. Armed with Praskovia's letter, her forged genealogy, and thousands of rubles for bribes, Merkulov left for White Russia at the end of the year.[14]

By 4 November, Praskovia and Nicholas had returned to Moscow from Kuskovo. They now faced the most important day of their lives. What they had finally decided to do had never before been done in Russia. By marrying they would be changing their lives, as well as those of their families, in unalterable and not yet fully comprehended ways.

Were there any second thoughts as the day approached? Did either of them get cold feet and try to convince the other that what they were planning was madness, likely to destroy them and quite possibly members of both their families? It's hard to imagine either Praskovia or Nicholas going to sleep on the night of the fifth without some voice inside their heads telling them not to go ahead with the wedding. But they had been through this uncertainty and second-guessing many times before — all the reasons for being cautious, for not taking this ultimate step and simply continuing on as they had been. They both must have known by now, however, that whatever doubts they might still harbor, they simply could no longer go on in the old way.

The spiritual suffering had taken too great a toll on Praskovia. She was filled with shame to the point of self-loathing, and this feeling, far from lessening over the years, only grew as time passed and her relationship with Nicholas remained unchanged. Nicholas could no longer bear to see Praskovia suffer. He knew that he was the cause of it and that he had the power to ease her pain. For years he had struggled with his own prejudices about noble birth and with the burden he felt to uphold the family name. He understood society's biases, indeed, he shared many of them. In the end, this wasn't enough to stop him. It had to have hurt Praskovia to think that marriage required denying the truth about her family and adopting the lie that she was the descendant of Polish nobility, but it was a concession she was willing to make, especially since she knew, most likely even better than Nicholas, how damaging her origins would be to any future offspring. Slaves typically know their masters better than they know themselves.

The lamps had already been lit outside the Corner House when a carriage pulled up before the main entrance. A footman opened the door and in climbed Praskovia, Tatiana, Nicholas, and Nicholas Bem. The carriage lurched forward out of the courtyard, turned right on the alley before the mansion and then quickly right again onto Vozdvizhenka Street. Across the street the cupolas of the Krestovozdvizhensky Monastery loomed in the darkness.

They drove a few short blocks up Vozdvizhenka away from the Kremlin, passed through a cut in the city walls, and then jogged right into Povarskaia Street. Within minutes they were at the church. The portico over the main door hung down low, making them feel as though they had to duck to keep from hitting their heads as they hurried inside. It was dark when they entered. At the far end, the gold iconostasis glowed dimly in the candlelight. The overall impression inside was one of warmth, intimacy, closeness to God. Five men came forward to greet them. Father Grigory Ivanov and Deacon Simon Ivanov of the Church of Nicholas the Miracle Worker presided over the ceremony, assisted by Stefan Nikitin, the priest of St. Simon Stylites. Prince Andrei Shcherbatov and Alexei Malinovsky, serving as witnesses, were also there.[15]

The clergymen had completed the necessary paperwork in advance. They had already made an entry in the metrical books of the Church of St. Nicholas, certifying, falsely no doubt, that the obligatory banns had been read aloud in the church on three separate occasions in advance of the wedding. The betrothed were listed as "Parishioner His Highness Sir Actual Privy Councilor of His Imperial Majesty's Court, Chief Chamberlain and Knight of Various Orders Count Nicholas Petrovich Sheremetev and the maiden Praskovia Ivanovna Kovalevskaia."[16] Sometime earlier both Nicholas and Praskovia had confessed their sins and received a deed attesting to the fact that their souls had been properly cleansed for marriage by Father Polikarp, patriarch of Jerusalem and Palestine.[17]

Next, Nicholas and Praskovia were presented with a document testifying to the fact that both were Russian Orthodox, were in no way related, were in their right mind, were undertaking this sacrament freely and without compulsion, were of sufficient age, and had never before been married. Nicholas and Praskovia were so nervous they didn't notice that the deacon had put down their incorrect ages—forty-eight for Nicholas, who had turned fifty that June, and thirty for Praskovia, who was thirty-three as of July.

After Deacon Simon read the document aloud, he turned to Nicholas and asked him to sign it. With bold, fat strokes of the pen, Nicholas signed—*Count Nicholas Petrovich Sheremetev,* his proud, cosmopolitan signature a mix of Cyrillic and Latin letters. Then Praskovia took the quill. Her signature could not be more different. In a neat and humble hand, free of any flourishes and swirling curlicues, Praskovia wrote—*To this warrant the above mentioned maiden and bride Praskovia Kovalevskaia, the daughter of Ivan, did herself sign.*[18] The strength it took to write these words, the immense degree of self-control, and the emotions fighting to break free have all left their traces on this scrap of paper. As she was completing the final letter, Praskovia succumbed. She lost control of the pen and scrawled a long trail of ink across the bottom of the page.

Next, Prince Shcherbatov and Alexei Malinovsky stepped forward and affixed their signatures as witnesses. There is a third signature as well, belonging to one Paul Narbekov. Who this was, other than a member of an old Russian noble family, remains a mystery. It is also possible his signature was affixed after the ceremony, for no other sources put him at the church.[19]

The paperwork done, the party moved to the front of the church just before the iconostasis. Standing directly behind Nicholas and Praskovia, Prince Shcherbatov and Tatiana held symbolic crowns over their heads while Deacon Simon conducted the wedding ceremony. Shortly after seven o'clock, the ceremony was completed. Nicholas and Praskovia were now husband and wife.

Before leaving the church, Nicholas handed the deacon two hundred rubles. "No matter where you are," he told him, "you will continue to receive the same amount from me every year for the rest of my life."[20] The gift and the promise were more than tokens of Nicholas's gratitude. They were intended to buy the deacon's silence. Four days later, Nicholas presented Father Nikitin and the Church of St. Simon Stylites with an exquisite jewel-encrusted silver service.

Back in the carriage, Praskovia and Nicholas were overcome by a confused jumble of emotions—joy, relief, and anxiety over the future. The others, seated next to them, must have had similar if less intense feelings as they rode back to the Corner House through the black Moscow night.

TWENTY-FOUR

Newlyweds

Nicholas awoke the next morning filled with joy, which took the form of a shower of gifts for Praskovia and others in the household. He wrote his Home Office to add fifteen hundred rubles to "Praskovia Ivanovna Kovalevskaia's" yearly salary, a bit impersonal, but then this was typically Nicholas's way of showing affection, and he raised the pay of his entire household staff. He also ordered a nice new house built for Praskovia's father at Ostankino. At the same time he directed nearly four thousand rubles for prayers at churches and monasteries across Russia in memory of his parents, grandparents, and great-grandparents. Nicholas had never done anything like this before. His motives seemed to have been contradictory—at once thanking the Lord for finally bringing him and Praskovia to this point of happiness and praying for his forefathers' forgiveness at having married a former serf.[1]

"Your Excellency, Count Nicholas Petrovich, My dear Sir!" wrote Father Platon two days after the wedding, "I congratulate Your Excellency on the successful completion of your intentions and wishes. Live in love and virtue under God's blessing. I shall pray to God with you that He may bless you with offspring and so continue the honor and glory of your distinguished family. With this zeal do I pay my respects to your love and that of your blessed family. I remain with true respect, etc., etc., Platon, Metropolitan of Moscow." With his letter Platon included a document testifying to their marriage, which Nicholas placed among his most guarded personal papers. Several days later Platon sent a marriage certificate with his signature and best wishes to "Countess Praskovia Ivanovna."[2]

Who else knew Praskovia had become "the countess"? Of course the attending clergy and witnesses. Prince Shcherbatov was incapable of keeping anything from his wife, and we don't know how good she was at keeping a secret. The coachman and postilions must have had an idea of what that night's mysterious trip had been about and probably talked about it to others in the household. The women living with Praskovia, who may have helped her dress for the ceremony, certainly knew. The men in his office soon knew something had happened when they received the instruction to no longer call her Parasha or Praskovia Kovalyova, but "Praskovia Ivanovna Kovalevskaia" in all communications.[3] And Dmitry Malimonov knew since he had worked with Merkulov on creating the false genealogy. It is impossible to say how far the secret spread beyond this small group. Rumors, however, of some sort of change in Count Sheremetev's relations with his serf Praskovia certainly made their way around society.

Although Nicholas was expected at court, he claimed to be too busy to leave Moscow. This was probably just an excuse to spend some time alone with Praskovia. It was late December when they set out from Moscow, again taking the long route via Rostov. They stopped to pray and give offerings to St. Dmitry's remains, and Nicholas told the priests of his plan to build a new church at the Yakovlevsky Monastery there. By 8 January 1802, Nicholas and Praskovia had arrived in St. Petersburg. The Fountain House was stale after their months-long absence, so Nicholas had some fragrant water of roses and orange blossoms made to freshen up Praskovia's rooms.[4] On the thirteenth, Nicholas made his first appearance at court.

The next morning Nicholas awoke with a runny nose and cough. He had come down with a cold. He reported sick and called the doctors. A Spanish fly was placed below his left shoulder, but this only made matters worse; when it was removed a large carbuncle formed, and the first signs of gangrene were evident. Nicholas was forced to bed, where he stayed throughout much of January and February. Finally, on 27 February, James Wylie, Alexander I's personal surgeon, cut out the carbuncle and had a lint applied over the wound. But the operation wasn't entirely successful, and he had to operate several more times, after which Nicholas succumbed to two bouts of intense fever. For weeks he was too feeble to get out of bed and missed the Easter celebrations. It was April before Nicholas revived. By then he was out of bed and able to walk slowly about his room with the help of a cane. Recalling the pain and suffering, Nicholas wrote to Prince Peter Urusov that he had been "on the edge of the grave and had been ready to plunge into eternity." There were rumors in Moscow that he had died, which piqued the greedy interest of members of his extended family.[5]

Nicholas rewarded Wylie with an expensive gold snuffbox; the medic who bandaged the wound received fifteen hundred rubles. All was not well, however. An itchy red rash that Nicholas couldn't keep from scratching broke out on the entire left side of his face. His skin became red and swollen, disfiguring him and making him loathe to show himself in public. Nicholas didn't leave his bedroom until the end of April. "The doctors," he complained to a friend, "have been tormenting me with their medicines."[6]

Troubles with his family exacerbated his illness. Upon returning to the capital he had been visited by his nephews' numerous creditors demanding money. Nicholas paid them twenty thousand rubles, but this was not enough. They threatened to go to the city commandant unless they were made whole. An angry Nicholas wrote to his sister insisting she send another twenty thousand rubles or else the entire family, himself included, would be threatened by state action, an "unpleasantness" he had no wish to be exposed to. It didn't help that although Kirill had shown enough concern to visit the Fountain House and enquire after his uncle's health, Peter, Nicholas informed his sister, not once bothered to come see him.[7] Peter did, however, have time to write his uncle that same day and beg for five hundred rubles, adding that he was on the verge of being evicted from his house and thrown out into the street. To make matters worse Varvara informed Nicholas that her daughters, Catherine and Varvara Alexeevna, had racked up debts as well and needed money for their dowries since they both planned to wed soon. And if this wasn't enough, Catherine and Varvara now turned to Nicholas to buy them jewelry "since it is not proper to appear at court without diamonds."[8] At first Nicholas ignored his nieces and then wrote back to say he was through trying to help the lot of them. So fed up was Nicholas with his family that he changed his will, replacing Kirill and Peter as his heirs in favor of his cousin Vasily Sergeevich, a change none of them was ever aware of.

Next, he turned to Praskovia's fate. Convinced he had cheated death that spring but certain he would precede Praskovia to the grave, Nicholas wrote a testament outlining what was to be done when he died. "My dear wife, Countess Praskovia Ivanovna, Heeding the word of God commanding us to always be ready for death, I have prepared an instruction that I considered necessary upon the inevitable event of my death, including what is to be done with my body wherever I may happen to die, and present it to you, my dear friend, with whom I am attached by the Holy bonds of matrimony and share my life and my time."[9]

Nicholas gave Praskovia directions on exactly where to find two copies of his will that he kept in two sealed envelopes under lock and key in a small box. Upon his death Praskovia was to open the box and remove the wills along with letters addressed to a few of his closest friends. Nicholas had already asked these friends to look after Praskovia upon his death and see to it she was not harmed or denied her rights as his widow. She was to hand these letters to her most trusted servant and have them delivered immediately, "without wasting a minute." These letters instructed Nicholas's friends to go to Praskovia as soon as they get word and to remain by her. One will was for Praskovia to keep, the other for the Board of Guardians of the Imperial Foundling Hospital, one of whose directors was Nicholas's friend Prince Golitsyn, the same who had introduced him to Boris Merkulov. Praskovia was to send this copy of the will only with someone she, and his friends, felt could be trusted. All of this is to be done "in the first hour" of Nicholas's dying in order to safeguard Praskovia and his property.[10]

The reason for these precautions is understandable. Only a few knew that he and Praskovia had married, and few would believe her if she had stated that the late count had been her husband. Indeed, only a handful of people even knew that she was no longer a serf. Unless he took steps to protect Praskovia, she would be at the mercy of his sister, who had long resented Praskovia's place in the household, of his nephews, and of others in the family, none of whom wished her well. He didn't dare think what they might do to her. In time he would make their marriage public, but for now the main thing was to assure her safety.

These wills were destroyed the following year after Dmitry's birth, so we don't know what they contained. It seems likely that a good deal, most perhaps, of the estate was to go to Praskovia, the rest to his family and to charity. The outcry would have been loud, and Nicholas knew he had to have every detail prepared if the will was to be carried out. Powerful forces would have lined up to stop it.

In this same letter Nicholas instructed Praskovia to bury him "in the simplest coffin, painted black with a white cross on the top, and in the simplest clothes you can find in my wardrobe." She was to place in his hands his beloved icon of Christ the Savior depicted along with St. Dmitry of Rostov. Should he die in the capital, he asked to be buried alongside his sister Anna at the Alexander Nevsky Monastery; in Moscow, between his parents at the Novospassky Monastery. The funeral should be "simple . . . and without any vain magnificence." In the box with the wills he placed one hundred thousand rubles: three thousand to pay for the funeral, the rest to be given out to the sick, poor, and imprisoned.[11]

In early May 1802, Praskovia became pregnant. An elated Nicholas began showering her with gifts. He bought her comfortable spencers for lounging about the house, large bouquets of fresh-cut flowers for her rooms, two parrots, and even a pet monkey. He made further repairs to the pavilion in the garden in preparation for winter so that Praskovia could enjoy its peace and quiet during her later months of pregnancy. He had new rosebushes, raspberries, fragrant cherry trees, and two large poplars planted in the garden and ordered that all the gates and doors into the garden be kept locked and extra watchmen posted to protect their privacy.[12]

What Nicholas most loved to give her were jewels. He had been buying jewelry for Praskovia for years, but after their wedding he fairly buried her in a mountain of precious metals and gems. An inventory of Praskovia's jewelry from February 1802 runs sixty-five folios, detailing 270 items — she had chains, strings of diamonds, dozens of earrings, bracelets, rings, crosses, medallions, cuffs, pins, watches, diadems, coronals, clips, buckles, garlands, keys, etuis, and snuffboxes, all of gold or silver or ivory and all heavily encrusted with rare stones. Nicholas gave her several large pearls, including one weighing 331 carats worth eight thousand rubles.

Many of the pieces were personalized gifts from Nicholas. There was an octagonal gold ring with his cipher in diamond rosettes under blue glass; an initialed diamond bracelet totaling over 48 carats; a round gold and diamond snuffbox with a braided locket of Nicholas's hair; a portrait miniature of Nicholas with a locket of his hair on a long chain that Praskovia wears in her famous posthumous portrait with the red shawl. Notations in the inventory tell the fate of several of the objects. Some Praskovia gave away during her lifetime. Two coronals of silver with diamonds and colored gemstones she gave to the daughter of Count Alexei Sergeevich Sheremetev. The gift is revealing: Alexei was one of the most vocal of the claimants, and the gift suggests Praskovia was trying to reach out to him with a lavish olive branch. After her death Nicholas gave quite a few of the pieces to Tatiana and other women close to her. Some he saved for Dmitry, some for himself. Others were sold at auction to help pay off Nicholas's enormous debts.[13]

In 1802, Nicholas also rescinded his earlier order regarding Praskovia's salary; in fact he had it returned to him to be physically destroyed. From now on she would not be paid a salary but would be advanced large sums of money regularly from Nicholas's monthly installments. Ten women were assigned to Praskovia as her chambermaids, all of them from the troupe. Stepanida Muskosina, a former singer, was put in charge of the maids and of Praskovia's cook, Afrosinia.

There were changes in the lives of Praskovia's family. They had by now been given their freedom, and Nicholas set each of them up with schooling, a job, or social rank. Praskovia's brother Ivan Ivanovich was removed from a Petersburg pension where he had been living and sent to study at the Academy of the Fine Arts. Nicholas had Praskovia's father and brother Afanasy registered in the third merchant guild in Moscow and provided them with capital in excess of two thousand rubles, although they were not expected to do any work. Afanasy got his own home at Kuskovo, repaired and fixed up especially for him, and the overseer made sure he was supplied with plenty of meat, fish, salt, butter, and flour. Afanasy married Ivan Yakimov's half-sister Anna, thus creating for himself another bond with Nicholas, to the latter's displeasure. Michael, whose career as a tailor never worked out, was placed under Nicholas's "personal protection" and moved closer to Alexei Agapov with instructions to keep "an eye on him" at all times.[14] Praskovia's brother Nicholas had served as a clerk at Moscow University's typography office until retiring at the end of 1801 upon his emancipation. Nicholas then wrote to inquire about a position for him in "religious matters" under Count Dmitry Khvostov, noting that a salary wasn't a requirement, just a title of some sort.[15]

Nicholas and Praskovia returned to the previously abandoned project for a hospital at Sukharev Tower. Throughout the spring and summer they eagerly followed its progress, now under the supervision of Malinovsky, and Nicholas bemoaned not being able to devote more of himself to it since he was forever forced to waste time on "empty vanities."[16]

At the beginning of June 1802, Nicholas and Praskovia left the Fountain House for Pavlovsk. The weather was awful, cold and rainy, and Nicholas and Praskovia were both out of sorts and suffering from ailments. Nicholas had recurring "feverish paroxysms," and Praskovia's teeth hurt; Malinovsky promised to send her some medicine from Moscow.[17] Nicholas frequented the court of Dowager Empress Maria Fyodorovna, appearing only occasionally at the large court. On 25 July, he received Maria Fyodorovna and the grand duchesses at the dacha, treating them to dinner and a tour of his garden. Praskovia, now three months pregnant, had not yet begun to show. Days later they followed the court to Peterhof, then to Gatchina. Praskovia's teeth were still bothering her. On 11 September, Nicholas wrote to Malinovsky, "Praskovia Ivanovna earnestly requests you to send her three bottles of teeth rinse. That same kind you sent earlier. The approaching winter is requiring us to stock up on medicines."[18] At the end of October they returned to the capital.

The final weeks of 1802 Praskovia spent in expectation of giving birth. Now eight months pregnant, Praskovia was tired, uncomfortable, and ready to be relieved of the baby she was carrying. Still, she had been fortunate. Her health was good, and the fears of the doctors, who had apparently cautioned Nicholas of the threat childbirth posed to Praskovia's fragile condition, had proven unfounded, or so it appeared. She was happy to be back at the Fountain House and done moving about from place to place. She was settling in, waiting.

As before, she passed much of the time in prayer in the palace chapel. Its walls were covered with icons—some fifty-two in all—that she had collected over her life. As she prayed, the faces of the holy gazed down upon her—images of Christ the Pancrator, the Kazan and Tikhvin

Mother of God, Apostles Peter and Paul, Nicholas the Miracle Worker, and St. Paraskeva, her saint-name.[19] But the image that attracted her most was one of St. Dmitry of Rostov in a silver overlay. To this icon she prayed for the health and safety of her child. The murmur of her prayers echoed softly. The candles flickered and smoked in the cold air.

TWENTY-FIVE

Dmitry's Birth

Throughout the first week of January 1803, Nicholas suffered from recurring night fevers that made it impossible for him to sleep and left him exhausted and irritable. His throat was sore from a dry, hacking cough. On the eighth, his physicians prescribed port and bled him with leeches. None of this helped, and in the middle of the month he was forced to cancel meetings with both Dowager Empress Maria Fyodorovna and State Secretary Dmitry Troshchinsky.

Yet Nicholas managed to find the strength for more pleasant, personal matters. Although the theater had been closed for years, Nicholas continued to follow the goings-on in the world of opera, and on 3 January he wrote Monsieur Hyvart in Paris to have him send the score to an opera he had been hearing so much about—Wolfgang Amadeus Mozart's *The Magic Flute*. Nicholas also enclosed two thousand rubles in his letter and asked Hyvart in a postscript to pick out for him "the most beautiful jewelry of the latest design."[1]

Jewelry was on Nicholas's mind that day. After finishing his letter to Hyvart he began rummaging about in his bureaus, wardrobes, and cases in search of his best stones. From the star awarded him as a knight of the Order of St. Alexander Nevsky he pried off the largest diamond; from his dress shoes he removed the octagonal diamond-encrusted buckles; from his sumptuous caftan he snipped all the bejeweled buttons. To these he added a diamond clasp, two diamond rings, and a signet consisting of more than twenty diamonds and one massive emerald. Once he had finished he had a pile of jewels worth nearly eighty thousand rubles.

He packed all these up and sent them that day to Louis David Duval, the Swiss-born court jeweler whose creations were wildly popular in St. Petersburg, with instructions for five new pieces, namely, a pair of 40-carat diamond earrings; one diamond *bando* (to be worn on either the head or neck) comprising 2,490 stones and over 204 carats; one diamond fringe of 746 stones; a diamond and opal chain; and one diamond medallion. Nicholas intended these extravagant pieces as gifts for Praskovia in connection with the birth of their child. He didn't forget to include in his order a little something for himself too — a black tortoiseshell snuffbox with a portrait of Praskovia ringed by diamonds on its lid.[2]

Nicholas and Praskovia were no doubt anxious as she entered the final weeks of her pregnancy. They had to have been heartened by the relative ease with which she had passed the previous months and encouraged by her overall good health. Nevertheless, Nicholas and Praskovia knew they could not be certain she was out of danger until after the birth. Feeling the need to have someone they could trust with them, Nicholas wrote Vasily Sheremetev in December asking him to come stay. Vasily, then hundreds of miles away on his estate of Bogorodskoe southwest of Nizhni Novgorod, said goodbye to his wife and young children and came at once.[3]

Dealings with Boris Merkulov added to Nicholas's anxiety. Merkulov had botched his first trip to White Russia in 1801 and came back with nothing, which had caused Nicholas to question his ability to get the job done. Yet far from giving up, Nicholas had reinvigorated his efforts to obtain a noble patent for Praskovia and was now deeply immersed in discussions with Malinovsky on how best to complete the enterprise successfully.

On 3 January, the same day Nicholas had been selecting diamonds for Praskovia, Nikita Svorchaev, the head of Nicholas's personal office in St. Petersburg, sent a letter to his Moscow counterpart, Michael Smirnov, conveying Nicholas's latest thoughts on the matter. Svorchaev wrote that Nicholas was largely in agreement with Merkulov's recent letter in which he repeated the necessity of handling the matter himself and his request for thirty-five hundred rubles for bribes (one hundred per Polish noble signature) and travel expenses. This time Merkulov would avoid White

Russia, where his failure was known, and head to Poland instead. But before saying anything to Merkulov, Nicholas wanted Smirnov to first meet with Alexei Malinovsky, Nicholas's confidant in Moscow and the one in charge there on this important business, to see whether Merkulov was the best man to send to Poland.

Enclosed with the letter was a packet for Malinovsky from Nicholas. He was returning all the documents that had been drawn up in Praskovia's name in 1801 and repeated his request of late 1802 to have Merkulov draft new ones in the name of her brother Nicholas. The reason for the change was simple: by requesting the noble patent in her brother's name Nicholas hoped to hide better his connection to the affair. It was imperative that his name not be linked to this petition in any way, given the possibility of scandal and blackmail. He asked Merkulov to send his drafts back to St. Petersburg, where clean copies would be made. He also sent along the thirty-five hundred rubles Merkulov had requested and pleaded with Smirnov to press Malinovsky and Merkulov to finish the entire business as quickly as possible.[4]

Back in Moscow, Malinovsky had been busy trying to make sense of the information on Yakov Kovalevsky, the seventeenth-century Polish prisoner of war, found in the state archive and of details on Praskovia's family history supplied to him by Nicholas's secretaries. There were inconsistencies and gaps that he was having trouble reconciling. Moreover, he had found obvious mistakes in the counterfeit genealogy Merkulov had recently completed that the Russian Heraldry Department would be sure to spot.

Merkulov, too, was then going over the Kovalyovs' story about their Polish ancestors and had found problems in it that would need to be answered before he went to Poland. On 5 January, he sent a series of questions to St. Petersburg via Michael Smirnov. Based on what documents, he asked, can they claim their family once owned an estate in Poland? What documents can they cite that prove any connection between Yakov Kovalevsky and their more recent ancestors? Do any documents exist showing that this same Kovalevsky actually stayed in Russia and entered service here? Merkulov stressed that these questions would have to be answered before he could successfully carry out his commission. Bribes alone might not be sufficient. He finished by noting that the best thing would be for him to come to St. Petersburg and meet personally with

Nicholas and his secretaries to discuss these matters, something Nicholas had no intention of permitting.[5]

Upon receiving Svorchaev's letter of 3 January, Smirnov gathered up all the documents and went to see Malinovsky. The two discussed matters at length before deciding on the best course of action. Smirnov then rode to Merkulov's and told him to report the following day to Malinovsky. Merkulov duly arrived at Malinovsky's on 8 January, and the two men spent much of the day going over the fragmentary archival information, trying to weave it together into a story convincing enough to satisfy the Heraldry Office and any hesitant Polish official with whom bribes proved ineffective.

Late that afternoon, after Merkulov had left, Malinovsky wrote Smirnov, instructing him to send a letter to Svorchaev in Petersburg with the results of his investigations and his decisions on how to proceed. First, Malinovsky observed that while there were errors in the genealogy, these could be fixed to jibe with documents in the state archives. Second, despite Nicholas's misgivings, Merkulov was the only man for this "most delicate" assignment—no one knew the particulars of the case as thoroughly as he did, and it would be wise to limit knowledge of it to only one man. Merkulov would have to be sent to Poland. Third, it would be good not to promise to pay Merkulov too much or too little, for both could produce undesirable consequences. He advised waiting to see how reliable Merkulov proved to be in the coming weeks before agreeing on a fee. Finally, Malinovsky enclosed for Smirnov Merkulov's draft of the petition and warrant in the name of Nicholas Kovalyov.[6]

Smirnov immediately forwarded all this to Svorchaev in St. Petersburg. His letter arrived there on the thirteenth of January, and that same day Svorchaev informed Nicholas of the latest news from Malinovsky. He noted that he would have clean copies of both documents written out as soon as possible. He could make the copy of the warrant himself but was loathe to copy the petition since law required the name of the copyist be affixed to it, and this he wouldn't do "so that the name of Your Excellency appears nowhere on these papers." To keep the count's name out of the business, Svorchaev promised to have Michael Alekseev, an anonymous young scribe in Nicholas's office, come to him the next day and "force" him to make a clean copy.

The following day Svorchaev informed Nicholas that both documents had been copied as planned and, after some trickery on his part, signed by Praskovia's brother Nicholas. It was important that Nicholas Kovalyov not know that a petition for noble status was being prepared in his name. Although he wanted to ennoble Praskovia, Nicholas was wary about letting her brothers and father in on what he was doing, fearful that they might feel emboldened and begin making demands. And so Svorchaev had sent for Praskovia's brother Nicholas and without giving him a chance to inspect the documents instructed him to sign them, saying they were required as part of Nicholas's petition for obtaining a higher rank. Having no reason to doubt him, Nicholas Kovalyov promptly signed and then handed them back to Svorchaev, who was quite pleased with himself. On 15 January, Svorchaev sent the documents back to Smirnov in Moscow with instructions to deliver them as soon as possible to Malinovsky.[7]

During this flurry of activity, Nicholas decided to give Merkulov a permanent position on his staff with an extremely generous salary of three thousand rubles a year—less because of his abilities, which remained unproven, and more out of a fear that he might talk. To his agent negotiating the contract in Moscow, Nicholas wrote, "Do not upset Merkulov, but treat him with kid gloves."[8]

But before the documentation had been completed and Merkulov could set off for Poland, events at the Fountain House took a dramatic turn that forestalled further action.

The skies over St. Petersburg were clear on the morning of 3 February 1803. It was already well into the day before the anemic winter sun dragged itself high enough above the horizon to begin to dispel the night's darkness from Praskovia's rooms. Praskovia began experiencing contractions sometime early that morning. These became increasingly stronger, more intense, and frequent, and before long it was clear that she was going into labor. The delivery went smoothly and without complications, and a baby boy was born shortly before noon. They named him Dmitry after St. Dmitry of Rostov, who, Nicholas later said, "had showered them with his blessings on many occasions."[9] The infant was cleaned and then swaddled in blankets that Praskovia had laid out in advance together with an icon of Christ healing the weak. Father Dmitry Terentiev from the local parish church had arrived by now and said a prayer for the mother and son. Shortly after his birth, Praskovia blessed Dmitry with a large cross she had often prayed over during her pregnancy. Both mother and father were overjoyed at their son's birth, and tears streamed down Nicholas's face.[10]

Dmitry was handed over to the care of a wet nurse and two elderly women: the wife of Nicholas Bem and Avdotia Cherkassova, the widow of one of Nicholas's valets. Dmitry had been taken from Praskovia not simply because wealthy noblewomen at the time relied on wet nurses and a staff of baby maids to tend to their children. More important in this instance was Praskovia's illness. It was the common belief that consumption could easily be transmitted by mothers to their infants, and so for Dmitry's safety he was quickly removed from Praskovia's room.

Although she understood these precautions, his not being next to her seems to have caused Praskovia to worry. Part of this was a mother's natural concern for her child's well-being. But there were other causes for concern. Praskovia feared for Dmitry's safety. She wondered what the reaction would be to word of his birth and whether he might be in danger. Neither Nicholas nor her maids could reassure Praskovia that Dmitry was safe and well. Only the sound of his crying from the next room or the sight of him in the arms of his wet nurse by her door could ease her worry.[11]

Overwhelmed with emotion and busy seeing to Praskovia and little Dmitry, Nicholas did not find time to write to his friends of the news for two days. On 5 February, he sent three letters to Moscow—one to Malinovsky, another to Malinovsky's father and Nicholas's confessor, Priest Fyodor, and a third to Metropolitan Platon—informing them of his great "joy" and asking them to remember the family in their prayers. He also asked all three of them to keep the news a secret since owing to his illness he had not yet been well enough to tell the tsar, adding "though no doubt many here know about this already." Nicholas sealed all three letters and sent them to Agapov in Moscow with instructions to delivery them post-haste.

Nicholas then sent two similar letters to Rostov—one to Archimandrite Melkhisedek at the Yakovlevsky Monastery and another to Father Amfilokhy, in whose letter he enclosed an offering of ten thousand rubles to decorate his cathedral and to adorn the shrine of St. Dmitry. Nicholas asked them as well to keep the news of Dmitry's birth a secret.[12]

Dmitry's Birth

Dmitry was christened on 5 February by Father Dmitry in the palace chapel. A throng of friends, family, clergymen, house serfs, and other domestics packed the chapel, spilling over into the hallway. Holding Dmitry were his godparents, Admiral Count Grigory Kushelyov and Princess Antonina Shcherbatova. Kushelyov, the descendant of a poor yet ancient noble family, had served as an adjutant-general at the court of Tsar Paul, where he and Nicholas had become close. Shcherbatova, once one of Petersburg's great beauties, was the wife of Prince Andrei Shcherbatov, also there that day. Standing alongside them were Yakov Remetev, Paul Malinovsky (Alexei's younger brother), Dr. Lakhman, Nicholas Bem, and Dmitry Malimonov.

Following the ceremony Father Dmitry, the godparents, and a few friends went to congratulate Praskovia. She was still recovering from the ordeal of childbirth, so they stayed only briefly. As they left the palace, they could see clouds forming overhead.

TWENTY-SIX

Secrets Revealed

Praskovia, however, didn't regain her strength, and what everyone assumed to be the usual consequences of childbirth quickly proved to be something much more serious.

Not long after the baptism, Nicholas sent a footman to summon Dr. Rogerson. Rogerson read Nicholas's letter but did not reply. Nicholas sent the footman back a second time and then a third. Only then did Rogerson bother to respond, though simply to inform Nicholas that he could not see Praskovia. Could not or would not. Nicholas wasn't sure how to interpret Rogerson's reply.

Growing increasingly worried, Nicholas next sent for Drs. Wylie, Lakhman, and Robert Simpson, a Scotsman and former surgeon in the Russian navy. The doctors prescribed the usual treatments: bloodlettings, leeches, Spanish flies, purgatives, and baths in warm mare's milk. They tried them all, but nothing worked, and Praskovia grew weaker. Night sweats disturbed her sleep; in the morning she would awake feeling drained and cold in her damp bedclothes. She couldn't stop coughing, breathing was painful. At times Praskovia felt as if she were suffocating. Her skin had been drained of all color and turned a dull gray. She found it impossible to eat, and the lack of food made her ever more listless. Her dark eyes had sunk deep into their sockets. The flesh appeared to have fallen away from her bones, which now showed prominently under her skin.

Nicholas searched the doctors' faces for any sign of hope but found none. The ghost of Praskovia's dead sister Matryona seemed to be stalking them.

With the physicians' best efforts failing, Nicholas and Praskovia began to contemplate the worst. At nine o'clock on the morning of the seventh, Praskovia confessed to Father Paul Yefimov, Nicholas's home priest, and received the Sacrament.[1] Five days later they decided to seek the intercession of one of Petersburg's holiest relics. Throughout her life Praskovia had made generous sacrifices to various churches and monasteries. She now prepared to make her final and most lavish offering. On the twelfth she asked to see her collection of jewelry and selected from it a diamond and sapphire necklace Nicholas had recently given her. Praskovia handed the necklace to Nicholas and told him of her wishes.[2]

Nicholas left Praskovia and took the necklace to his stewards Peter Petrov and Paul Argunov. As soon as they had safely wrapped the necklace, the two men left the Fountain House and hurried down Liteiny Prospect to the Church of the Holy Mother of All-Lamenting Joys just off the Neva River near the Tauride Palace. The church took its name from its most famous icon. Brought to Petersburg in 1711 by Peter the Great's sister, Natalia, the icon was believed to have special healing powers. Pilgrims flocked to it from across Russia to be cured. Too ill to leave her bed, Praskovia sent an offering instead along with a plea that the church priests pray to the icon for her recovery.[3]

As the priests prayed, Praskovia told Nicholas of her final wishes. First, that he take care of her family, especially her father. Next, she told him of her wish to establish a charity to help poor and orphaned girls and to see that the hospital at Sukharev Tower be finished. She asked Nicholas to free the rest of her family and friends, including her nephew Nicholas Kalmykov, Tatiana, Tatiana's entire family, and the women living with her at the Fountain House. Last, she asked him to look after three old widows, possibly mothers of some of the performers, in her home village of Voshchazhnikovo.[4]

Nicholas and Praskovia also discussed Dmitry. Nicholas had planned to make their marriage public and to recognize their son as his sole heir, but he had hoped to have more time before making any announcement. Yet he knew that if he didn't act soon, the news would quickly spread on its own. By now the domestics in the Fountain House already knew, as did several of their friends and members of the clergy. Before long word would get around the city. If he were to tell the world of their secret, he had to do it soon. The business with Merkulov was also eating at him. Malinovsky had been writing Nicholas with updates. "I shall say in reply," wrote Nicholas on 19 February, "that the caution that you are taking is very good, and I, knowing how important it is in this instance to do everything possible to avoid the misuse of these documents, humbly request that you continue to keep a close watch on this matter." Then he added, "I am in great despair; my sick one is in quite a bad way."[5]

The pressure began to affect his health. Around the middle of the month Nicholas took to bed complaining of tightness in his chest. The physicians began shuttling back and forth between Praskovia's and Nicholas's rooms. Vasily Sheremetev was also hurrying back and forth between the two of them, sitting at their bedsides and doing his best to keep up their spirits. They had another visitor as well. Giacomo Quarenghi, the Italian architect who had worked on the designs for Ostankino, came regularly to the Fountain House. He would check on Nicholas first and then install himself in a chair outside Praskovia's anteroom, asking the doctors coming and going how she was faring.

Shortly after midnight on Saturday the twenty-first, Praskovia received the sacrament of the anointing of the sick. After blessing the oil, Father Yefimov anointed Praskovia's forehead and cheeks and chin as well as her nostrils, hands, and breast as he prayed: "Holy Father, physician of souls and of bodies, Who didst send Thy Only-Begotten Son as the healer of every disease and our deliverer from death, heal also Thy servant Praskovia from the bodily infirmity that holds her, and make her live through the grace of Christ, by the intercessions of St. Dmitry and of all the saints." Nicholas and the others in attendance were moved by the inner peace that came over her during the sacrament. At five o'clock that morning, Praskovia asked for a cross. Cradling it in her weak hands, she prayed over it for a time. Later that afternoon, Praskovia turned to Father Yefimov and asked him to perform the Acathistus, an ancient hymn or office in honor of the Mother of God. When he had finished she requested a prayer for the dead. As the priest spoke Praskovia softly repeated his words. Throughout these days Praskovia prayed to St. Nicholas the Miracle Worker—"You are my helper, you lead me thither, I place all my hope in you. O Lord! I place my spirit in your hands."[6]

At one point Praskovia motioned toward Nicholas and asked those gathered around her bed to look after him when she was gone. "He's a Christian," she whispered, "he knows God." She told them to pray for Nicholas and not to pity her. Next, Praskovia asked them to bring her the icon of the Kazan Mother of God that Nicholas kept in his room. But as one of the girls was about to fetch it, she appeared to change her mind and to ask for a different icon. Praskovia was becoming incoherent, and no one could tell which icon she was referring to. After several minutes of pained confusion, Nicholas ordered the girl to retrieve the Kazan icon from his room. She hurried out and returned a few minutes later, placing the icon in Praskovia's hands. Praskovia had now begun to slip in and out of consciousness; still, she managed to ask them to place the icon in her coffin after her death.[7]

There was no doubt now that the end was approaching. Nicholas left Praskovia and returned to his room. He finally realized that he could wait no longer and sat down to write a letter to the tsar. It didn't come easily. He kept crossing out what he had written as he searched for the right words. After a few drafts, Nicholas was satisfied.

Your Most Gracious Majesty!

My pitiful and most wretched condition has not yet deprived me of the hope of still having the pleasure of informing Your Imperial Majesty myself that I have taken up the bonds of holy matrimony and that this February 3rd God blessed me with a son and heir, Count Dmitry. Nevertheless, the desperate condition of my wife, Countess Praskovia Ivanovna, whose cruel illness has pushed her to the edge of the grave, compels me not to delay for a minute to inform Your Imperial Majesty that I did indeed wed on 6 November 1801 in Moscow at the Church of St. Simon Stylites on Povarskaia Street, in complete accordance with all the sacred rites, of which I possess indisputable written proof.

My wife, Countess Praskovia Ivanovna, received the finest possible upbringing in my father's home, and through my gentle care for her did with time develop into a woman who, judging by her most decorous sentiments, became fully worthy of her current station. She is of irrefutable noble origin, and her forefather was a native Polish nobleman by the name of Kovalevsky. My late aunt, who took a special interest in her education, never had any doubt that she belonged to the nobility.

Having full knowledge of Your Imperial Majesty's sublime enlightenment and love for all humanity, I give no consideration to the thought that I might incur Your Majesty's disfavor for having breached established court protocol by having failed to inform you prior to my wedding. And so, prostrating myself at the feet of Your Imperial Majesty, I dare to request, in the midst of my sorrow, one single act of charity, namely that you make me happy and comfort me, even if it be only by writing me one Sacred Word, that this does not contradict your will and may be deemed worthy of favorable acceptance.

Most Gracious Sovereign!

Your Imperial Majesty's most loyal subject,

Count Sheremetev[8]

He slipped the letter in an envelope addressed to State Secretary Dmitry Troshchinsky, affixing a brief note—"My dear Sir, Dmitry Prokofievich, Having written a letter of special importance to the Emperor, I humbly request you deliver it to His Imperial Majesty."[9]

Next, he wrote a similar letter to Empress Elizabeth. He asked her to extend to his infant son the benevolence she had shown him and to become Dmitry's patron and protector. He ended with a plea for Praskovia. "Deign, Madame, to honor my spouse, Countess Praskovia Ivanovna, with Your August benevolence, by permitting sentiments of your touching humanity, that I and all your subjects have admired for a long time, to freely flow. It is on this that all her hope is based, as said by one who, with the most perfect submission, remains, Madame, Your Imperial Majesty's most humble, most obedient servant and subject, Count Nicholas Sheremetev."[10]

Nicholas then wrote a final letter to Dowager Empress Maria Fyodorovna.

That Sunday, 22 February, was a typical day at the Winter Palace. In the morning, Alexander and his brother, Grand Duke Constantine, witnessed the mounting of the guards and then made a brief visit to their mother in her private apartments before joining Empress Elizabeth for services in the main chapel. By now the palace's ceremonial halls had filled with courtiers and their wives, officers, and prominent members of the nobility, as was common on Sundays. He greeted them upon leaving the chapel, and a few of them were presented to the tsar.

Among them was Vasily Sheremetev. It is tempting to speculate whether the subject of Nicholas and Praskovia came up during their brief conversation. The tsar may have been aware that Vasily was staying at the Fountain House, and it would have been awkward not to inquire about his host. Alexander had possibly heard rumor of Dmitry's birth and the drama unfolding at the Fountain House. Given that gossip was the currency of court life, it would be remarkable if by now, almost three weeks after Dmitry's birth, he hadn't. Unfortunately, no record of their conversation survives, and we can only guess at what passed between them.

After another visit to the dowager empress's apartments, Alexander, Elizabeth, Constantine, and various grand dukes and duchesses, accompanied by many courtiers, attended another service in the chapel. Lunch for eighteen was then served in Maria Fyodorovna's rooms. The rest of the day the tsar spent alone in his private apartments and dined that evening at the usual hour with the empress and Countess Stroganova.

Nicholas's letter probably reached Troshchinsky sometime that afternoon, and he presented it to the tsar the same day. Sensing the urgency of the situation and Nicholas's anguish, the tsar sent Troshchinsky back to the Fountain House to tell Nicholas in person that he had received his letter and given his blessing to the secret marriage and recognized the birth of Nicholas's son. Although the tsar graciously accepted what Nicholas had told him, it did not please him. Given Alexander's later cold treatment of Dmitry, it can be assumed that the emperor found the entire affair rather distasteful and wished to put it out of his mind. The empress did not even deign to acknowledge Nicholas's letter. Only Maria Fyodorovna had any sympathy for Nicholas and his family. In the coming years the dowager empress took an active role in Dmitry's upbringing, especially after his father's death.

After Troshchinsky left the Fountain House, Nicholas told Praskovia of the tsar's reaction. It must have come as a relief to know that after so many years of leading a secret life, she could die an honest death as Nicholas's wife and not his concubine and that their son had been recognized for who he was.

TWENTY-SEVEN

Death

Praskovia died shortly after two o'clock in the morning on 23 February 1803, having regained consciousness long enough to say one last
prayer and receive the sacred final rites. The cause of death may have been
sepsis. The strains of pregnancy and the bloody act of childbirth could
have allowed the bacterial pneumonia (if that was indeed the illness that
had afflicted her for so long) to cross over into her bloodstream, resulting in a dangerous drop in blood pressure, major organ failure, and then
death.[1] She was months shy of her thirty-fifth birthday. Praskovia's body
lay in bed for two hours as Nicholas, Tatiana, and her other friends wailed
beside it in grief. At one point Nicholas held over her body the cross used
to bless their son weeks earlier. Finally, Tatiana had to be helped from the
room so great was her despair and exhaustion.[2]

At four o'clock Praskovia was placed on a table in the center of the
room. Her maids removed her bedclothes, washed her body, and then
dressed it in clean, simple garments. Next, they draped her body with
fresh white sheets trimmed with a calico frill. Her wedding ring was
taken off and given to Nicholas; the large diamond ring on her small finger was placed in a special case for Dmitry. A few locks of her auburn hair
were cut for mementos. Two icons—one of Christ the Savior, the other
of the Great Martyr St. Varvara—were placed on a lectern covered in a
satin shroud at the head of the table. Around her body they lit candles

decorated with black crepe that flickered dimly, casting faint shadows about the room.

As soon as the body had been prepared, Father Yefimov performed the requiem, attended by Yakov Remetev, Dmitry Malimonov, Nicholas Bem, the stewards, and Nicholas's closest male and female servants. After the ceremony an honor guard of thirteen took its place around the body. The guard would remain there for the next three days, with only short breaks to eat and sleep. At ten a.m., Father Yefimov and the others assembled again in Praskovia's room to perform the requiem once more. By now the sun was up. It was a glorious morning—bright, clear, and cold, the thermometer straining to rise above zero degrees Fahrenheit. Yefimov repeated the requiem twice a day, every morning and every evening, until Praskovia's funeral on the twenty-sixth. In between the services clergymen from the local parish church, dressed in funeral albs, read the Psalter around the clock.[3]

In Moscow that day Metropolitan Platon, unaware of Praskovia's death, sent Dmitry a small wooden cross and a nightshirt.

On the twenty-fourth, Praskovia's body was placed inside an oak coffin lined with white satin and sheathed on the outside with swatches of crimson and silver velvet. Two white pillows cradled her head. Nicholas Argunov, a serf artist, was brought in to make sketches for a death portrait. After he had finished, the lid was closed, sealed, and covered with a thick gold brocade cloth. Finally, a large silver cross was placed on top.

That same day a letter arrived from Troshchinsky with the tsar's official reply to Nicholas's letter of the twenty-second. It was brief: "My dear Sir, Count Nicholas Petrovich . . . You were in your authority to marry whenever and whomever you wanted. The conditions pertaining to your marriage do not alter His Imperial Majesty's benevolence toward you, which you have always enjoyed." Oddly, Alexander did not mention Praskovia's death or Nicholas's wish to have Dmitry recognized as his heir.

Still, Nicholas was relieved to have Alexander's blessing in writing. But the tsar's terse reply left little doubt as to his feelings about the affair. And then there were these words that Troshchinsky affixed at the end: "All that remains is for me to add to this my own desire, namely that your newborn son grow up to be your comfort, that he may enjoy all the rights of his family, and that he has inherited all of its virtues. And may I also convey my sincere condolences on the untimely death of your spouse, whom your heart chose and your love placed above her station."[4] Troshchinsky, and apparently the tsar too, did not believe the story of Praskovia's noble ancestry. Nor would the rest of society once they heard it.

After reading Troshchinsky's letter, Nicholas dictated from bed a reply requesting that because of his poor health he be allowed to resign his court duties. The tsar granted his request.[5]

Later that day Nicholas sent letters to his offices in Petersburg and Moscow informing them of his marriage, of Dmitry's birth, Praskovia's death, and the tsar's blessing. Nicholas ordered his secretary to make several copies of the tsar's letter. He then placed the original in an envelope together with a copy of his letter to his offices and sealed it five times, making certain to cover every seam in heavy black wax with the Sheremetev crest. He handed this envelope to his secretary and instructed him to place it in the office's metal box that contained the most important documents pertaining to the history of the Sheremetev family. Copies of all these documents were also sent that day to the count's Moscow office, where they were stored under lock and key in a special iron trunk along with other significant family documents.[6]

Nicholas's final act that day was to honor Praskovia's wish to free several of his serfs. He had his secretary draft documents freeing Peter Kalmykov and his son Nicholas; Stepanida Mukosina; and Tatiana, her mother, Yelena, and her two brothers, Grigory and Gavril. He also instructed that they continue to receive their regular salaries and be permitted to live in his homes.[7]

The following day Nicholas issued a directive to his office establishing a set of strict procedures for ensuring Dmitry's safety.[8] Nicholas Bem was put in charge and given authority over everyone who came near Dmitry or his rooms. A servant named Peter Solovyov was chosen as his assistant and ordered to remain constantly at Dmitry's side and to follow no one's instructions but Bem's. Four guards were posted outside the door to Dmitry's room—two on duty, two off duty resting on cots next to the door. Bem and Solovyov were instructed to oversee the regular changing of the guards and to check at night that the guards had not fallen asleep. Peter Smagin, now a servant but once a performer who had sung alongside Praskovia at the Ostankino premier, was posted on the inside. The door was to remain locked from within at all times. Smagin was to open it only after the person outside had been questioned and slid under the door a note signed by Nicholas himself granting access to Dmitry's room. Each morning and evening Bem and Solovyov were to report to Nicholas on Dmitry's health and everything that had taken place in his room. Should Dmitry become ill or anything out of the ordinary happen, they were to notify Nicholas immediately. So that there could be no confusion, a copy of the order was sent to first steward Peter Petrov and also to the home office in Moscow.

At first glance Nicholas's precautions appear to be the product of a febrile mind. Having just lost Praskovia and in the throes of grief and illness, Nicholas seems to have imagined all sorts of dark threats directed against Dmitry. But this was not just baseless paranoia. Nicholas had reason to fear the reaction of some in his family. His nephews' money troubles had grown direr in the past months. Their father had cut them off for good, and they had stepped up their entreaties to Nicholas for money. Word of Dmitry's birth came as a terrible shock. The brothers were thrown into confusion over what this meant for their inheritance, not knowing that they had already been replaced as his heirs. Kirill wrote Nicholas pleading for a meeting with him at the Fountain House.[9] His nephews were not the only ones Nicholas worried about. The claimants, too, were outraged at the news. For over half a century they had been fighting for what they considered their rightful share of the Sheremetev fortune, and now it all stood to be inherited by the son of a serf.

Were members of his own family capable of killing Dmitry? The thought crossed Nicholas's mind. He knew it wouldn't be hard to do if they were. He had had trouble in the past with thieves and suspicious persons coming onto his property. Some had even managed to get inside the Fountain House and wander about for some time before being caught. Nicholas had tried to increase the security, but with so many servants it was nearly impossible to control access to the palace. A few well-placed bribes could easily buy accomplices on the inside among the army of domestics, some of whom nursed their own silent grudges against Nicholas for slights and affronts, both real and imagined.

Nicholas decided he wouldn't take any chances. He couldn't be certain how far the Razumovskys or others might go in their shock and anger. He had lost Praskovia; he was not going to lose Dmitry.

Death

The residents of St. Petersburg awoke on the morning of the twenty-sixth to snow. It had been falling heavily since the early hours and by midday lay thick in the streets. A gusty wind sculpted elegant mounds as teams of men with brooms and crude shovels struggled to clear entrance-ways and courtyards.

At one o'clock that afternoon a number of Nicholas's friends arrived at the Fountain House and were shown upstairs to Praskovia's room to pay their final respects. It wasn't a large group; most of society, including many whom Nicholas had considered friends, stayed away. Counts Peter and Paul Shuvalov were there, as were Count Alexander Samoilov (the late Prince Potemkin's nephew) and his wife. The decorated war hero and brother of Catherine the Great's influential advisor, Count Ilia Bezborodko, came with his wife too. The head of the Russian Orthodox Church, Chief Procurator Yakovlev, visited, along with Dr. Lakhman, Quarenghi, and Prince Andrei Shcherbatov and his family. After paying their respects, they visited briefly with Nicholas in his room. All of them, except for Quarenghi, who would take part in the funeral, departed around six o'clock that evening.

By then the snow had stopped falling and the wind died down. It was quiet, the sounds of the city muffled by the fresh snow. The lamps around the Fountain House had all been lit, and only faint traces of light could still be detected in the gray sky. Shortly before seven o'clock, three Orthodox priests in black arrived at the palace. Father Ambrose, the metropolitan of Novgorod and St. Petersburg, Father Paul, the archbishop of Yaroslavl and Rostov, and Father Varlaam, the archbishop of Georgia, had been invited by Nicholas to say final prayers for the soul of the deceased before her body was taken for burial. They climbed the front stairs to the palace chapel, where a deacon from the parish church was waiting for them. After a polite greeting, the deacon led the clergymen to Praskovia's room.

Once they had finished the short service, the coffin was carried from the room, down the staircase, and out into the courtyard. The pallbearers slid the coffin onto the waiting coach and replaced the brocaded gold cloth over it. On the box sat Praskovia's coachman, Natin, sheathed in a black cloak and flowing black hat, his face hidden behind a dark veil. Six stable hands similarly attired stood alongside six steeds caparisoned in black horse cloth. Their torches crackled and vainly beat back the encroaching darkness. Atop the runners stood six valets also in black. Another two dozen of Nicholas's men bearing torches flanked the coach. At the head of the cortege rode a mounted police officer, behind him dozens of officers followed on foot together with a collection of priests and high clergy. Praskovia's confessor bore aloft an icon of St. Sergius, and three separate choirs—Nicholas's, the archbishop of Yaroslavl's, and the metropolitan's—intoned Orthodox hymns. A small number of friends and servants, including Remetev, Malimonov, Quarenghi, Dr. Lakhman, and Praskovia's maids, followed the funeral coach. The procession comprised over two hundred persons.[10]

The cortege set out down Liteiny Prospect and then turned left onto Nevsky Prospect, the capital's main boulevard, for the long ride to the Alexander Nevsky Monastery at the street's terminus, where Praskovia was to be interred in the Sheremetev family crypt.

Crowds gathered along the route to watch the somber procession as it made its way through the city. It was the grandest funeral St. Petersburg had seen in years. This, combined with the fact that there had been no prior announcement of the funeral, no mention in the *St. Petersburg Gazette* about the death of anyone of importance, served to intensify the curiosity of the onlookers. One group was noticeably absent from the funeral. No one from noble society deigned to attend even though by now all had heard the news about Nicholas and Praskovia. Some were furious by what they had heard, some dismayed, and others saddened, yet whatever the reaction, all of them, save his closest friends, turned their backs on Nicholas, abandoning him in his despair. Nicholas was also not there. Sick and crushed by grief, he stayed home in bed, tended to by his cousin Vasily.

About an hour after leaving the Fountain House, the cortege arrived at the Alexander Nevsky Monastery. The coffin was unloaded from the funeral coach and carried along the narrow walk through the cemetery and up the steps of the Cathedral of the Holy Trinity, where it was placed upon a catafalque. Praskovia's confessor set the icon of St. Sergius on a small altar before the coffin. In the dim candlelight, a bearded monk in black read the Psalter, his voice echoing in the lofty expanse. Sixteen brothers stood watch like ghostly specters from the shadowy recesses of the cathedral. They were joined by steward Petrov and his wife, maître d'hôtel Terekhov, Nikita Svorchaev, and several footmen and female servants. All of them stayed with Praskovia through the night.

At eleven o'clock the next morning, Father Ambrose together with Archbishops Paul and Varlaam and the other priests from the monastery performed the final liturgy. The coffin was then carried to the adjacent cemetery for interment in the Church of St. Lazarus. A light snow was falling, and the pallbearers had to step cautiously on the slick stones underfoot. Praskovia was laid to rest at the feet of Nicholas's grandfather, the Field Marshal, and surrounded by members of the Romanov royal family and assorted Russian grandees. At the base of her marble grave the Sheremetev coat of arms was affixed and atop it a bronze plaque that read,

> Here lies the body of Countess Praskovia Ivanovna Sheremeteva, a descendant of the Polish noble family Kovalevsky. She was born 20 July 1768, married 6 November 1801 in Moscow, and died shortly after two o'clock on the morning of 23 February 1803 in Petersburg.

> This plain marble, unfeeling and impermanent,
> Hides the priceless remains of a wife and mother.
> Her soul was a temple of virtue
> In which peace, piety, and faith resided,
> Where pure love and friendship dwelled.
> Even in her final hour she remained devoted,
> Feeling the full grief of those she was leaving behind.
> What is to become of her wretched spouse,
> Fated to drag out the rest of his days without his friend?
> His heart lives on nothing but barren sighs, wailing, sorrow,
>   and heavy moans.
> Yet her death was the path to immortality,
> Her innocent spirit is now in God's embrace,
> Robed in the radiant cloak of imperishability
> And forever surrounded by the faces of angels.
> Fill this dwelling place with righteous blessings,
> O God, and lay her pure soul to rest for all eternity.

Six years later Nicholas would be laid to rest here alongside Praskovia. Today their graves are forgotten, and tourists come instead to see where the mighty figures of nineteenth-century Russian music lie buried—Nikolai Rimsky-Korsakov, Modest Mussorgsky, Arthur Rubenstein, Peter Tchaikovsky. Yet it was Praskovia, one of the first great stars of the Russian opera, who broke the barrier separating talent and birth and was deemed worthy of this burial place.

One night shortly after her death, Praskovia came to Tatiana in a dream. Tatiana found herself in an unfamiliar place that appeared to be some sort of church. As she looked about she spied Praskovia in a white gown standing in the near distance before the Pearly Gates. Praskovia gazed at her and then spoke, telling Tatiana not to grieve and not to weep for her. "I am very well now," she said. And with that, Tatiana awoke.[11]

TWENTY-EIGHT

Scandal

On 6 March, eleven days after Praskovia's death, the serfs at Kuskovo were called out of their huts and told to gather in front of the over-seer's office to listen to a letter from their lord and master:

> It pleased Almighty God to foreordain that I should marry, in complete accordance with the rites of our church, on the 6th day of November 1801 in the Church of St. Simon Stylites during my stay in Moscow. . . . My lawful spouse, Countess Praskovia Ivanovna Sheremeteva, was born a Kovalevsky, and irrefutable documents attest to her being the descendant of that ancient Polish noble family. On the 3rd day of February of this year 1803 she was delivered of a son, Count Dmitry, who was given to us by God and has been rightfully recognized as my legal heir. He was christened, according to our Christian faith, in my home chapel, located in my home on the Fontanka in the parish of the Church of St. Simon and Anna, before the entire clergy of that parish and in the witness of many state officials and all my stewards, footmen, and as many house serfs as the church could accom-modate. On the 23rd day of this same February my beloved and much revered spouse, Countess Praskovia Ivanovna, passed away to my ineffable grief following a cruel illness that struck her from the very day of her delivery. She was buried with all the honors

befitting her station at the Nevsky Monastery in the Church of St. Lazarus where the bodies of the deceased Counts Shereme- tev and their families lie. My marriage to Countess Praskovia Ivanovna has been approved and recognized in writing to me by His Most Merciful Imperial Majesty, Our Emperor Alexander Pavlovich, and by the entire Imperial Family.[1]

Next, the overseer read the letters of the tsar and Dmitry Troshchen- sky recognizing the count's marriage and Dmitry's status as his sole, rightful heir. Nicholas knew the news would be met by disbelief, so he had ordered the letters read three times "in the clearest voice and so that all are listening attentively."[2] Then all the men were called forward to sign their names testifying that they had heard the news. Most of the men couldn't write, so a scribe signed for them. Many of the serfs listen- ing that day knew Praskovia. Word of her marriage to their master and of her sudden death must have stunned them into silence. Among the signatures is her Uncle Maxim's. Standing in the crowd with him were his wife, Anisia, and their daughter and son-in-law, Akulina and Lukian. Neither Praskovia's father nor her brother Afanasy's signatures are on the list. The overseer must have informed them in private sometime before.[3]

The following day the serfs at Kuskovo assembled again, this time in the estate church to listen to the village priest read the letters for a fourth time, followed by a liturgy and requiem for Praskovia, for whom the serfs were directed to "bewail their unspeakable grief." Next, the priest led them in prayers for the health and long life of Nicholas and his newborn son and so that they might all "imprint in their hearts their undivided loyalty to both Our Benefactor and Master Count Sheremetev and to His Heir."[4]

This scene was repeated on all the Sheremetev estates across Russia in early March. On the fifth, the serfs of Voshchazhnikovo gathered to hear the news. Among them was Anna Andreeva, Praskovia's godmother, to whom Nicholas sent two hundred rubles the next day at Praskovia's re- quest. The news was read at the Konstantinova estate, home to Prasko- via's Aunt Lukeria, her husband, Rodion, and their nine children; at Ostrovtsy, where her father's other sister, Martha, lived with her son, as well as the children of her late Uncle Matvei. Within two weeks of Praskovia's death, all the hundreds of thousands of Nicholas's serfs had been informed.[5]

The serfs in the Fountain House assembled in the chapel at two o'clock on the afternoon of 4 March to take part in the same ceremony. They prayed for Praskovia's soul—"Omnipotent God! Most Merciful God! . . . Although you sent your slave to her death for her sins, still we pray to you for her. . . . Dear God! . . . Lay to rest the soul of your deceased slave Praskovia in the heart of Abraham, accept her among the righteous, who know neither sickness nor lamentation, but eternal life." They prayed to St. Dmitry of Rostov—"We deliver up our prayers to you in the Lord's cathedrals, the Holy Church praises you, the soul of God's deceased slave Praskovia maintained to the grave its heartfelt faith and sacred devotion to you: Hear my prayer, O great servant of God! Pray for her before the throne of our Most Holy God that she may be cleansed of all her sins." And they pledged their allegiance to Nicholas and his son.[6]

On 26 March, Nicholas sent letters to thirty-six friends, acquaintances, and family members. One of these went to his sister Varvara. He feared breaking the news to her all of a sudden and so sent his letter to an old friend of Varvara, the scholar and archivist Nicholas Bantysh-Kamensky. He wrote Bantysh-Kamensky that he worried Varvara, upon hearing the news, might think something dreadful had happened to Nicholas himself. He apprised Bantysh-Kamensky of the contents of the letter and asked him to first prepare her gently for the news before giving her the letter. The letter to his sister was brief, describing in laconic terms the facts of his marriage, the birth of his son, and Praskovia's death and making certain to mention the tsar's recognition of his marriage. The letter was written out by one of his secretaries; at the bottom Nicholas penned in his own hand: "Have pity on me, I truly am beside myself, my loss is too great. I've lost a most worthy wife, and in my late Countess Praskovia Ivanovna I had a most worthy friend and companion. I end my mournful confession and remain, Count Sheremetev."[7] Varvara did not reply. She did not write her brother again for two months, and when she did, she made no mention of Praskovia. She was unable to bring herself to mention Dmitry in her letters until the middle of September.

The news stunned society and turned many against Nicholas. One

of them was Prince Ludwig of Württemberg, the brother of the dowager empress and once someone Nicholas had considered a friend. Days
passed, and the prince did not deign to reply or visit. On 8 March, an
anxious Nicholas wrote, "Monseigneur, in misfortune one is always more
sensitive and worried than at other moments. It causes me great pain to
imagine that I am to be deprived of your flattering me with a visit for so
long. . . . Is it possible, Monseigneur, that in the unfortunate circumstances in which I find myself, you could have changed in regards to me,
and that you could have lessened your benevolence towards me? No, I
refuse to believe that."[8]

Countess Dorothée de Lieven, the sister of Tsar Alexander's aide-
de-camp Alexander von Benckendorff and an influential St. Petersburg
salon hostess, wrote to her brother with barely concealed disgust that
"Sheremetev has married one of his slaves whom he declared his legitimate wife as soon as she gave birth to a son. . . . The son's name is Dmitry, and he shall inherit the count's immense wealth."[9] Countess Lieven's
contempt for Nicholas's behavior seems to have been shared by most in
her set.

On 2 March, the sixteen-year-old Sergei Vasilievich Sheremetev
wrote to his parents from the capital,

> The biggest news here is that the Countess Praskovia Ivanovna
> Sheremeteva has died and the count is consumed by grief. I
> went to see him the day after she died, but he was ill and in bed
> and so didn't receive me. Upon the advice of Vasily Sergeevich
> [Sheremetev] I'm now wearing mourning, and he also advised
> me to visit the count often so that he sees I am not indifferent to
> his suffering. The funeral was most magnificent, the Metropoli-
> tan and all the distinguished clergymen were on hand to bury the
> countess at the Nevsky Monastery.
>
> She left behind a son named Count Dmitry Nikolaevich,
> and the Count has already hired several foreigners to oversee his
> upbringing.[10]

Sheremetev's letter betrays a combination of teenage obliviousness to
others' feelings and his class's inability to conceive of serfs as being fully
human, as actual people whose death could be the occasion for grief and
warrant the wearing of mourning clothes.

The shrill sounds of vituperation and outrage occasioned by Nicholas's scandalous actions filled the salons and drawing rooms of St. Petersburg and Moscow that year. Like all gossip, they have left behind hardly a trace.[11]

Perhaps the best place to gain a sense of society's reaction is in fiction. The writer Nicholas Leskov captured the nobility's disdain for Praskovia in his story "An Impoverished Family." Set in the middle of the nineteenth century, the story reveals that the shock of Nicholas's actions had still not faded away decades after Praskovia's death. The story's narrator comments how even then, so many years later, men and women in some circles continued to be outraged by Nicholas's marriage and loved to heap scorn on Praskovia. A dissenter from the noble consensus was Princess Varvara Chestunova, a descendant of a minor noble family and the narrator's grandmother. "Woe to him who considers name more important than deeds," the princess liked to say:

> Yes, it's not true that Countess Praskovia Ivanovna was a Polish noble illegally forced into serfdom under the Sheremetevs. . . . Praskovia Ivanovna was a real peasant, and a song about her arose—"Late yesterday eve, whilst driving the cows home from the wood"; but that Countess Praskovia, as well as having had an unappreciated beauty, was smart, good, and had a noble soul, and so is worthy of everyone's respect—that's the truth. It was her idea that the count build the almshouse in Moscow and that he do good for people. That, if you will, is better than strutting about simply because of one's name and putting on airs and spending all one's time making social calls. . . . No, may God grant us more women with a heart like Praskovia Ivanovna, the girl "from the wood."[12]

Princess Chestunova found few supporters among her contemporaries, but as time passed more and more nobles came to share her views about the remarkable Countess Praskovia Ivanovna.

TWENTY-NINE

Saint Praskovia

In a letter to Father Amfiloky days after Praskovia's funeral, Nicholas wrote, "Pray for a man buried in grief. I truly need your help. My only desire is to be with God, to fulfill his Holy will, to confess my sins, and to save my soul."[1]

To that end Nicholas dedicated himself to helping others. The first thing he did that March was to begin paying for poor and orphaned girls to go to schools in St. Petersburg and Moscow, as Praskovia had asked. "This loss which is more painful than I can express leaves me no other consolation than to participate in the happiness of others," he explained to the director of the Smolny Institute for Girls. "Please offer me all possible opportunity to do good, and I shall owe you for the only joy that is remaining to me."[2]

The main focus of Nicholas's charity was the Moscow almshouse he had begun with Praskovia years earlier. On 16 April, Nicholas sent a proposal for the project to the tsar requesting official recognition. He noted Praskovia's role in its creation and promised to support it with over one million rubles of his own money, all the income generated by his village of Molodoi Tud, and the proceeds from the sale of two of his homes in Moscow. The almshouse would care for the sick and the poor; every year six thousand rubles would be handed out to orphaned girls as dowries. The structure was nearly completed, and state support would allow it to flourish. As a purely private enterprise, Nicholas feared, it would not succeed. Nine days later the tsar issued an ukase granting his request.[3]

Nicholas was overjoyed at the news. He immediately donated thousands of rubles for "prayers of thanksgiving" at monasteries across Russia.[4] Word of Nicholas's act unleashed a wave of praise. The poet Gavrila Derzhavin was moved to commemorate his deed in verse, contrasting the former ways of the Sheremetevs, when millions were spent on magnificent entertainments, to this new spirit of charity: "So did he acquire everyone's love,/By giving money to the poor, comfort to the sick."[5] Russians as far away as Naples drank his health. "May every Russian be filled with such sentiments, and may they not be motivated by the desire for ribbons, for sparkling and distinguished Imperial orders, but by sincere devotion to the Fatherland," exhorted Alexander Bulgakov in a letter home from Italy.[6]

There was more work to be done than Nicholas realized, and the hospital did not open until after his death in 1810. By the time it was shut down by the Bolsheviks in 1917, the Sheremetev Almshouse had cared for over two million sick, poor, and elderly at a cost of six million rubles. Every year on the anniversary of Praskovia's death dowries were given out to orphans in front of her bust in the main gallery. Some three thousand girls in all were helped, making it one of the most beneficial institutions in all Russia.

The almshouse was just one way Nicholas memorialized Praskovia. He also had matins performed at her grave every day of the year and spent tens of thousands of rubles on prayer services for her soul in churches and monasteries throughout Russia. The prayers were to continue, Nicholas instructed, "forever."[7] On Praskovia's birthday, name day, and the anniversary of her death Nicholas handed out to the poor six thousand rubles, twice the amount of Praskovia's pocket money, which she had never kept for herself but always gave away to others. He left an instruction that all of his descendants were to adhere to this practice: "Such is my directive, and you will all have to meet with me on the day of Our Lord's Second Coming. If anyone should repeal this or out of greed for money not carry it out, he will have to answer on the great Day of Judgment and for such lack of compassion he will immediately receive God's wrath, which he will already feel in this life."[8]

The charity and memorials were the result of a complicated mix of motives, emotions, and promises. He was carrying out Praskovia's final wishes. He also wanted to do good for its own sake, largely owing to Praskovia's influence, which had opened his eyes to the gospels' profoundly egalitarian message of love.

But there were darker forces at work as well. Nicholas was plagued by guilt at having taken so long to free and then marry Praskovia. He knew how important the church's blessing had been to her, yet he had been reluctant to confront his own prejudices, doubts, and fear. He knew he had gone to great lengths to conceal the truth of their relationship, had concocted an unbelievable lie about her past, and had convinced her to go along with it. She had given him an heir, which he wanted, and this had led directly to her death. Nicholas was overcome with shame and felt a need to atone. And there must have been some anger in him too, anger at a society that had forced him to make such decisions, a society that had never been willing to accept Praskovia as anything more than a serf with a remarkable voice. He was angry about the slights and affronts, the spiteful gossip and rumors that had followed Praskovia most of her life. Having kept his life with Praskovia hidden for decades, he now wanted everyone to know about it and to revere her memory.

It was then that the image of Praskovia as a living saint was created. Nicholas was its author. As he had determined so much of her life, so he determined her legacy. Tragically, she was never allowed to be fully human. In her lifetime Praskovia's freedom was at first denied and then limited, circumscribed; in her afterlife, she was stripped of all human frailty, of the contradictory emotions, impulses, drives that make us perfectly flawed human beings. She went from serf to saint without ever being an ordinary woman.

The Fountain House was turned into a shrine to Praskovia. In the garden Nicholas placed a large marble monument with a bronze plaque that read: "I believe I see her waiting shadow/Wandering about this place./I approach! But soon this cherished image/Brings me back to my grief/ And flees, never to return."[9] The monument remained until the 1930s, when it was replaced by one to Stalin. Another plaque was mounted on the pavilion: "In this place we spent time together as a family in peace and quiet. To the right is a maple, to the left two willows, all planted by Countess Praskovia Ivanovna Sheremeteva in 1800."[10]

Praskovia's rooms became the holy of holies. Over the door to her antechamber Nicholas hung a sign — "Recall Your Lord's gifts and blessings, which have been for all time. Do not recall the sins of youth and omission of Your Slave Countess Praskovia, who died here, but given Your mercy and Your benevolence, bless her. God's inscrutable foreordainment, which imprints in our hearts the memory of the one who has moved on to eternity, makes this little temple, in which her devout soul ended its life, precious."[11]

In the antechamber Nicholas arranged her favorite icons. He had his artist Nicholas Argunov paint three large-scale portraits to commemorate their wedding, Praskovia's pregnancy, and her death. Nicholas had intended to hang the last one in this room where she had died, but the gruesome effect of the image was too much, and Nicholas made Argunov paint a smaller version, which he placed between the windows in her room. The other two portraits were hung in their private rooms as well. In the center of the room on a lectern stood a small sepulcher of silver and glass based on a sketch by Quarenghi. In it lay a locket of Praskovia's hair and letters from Nicholas to his son:

This place was the cloister of your mother, Countess Praskovia Ivanovna Sheremeteva (*née* Kovalevskaia), who now rests for all eternity with God and whom I honored and worshiped as my wife. This room was the sanctuary of all her joys, sorrows, and illnesses. On this spot she bore with magnanimity two nearly fatal illnesses. Yet most gracious God, in all His ineffable mercy, heard her prayers and miraculously spared her from death. Her sense of gratitude for the Almighty's munificence impressed on her grateful heart these lines of Scripture which she often repeated: "The Lord hath punished me severely, but He hath not given me over to death." (Psalm 118, verse 18) This is the very chamber where your venerable mother, having given birth to you, her only son, placed her soul in the hands of the living God after 27 [*sic*] days of suffering that she bore with the most courageous patience. You never had the pleasure of gazing upon the face of this venerable woman who gave you life, nevertheless, this place should instill in your tender soul respect and deference for her eternal memory. Do not dare to either destroy or make any changes to this room. Leave this mournful chamber, entrusted to your reverential care, just as it is, and may it serve as a holy memorial to her virtues, and when bitter tears flow from your eyes, then with all your heart repeat these words: Dear Lord, do not forget your slave who died here in this place and has entered Your Kingdom, and ensure that she be remembered for all eternity.

Upon entering this room you should remember what you owe your mother. She was virtuous, imbued with honor, and endowed with intelligence . . . which is why during her life she was respected by honest people, loved by our household, and blessed by the poor. I say nothing about me, for I loved her more than my own life, and not only here but beyond this life shall not stop loving her, and *I am certain that I shall go on loving her even until my last breath.* . . . And you, having heard this, must not only go out in the world, but be careful not to be infected by its false charms, but to shine by imitating your worthy mother and to fear all passions and intoxications. . . . Or else you can expect nothing but eternal ruin and the abyss before which even the demons quiver.

As you enter this dwelling place where your beloved and virtuous mother lived and ended her life, remember that your life was bought at a high price. Your first glimpse of this turbulent and dangerous world cost your mother her life, and inflicted on me unending sorrow, grief, and anguish that will accompany me to my grave and, as God has planned, has destroyed my health, ruined my peace, and my life itself.[12]

It is not difficult to imagine Dmitry's pain and self-reproach upon reading these words.

On 24 April, Nicholas wrote Agapov to go out to Ostankino, find Praskovia's costume from *The Marriage of the Samnites,* carefully wrap it, and send it to him. In late June, Konstantin Gusiatnikov, a serf from the village of Voshchazhnikovo, arrived at the Fountain House with the dress and helmet in a large crate. Nicholas removed them and gave them to Tatiana to keep.[13]

He began giving away other mementos of Praskovia. To Tatiana, he also presented some pearl and diamond earrings, a gold chain, and a French watch. To Dr. Lakhman's daughter, a gold wreath. To Prince Shcherbatov's daughter, a gold chain and medallion. To Count Alexei Sergeevich Sheremetev's daughter, Praskovia's harp. To Nicholas Kalmykov, a snuffbox with a locket of Praskovia's hair. To Taniusha, gold earrings. To Stepanida Mukosina, a watch, snuffbox, and a portrait miniature of Praskovia. Stepanida lovingly braided a locket of Praskovia's hair into a neat pattern of squares and tucked it between the image and the frame.[14]

Nicholas took Praskovia's wedding ring and placed it on a gold chain around his neck. He had a gold ring made with a tiny locket of her hair under glass. And he had Praskovia's final needlework mounted in a mahogany frame and hung on the wall of his study, next to portraits of himself, little Dmitry, and Praskovia.

In early March, Vasily Sheremetev left Nicholas to return to his family. He wrote upon arriving home to inquire about Nicholas's health; when he departed Vasily believed Nicholas might not survive the loss of Praskovia.[15] Nicholas missed Vasily and felt miserably alone. "My soul is as sick now as it was before your departure," he replied. "The recent Easter holiday only served to make me that much more aware of what I have lost. My grief cruelly torments me, and my crushed spirit has caused my health to suffer as well. That's all I can tell you. . . . My son is, thank God, as well as can be expected at his tender age."[16]

Nicholas was confined to bed for the holiday. Along with his usual ailments, he began complaining of strange pressure in his chest and abdomen and a general malaise.[17] The doctors proved helpless, angering him and bringing back memories of their failure to save Praskovia. "Given my heartfelt devotion to you," he wrote Father Platon,

I shall tell you openly that the doctors are largely responsible for my misfortune. They were most negligent and made more

mistakes than any old midwife would ever be capable of. I intend
to send you a detailed account of everything, although it must
be recognized that none of this would have happened had it not
been God's will. Nevertheless, what grieves me most is having
lost something that can never be returned. My soul suffers without interruption, but my faith in God's mercy remains strong—if
not in this world, then in the next shall I not be abandoned, and
this has always been, and will always be, my sole desire. Do not
forget me in your prayers. I have no small need of them: my soul
is quite weakened, and I am unable to find anything that might
give it peace or comfort.[18]

Nicholas's mood became increasingly gloomy. His mind dwelled
on death. He began reading Edward Young's *The Complaint, or Night-
Thoughts on Life, Death, and Immortality* and the works of other graveyard poets. He ordered his gravestones cut and sent to the Alexander
Nevsky Monastery, convinced he would soon need them. Nicholas also
had a bronze plate made with the appropriate biographical information;
the only thing left to be added was the date of his death. The plate was
placed with the stones in the monastery's cellar. "Since my spirit is there,"
Nicholas said, "so shall my bones be."[19]

That spring Nicholas thought he might escape his grief by leaving St.
Petersburg. He wrote Hyvart of his plans to travel, implying he might go
as far as Paris. He bought a dacha called Ulianka outside the city on the
Peterhof Road. It was situated in a dense birch forest; in the evenings
a thick, black fog emanated from the damp ground, shrouding everything in mist and lending the area a moody, melancholic aura that suited
Nicholas's depression.

He had considered returning to Ostankino, but this would have
evoked too many memories of Praskovia. In June, he began plans for a
new refuge at his estate of Zhikharevo a ways from Moscow. The village
sat perched atop a high bluff overlooking the Malaia Istra River with a
view of the New Jerusalem Monastery. He wrote Alexei Malinovsky that
he had decided to build "a peasant hut" that might "serve me as a pleasant sanctuary. . . . I see it as some sort of a dream place where, should
my melancholy compel me to wander the great wide world, I might

live for a few weeks or so at a time near Moscow, without having to set foot in it." Here he intended to spend "the final days of my life in peace and quiet."[20] Work at Zhikharevo was completed in 1805, but Nicholas never visited. The buildings fell into disrepair and were sold as scrap in 1827.

Nicholas did leave St. Petersburg in June on a pilgrimage to Rostov, where he and Praskovia had visited a little over a year earlier. He had returned by mid-July.

From the day Praskovia died Nicholas showed great care in looking after her family. He increased all their yearly salaries, including those of her Uncle Maxim and nephew Nicholas. He was particularly concerned with her father's well-being. Displeased with Agapov's haphazard supervision, he asked Alexei Malinovsky to check on matters and to try to impress on Agapov the importance of the assignment. That autumn Nicholas sent a detailed list of new clothing for Ivan Stepanovich (a heavy sheepskin coat, leather boots, woolen socks, fresh underwear, a silk scarf, and a comfortable house coat) and provisions, with a modest daily ration of wine, enough to make him happy but not drunk.[21]

Nicholas looked after the brothers too. Michael was back in Moscow by now, living in the Corner House. He appears to have been causing trouble and so was also being watched by Agapov, who sent regular reports to Nicholas on his behavior. Michael was sent to Nicholas in St. Petersburg, where Nicholas could keep an eye on him and where his brother Ivan was still studying at the academy.[22] Afanasy was the most trouble of all the brothers. He had begun to show his father's fondness for the bottle and began acting out and refusing to recognize the authority of Nicholas's overseers. He saw in the story of his family's Polish noble origins an opportunity to demand his due and wrote Nicholas cloying letters expressing his profound admiration for him and his fervent desire to come visit Nicholas. Nicholas was not about to let this happen, and he increased Afanasy's salary to eight hundred rubles, much more than anyone else in the family received, just to keep him away.[23]

Eighteen hundred and three had been the worst year of Nicholas's life. The birth of his son could in no way compensate for the death of

Praskovia; Nicholas couldn't take consolation in Dmitry since he saw in him the cause of all his suffering. In December, he unburdened himself once more to Vasily: "I shall say to you that my feelings of misery born from my great loss have in no way diminished, and I shall go to the grave with them. I truly have lost everything."[24]

THIRTY

Putrid Bones

The cloud that had settled over the Fountain House with Praskovia's death never lifted, and there was an unmistakable feeling that the life of the household was moving toward its end.

Nicholas lived quietly, largely out of sight. Although he still appeared occasionally at court, he rarely went out into society, preferring the isolation of Ulianka or his private apartments in the Fountain House. Nicholas found it difficult to be around people. He had become anxious and increasingly melancholic; his frequent illnesses intensified his sour demeanor. He got rid of most of the domestics, assigning them elsewhere. The remaining actors and actresses married and left, and the once crowded palace grew strangely empty and quiet.

On the morning of the first anniversary of Praskovia's funeral, his son Ivan Yakimov collapsed while climbing the stairs of the Fountain House on his way to see Nicholas. Shortly after being put to bed, Ivan was convulsed by seizures and then lost consciousness. He died shortly before noon on 1 March and was buried near the entrance to the Church of St. Lazarus. The death of his son and companion added greatly to Nicholas's woes.[1]

Yakov Remetev had left the Fountain House soon after Praskovia's death, quitting his position at the College of Foreign Affairs and heading for Moscow and a life of his own. It had never been easy being the illegitimate half brother of a distinguished aristocrat, and Yakov had had enough. In Moscow, Yakov began denouncing Nicholas, claiming he had unjustly taken his servants, had been withholding his money, and kept him from assuming possession of the estate of Spasskoe promised him. He threatened to bring a lawsuit against Nicholas.

Nicholas threw up his hands at Yakov's "harsh manner and his childish impetuosity."[2] He asked Malinovsky and Prince Peter Urusov to track him down and see what might be done to come to some sort of accommodation. All efforts proved futile, however, and by the spring of 1805, Nicholas and Yakov had parted company for good. Yakov let it be known that he didn't want to have anything to do with his half brother or the Sheremetevs and requested that he be attached to Count Golovkin's embassy to China. Nicholas wrote Agapov that his half brother was no longer to be granted access to Kuskovo, Ostankino, or any of his other properties in Moscow. Margarita Remeteva left the Fountain House as well, although under much better circumstances. In January 1806, she married State Counselor Alexei Putiatin and shortly thereafter they moved to the Spasskoe estate.[3]

Every year the anniversaries of Praskovia's birth and death continued to be solemnly recognized with prayer services in churches across the country, and Nicholas often visited her grave. He increasingly sought comfort in religion and immersed himself in sacred texts, turning away the secular writings of his youth, writings that he now claimed "fill your mouth with honey and your heart with poison." He found the greatest solace in a French tract titled *La consolation du chrétien*, which counseled quiet acceptance of death. His thoughts dwelled on "the putrid bones and awful stench" that he was soon to become inside his own coffin.[4]

As Dmitry grew, Nicholas came to take pleasure in him, and his presence no longer served solely as a reminder of the tragic events surrounding his birth. He bragged to his friends with a father's pride the first time Dmitry called him Papa.[5] He enjoyed sharing anecdotes with Malinovsky—like the time he dressed Dmitry in the uniform of the Knights of the Order of Malta (Nicholas belonged to the order), and Dmitry promptly proceeded to wet himself and his costume, or the time when Dmitry was teething and had turned the household upside down with his antics.[6]

Dmitry had two nannies, Stepanida Mukosina and Yelena Kazakova, both former performers and maids of Praskovia. Nicholas was not the kind of man to live for long without a woman, and sometime in 1804, after a year of mourning, he took Yelena to his bed. Their first son, Nicholas, was born on 13 July 1805; a second son, Sergei, followed the next year, and a third, Alexander, in 1809, months after Nicholas had died. None of them were recognized as legitimate but were treated as "charges," just like the Remetevs. Nicholas petitioned the tsar to grant them Russian noble status, which he refused, so he purchased a baronetcy in the name of Istrov from the Holy Roman Emperor in Vienna for one thousand gold ducats.[7]

After becoming pregnant, Yelena was removed as Dmitry's nanny and given a large reward for her service. Her standing in the household grew, much to the displeasure of Tatiana, who saw in the new mistress a usurper and an affront to Praskovia and her memory. The two women circled each other like wary cats, and their mistrust added an air of tension to the grim mood of the Fountain House.

On a visit to the Winter Palace in December 1808, Nicholas was approached by the tsar, who informed him of the upcoming visit of the king and queen of Prussia in connection with the engagement of Grand Duchess Elizabeth Pavlovna and Prince Georg of Oldenburg. Wishing to impress his visitors, Alexander asked Nicholas to throw a large ball in their honor at the Fountain House. Nicholas had not entertained in years and had no desire to open his house anymore to large crowds; what's more, he had not been feeling well since October and organizing a ball would weigh on his fragile health. But the tsar insisted and impressed on Nicholas the importance of the visit, and in the end Nicholas agreed.

Upon returning home and viewing the palace with fresh eyes, Nicholas realized considerable work needed to be done to ready the Fountain House. Nicholas, Dmitry, Tatiana, Yelena, and the rest of the remaining household packed up and moved across the Fontanka River to the home of Countess Pushkina until the renovations could be completed.

Nicholas's health continued to decline throughout December. Nevertheless, on the morning of the twenty-sixth, Nicholas dutifully pulled himself out of bed to make his appearance at court. The dowager empress noticed the poor color of his face and knew at once that he was seriously ill. She told him to go home that instant and retire to bed, which he did. Nicholas knew he was going to die. Before going to sleep that night he made an addendum to his will, setting aside 550,000 rubles for Yelena and the Istrov boys and stipulating that they were to remain in the Fountain House after his death.[8]

Alexander visited Nicholas on the first day of the New Year. The official reason for his visit was to enquire about his health, although what he really wanted to know was how preparations were coming for the ball. Nicholas died the next day. He was fifty-seven years old. Tatiana was with him when he died. She had been holding his hand, yet, fearful that he might be contagious, Nicholas pulled it away and had her cover it with a handkerchief before allowing her to touch him again. He made her promise to stay with Dmitry. "Oh, God, deliver me from this madness!" were his final words.[9]

Several causes for his death have been given. The wicked story that went about the city in the days after was that Nicholas had been killed so that the Prussian royal couple could be entertained by the sight of the magnificent funeral of Russia's most distinguished aristocrat. Alexander Pushkin claimed he had been killed by the excesses of his youth: "You knew the Trianon and outrageous parties,/But their sweet poison did you in."[10] The attending doctors claimed it was nothing more than "an intense fever." Nicholas's grandson Sergei believed he died when "the guiding star of his life was taken from him, without whom he couldn't live and for whom he wept until his death."[11]

As he had ordered, Nicholas's funeral was modest, and despite the gaiety surrounding the king and queen's visit, many turned out to pay their final respects. He was buried alongside Praskovia in a simple black jacket, white trousers, and English leather boots. On his finger he wore his wedding ring; around his neck hung the gold chain with Praskovia's ring that he had worn since her death. Large gifts were made to charity.

Nicholas freed twenty-two of his house serfs in his will and directed that all of them be permitted to remain at the Fountain House. Special care was to be shown Tatiana, Taniusha, Yelena, and her sons. Praskovia's family was to continue to receive their yearly salaries in addition to a onetime gift of fifty thousand rubles. The bulk of his estate Nicholas left to his son. In the event of Dmitry's death, it was to skip Nicholas's sister, her sons and daughters, and pass instead to his cousin Vasily.

A lifetime of extravagance had left Nicholas with enormous debts totaling nearly three million rubles. The executors of his estate sold much of his wardrobe, his collection of cellos, and other personal effects to begin to pay it down. The finest pieces of the Sheremetev jewels, some of which had belonged to Praskovia, were auctioned off in St. Petersburg in December 1809. A man by the name of Lemberg bought many of them. According to family legend, he took the jewels to Paris, where he sold them to Napoleon for his new bride, the empress Marie Louise.

THIRTY-ONE

Fatherly Advice

Nicholas had sensed he would not live to see Dmitry reach manhood. He worried about how his son would fare without either parent and surrounded by an extended family and society that viewed him with a mixture of arrogance, condescension, and greed. Nicholas feared Dmitry would face temptation and prejudice and be besieged by sycophants who would flatter him to his face and mock his peasant roots behind his back.

Nicholas composed two lengthy letters to his son explaining the story of his parents' love for one another, the circumstances of their lives and Dmitry's birth, the challenges Dmitry would face in his life, and Nicholas's hopes for him. Nicholas believed this was his sacred obligation as a father, a Christian, a friend, and a husband, in keeping with Praskovia's wishes. He left the letters in the sepulcher in Praskovia's room for his son to read when he was old enough.[1]

Writing of his own life, Nicholas hoped to offer Dmitry an example from which to learn. Nicholas came to see his life as a journey of moral self-improvement, a Christian Bildungsroman in which the arrogant and venal young aristocrat, enslaved to status, wealth, and the temptations of the flesh, finds his way to true happiness, well-being, and inner peace through the acceptance of God and adherence to his laws.

"In order to answer my main purpose in confiding in you, my son," Nicholas wrote, "all the circumstances that have come together to form the thread of your life, there is no need to give as an example those celebrated events of bygone days, to use them to support my soulful conversation with you, for everyone is already convinced of what has been just as it is well known to all that I have but one heir, and that is you. But should indiscrete talk, in the days of my oblivion, upset your peace and the purity of your feelings, then may this revelation of my heart be a calming truth, a defense against enmity, a solid support of that holy union, the author of all your days."

As a young man, he confessed,

> I was carried away by the desire for sensations, be they delicate or intoxicating, I craved all that was pleasing and gay, magnificent and amazing. . . . A certain knowledge I had, added to my taste and my passion for the rare and the unusual aided this desire: my wish to captivate and astound people who had neither seen nor heard of my magnificent creation [Ostankino] reflected my vanity and impetuous feelings. Then I became aware that the splendor of such a creation satisfied these feelings only for the shortest time, and all vanished instantaneously in the eyes of perfection, not leaving the slightest impression in my soul, save emptiness.
>
> There were magnificent feasts, during which I forgot all moderation in food and drink, in which luxury and vanity lorded over my mind and heart, and at which in one day for the mere sake of caprice, the greatest wealth was wasted, wealth acquired from years of human labor capable of providing prosperity for thousands of the poor for their entire lives. There were theatrical spectacles that had long since given up all moral principles and touched us more for their corrupting and ruinous quality than for their virtue.

And then Nicholas grew close to Praskovia—

> This time my soul could not resist or overcome these ardent feelings, still I was guided by the best intentions, and if on one hand the general prejudices provided me with sickening notions, then on the other having already once in my life been conquered by love's passion, I decided it best to fall back on what was good; marriage gave me a sense of calm, and led to a place sanctioned

by law and blessed by God. This true friend, loyal to me with all her emotions, who breathed devotion and a passionate affection for me, dedicated her entire life to pleasing my will, and combining all possible virtues, she obtained for herself all of my respect and reverence for her; at first our situation lacked the pleasant aspects of life; it could not provide true happiness; conscience, God's Holy Laws, and the prospect of illegitimate offspring all cast a shadow over this false happiness.

For a long time I fought with the voice inside me that is God's Law and with the transitory prejudices of this world about the inequality of caste and estate. At the same time, the humble sentiment and strict religious principles that filled your mother's soul had a strong influence on her peace of mind. Her health began markedly to wither, her fears about God's inevitable judgment troubled both our consciences, the cruel illness that struck her in 1800, and God's miraculous mercy that pulled her from the very jaws of Death, my own advanced age, and the fact of our having grown accustomed to each other over more than twenty years—all these combined and made clear to me that the only way to set all this right was to ignore the recriminations of this world and to resort to the healing power of Christian faith and to do what honesty demanded, which I finally did, purifying my soul and entering into the bonds of Holy matrimony with her.

Nicholas returned repeatedly to the reasons for his marrying Dmitry's mother. He wanted his son to know that Praskovia had been an extraordinary woman deserving of this distinction—"Her qualities compelled me to flout society's prejudices concerning noble title and birth and to make her my wife. And what better offering could I have made to her dignity and to my love for her than to join together our hearts and our lives through the bonds of holy matrimony?

"Her spiritual goodness expressed itself first of all in a love for God, a strict adherence to faith, loyalty to her husband, and help for the suffering. She never hid her gold, and always extended her hand to the poor and destitute; her purse, filled again and again from many sources, was always empty. She gave it all away, she used it all to help humanity."

Nicholas did not leave it at that and looked to the past for further justification.

> All history gives us examples of society's most important personages, such as Tsars, Kings and Queens, and famous pillars of the Fatherland, all expected to follow the strictest standards, having overcome prejudices and followed nothing but the voice of their heart. Refusing to please man-made customs concerning marriage based on the status of one's kin, they were nourished by their spouses and by God's goodness that acts on all human behavior, and so were they successful and were they comforted by the offspring of their unions.

Here Nicholas provided examples: Roman Emperor Constantine married a peasant girl; Russian Prince Yaropolk married a Greek prisoner of low birth in AD 880; Grand Prince Yaroslav married the daughter of a Novgorod commoner in 1264; King David of Georgia married a peasant in 1205; and perhaps most compelling for Nicholas's purposes, Peter the Great married a former pastor's daughter who later ruled Russia as Catherine I.

But Nicholas knew well enough that these examples meant little in the Russia of their day—

> I have myself experienced the mendacity of my acquaintances, to my heart's great disappointment. It seemed they loved and respected me; they took part in my pleasures, but when my wife's death reduced me to despair, few could be found to comfort me or share in my grief when all it took to give my soul the slightest comfort was one small tear, the least sigh, or one heartfelt word of a true friend, an honest man. . . . Nothing gave me the least comfort after being deprived of my best friend, nothing lessened the cruel illness that soon descended upon me: I found nothing in my wealth and magnificence to calm and heal my exhausted soul, and then I realized they were nothing but vanity. . . . I was beyond feeling.

Nicholas instructed Dmitry that with his proud name and immense fortune came great obligations. It was his duty to use his advantages to serve God, the tsar, Russia, and his fellow man. All eyes would be upon him, but he would not fail should he maintain an unshakeable faith in God.

At the heart of Nicholas's words, however, lay a strikingly radical notion about the equality of all people and the need to heed one's inner voice, rejecting tradition when one knew it to be at odds with the truth. True happiness and spiritual peace, he stressed, are to be found by sticking to "the path of one's conscience and the truth," for only then will "no temptation, enticing earthly pleasures, or pangs of conscience have any power to control you." He told Dmitry, "Tradition is not law. One mustn't submit one's mind and will to it, especially in those instances when one can free oneself from our age-old errors. All people were created one and the same; they are all equal by their common origin; they differ only in their character or their actions, be they good or bad. He who has greater advantage has greater means to do good. Your soul will never know sweet pleasure and peace if it remains unfeeling to virtue."

Nicholas requested that wherever he should die, Dmitry make certain Nicholas's body was laid to rest next to Praskovia's, and he expressed the hope that Dmitry would wish to be buried alongside them. "If, dear son," Nicholas ended, "your sensitive heart causes you to shed tears for me, then remember, that if I was able to spend my few remaining days well and died with true repentance, then I am not entirely worthy of pity."

THIRTY-TWO

Separate Fates

Praskovia's father died an old man in his seventies at Ostankino in the spring of 1813. After years of gradual decline Ivan Stepanovich had become recalcitrant, refusing to eat or accept any help, and the estate managers had trouble finding reliable people to watch him. One couple assigned to Ivan beat him savagely and then abandoned him in his cottage for a month with a broken rib. The overseers were instructed to make sure Ivan had enough food, plenty of firewood and candles. Every two or three days a half liter of vodka was placed on his doorstep.

A German traveler happened upon him outside his Ostankino cottage not long before his death. Ivan Stepanovich told him he was the count's father-in-law and claimed to be the estate manager for which he was paid several hundred rubles a year. The traveler was skeptical, noting that wherever he got his money from, it did enable the old man "to live in perpetual intoxication, which seems to be his happiest condition."[1]

Afanasy lived out his days at Kuskovo with his wife and teenage son in an alcohol-induced haze, indolent, surly, and unsusceptible to the overseers' threats to exile him to a distant estate unless his changed his ways. When Napoleon's troops came in 1812, they robbed the family of everything but the shirts on their backs.[2] Brother Ivan Ivanovich had never shown any aptitude while studying at the Academy of Fine Arts and so was sent to work at the Sheremetev Almshouse as a scribe. He felt the work was beneath him, and, in 1814, after falling deeply into debt and facing being sent off to the army, he suddenly vanished from Moscow. Ivan turned up again two years later in nothing but rags, unable to account for his whereabouts. Realizing he was incapable of caring for himself, the trustees of Nicholas's estate bought him some new clothes and settled him in one of the Sheremetev homes together with a manservant to look after him.[3]

Boris Merkulov's second mission to acquire patents of Polish nobility for Praskovia and her family failed. Nevertheless, Nicholas had kept him on his staff, paying him a generous salary of four thousand rubles a year. This didn't suit Merkulov for long, and he decided the fair price for his silence was twenty thousand rubles. The last thing Nicholas wanted was for Merkulov to make public this unflattering story, and so they settled and Merkulov remained in his employment. In the end no noble patent was ever issued for any of the "Kovalevskys."[4]

Taniusha Orlova remained in the Fountain House in the care of Tatiana Shlykova and was educated alongside Dmitry and the Istrov brothers, excelling in French and the fortepiano. In November 1810, Vasily Pogodin, a junior official in the Ministry of Police, proposed marriage, even though Taniusha was just fourteen. After receiving assurances of his good character, the trustees granted permission.

Excited and deeply in love, Taniusha and Vasily began making their wedding plans early the following year. She had already been to the tailor to purchase taffeta, muslin, and cambric for her wedding dress, when in February she came down with a severe cold. Her illness worsened, and on 10 April she died of consumption in the Fountain House. The fabric intended for her wedding dress was used to make her burial costume.[5]

Despite the ill will between them, Nicholas left Yakov Remetev seventeen thousand rubles upon his death. Yakov needed the money after his two villages burned to the ground and he had no one else to turn to for help. He later had a son named Peter, probably after Yakov's father, and a grandson, Alexander, alive in Oryol in the 1890s. Nothing is known about Yakov's fate. His sister Margarita left Spasskoe for St. Petersburg after her husband's death. She died there childless and alone in August

1848 at the age of sixty-nine. Her estate, some three thousand rubles, two dachas, and twenty-seven serfs, she left to her nephew, Peter Remetev.

The fates of Nicholas's nephews are perhaps the saddest. When it finally sunk in that the fortune he had been counting on would go to Dmitry, Kirill Razumovsky considered fleeing to Vienna but was detained by his creditors. Kirill's father had by now stopped advancing his sons any money and replying to their letters. His situation appeared hopeless.

Kirill began to show signs of mental derangement, and there was talk of bizarre outbursts and attacks. In the autumn of 1804, he was hurriedly sent to Scotland, the stated purpose of the trip being to cure him of his illness, though it seems the family chiefly wanted to remove this embarrassment from the capital and hope his debts and antics would be forgiven and forgotten.

In 1806, Kirill returned, utterly mad. He was seen walking about the city with a knife in his hand threatening passersby and screaming wildly. At other times he would suddenly burst into song. Once he shot his coachman with a pistol. He was drinking heavily. The cause of his madness was unknown, but many began to suspect the work of the secret society of the Illuminati, who, it was said, had gained control over his mind through the use of black magic. On 21 August 1806, the tsar ordered his arrest, and he was locked up in the Schlüsselburg Fortress. The authorities searched his papers for proof of any connection to the Illuminati (they found none), confiscated his razors, and confined him to a small cell. Upon his request a lamp was kept burning at night so he could be certain there were no evil spirits lurking in the corners.

Kirill was transferred two years later to Suzdal's Yefimievsky Monastery, the so-called Russian Bastille, and placed in the monks' care. He joined nine other "secret" prisoners and was never referred to by name, but only as a "certain individual." The monks subjected him to heavy doses of Orthodox teachings in the conviction that God alone could save him. He was often tormented by strange visions and violent rages. His father had been the one responsible for Kirill's incarceration, and following his death in 1822 Kirill was released to his sisters. He lived another seven years, never regaining his mental health. Kirill died and was buried in Kharkov. With no family there to tend to his grave it quickly became overgrown with grass and weeds, fell into disrepair, and was lost.[6]

His brother experienced a similar, if not so extreme, downfall. After Praskovia's death, Peter underwent a remarkable transformation from a sociable man-about-town to a morose misanthrope. By 1806, his debts had grown to twenty-five thousand rubles, more than he could even begin to repay. To rescue Peter, his father spirited him out of Petersburg and into a sort of exile in Odessa, about as far away as he could possibly send him. There he lost contact with the rest of his family.

Peter managed to buy a large house outside the city and became a recluse. He let his beard and hair grow long and straggly and holed up there, never leaving and never letting anyone come to see him. When his father died Peter inherited his estate, which wasn't very much; Count Alexei Razumovsky had gone through nearly all his money and been forced to petition the tsar for an annual pension not long before his death. What remained Peter used to build a labyrinth of caves and passageways under his house, the sole access to which was through a secret door in his bedroom.

In 1827, his creditors sued Peter for fifty-five thousand rubles of bad debt. He ignored their suits and was eventually evicted from his house by the police, taking up residence in a nearby dirty inn. He died in 1835, and with him the male line of the Razumovskys in Russia came to a pathetic end.[7]

Their mother's remaining years are no less painful to consider. For decades Varvara had relied on her brother for everything, and after Nicholas died she was left utterly helpless. Other than the requests for money from her son Peter she had no more contact with the family. With time she eventually forgave her estranged husband for destroying her life and wept when she learned of his death. She became a virtual prisoner in her own home at the hands of her servants. All the windows of her sprawling, ramshackle mansion on Lubianka Square were kept sealed up year-round; inside, the stuffy rooms were in perpetual disarray, dust motes floated slowly in the thick air, and piles of priceless artworks, of statues, paintings, porcelain, silver, and jewelry lay about in jumbled heaps.

Managing all this was more than Varvara could handle, so she entrusted her affairs to her head servant, Ivan Syrov, and her favorite maid, Marfushka. Syrov robbed her blind. He deceived Varvara into willing him her entire estate, bits of which he doled out to the rest of the servants to buy their complicity. When she died alone in 1824 the rumor in Moscow was that not a single silver spoon was left in the house.

Yelena Kazakova and her sons Barons Sergei and Alexander Istrov (their brother Nicholas had died in 1811) remained at the Fountain House until 1814, when she married Titular Counselor Pogodin and moved out, much to Tatiana's and Dmitry's relief. After that Tatiana made it a point never to mention Kazakova's name and treated the Istrovs coldly.

Baron Sergei became an official in the College of Foreign Affairs and eventually rose to the rank of court counselor. He was apparently the only one of the three Istrovs who maintained a relationship with Dmitry. A small man with an odd gait and irascible temperament, he frequently came by for dinner, when he and Tatiana would get in terrible rows.

Even though the Istrov boys were given their fair share in Nicholas's will and Dmitry paid them an annual pension, they and their offspring were forever short of money and begging Dmitry for more. Letters would arrive filled with hard luck stories of dire need, ruthless creditors, threats of eviction, debtor's prison. In 1850, Sergei's daughter Lydia wrote Dmitry from Paris for five thousand rubles, adding with an impressive touch of melodramatic effect that she had reached "the point of putting a noose around my neck."[8]

Baron Alexander Istrov died in 1855, his brother Sergei four years later. Dmitry paid for Sergei's funeral.

Tatiana kept the promise she made to Nicholas on his deathbed and stayed with Dmitry. For almost half a century she lived on the ground floor of the Fountain House in two rooms decorated with icons, paintings of Kuskovo and Ostankino, and a portrait of Praskovia. Tatiana spent most of her days here reading newspapers with her maid. On her name day, well-wishers, many of them friends of Dmitry, including Alexander Pushkin, would crowd into her rooms. Tatiana became Dmitry's second mother. They shared an emotional bond and loved each other dearly. She knew better than anyone how much his parents had suffered in their lives and wanted Dmitry's life to be free of such pain, although she knew too well the hostility his family and society felt toward him.

For years Dmitry tried to talk Tatiana into making one last trip back to Moscow. Finally, in 1851, she agreed to go. Tatiana had not been to Moscow in half a century; her last visit had been in 1801 when Nicholas and Praskovia married. She stayed at the Corner House with Dmitry and his son Sergei. They visited the city's churches and monasteries and rode out to see Ostankino. The Old Home where she had lived with Praskovia and the other females in the 1790s was gone, having been torn down in the 1830s.

Several times they prepared to make the trip out to Kuskovo, but each time Tatiana changed her mind. Encouraged by Dmitry and Sergei, she eventually overcame her apprehension. Sergei recorded Tatiana's reaction to her youthful home, which had by now changed almost beyond recognition: "Tatiana Vasilievna looked all around and went everywhere with an attentive and sorrowful look on her face . . . it was doubly grievous for her to see these beloved places of her past and to be alone with her remembrances, no longer in the old Kuskovo, but in this now-abandoned, overgrown, and woeful one."⁹

Tatiana died in bed on the morning of 25 January 1863 at the age of ninety. Dmitry and Sergei sat together at her bedside for several hours recalling her remarkable life. In her rooms they found a small box with a note inside describing Nicholas's and Praskovia's wedding and Praskovia's copy of her favorite prayer by St. Dmitry of Rostov. There was also a locket of Nicholas's hair and a gold ring engraved with the words "Save and keep me."¹⁰

Dmitry's earliest childhood memories were of playing games with Tatiana. After his father's death, Dmitry looked to Tatiana as the one adult he could trust and love. She had, however, no legal authority over him or the household, which lay with a board of trustees put in place by Nicholas's will. The board deemed it inappropriate for a former serf ballerina to have so much influence over the boy and decided to have her removed from the Fountain House. Dowager Empress Maria Fyodorovna, who knew of Nicholas's respect for Tatiana, came to her aid and convinced the trustees to change their mind.

As a boy Dmitry displayed artistic talent, which his teachers encouraged, and he became a fine dancer—particularly good at the mazurka—an amateur thespian, and singer, combining perfect pitch and a pleasing, beautifully mannered tenor voice. He enjoyed singing romances, accompanying himself on the piano. Dmitry described himself as "fanatico per la musica." Sergei observed, "Music acted on him in a magical way."[11]

Dmitry began his service in 1823 as a cornet in the Chevalier Gardes, and though he continued to serve for many years, his heart was never in it and his record never amounted to much. His fellow guards officers took advantage of their comrade's weak nature and turned the Fountain House into their private club. It became the scene of drunken revelry and carousing, paid for by the host, who never enjoyed himself but was too shy and insecure to tell them to leave.

Seeing this pained some in his family. "What a poor young man. It's so sad to see how they rob him, it's simply terrible," sighed his future mother-in-law. "Just imagine, his income isn't enough. He's almost always at home, and the people who are living with him there . . . have taken such control over him that he cannot make a move without them. . . . He doesn't have a single kopeck left to cover his expenses, and he's had to borrow two million rubles to get by. . . . Woe to rich orphans."[12]

Such honest concern for Dmitry was rare. Sergei noted with sadness that Dmitry's birth had upset the entire family and his descent "from 'a peasant'" was something it never got over.[13] When, in 1835, a false rumor reached St. Petersburg that Dmitry had died of scarlet fever in Voronezh, the expectation this produced among his grasping relatives inspired Pushkin's mocking poem "On Lucullus's Recovery."[14]

Although he did not share his parents' passion for opera, Dmitry did revive the family choir, which, by the 1850s, numbered over ninety singers. The choir's concerts in the Fountain House were popular with members of the tsarist family as well as some of Russia's finest composers—Mikhail Glinka, César Cui, and Mily Balakirev. Franz Liszt heard the choir perform and was inspired to dedicate a composition to it, as did Hector Berlioz.

Tsar Alexander II stayed with Dmitry at Ostankino before his coronation in 1855. One can imagine Alexander visiting the theater and inquiring about Dmitry's mother and her famous career. According to family legend, it was during this stay at Ostankino, in the palace built to showcase a serf, that Alexander signed the initial decree that began the process of emancipating Russia's serfs.[15]

In 1849, Dmitry's first wife, Anna, died. Even though Dmitry would later remarry, her death left him a changed man. He adopted an almost monastic existence, spending long hours alone in his room in prayer. Life at the Fountain House became centered on the careful observance of Orthodox rites and services conducted with reverent solemnity. The sound of sacred hymns echoed throughout the home. While Anna's death played a role in Dmitry's turn toward religion, it cannot account for everything. It seems as if Dmitry felt the need to atone for some past sin. It was said faces of the dead haunted him in his dreams.[16]

Sergei wrote that Dmitry rarely spoke of his parents and then only in a hushed voice as if out of respect. Not surprisingly, he talked more of Nicholas, always referring to him as *batiushka*, beloved father. Dmitry almost never mentioned his mother, although when he did, his voice would drop to a whisper. His calendar entries show that he visited the Church of St. Simon Stylites and the Church of St. Lazarus; he and Tatiana never failed to attend prayers for the dead in remembrance of his parents at the Alexander Nevsky Monastery. But if the visits to these places so important to his parents' lives meant anything, he never let it be known. He once told Sergei that he was saving all his personal papers for him in a large box. Sergei found the box after his father's death, but it had been emptied and its contents presumably destroyed.

Unable to speak his heart Dmitry expressed himself through charity. As soon as he came into his rights Dmitry increased the funding for the Sheremetev Almshouse and improved its facilities. Although the almshouse remained the focus of his philanthropy throughout his life, Dmitry also gave generously to many churches, monasteries, and schools. After Tsar Alexander II freed the serfs in 1861 and Dmitry's income declined, he continued to give away as much money as before and made up for the shortfall by reducing his personal spending. He did not seek recognition for his charity, but it became well known across Russia nonetheless, giving rise to the expression "to live on the Sheremetev account."

Dmitry's obsessive religiosity and insistent charity appear to be the methods he developed for coping with the scandal of his birth. They were his way of seeking forgiveness for his mother's death and, in his own mind, the penance expected of him by society for having been born the son of a serf.

Dmitry died of a heart attack at Kuskovo on 12 September 1871. His coffin was placed on a train and taken to St. Petersburg, where he was laid to rest alongside his parents. Before they closed the coffin, Sergei took one final look at the body and was struck by something he had never noticed before—how much his father resembled Praskovia.[17]

Coda

The magic theater has been torn down,

The slaves no longer perform opera there.

Parasha's voice has broken off,

The princes applaud her no more —

The delicate sounds of her breast have fallen silent,

And Croesus the Younger has died bored and alone.

Oh, time, cruelest of foes!

You spare nothing.

—PRINCE IVAN DOLGORUKY, *A Walk at Kuskovo*

The Sheremetevs' musical traditions lived on after Dmitry's death. The writer Andrei Muravyov, who was close to many in the family, even Nicholas's sister in her last years, observed, "The Sheremetevs are songbirds," they have the tendency "to speak in a sing-song voice."[1] Dmitry's son Sergei was given musical instruction and dance lessons as a boy by Auguste Poireaux, whose grandfather, the famous Le Picq, had earlier taught Tatiana Shlykova. Nothing made little Sergei happier than when Tatiana would come watch him dance.

Although his father's choir was disbanded, Sergei managed to put together a smaller one of some fourteen singers. It became one of the capital's finest, and Tsar Alexander II frequently came to the Fountain House to hear it. Sergei also put on musical evenings in the Fountain House in which stars from the Mariinsky Opera would perform. He saw that his children were taught to play the balalaika, which came in handy after the revolution, when some of them were forced to play in small orchestras in Petrograd to earn a living. Sergei was the last Sheremetev to live in the Fountain House. He died in 1918.

Sergei always honored his grandmother Praskovia. He proudly hung the portrait of her in her red shawl in the state bedroom at Kuskovo. When Tsar Alexander III, Empress Maria Fyodorovna, and their son Grand Duke Nicholas, the future (and last) tsar, visited in May 1883, Sergei showed it to them and spoke reverently of his grandmother. He tried to inculcate the same respect in his children and grandchildren. One granddaughter, Xenia Saburova, recollected as an old woman in her nineties, "Everyone in our family held Praskovia Ivanovna in the greatest respect. Grandfather did not allow anyone to call her Parasha. I remember that in the Fountain House was a large hinged icon atop a lectern. It held an image of Praskovia Ivanovna in her coffin, and in the center were two portraits of her—one in a cap with a miniature on her breast, the other, her last portrait, just before giving birth, in the striped dress, with that bittersweet look on her mouth. . . . The icon was opened only on important holidays, and the children were led past it. Those of the younger generation who made mischief lost this honor, and usually the 'little sinner' wept bitterly."[2]

Another granddaughter, Yelena Golitsyna, recalled that Praskovia's room was kept in a state of "inviolability" and that all the children were led into it every Sunday. "We bowed down to her memory, tenderly and with devotion," she remembered. "It seems to me love for her inspires us even to this day."[3]

Count Alexander Sheremetev, Dmitry's younger son, carried on the family's musical traditions as well. Music was his passion—he became a music patron, director, and even composer. He founded a choir and, in 1882, a symphony in St. Petersburg that survived up until the revolution. In 1910, the orchestra was renamed the A. D. Sheremetev Musical-Historical Society in his honor. In its hall on Nevsky Prospekt the society put on free concerts (150 between 1898 and 1910), readings, and lectures. In 1906, the society staged the first Russian performance of Richard Wagner's *Parsifal* under his direction. In the years 1901–17, Alexander also served as one of the directors of the tsar's court choir. After the revolution, he left Russia with his family, settling in Paris, where he continued to organize concerts.

A few of Sergei's descendants heard Euterpe's song. His grandsons, the brothers Peter and Nicholas Sheremetev, a cellist and violinist, respectively, played together in the orchestra of Moscow's Vakhtangova Theater. Nicholas, named in honor of his great-great-grandfather, was the concertmaster of the orchestra for many years and also composed music for a production of Nikolai Gogol's *Inspector General*. He was married to an actress who performed under the name Mansurova, and he shared his namesake's love of hunting. In 1924, Peter Sheremetev left Russia for France, taking with him only his Italian cello.

Members of the family who remained in Russia had it harder. Sergei's grandson Boris was arrested by the Bolsheviks in 1918 and thrown into Moscow's Lefortovo prison. One night in November 1918, the secret police showed up at the Corner House, barged in, and locked the doors so no one could get out. They ransacked the home well into the next morning before carting off millions of rubles worth of gold, silver, china, and art, taking several of Sergei's grandsons with them too. Xenia Saburova's father was executed by the Bolsheviks in 1919, and the rest of the family forced into internal exile; Xenia was swept up in Stalin's Great Terror in 1937 and sent to the Gulag as an English spy. She wasn't released until a year after Stalin's death in 1954. She reminisced about how thoughts of Praskovia kept her alive through those dark years. "There, in the camp," she said shortly before her death, "I often thought about Praskovia Ivanovna, and the way she determined her own fate filled me with admiration."[4]

Praskovia was also credited with saving the life of Xenia's cousin, Vasily Sheremetev. Born in 1922, Vasily was the last representative of the male line of the family in Russia. In 1941, he left for the front to fight the Nazis. He was wounded several times and then taken prisoner. Vasily later said he never feared for his life since the amulet he wore around his neck with a portrait of Praskovia kept him safe. After the war, he became increasingly preoccupied with thoughts about Russia's past and his family's role in it. He was convinced that all the catastrophes that had befallen the family were just recompense for the lives of so many serfs they had crushed. He later worked as a tour guide at Ostankino.

In recent years music has returned to the Sheremetev palaces. In 1989, the Fountain House became the home of the Museum of the Theatrical and Musical Arts and began hosting concerts of choral music once sung by the Sheremetev choir. The theater at Ostankino has been restored, and operas are again being performed there. And during the warm summer months thousands of visitors flock to Kuskovo to stroll the gardens, tour the palace, and attend evening concerts in the renovated white hall.

There is one place at Kuskovo, however, where few visitors go. It lies out past the Italian house in the direction of the orangerie, in a stand of oaks, lindens, and birch a few yards beyond the border of the formal garden and close by the main road running past the estate. It's dark here and cool, even on the hottest days. The ground, covered in thick grass, is uneven and marked by undulating mounds and depressions. This is all that remains of the outdoor theater where Praskovia performed centuries ago. On summer nights the faint sounds of the palace concerts can be heard out here, twining through the trees, interrupted only by the heavy rumble of the occasional passing truck.

Notes

ABBREVIATIONS USED IN
THE NOTES AND BIBLIOGRAPHY

AKK	*Arkhiv kniazia F. A. Kurakina*
AKV	*Arkhiv kniazia Vorontsova*
ARO GTsTM	Arkhivno-rukopisnyi otdel, Gosudarstvennyi tsentral'nyi teatral'nyi muzei im. A. A. Bakhrushina
bk.	book
d.	delo (dela) [file (files)]
ERD-R	Ermitazhnye redkie dokumenty-rukopisi
f.	fond [collection]
GARF	Gosudarstvennyi arkhiv Rossiiskoi Federatsii
GAVO	Gosudarstvennyi arkhiv Vladimirskoi oblasti
IV	*Istoricheskii vestnik*
KfZh	*Kamer-fur'erskii tseremonial'nyi zhurnal*
KR RIII	Kabinet rukopisei, sektor istochnikovedeniia, Rossiiskii institut istorii iskusstv
l. (ll.)	list (listy) [folio (folios)]
Memuary	Sheremetev, S. D. *Memuary*. Edited by L. I. Shokhin (Moscow, 2001)
NA	National Archive (London)
NA MMUO	Nauchnyi arkhiv, Moskovskii muzei-usad'ba Ostankino

No.	nomer [number]
O18v	Sheremetev, S. D., ed. *Otgoloski 18. veka.* 11 vols. (Moscow, 1896–1905)
ob.	oborot [verso]
OIRK GE	Otdel istorii russkoi kul'tury, Gosudarstvennyi Ermitazh
op.	opis' [register]
OPI GIM	Otdel pis'mennykh istochnikov, Gosdarstvennyi istoricheskii muzei
OR RGB	Otdel rukopisi, Rossiiskaia Gosudarstvennaia Biblioteka
OR RNB	Otdel rukopisi, Rossiiskaia Natsional'naia Biblioteka
PIS	Bezsonov, P. *Praskov'ia Ivanovna Sheremeteva. Eia narodnaia pesnia i rodnoe eia Kuskovo* (Moscow, 1872)
pt. / pts.	part / parts
RA	*Russkii arkhiv*
Repertuar	Lepskaia, L. A. *Repertuar krepostnogo teatra Sheremetevykh: katalog p"es* (Moscow, 1996)
RGADA	Rossiiskii gosudarstvennyi arkhiv drevnikh aktov
RGIA	Rossiiskii gosudarstvennyi istoricheskii arkhiv
RGVIA	Rossiiskii gosudarstvennyi voenno-istoricheskii arkhiv
RS	*Russkaia starina*
SO	Sheremetev, S. D., ed. *Stoletnie otgoloski, 1801, 1802, 1803* (Moscow, 1901–03)
st. inv.	staryi inventar' [old inventory]
Teatry	Elizarova, N. A. *Teatry Sheremetevykh* (Moscow, 1941)
TIS	Sheremetev, S. D. *Tat'iana Ivanovna Shlykova, 1773–1863* (St. Petersburg, 1889)
TsIAM	Tsentral'nyi istoricheskii arkhiv Moskvy

PRELUDE

1. Akhmatova, *Complete Poems*, 583.
2. Popova, *Krepostnaia aktrisa*, 5.
3. Alekseeva, ed., *Sheremetevy*, 397.
4. RGIA, f. 1088, op. 9, d. 2899.
5. *PIS*, 23–24, 24n.
6. RGIA, f. 1088, op. 1, d. 66, 69, 70, 71, 72.
7. Sholok, *Ostankino*, 111; Elizarova, *Krepostnaia aktrisa*, 6.
8. Tomalin, *Mrs. Jordan's Profession*, xviii.

9. Holmes, *Footsteps,* 120.
10. *TIS,* 41. Ellipsis in original.
11. RGIA, f. 1088, op. 9, d. 2883.
12. Holroyd, *Works,* 16, 19. And see Holmes, *Footsteps,* and idem, *Sidetracks.*
13. RGIA, f. 1088, op. 1, d. 115, ll. 280b–29.
14. RGIA, f. 1088, op. 1, d. 69, ll. 1–2; d. 72, l. 6.

CHAPTER 1. AN ARISTOCRATIC BOYHOOD

1. Vdovin, ed., *Graf Nikolai,* 12.
2. Dologorukov, *Povest',* 145.
3. Shcherbatov, *Corruption,* 205.
4. Vdovin, ed., *Graf Nikolai,* 12–21; *O18v,* 2:4; 6:32–33.
5. Vdovin, ed., *Graf Nikolai,* 21–30; RGIA, f. 1088, op. 1, d. 906, l. 1.
6. Vdvoin, ed., *Graf Nikolai,* 33–36; *Zimnyi dvorets,* 136, 176.
7. Vdovin, ed., *Graf Nikolai,* 36–38; Kobeko, *Tsesarevich Pavel,* 42.
8. Dynik, *Krepostnoi teatr,* 58–59, 61; *Teatry,* 18, 153–54; RGADA, f. 1287, op. 1, ch. 2, d. 3739a, ll. 1–2.

CHAPTER 2. THE BLACKSMITH'S DAUGHTER

1. Searches of the archives in Moscow, St. Petersburg, and Yaroslavl' by me and several other scholars have yet to yield any information on the details of Praskovia's birth.
2. Details on the family are from RGIA, f. 1088, op. 1, d. 105; op. 3, d. 1549.
3. *PIS,* 44–45.
4. Ibid., 44; RGIA, f. 1088, op. 17, d. 73, l. 4.
5. *Kuskovo i ego okrestnosti,* 62–65.

CHAPTER 3. GRAND TOUR

1. Details on the men's travels are from *AKK,* bk. 5, 333–425; bk. 6, 205–443.
2. D. N. Sheremetev, *Opis' biblioteki,* 245, 246; *Odna iz domashnikh bibliotek,* 13.
3. *AKK,* bk. 6, 338.
4. Ibid., 339.
5. Thomas, *Aesthetics,* 225.
6. *Dissertation sur le drame lyrique* (The Hague and Paris, 1775 [1776]), 37. Cited in Charlton, *Grétry,* 140.
7. Charlton, *Grétry,* 56–57, 62; Mooser, *L'Opéra-comique,* 60–61, 134–35.
8. Quoted in Thomas, *Aesthetics,* 228.
9. *AKK,* bk. 6, 402, 452.
10. *O18v,* 7:24–31.
11. Corberon, *Diplomat français,* 1:271–72, 275.

12. Dr. Andrean Frese, "Description des maladies de Son Excellence Monsieur le Comte," OIRK GE, ll. 3–40b.
13. RGIA, f. 1088, op. 1, d. 69, ll. 42–43ob.
14. *AKK*, bk. 7, 287–89; N. P. Sheremetev, "Zametki," 678.

CHAPTER 4. THE BIG HOUSE

1. NA MMUO, No. st. inv. 364, ll. 5–6.
2. RGIA, f. 1088, op. 1, d. 70, ll. 2–20b.
3. RGIA, f. 1088, op. 17, d. 69, ll. 219–33; *O18v*, 6:3.
4. *O18v*, 6:124–26.
5. RGADA, f. 1287, op. 1, d. 4853, l. 4.
6. D. N. Sheremetev, *Opis' biblioteki*, n.p.
7. OR RGB, f. 54, d. 4.8, ll. 34–34ob; RGADA, f. 1287, op. 1, d. 4853, ll. 3–4.
8. RGADA, f. 1287, op. 1, d. 4851, ll. 6–60b; *TIS*, 2–3.
9. RGADA, f. 1287, op. 1, d. 4853, ll. 3–4.
10. RGIA, f. 1088, op. 1, d. 70, l. 2.

CHAPTER 5. FIRST MEETING

1. *PIS*, 51–52.
2. *Moskovskie vedomosti*, no. 34, 26 September 1785, 442; *Teatry*, 19.
3. RGIA, f. 1088, op. 1, d. 72, ll. 20b–30b.
4. RGIA, f. 1088, op. 1, d. 70, ll. 2–20b.
5. *Repertuar*, 19.
6. Prokopenko, "Istoriia sozdaniia," 60.

CHAPTER 6. PRASKOVIA'S DEBUT

1. *Repertuar*, 21–22.
2. Marinchik, *Nedopetaia pesnia*, 51–52.
3. Ibid., 48–49; Voroblevskii, *Opyt druzhby*, title page.
4. RGIA, f. 1088, op. 1, d. 72, l. 30b.

CHAPTER 7. EARLY SUCCESS

1. Kuz'min, "Krepostnoi literatur," 152; *Teatry*, 118.
2. [Sédaine], *Begloi soldat*.
3. Ibid., act 3, scene 10; Elizarova, *Krepostnaia aktrisa*, 15–16.
4. Kolychev, *Tshchetnaia revnost'*, 5.
5. Ibid., act 1, scene 3.
6. *AKV*, bk. 11, 37; RGADA, f. 1287, op. 1, d. 4855, ll. 3–30b; d. 4811, l. 229; d. 4720, ch. IV, ll. 18–190b.

7. RGIA, f. 1088, op. 1, d. 876, ll. 10b–2.
8. NA MMUO, No. st. inv. 364, l. 45.
9. *Repertuar*, 156; *TIS*, 23–24; RGIA, f. 1088, op. 1, d. 759, l. 51; RGADA, f. 1287, op. 1, d. 4811, l. 166; d. 4720, ch. IV, ll. 18–190b.
10. [Malzeville], *Loretta*, scenes 5–6.
11. Ibid., scene 11.
12. Ibid., scenes 13–15.
13. *O18v*, 6:43, 48–49, 62.
14. Ibid., 87.
15. Ibid., 39.

CHAPTER 8. SERF DIVA, SERF MISTRESS

1. RGIA, f. 1088, op. 1, d. 72, ll. 4–50b.
2. RGIA, f. 1088, op. 1, d. 72, l. 8.
3. RGADA, f. 1287, op. 1, d. 4827, ll. 15–16.
4. RGIA, f. 1088, op. 1, d. 70, ll. 2–20b.
5. *Razluka*, act 1, scene 1.
6. RGADA, f. 1287, op. 1, d. 4855, ll. 7–8.
7. Dr. Andrean Frese, "Description des maladies," OIRK GE, l. 40b.
8. I wish to thank Dr. Thomas Pozefsky, M.D., of Johns Hopkins University for reviewing Dr. Frese's detailed descriptions of Nicholas's health problems and treatments and for offering his best opinion of Nicholas's physical condition.
9. *Teatry*, 391–478; NA MMUO, No. st. inv. 364, l. 49.
10. *Teatry*, 407.
11. Ibid., 408.
12. Ibid., 397.
13. KR RIII, f. 2, op. 1, d. 787; d. 1284.
14. KR RIII, f. 2, op. 1, d. 831; d. 832, ll. 580b–640b, 68; *Teatry*, 407.
15. OIRK GE, ERD-R, No. 315, ll. 5–50b, 70b, 8.
16. RGADA, f. 1287, op. 1, d. 4812, ll. 113–15.
17. RGIA, f. 1088, op. 1, d. 69, ll. 390b–40.
18. RGIA, f. 1088, op. 1, d. 69, ll. 40–400b.
19. RGADA, f. 1287, op. 1, d. 4811, l. 172; *O18v*, 2:11.
20. RGIA, f. 1088, op. 1, d. 70, l. 80b.

CHAPTER 9. ENTERTAINING CATHERINE

1. RGADA, f. 1287, op. 1, d. 4812, l. 1620b.
2. *Teatry*, 425, 428.
3. *Repertuar*, 28, 32.
4. The events of the day are described in *KfZh*, 1787, 637–40; NA MMUO, No. st. inv. 328, ll. 19–20; *Moskovskie vedomosti*, 30 June; 2, 3, 7 July 1787; Komarovskii, *Zapiski*, 14.

5. On the theater, ARO GTsTM, f. 486, L/620, Opis' selu Kuskovu, ll. 3, 11–12.

6. RGIA, f. 1088, op. 17, d. 186, ll. 1–10b.

7. Rosoi, *Braki*, act 2, scenes 1–3; Charlton, *Grétry*, 143.

8. Starikova, *Teatral'naia zhizn'*, 225.

9. RGADA, f. 1287, op. 1, d. 4812, l. 14; *TIS*, 2.

10. Ségur, *Memoirs*, 2:189–90. Ségur is mistaken about the composer and librettist.

11. Ibid., 189–90.

12. *KfZh*, 1787, 643, and Prilozhenie, 66–67; RGADA, f. 10, op. 3, d. 263, l. 36; Khrapovitskii, *Zapiski*, 33.

13. *Teatry*, 445.

CHAPTER 10. THE SHEREMETEVS AND THEIR SERFS

1. OR RGB, f. 54, d. 4.8, l. 34.

2. RGIA, f. 1088, op. 1, d. 309, l. 16.

3. Dmitrieva, *Zhizn'*, 23–24.

4. Shchepetov, *Iz zhizni*, 12–13; Hartley, *Social History*, 9, 18–26, 39–40; Blum, *Lord*, 367–68; Kolchin, *Unfree Labor*, 52, 54. The number of serfs owned by the Sheremetevs is not known precisely, and some sources give a much higher number, but this figure is the most accurate.

5. Lepskaia, "Krepostnye shkoly," 88.

6. Mikhnevich, *Russkaia zhenshchina*, 397.

7. Staniukovich, *Biudzhet*, 11–13; Shchepetov, *Krepostnoe pravo*, 85.

8. Shchepetov, *Krepostnoe pravo*, 109. And see Iatsevich, *Krepostnye*, 26.

9. Iatsevich, *Krepostnye*, 24.

10. Ibid., 24–25.

11. Blum, *Lord*, 456.

12. Kolchin, *Unfree Labor*, 354–55.

CHAPTER 11. THE OLD COUNT'S DEATH

1. *O18v*, 8:19–41.

2. OR RGB, f. 54, d. 4.8, l. 34; RGADA, f. 1287, op. 1, d. 4786, ll. 1–20b.

3. RGADA, f. 1287, op. 1, d. 4812, ll. 184, 190, 196.

4. *O18v*, 9:21.

5. *O18v*, vol. 9; 11:219–21.

6. *O18v*, 2:10; Staniukovich, *Domashnii*, 33.

7. RGIA, f. 1088, op. 17, d. 69, ll. 204–10.

8. *PIS*, 77.

9. S. D. Sheremetev, *Kuskovo*, 29–40.

10. RGADA, f. 1287, op. 1, d. 4856, l. 60b.

11. *Razluka,* act 1, scene 1.
12. RGADA, f. 1287, op. 1, d. 4812, ll. 16, 76.

INTERLUDE I. SERF THEATER

1. Roosevelt, "Emerald Thrones," 7.
2. Kashin, *Teatr,* 61.
3. Senelick, *Serf Actor,* 38.
4. Ibid., 33–35.
5. Afanas'ev, "Vospominaniia," 41–42.
6. Roosevelt, "Emerald Thrones," 7.
7. Plavil'shchikov, *Sochineniia,* pt. 4, 32.
8. Molebnov, *Penzenskii teatr,* 20.
9. Beskin, *Krepostnoi teatr,* 6–7.
10. Bestuzhev, *Krepostnoi teatr,* 46–47.
11. Passenans, *Russie,* 91–92.
12. Sakulin, "Krepostnaia intelligentsiia," 88; Leskov, "Tupeinyi khudozhnik"; Molebnov, *Penzenskii teatr,* 10–11; Senelick, *Serf Actor,* 38.
13. Bestuzhev, *Krepostnoi teatr,* 42–44.
14. Sakulin, "Krepostnaia intelligentsiia," 79–80.
15. Malnick, "Russian Serf Theater," 409.
16. Senelick, "Erotic Bondage of Serf Theater."
17. Beskin, *Krepostnoi teatr,* 5–6, 22.
18. Kashin, *Teatr,* 16–17.
19. Shalikov, *Puteshestvie,* 74–85; Bestuzhev, *Krepostnoi teatr,* 33–35.
20. Rosslyn, "Female Employees"; idem, "Petersburg Actresses."
21. Senelick, *Serf Actor,* xiii–xv, 4, 249.
22. Sholok, *Ostankino,* 751.

CHAPTER 12. "I INTEND TO BUILD . . ."

1. RGIA, f. 1088, op. 3, d. 136, l. 250b.
2. Lepskaia, "Ostankinskii teatr," 69–70; Vdovin, ed., *Graf Nikolai,* 227–48.
3. L. I. Prokopenko, "Istoriia sozdaniia," 70.
4. NA MMUO, No. st. inv. 131, l. 20b.
5. Dolgorukov, *Kapishche,* 178–79; idem, *Povest',* 191–93. This citation combines two versions of the same event.
6. RGADA, f. 1287, op. 1, d. 4851, ll. 1, 70b.
7. RGIA, f. 1088, op. 1, d. 84, ll. 140b–18.
8. P. S. Sheremetev, *Vasilii,* 28–29.
9. RGIA, f. 1088, op. 1, d. 84, l. 19.
10. Deviatova, "Dlia kogo dekol'te," 102n1.

11. *Teatry,* 469.
12. Ibid., 470.

CHAPTER 13. FAREWELL TO KUSKOVO

1. Tumanskii, "Opisanie," 506.
2. Ibid.
3. Ibid., 512.
4. N. P. Sheremetev, "Pis'ma," *RA* 1 (1899): 391–94.
5. Ibid., 394. On Praskovia's handwriting, 394n2; and idem, "Zametki," 676–78.
6. RGIA, f. 1088, op. 3, d. 141, ll. 650b–67.
7. RGIA, f. 1088, op. 1, d. 86, ll. 130b–14, 230b–24.
8. RGIA, f. 1088, op. 1, d. 86, ll. 210b–23.
9. RGIA, f. 1088, op. 12, d. 80, ll. 1–20b, 8–90b, 10–110b, 13–130b.
10. RGIA, f. 1088, op. 1, d. 86, ll. 80–800b.
11. RGIA, f. 1088, op. 3, d. 141.
12. RGIA, f. 1088, op. 3, d. 141, ll. 60–630b, 870b–91.
13. RGIA, f. 1088, op. 3, d. 141, ll. 870b–91.
14. Shchepetov, *Selo Ostankino,* 33.
15. RGIA, f. 1088, op. 1, d. 87, ll. 290b–300b.
16. RGIA, f. 1088, op. 12, d. 82, ll. 4–40b.

CHAPTER 14. OSTANKINO'S PREMIER

1. Room inventories: NA MMUO, No. st. inv. 60 and 279.
2. RGIA, f. 1088, op. 3, d. 150, ll. 370b, 72, 750b, 2060b–07.
3. RGIA, f. 1088, op. 3, d. 150, ll. 910b–92.
4. RGADA, f. 1287, op.1, d. 4824, l. 11.
5. Shchepetov, *Selo Ostankino,* 37.
6. Reinbeck, *Travels,* 103–05.
7. *O18v,* 4:84–85.
8. OPI GIM, f. 56, d. 167, l. 20.
9. *AKV,* bk. 9, 336.
10. RGIA, f. 1088, op. 3, d. 150, ll. 1470b–1480b.
11. RGIA, f. 1088, op. 1, d. 159, ll. 2, 17–170b.
12. RGIA, f. 1088, op. 1, d. 304, ll. 12–13.

CHAPTER 15. TRAINING THE TROUPE

1. *Teatry,* 260; RGIA, f. 1088, op. 9, d. 1900.
2. RGIA, f. 1088, op. 3, d. 150, l. 40.
3. RGIA, f. 1088, op. 1, d. 85, ll. 260b–27.

4. *Teatry*, 285.

5. RGIA, f. 1088, op. 3, d. 165, l. 37.

6. *Teatry*, 275–76.

7. Ibid., 291.

8. Ibid., 274–75.

9. Ibid., 282.

10. RGIA, f. 1088, op. 3, d. 164, l. 54.

CHAPTER 16. LIFE IN THE TROUPE

1. *Teatry*, 313.

2. Ibid., 323.

3. Ibid., 317. A zolotnik is approximately 4.25 grams or .15 ounces.

4. OIRK GE, No. 969, ll. 410b–430b.

5. *SO, 1801*, 46, 48; *Teatry*, 319, 327; RGIA, f. 1088, op. 3, d, 150, ll. 1600b–610b, 1620b–640b, 2390b; NA MMUO, No. st. inv. 131, ll. 3, 4.

6. RGIA, f. 1088, op. 3, d. 141, ll. 50–51.

7. RGIA, f. 1088, op. 3, d. 164, l. 54.

CHAPTER 17. TO ST. PETERSBURG

1. RGIA, f. 1088, op. 1, d. 69, l. 380b.

2. On Taniusha, RGIA, f. 1088, op. 3, d. 1602.

3. Golovine, *Memoirs*, 107–08.

4. RGIA, f. 1088, op. 2, d. 891, ll. 10b–2.

5. RGADA, f. 1287, op. 1, d. 6482, ch. 2, ll. 9180b, 9490b, 995, 1049, 1090; *O18v*, 11:49.

6. Report of Charles Whitworth to Lord Grenville, 5 December 1796 (n.s.), NA, FO 65/35, No. 62 (unfoliated); RGADA, f. 1287, op. 1, d. 4813, l. 4; Shil'der, *Imperator Pavel*, 281.

CHAPTER 18. TSAR PAUL

1. Czartoryski, *Memuary*, 1:119; Charles Whitworth to Lord Grenville, NA, FO 65/35, No. 57 (unfoliated), 18 November 1796 (n.s.).

2. Prilozheniia k *KfZh, 1796*; *Zimnyi dvorets*, 229–31; *O18v*, 11:110–11; N. P. Sheremetev, "Iz bumag i perepiski," 309, 311, 316.

3. RGIA, f. 1088, op. 1, d. 117, ll. 23–230b.

4. N. P. Sheremetev, "Iz bumag i perepiski," 312.

5. RGIA, f. 1088, op. 3, d. 160, ll. 43–46, 102–030b, 1120b–140b, 132–390b.

6. Pribavleniia, *Moskovskie vedomosti*, 8 April 1797, 1–12.

7. *O18v*, 4:13–14.

8. Stanislas II, *Memoires secrets*, 121–24.

9. K. L. Blum, *Ein russischer Staatsmann*, 4:320–21.

10. RGADA, f. 1287, op. 1, d. 6483, ll. 81, 87.
11. RGIA, f. 1088, op. 12, d. 86, ll. 1–180b.
12. RGIA, f. 1088, op. 1, d. 196, ll. 9–100b.
13. RGIA, f. 1088, op. 1, d. 53, l. 6.
14. RGIA, f. 1088, op. 1, d. 117, ll. 33–360b. The last sentences of the second and third paragraphs of Nicholas's "Note" are approximations. The handwriting in these places is too illegible to decipher with complete accuracy. *Les mouches cantarides* refer to Spanish fly. Cantaridin is the active ingredient in the crushed blister beetle.
15. RGIA, f. 1088, op. 1, d. 277, l. 60b.

INTERLUDE II. SERF ACTRESS STORIES

1. Gertsen, "Soroka-vorovka"; Shchepkin, *Zapiski,* 370–71; Grits, "K istorii," 655–59.
2. Iushkov, *K istorii,* 6–19.

CHAPTER 19. FREEDOM

1. Georgel, *Voyage,* 368–69.
2. N. P. Sheremetev, "Iz bumag i perepiski," 322; RGIA, f. 1088, op. 1, d. 53, ll. 15–150b.
3. *TIS,* 22–25, 28, 39.
4. RGIA, f. 1088, op. 1, d. 92, l. 120b.
5. RGIA, f. 1088, op. 1, d. 79, ll. 3–8. I would like to thank Sofiya Yuzefpolskaya for this English translation.
6. RGIA, f. 1088, op. 1, d. 96, ll. 30–300b.
7. RGIA, f. 1088, op. 1, d. 5, ll. 1–10b; d. 202, ll. 5, 7; NA MMUO, No. st. inv. 131, l. 100b.
8. RGIA, f. 1088, op. 1, d. 245, ll. 40b–5.
9. RGIA, f. 1088, op. 3, d. 1549, ll. 500b–51.

CHAPTER 20. THE CURTAIN FALLS

1. P. S. Sheremetev, *Vasilii,* 128–29.
2. The letters between Peter and his father are in RGVIA, f. 53, op. 1, sviazka 149, d. 14; and RGADA, f. 11, d. 1311, ll. 1–6; Vasil'chikov, *Semeistvo,* 2:118–20.
3. RGVIA, f. 53, op. 1, sviazka 149, ll. 300b, 390b, 430b.
4. RGVIA, f. 1088, op. 1, d. 241, ll. 7–80b.
5. RGIA, f. 1088, op. 3, d. 172, l. 25.
6. *O18v,* 11:240–41.
7. RGIA, f. 1088, op. 17, d. 527, l. 6
8. RGADA, f. 1287, op. 1, d. 4813, ll. 40b–5; Shil'der, *Imperator Pavel,* 337–38.
9. Czartoryski, *Memuary,* 160.
10. NA, Foreign Office, Russia, FO 65/46, ff. 225–225v.

CHAPTER 21. THE SPECTER OF DEATH

1. RGADA, f. 1287, op. 1, d. 4851, ll. 50b–6; N. P. Sheremetev, "Iz bumag i perepiski," 503; idem, "Pis'mo," 326.
2. Author conversation with Nikita Cheremeteff. Bridgeport, Connecticut, 6 December 2004.
3. N. P. Sheremetev, "Pis'mo," 326–27; idem, "Dopolneniia," 526–27.
4. RGADA, f. 1287, op. 1, d. 4851, ll. 5–60b; N. P. Sheremetev, "Iz bumag i perepiski," 503.
5. RGIA, f. 1088, op. 1, d. 97, ll. 120b–13, 150b, 22–230b.
6. *SO, 1801*, 9, 11, 40–43.
7. RGIA, f. 1088, op. 3, d. 192, l. 4.
8. RGIA, f. 1088, op. 1, d. 68, ll. 7–70b.

CHAPTER 22. CORONATION

1. *SO, 1801*, 53–64.
2. RGIA, f. 1088, op. 9, d. 2725; S. D. Sheremetev, *Vozdvizhenskii dom.*
3. *SO, 1801*, 38, 70
4. Nikolai Mikhailovich, *Imperatritsa Elizaveta*, 51–52.
5. Paget, *Papers*, 2:19–20.
6. Vigel, *Zapiski*, pt. 7, 193; Komarovskii, *Zapiski*, 75.

CHAPTER 23. THE WEDDING

1. *SO, 1801*, 79.
2. RGIA, f. 1088, op. 3, d. 169, l. 17.
3. RGIA, f. 1088, op. 1, d. 96, ll. 300b–31; d. 241, ll. 11–120b, 13–16; RGADA, f. 1263, op. 1, d. 2887, ll. 3–4.
4. On the Batoni affair, RGADA, f. 1263, op. 1, d. 2887, ll. 1–2, 3–4, 5; d. 2918, ll. 4–40b; d. 5184, l. 1; RGVIA, f. 53, op. 1 sviazka 149, d. 19, ll. 17–18.
5. RGVIA, f. 53, op. 1 sviazka 149, d. 10, ll. 3–4; d. 19, ll. 17–18; *Moskovskie vedomosti*, 27 February 1801, 407, 417; repeated on 2 March, p. 450.
6. On the tangled history of Praskovia's bogus genealogy and the attempt to acquire proof of Polish noble status, RGIA, f. 1088, op. 1, d. 71, ll. 18–180b; op. 3, d. 605, ll. 11–120b; d. 54, ll. 25–250b; d. 159, ll. 62–630b; d. 1549, ll. 1–76; d. 1563, ll. 1–210b; RGADA, f. 180 Kantseliariia MGAMID, op. 1, d. 79, ll. 29–300b.
7. RGIA, f. 1088, op. 3, d. 1549, ll. 62–620b; d. 1563, ll. 18–180b.
8. RGIA, f. 1088, op. 3, d. 54, ll. 25–250b.
9. RGIA, f. 1088, op. 1, d. 99, ll. 410b–42; op. 3, d. 98, ll. 200b–22.
10. Goldoni, *Dobraia devka*, act 1, scene 4.
11. Ibid., act 1, scene 9. Ellipsis in original.
12. Ibid., act 2, scenes 8, 11.

13. Glagoleva, "Illegitimate Children;" Savelov, *Lektsii,* 90–93. I am most grateful to Professor Olga Glagoleva for generously sharing her knowledge of these matters with me.
14. RGIA, f. 1088, op. 3, d. 1549, l. 6(b)ob.
15. OIRK GE, ERD-R, No. 310, ll. 1–4; No. 311, ll. 1–8; OPI GIM, f. 56, d. 173, ll. 3–4; RGIA, f. 797, op. 84, d. 203, ll. 1–5.
16. TsIAM, f. 203, op. 745, d. 130, ll. 115, 1190b.
17. RGIA, f. 1088, op. 1, d. 64, ll. 1–20b.
18. RGIA, f. 1088, op. 1, d. 65, ll. 1–4.
19. RGIA, f. 1088, op. 1, d. 65, l. 4.
20. OPI GIM, f. 56, d. 173, ll. 3–4; RGADA, f. 1287, op. 1, d. 4815, l. 24a.

CHAPTER 24. NEWLYWEDS

1. *SO, 1801,* 83, 86–96.
2. OIRK GE, ERD-R, No. 310, ll. 1–3.
3. RGADA, f. 1287, op. 1, d. 4820, ll. 116–17.
4. OIRK GE, ERD-R, No. 970, l. 340b; *SO, 1802,* 16.
5. RGIA, f. 1088, op. 1, d. 98, ll. 220b–270b; RGADA, f. 1287, op. 1, d. 4837, l. 8; *SO, 1802,* 62–63.
6. RGIA, f. 1088, op. 1, d. 99, ll. 7–70b; d. 230, ll. 6–60b.
7. RGIA, f. 1088, op. 3, d. 98, ll. 23–230b, 28–30.
8. RGIA, f. 1088, op. 1, d. 244, ll. 2–3.
9. RGIA, f. 1088, op. 3, d. 54, l. 2.
10. RGIA, f. 1088, op. 3, d. 54, ll. 4–60b.
11. RGIA, f. 1088, op. 3, d. 54, ll. 7–110b.
12. OIRK GE, ERD-R, No. 970, ll. 1580b–159, 164, 210.
13. RGIA, f. 1088, op. 3, d. 1314, ll. 56–79; OIRK GE, ERD-R, No. 312, l. 7; No. 970, l. 20; RGADA, f. 1287, op. 1, d. 4820, ll. 121–2.
14. RGADA, f. 1287, op. 1, d. 4820, ll. 110, 111, 121. On Anna Yakimova: RGIA, f. 1088, op. 3, d. 185, l. 1.
15. RGIA, f. 1088, op. 3, d. 1549, l. 49; d. 1614, ll. 5–6.
16. RGIA, f. 1088, op. 1, d. 99, ll. 420b–430b, 70–71, 71–72, 79–80; op. 3, d. 605.
17. RGIA, f. 1088, op. 1, d. 99, ll. 27–28; d. 101, l. 6; d. 245, l. 174.
18. RGIA, f. 1088, op. 1, d. 99, l. 59.
19. RGIA, f. 1088, op. 12, d. 115, ll. 107–08.

CHAPTER 25. DMITRY'S BIRTH

1. N. P. Sheremetev, "Iz bumag i perepiski," 473.
2. RGIA, f. 1088, op. 3, d. 1314, ll. 40b–5, 10–11, 210b–28.
3. RGIA, f. 1088, op. 1, d. 295, l. 39.
4. RGIA, f. 1088, op. 3, d. 1549, ll. 46–470b.
5. RGIA, f. 1088, op. 3, d. 1563, ll. 1–40b.

6. RGIA, f. 1088, op. 3, d. 1563, ll. 5–6.

7. RGIA, f. 1088, op. 3, d. 1563, ll. 9–12.

8. RGIA, f. 1088, op. 1, d. 103, ll. 200b–21.

9. RGIA, f. 1088, op. 1, d. 72, ll. 7–70b.

10. *SO, 1803,* 103.

11. *PIS,* 84.

12. RGIA, f. 1088, op. 1, d. 102, ll. 20–24; op. 3, d. 604, ll. 14–150b.

CHAPTER 26. SECRETS REVEALED

1. RGIA, f. 1088, op. 1, d. 68, l. 50b.

2. RGIA, f. 1088, op. 1, d. 120, ll. 7–70b; op. 3, d. 1828.

3. RGIA, f. 1088, op. 3, d. 1828, ll. 1–4; d. 217, l. 46.

4. OIRK GE, No. 971, ll. 110b, 440b, 46; RGIA, f. 1088, op. 1, d. 104, ll. 34–360b; op. 3, d. 217, l. 770b.

5. *SO, 1803,* 26–27.

6. RGIA, f. 1088, op. 1, d. 68, ll. 50b–6.

7. RGIA, f. 1088, op. 1, d. 68, ll. 6, 70b.

8. RGIA, f. 938, op. 1, d. 247, ll. 3–30b. Draft: f. 1088, op. 1, d. 66, ll. 2–20b.

9. N. P. Sheremetev, "Iz bumag i perepiski," 474.

10. RGIA, f. 1088, op. 1, d. 115, ll. 260b–28.

CHAPTER 27. DEATH

1. Rakina, "Nikolai Argunov," 62n122. I would like to thank Varvara Rakina for sharing her knowledge of and insight into Praskovia's life and death.

2. RGIA, f. 1088, op. 1, d. 68, ll. 70b–8; *SO, 1803,* 103, 105.

3. RGIA, f. 1088, op. 1, d. 70, ll. 40b–5; d. 79, ll. 2a/ob–2b; d. 72, ll. 130b–14; op. 3, d. 1314, l. 58.

4. RGIA, f. 1088, op. 1, d. 66, l. 3; op. 17, d. 544, l. 3.

5. RGIA, f. 1088, op. 1, d. 102, ll. 10–100b, 62.

6. RGIA, f. 1088, op. 1, d. 66, ll. 5–90b.

7. RGIA, f. 1088, op. 3, d. 217, ll. 27–28; d. 1549; *SO, 1803,* 32.

8. RGIA, f. 1088, op. 1, d. 67, ll. 34–39; op. 3, d. 217, ll. 31–32; *SO, 1803,* 32–34.

9. RGIA, f. 1088, op. 1, d. 242, ll. 1–3; d. 243, l. 3.

10. On Praskovia's burial, RGIA, f. 1088, op. 1, d. 70, ll. 60b–8; d. 72, ll. 11–20; d. 77, ll. 8–110b.

11. N. P. Sheremetev, "Iz bumag i perepiski," 509.

CHAPTER 28. SCANDAL

1. RGIA, f. 1088, op. 1, d. 66, ll. 4–70b.

2. RGIA, f. 1088, op. 1, d. 66, l. 90b; RGADA, f. 1287, op. 2, d. 3879, l. 2.

3. RGIA, f. 1088, op. 1, d. 76, ll. 11–12.
4. RGIA, f. 1088, op. 1, d. 76, l. 11–110b; d. 67, ll. 220b–23.
5. RGIA, f. 1088, op. 1, d. 67, ll. 7–16; RGADA, f. 1287, op. 2, d. 3879, l. 2; *SO, 1803,* 38.
6. RGIA, f. 1088, op. 1, d. 76, ll. 24–250b.
7. RGIA, f. 1088, op. 1, d. 103, l. 350b.
8. RGIA, f. 1088, op. 1, d. 115, ll. 31–320b.
9. Daudet, "Une vie," 180.
10. RGADA, f. 1287, op. 1, d. 3041, ll. 2–30b.
11. For one indirect reaction, see *AKV,* bk. 17, 61–62.
12. Leskov, "Zakhudalyi rod," 112–13.

CHAPTER 29. SAINT PRASKOVIA

1. RGIA, f. 1088, op. 1, d. 103, ll. 370b–39.
2. RGIA, f. 1088, op. 1, d. 115, ll. 290b–30.
3. RGIA, f. 1088, op. 1, d. 102, ll. 130b–140b, 170b–180b, 26–34, 59, 71.
4. RGIA, f. 1088, op. 1, d. 103, ll. 660b–77.
5. Derzhavin, *Sochineniia,* 2:451–56.
6. Bulgakov, "Iz pisem," 223.
7. RGIA, f. 1088, op. 1, d. 76, ll. 7–80b.
8. OIRK GE, No. 971, ll. 440b–450b.
9. *SO, 1803,* 59; N. P. Sheremetev, "Iz bumag i perepiski," 508; Staniukovich, *Fontannyi dom,* 21.
10. Lansere, "Fontannyi dom," 79.
11. *O18v,* 2:12.
12. RGIA, f. 1088, op. 1, d. 73, ll. 50b–6; *SO, 1803,* 100–02.
13. RGADA, f. 1287, op. 1, d. 6484, ll. 61–610b, 80, 830b, 174.
14. RGIA, f. 1088, op. 3, d. 1314, ll. 11, 570b–76; author interview with Varvara Rakina at Ostankino Museum, 3 April 2003.
15. RGIA, f. 1088, op. 1, d. 295, ll. 40–400b.
16. P. S. Sheremetev, *Vasilii,* 166–67.
17. RGIA, f. 1088, op. 1, d. 326, ll. 2–30b.
18. RGIA, f. 1088, op. 1, d. 103, l. 49–490b.
19. RGIA, f. 1088, op. 1, d. 73, ll. 5–50b; d. 120, ll. 12, 13; N. P. Sheremetev, "Iz bumag i perepiski," 504.
20. Springis, "Usad'ba," 231, 233.
21. RGIA, f. 1088, op. 3, d. 1549, ll. 99–1000b, 103–05.
22. RGADA, f. 1287, op. 1, d. 6484, ll. 17, 19–190b, 46, 54.
23. RGIA, f. 1088, op. 3, d. 1546, l. 3; d. 1549, ll. 101–010b.
24. RGIA, f. 1088, op. 1, 102, ll. 77–770b.

CHAPTER 30. PUTRID BONES

1. OIRK GE, No. 971, l. 490b; RGIA, f. 1088, op. 1, d. 325, ll. 1–2, 5–100b; d. 68, ll. 60b, 8–80b; d. 876, ll. 2, 3–60b.
2. N. P. Sheremetev, "Iz bumag i perepiski," 497.
3. RGIA, f. 1088, op. 1, d. 277, ll. 42–43, 48–49; d. 324, ll. 10, 12, 13; d. 105, ll. 35–360b, 50–51; op. 1, d. 238, ll. 39–40.
4. P. S. Sheremetev, *Vasilii,* 176–81; RGIA, f. 1088, op. 1, d. 295, l. 74; RGADA, f. 1287, op. 1, d. 4837, ll. 139–40; d. 4815, ll. 21–210b.
5. RGIA, f. 1088, op. 1, d. 277, ll. 37–370b.
6. RGIA, f. 1088, op. 1, d. 104, ll. 100b–11, 51–520b.
7. RGIA, f. 1088, op. 1, d. 325, ll. 12–71.
8. RGIA, f. 1088, op. 3, d. 55, ll. 68–72.
9. *O18v,* 11:20; RGADA, f. 1287, op. 1, d. 4815, ll. 57–61, 64.
10. *O18v,* 2:title page.
11. Bogoliubov, "Pis'ma," 303; RGADA, f. 1287, op. 1, d. 4815, l. 69.

CHAPTER 31. FATHERLY ADVICE

1. All quotations from RGIA, f. 1088, op. 1, d. 69, ll. 1–12, 36–510b; d. 72, ll. 1–10.

CHAPTER 32. SEPARATE FATES

1. Reinbeck, *Travels,* 105.
2. RGADA, f. 1287, op. 1, d. 6485; RGIA, f. 1088, op. 3, d. 1614, ll. 2–20b, 70b, 18–20.
3. RGIA, f. 1088, op. 1, d. 71, ll. 6–100b, 18; d. 113, ll. 130b–14; op. 3, d. 1614, ll. 7–70b, 8, 9.
4. RGIA, f. 1088, op. 1, d. 71, ll. 18–180b; d. 104, ll. 17–18, 460b–49, 100; d. 110, l. 30.
5. RGIA, f. 1088, op. 3, d. 1602.
6. RGIA, f. 1088, op. 1, d. 241, ll. 23–240b; d. 245, ll. 79–790b, 1000b, 105, 108, 144–46; RGADA, f. 1203, op. 1, Viazka 273, d. 183, l. 130b; d. 187, ll. 1–120b; Viazka 274, d. 58, l. 4; d. 69, l. 1; Viazka 278, d. 63, ll. 1–2; Viazka 280, d. 38, l. 30b; d. 172, ll. 50b–6; d. 181, l. 2; GARF, f. 98, op. 1, d. 11, ll. 9–11; d. 15, ll. 1a–2; GAVO, f. 578, op. 1, d. 78, ll. 1–19; Vasil'chikov, *Semeistvo,* 2:123–25, 140; *AKV,* bk. 14, 189–90; "Vyderzhki iz staroi zapisnoi knizhki," 452–53; *Russkii biograficheskii slovar',* s.v. "K. A. Razumovskii"; Gernet, *Istoriia,* 52–54, 280–86.
7. *AKV,* bk. 38, 428–29; *Russkii biograficheskii slovar',* s.v. "P. A. Razumovskii."
8. RGIA, f. 1088, op. 1, d. 780, ll. 24–250b, 30–330b, 75.
9. S. D. Sheremetev, *Vospominaniia detstva,* 45.
10. RGADA, f. 1287, op. 1, d. 4851, l. 80b.
11. S. D. Sheremetev, *Graf Dmitrii,* 6–7, 10, 15; Alekseeva, ed., *Sheremetevy,* 159.
12. Sheremeteva, *Dnevnik,* 59, 86–87; Alekseeva, ed., *Sheremetevy,* 176.
13. *Memuary,* 180.
14. Pushkin, *Polnoe sobranie,* 3:404–05.

15. S. D. Sheremetev, *Ostankino,* 20–21.
16. Alekseeva, ed., *Sheremetevy,* 155.
17. Ibid., 151–52.

CODA

1. *Memuary,* 209.
2. Alekseeva, ed., *Sheremetevy,* 143.
3. Alekseeva, *Ostavit',* 190.
4. Alekseeva, ed., *Sheremetevy,* 143.

Bibliography

MANUSCRIPT SOURCES
Iaroslavl'

State Archive of Iaroslav Province

London

The National Archives

Moscow

A. A. Bakhrushin State Central Theater Museum, Library and Archive
Central Historical Archive of Moscow
Moscow Country Estate Museum Ostankino, Research Archive
Russian State Archive for Ancient Acts
Russian State Library, Manuscript Division
Russian State Military-Historical Archive
State Archive of the Russian Federation
State Historical Museum, Division of Printed Sources
State Museum of Ceramics and "The Kuskovo Estate of the Eighteenth Century," Library

Bibliography

St. Petersburg

Central Historical Archive of St. Petersburg
Russian Institute for the History of the Arts, Manuscript Division
Russian National Library, Manuscript Division
Russian State Historical Archive
State Hermitage Museum, Division of the History of Russian Culture

Vladimir

State Archive of Vladimir Province

NEWSPAPERS

Moskovskie vedomosti
Sanktpeterburgskie vedomosti

PUBLISHED SOURCES

Adres Kalendar'. St. Petersburg, 1769–1809.
Afanas'ev, N. Ia. "Vospominaniia." *IV* 41 (1890): 23–48, 255–76.
Akhmatova, A. *Zapisnye knizhki Anny Akhmatovoi (1958–1966)*. Edited by
    K. N. Suvorova. Moscow, 1996.
———. *The Complete Poems of Anna Akhmatova*. Translated by Judith
    Hemschemeyer. Edited by Roberta Reeder. Boston, 1997.
———. *The Word That Causes Death's Defeat: Poems of Memory*. Translated by
    Nancy K. Anderson. New Haven, 2004.
Akimov, A. F. *Kuskovo*. Moscow, 1946.
Aksakov, Sergei. *A Russian Schoolboy*. Translated by J. D. Duff. Oxford, 1978.
*Akty uchrezhdeniia grafom N. P. Sheremetevym dvukh komandirstv v Rossiiskom
    Velikom Priorstve Ordena Sviatogo Ioanna Ierusalimskogo*. [St. Petersburg,
    1799].
Alekseeva, Adel'. *Dolgoe Ekho: N. P. Sheremetev i P. I. Zhemchugova*. Moscow,
    2000.
———. *Kolokol'nik: rasskaz ob aktrise russkogo krepostnogo teatra P. I. Kovalevoi-
    Zhemchugovoi*. Moscow, 1988.
———. *Kol'tso grafini Sheremetevoi*. Moscow, 1995.
———. *Ostavit' plamen' svoi*. Moscow, 1986.

Bibliography

———. "Sheremetevy." In *Moskva rodoslovnaia*. Moscow, 1998.

Alekseeva, Adel', and M. D. Kovaleva, eds. *Sheremetevy v sud'be Rossii: vospominaniia, dnevniki, pis'ma*. Moscow, 2001.

Alpatov, M. V., and V. A. Kulakov. *N. I. Argunov*. Moscow, 1976.

Andreev, A. Iu. *Russkie studenty v nemetskikh universitetakh XVIII–pervoi poloviny XIX veka*. Studia Historica. Moscow, 2005.

Anisimov, Iu., and G. Novitskii. *Ostankino*. Moscow, 1927.

[Anseaume, Louis]. *Zhivopisets, vliublennyi v svoiu model'*. Translated by V. G. Voroblevskii. [Moscow, 1779.]

Antonova, L. V. *Krepostnye talanty v usad'be Sheremetevykh*. Leningrad, 1964.

Arkhiv Kniazia Vorontsova. 40 vols. St. Petersburg, 1870–95.

Aseev, B. N. *Russkii dramaticheskii teatr ot ego istokov do kontsa XVIII veka*. Moscow, 1977.

Bantysh-Kamenskii, D. N. *Slovar' dostopamiatnykh liudei russkoi zemli*. 3 vols. Moscow, 1847.

Barsukov, A. P. *Rod Sheremetevykh*. 8 vols. St. Petersburg, 1881–1904.

Bashilova, M. P., and T. S. Sternina. *Ostankino*. Moscow, 1969.

Baturin, P. S. "Zapiski P. S. Baturina." *Golos minuvshego* 1/3 (1918): 45–78; 4/6 (1918): 173–210; 7/9 (1918): 99–132.

Baye, Joseph de. *Kouskovo: La Résidence d'un grand seigneur russe au Xviiie siècle*. Paris, 1905.

Beliakaeva-Kazanskaia, L. V. *Siluety muzykal'nogo Peterburga: Putevoditel' po muzykal'nym teatram, muzeiam, kontsertnym zalam proshlogo i nastoiashchego*. St. Petersburg, 2001.

Beskin, E. *Krepostnoi teatr*. Moscow-Leningrad, 1927.

Bestuzhev, K. *Krepostnoi teatr*. Moscow, 1913.

Bezsonov, P. *Praskov'ia Ivanovna Sheremeteva. Eia narodnaia pesnia i rodnoe eia Kuskovo*. Moscow, 1872.

Blagotvoritel'nomu vel'mozhe, uchrediteliu v Moskve doma dlia prizreniia bednykh i bol'nykh svoim izhdiveniem. St. Petersburg, 1803.

Bludova, A. D. "Vospominaniia." *RA* 1 (1889): 39–106.

Blum, Jerome. *Lord and Peasant in Russia: From the Ninth to the Nineteenth Century*. Princeton, 1961.

Blum, Karl Ludwig. *Ein russischer Staatsmann: Des grafen Jakob Johann Sievers Denkwürdigkeiten zur Geschichte Russlands*. 4 vols. Leipzig, 1857–58.

Bogoliubov, V. F. "Pis'ma V. F. Bogoliubova k kn. Kurakinu." *RA* 3 (1893): 303–04.

Borinevich, S. "Eshche dva slova ob Odesse v 30-kh godakh." In *Iz proshlogo Odessy: Sb. Statei*. Odessa, 1894.

Brodskii, B. *Svideteli strannogo veka*. Moscow, 1978.

Bulgakov, A. Ia. "Iz pisem A. Ia. Bulgakova k ego ottsu." *RA* 3 (1898): 223.

Cassiday, Julie A. "The Precious Pearl of Our Theater: The Early Nineteenth-Century Russian Actress as Public Woman." Unpublished paper, 2006.

Chaianova, O. E. *Teatr Maddoksa v Moskve, 1776–1805*. Moscow, 1927.

Charlton, David. *Grétry and the Growth of Opéra-Comique*. Cambridge, 1986.

Chebotarev, Kh. A. *Istoricheskoe i topograficheskoe opisanie gorodov Moskovskoi gubernii s ikh uezdami*. Moscow, 1787.

Chemerovtsev, Aleksei. "Krest'ianin vol'nodumets." *RS* 107 (1901): 284.

Chereiskii, L. A. *Pushkin i ego okruzhenie*. Leningrad, 1989.

Cherviakov, A. F. *Fans, from the 18th to the Beginning of the 20th Century: Collection of the Palace of Ostankino in Moscow*. Bournemouth, England, 1998.

———. *Ostankinskii Dvorets-Muzei: putevoditel'*. Moscow, 1985.

Corberon, Marie-Daniel Bourrée, Chevalier de. *Un Diplomat français à la cour de Catharine II 1775–1780. Journal intime*. Edited by L. H. Lablande. 2 vols. Paris, 1901.

Czartoryski, Prince Adam. *Memuary kniazia Adama Chartorizhskago i ego perepiska s Imperatorom Aleksandrom I*. Vol. 1. Moscow, 1912.

Daniel, Thomas A. *Captain of Death: The Story of Tuberculosis*. Rochester, N.Y., 1997.

Daudet, Ernest. "Une vie d'ambassadrice au siècle dernier: A la cour de Russie." *Revue des deux mondes* 13, series 5 (1 January 1903): 154–88.

Dediukhina, V. S. "Istoriia formirovaniia sela Ostankina." In *Problemy Istorii SSSR*. Moscow, 1979.

———. "K voprosu o roli krepostnykh masterov v istorii stroitelstva dvorianskoi usad'by XVIII v. (Na primere Kuskovo i Ostankino)." *Vestnik Moskovskogo Universiteta*, series 8 (Istoriia), no. 4 (1981): 83–94.

Demidov, N. A. *Zhurnal puteshestviia ego vysokorodiia . . . N. A. Demidova*. Moscow, 1786.

Demina, G. V. "Selo Kuskovo, gde boiarin zhil bol'shoi." In *Otechestvo: Kraevedcheskii al'manakh*. Moscow, 1994.

Dennison, Tracy K. "Did Serfdom Matter? Russian Rural Society, 1750–1860." *Historical Research* 79, no. 203 (February 2006): 74–91.

———. "Serfdom and Household Structure in Central Russia: Voshchazhnikovo, 1816–1858." *Continuity and Change* 18, no. 3 (2003): 395–429.

Derzhavin, G. R. *Sochineniia.* Edited by Ia. Grot. 2d ed. 7 vols. St. Petersburg, 1864–78.

Deviatova, S. "Dlia kogo dekol'te sheiu myt'? Kak razvivalas' gigiena v XVIII veke." *Rodina* 7 (2003): 101–02.

Dmitrieva, E. E., and O. N. Kuptsova. *Zhizn' usadebnogo mifa: utrachennyi i obretennyi rai.* Moscow, 2002.

Dmitrii, Saint, Metropolitan of Rostov. *Sochineniia Sviatogo Dmitriia, Mitropolita Rostovskogo.* Vol. 1. Moscow, 1842.

Dolgorukov, I. M. *Kapishche moego serdtsa ili slovar' vsekh tekh lits, s koimi ia byl v raznykh otnosheniiakh v techenie moei zhizni.* Edited by V. I. Korovin. Moscow, 1997.

———. *Povest' o rozhdenii moem, proiskhozhdenii i vsei zhizni.* Edited by A. Poliakov. Petrograd, 1916.

———. "Zhurnal puteshestviia iz Moskvy v Nizhnii 1813 goda." *Chentiia v obshchestve istorii i drevnostei rossiiskikh* 1, sect. 2 (1870): 1–122.

Dolgorukov, P. V. *Rossiiskaia rodoslovnaia kniga.* 4 vols. St. Petersburg, 1854–57.

Dormandy, Thomas. *The White Death: A History of Tuberculosis.* Washington Square, N.Y., 2000.

Duval, Alexandre. *A l'ombre de Prascovia, comtesse de Schérémetoff. Élégie.* Paris, 1804.

———. *Elegiia k teni grafini Praskov'i Ivanovny Sheremetevoi.* Translated by Iakov Bardovskii. Moscow, 1805.

"Dva Obeliska." *RA* 2 (1911): 109–12.

Dynik, Tat'iana. *Krepostnoi teatr.* Moscow, 1933.

Efremova, I. K., and A. F. Cherviakov. *Ostankino.* Moscow, 1960.

Elizarova, N. A. *Teatry Sheremetevykh.* Moscow, 1944.

———. *Krepostnaia aktrisa P. I. Kovaleva-Zhemchugova. (K osmotru vystavski muzeia), Ostankinskii dvorets-muzei.* Moscow, 1950.

———. *Ostankino.* Moscow, 1955.

———. *Ostankino, khudozhestvennye sokrovishcha dvortsov-muzeev.* Moscow, 1966.

Ertaulov, Gurii. "Vospominaniia o teatre grafa Kamenskogo v Orle." *Delo* 6 (1873): 184–219.

Evreinov, N. N. *Krepostnye aktery: Populiarnyi istoricheskii ocherk.* Leningrad, 1925.

Fadeev, A. M. "Vospominaniia." *RA* 3 (1891): 465–94.

Ferriéres, A. *Bashmaki mordore, ili nemetskaia bashmachnitsa, liricheskaia komediia v dvukh deistviiakh.* Translated by V. G. Voroblevskii. Moscow, 1779.

Findeizen, N. F. *Ocherki po istorii muzyki v Rossii s drevneishikh vremen do kontsa 18. v.* 2 vols. Moscow-Leningrad, 1928–29.

Fomichev, S. A., ed. *A. S. Griboedov v vospominaniiakh.* Moscow, 1929.

Framery, N., *Infanta Zamory, komediia v trekh deistviiakh s peniem.* Moscow, [1784].

Fubini, Enrico. *Music and Culture in Eighteenth-Century Europe: A Source Book.* Translated and edited by Bonnie J. Blackburn. Chicago, 1994.

Gakkel', E. V. "Krepostnaia intelligentsiia v Rossii vo vtoroi polovine XVIII–pervoi polovine XIX v." Dissertation [Kandidatskaia stepen'], Leningrad State University, 1953.

Garnovskii, I. A. "Krepostnoi teatr pomeshchika I. O. Khorvata." *Nasha starina* 4–5 (1916): 289–305.

Gavrilova, E. I. "Al'bom miniatiurista Deshatobura." In *Pamiatniki kul'tury. Novye otkrytiia. Pis'mennost', iskusstvo, arkheologiia. Ezhegodnik 2000.* (2001): 287–99.

Georgel, Jean François. *Voyage à Saint-Petersbourg en 1788–1800, fait avec l'ambassade des Chevaliers de l'ordre de St.-Jean de Jerusalem.* Paris, 1818.

Gernet, M. N. *Istoriia tsarskoi tiur'my.* Vol. 1. Moscow, 1960.

Gertsen, A. I. "Soroka-vorovka." In *Sobranie sochinenii.* Vol. 4. Moscow, 1955.

Glagoleva, Olga E. "Illegitimate Children of the Russian Nobility: Law and Practice in 1700–1860." *Kritika* 6, no. 3 (Summer 2005): 461–99.

Goldoni, Carlo. *Dobraia devka, komicheskaia opera.* Translated by I. A. Dmitrevskii. Moscow, 1782.

Golitsyn, A. L. *Iz proshlogo: Materialy dlia istorii krepostnogo teatra.* Orel, 1901.

Golovine, V. N. *The Memoirs of Countess Golovine: A Lady at the Court of Catherine II.* Translated by G. M. Fox-Davies. London, 1910.

Gorbunov, I. F. *Polnoe sobranie sochinenii.* Vol. 1. St. Petersburg, 1904.

Glozman, I. *Kuskovo.* Moscow, 1956.

Glozman, I., and L. V. Tydman. *Kuskovo.* Moscow, 1966.

Glozman, I., V. L. Rapoport, I. G. Semenova, L. V. Tydman, and N. T. Unaniants. *Kuskovo. Ostankino. Arkhangelskoe.* Moscow, 1976.

Grabar, I. E. "Ostankinskii dvorets." *Starye gody* (May–June 1910): 5–37.

———. *Zagadka Ostankinskogo dvortsa: neizvestnye i predpolagaemye postroiki V. I. Bazhenova.* Moscow, 1951.

Grinval'd, Ia. *Tri veka moskovskoi stseny: Ocherki po istorii teatral'noi Moskvy.* Moscow, 1949.

Grits, T. S. "K istorii 'Sorovka-vorovka.'" *Literaturnoe nasledstvo* 63 (1955).

Hartley, Janet. *A Social History of the Russian Empire, 1650–1825.* London and New York, 1999.

Hilton, Alison. *Russian Folk Art.* Bloomington, Ind., 1995.

Holmes, Richard. *Footsteps: Adventures of a Romantic Biographer.* New York, 1985.

———. *Sidetracks: Explorations of a Romantic Biographer.* New York, 2000.

Holroyd, Michael. *Works on Paper: The Craft of Biography and Autobiography.* Washington, D.C., 2002.

Iakushkin, E. I. "Pis'mo M. A. Iakushkinoi." In *Dekabristy,* edited by N. P. Chulkov. Moscow, 1938.

Iatsevich, A. G. *Krepostnye v Peterburge.* Leningrad, 1933.

Iazykov, D. *Grafinia Praskovia Ivanovna Sheremeteva: Biograficheskii ocherk.* Moscow, 1903.

Imperial Russian Historical Society. *Sbornik Imperatorskogo russkogo istoricheskogo obshchestva.* 148 vols. 1867–1916.

Insarskii, V. A. *Polovod'e: Kartiny provintsial'noi zhizni.* St. Petersburg, 1875.

Isarova, L. *Krepostnaia idilliia.* Moscow, 2000.

Iushkov, N. F. *K istorii russkoi stseny: Ekaterina Borisovna Piunova-Shmidgof v svoikh i chuzhikh vospominaniiakh.* Kazan', 1889.

Ivanov, A. "Zametka o grafakh Sheremetevykh ponamaria Alekseia Ivanova." In *Shchukinskii sbornik* 2 (1903).

Ivanovskii, A. "Krepostnye aktery i aktrisy." *Kolos'ia* 11 (1886): 244–68.

Karamzin, N. M. "Puteshestvie vokrug Moskvy." In *Zapiski starogo moskovskogo zhitelia: Izbrannaia proza.* Moscow, 1986.

Karnovich, E. P. *Zamechatel'nye bogatstva chastnykh lits v Rossii.* St. Petersburg, 1885.

Kashin, N. P. *Teatr N. B. Iusopova.* Moscow, 1927.

Katalog biblioteki grafa S. D. Sheremeteva. St. Petersburg, 1892.

Khodiakova, O. A. "Peterburgskaia usad'ba grafov Sheremetevykh v 20–60-e gg. XX v." *Peterburgskie chteniia—96* (1996): 433–35.

———. "Traditsii blagotvoritel'nosti grafskogo roda Sheremetevykh v Sankt-Peterburge XIX veka." *Peterburgskie chteniia (Peterburg i Rossiia)* (1994): 123–25.

Khrapovitskii, A. V. *Zapiski.* Edited by G. N. Gennadi. 1874. Reprint, Moscow, 1990.

Klinchin, A. P. *M. S. Shchepkin: Letopis' zhizni i tvorchestva.* Moscow, 1966.

Kobak, A. V, and Iu. M. Piriutko, compilers. *Istoricheskie kladibshcha Peterburga: Spravochnik-putevoditel'.* St. Petersburg, 1993.

Kobeko, D. F. *Sheremetevy i kniazia Uriusovy: genealogicheskii etiud.* St. Petersburg, 1900.

———. *Tsesarevich Pavel Petrovich.* St. Petersburg, 1887.

Kolchin, Peter. *Unfree Labor: American Slavery and Russian Serfdom.* Cambridge, 1987.

Kolychev, V. *Tshchetnaia revnost', ili Kuskovskoi perevoshchik.* Moscow, 1781.

Komarovskii, E. F. *Zapiski.* Moscow, 1990.

Kopytova, G. V. "Sheremetevskoe Sobranie." *Iz fondov kabineta rukopisei Rossiiskogo instituta istorii iskusstv. Publikatsii i obzori.* St. Petersburg, 1998.

Kostikova, N. "Novoe ob 'Amure' N. Argunova." *Iskusstvo* 3 (1973): 68–69.

Kots, E. S. *Krepostnaia intelligentsiia.* Leningrad, 1926.

Kovaleva, M. D. "Kuskovo: Zametki o dvorianskoi usad'be kontsa XIX–nachala XX vekov." *Dvorianskoe sobranie* 2 (1995): 207–14.

Krasko, A. "Grafy Sheremetevy." In *Dvorianskaia sem'ia: Iz istorii dvorianskikh familii Rossii,* edited by V. P. Stark. St. Petersburg, 2000.

Kublitskii, K. P. *Kuskovo.* St. Petersburg, 1902.

Kurakin, Aleksandr Borisovich. "Bumagi kn. A. B. Kurakina, 1763–1777." In *Arkhiv Kn. F. A. Kurakina.* Edited by F. A. Kurakin. 5 (1894): 333–425; 6 (1896): 205–443; 7 (1898): 95–431; 8 (1899): 99–413.

Kurakin, Aleksei Borisovich. "Pis'ma." In *Arkhiv Kn. F. A. Kurakina: Vosemnadtsatyi vek: istoricheskii sbornik* 1, bk. 11. (1904).

Kurmacheva, M. D. *Krepostnaia intelligentsiia Rossii: vtoraia polovina XVIII–nachalo XIX veka.* Moscow, 1983.

Kuskovo i ego okrestnosti. Moscow, 1850.

Kuskovskaia Nimfa, Prolog. N.p., 1782.

Kuz'min, A. I. "Krepostnoi literatur V. G. Voroblevskii." *XVIII vek* 4 (1959).

Kuznetsov, A. Ia. *V. G. Voroblevskii.* Moscow, 1949.

[La Ribadière, de]. *Dve sestry, ili khoroshaia priiatel'nitsa.* Translated by V. G. Voroblevskii. Moscow, [1779].

Lansere, N. E. "Fontannyi dom. (Postroiki i peredelki)." In *Zapiski istoriko-bytovogo otdela Gosudarstvennogo Russkogo muzeia* (1). Leningrad, 1928.

Lents, E., compiler. *Opis' sobraniia oruzhiia grafa S. D. Sheremeteva.* St. Petersburg, 1895.

Leonid, Arkhimandrit. "Istoricheskoe opisanie Borisovskoi Tikhvinskoi Devich'ei Pustyni." In *Chteniia v Imperatorskom obshchestve istorii i drevnostei Rossiiskikh pri Moskovskom universitete* 2 (1872).

Lepskaia, L. A. "'Ia pital k nei chuvstva samye nezhnye, samye strastnye . . .'" Unpublished paper, 2005.

———. "Krepostnye shkoly Sheremetevykh vo vtoroi polovine XVIII veka." In *Problemy istorii SSSR.* Moscow, 1979.

———. "Mashineriia Ostankinskogo teatra." In *Teatral'noe prostranstvo: materialy nauchnoi konferentsii* (1978). Moscow, 1979.

———. "N. P. Sheremetev. Ostankino. Prem'era." In *XVIII vek: assambleia iskusstv: vzaimodestvie iskusstv v russkoi kul'ture XVIII veka: sbornik statei,* edited by N. A. Evsina et al. Moscow, 2000.

———. "Novoe o krepostnykh shkolakh kontsa XVIII–nachala XIX v. v votchinakh Sheremetevykh." *Pamiatniki kul'tury. Novye otrkrytiia. Pis'mennost', iskusstvo, arkheologiia. Ezhegodnik 1987* (1988): 71–76.

———. *Ostankino.* Moscow, 1976.

———. *Ostankinskii dvorets muzei tvorchestva krepostnykh.* Leningrad, 1982.

———. "Ostankinskii teatr. Predystoriia. Zamysel. Voploshchenie." In *Novye materialy po istorii russkoi kul'tury. Sbornik trudov.* Moscow, 1987.

———. "Prem'era v Ostankine." In *Panorama iskusstv.* Moscow, 1980.

———. "Repertuar krepostnogo teatra Sheremetevykh." In *Starinnye teatry Rossii: XVIII–pervaia chetvert' XIX v. Sbornik nauchnykh trudov.* Moscow, 1993.

———. *Repertuar krepostnogo teatra Sheremetevykh: katalog p"es.* Moscow, 1996.

———. "Teatral'naia shkola Sheremetevykh vo vtoroi polovine XVIII veka." *Vestnik Moskovskogo universiteta* series 8 (Istoriia), no. 3 (1980): 46–56.

Leskov, N. S. "Tupeinyi khudozhnik (Rasskaz na mogile)." In *Izbrannye sochineniia,* edited by A. N. Keskov. N.p., 1946.

———. "Zakhudalyi rod." In *Sobranie Sochinenii,* edited by V. Iu. Troitskii. Moscow, 1989.

[Levshin, V. A.]. *Zhizn', anekdoty, voennyia i politechskiia deianiia rossiiskogo general-fel'dmarshala Grafa Borisa Petrovicha Sheremeteva.* St. Petersburg, 1808.

Liubetskii, S. N. *Selo Ostankino s okrestnostiami svoimi: Vospominaniia o starinnykh prazdnestvakh, zabavakh i uveseleniiakh v nem.* Moscow, 1868.

Loparev, Kh. M. *Biblioteka gr. S. D. Sheremeteva.* Vol. 2. St. Petersburg, 1892.

Maikov, L. "Kniazhna Mariia Kantemirova." *RS* 39 (1897): 401–17.

Makhaev, M. M. *Podlinnoe predstavlenie stroeniev i sadu, nakhodiashchikhsia v odnom iz uveselitel'nykh domov, nazyvaemom selo Kuskovo, prinadlezhavshchee Ego Siiatel'stvu Grafu Petru Borisovichu Sheremetevu.* N.p., n.d.

Malnick, Bertha. "Russian Serf Theater." *Slavonic and East European Review* 30, no. 75 (1952): 393–411.

[Malzeville, Danzel de]. *Loretta, komediia s pesniami v odnom deistvii.* Translated by K. V. U. [Moscow], 1781.

Marinchik, P. F. *Nedopetaia pesnia: Neobychnaia zhizn' P. I. Zhemchugovoi.* Leningrad-Moscow, 1965.

Marrese, Michelle Lamarche. *A Woman's Kingdom: Noblewomen and the Control of Property in Russia, 1700–1861.* Ithaca, 2002.

Matveev, B. M., and A. V. Krasko. *Fontannyi dom.* St. Petersburg, 1996.

Mikhailov, B. B. *Ostankino.* Moscow, 1976.

———. *Tserkov' Troitsy v Ostankine.* Moscow-Kozel'sk, 1993.

Mikhnevich, V. O. *Russkaia zhenshchina XVIII stoletiia: Istoricheskie etiudy.* Kiev, 1895.

Ministerstvo imperatorskogo dvora. *Kamer-fur'erskii tseremonial'nyi zhurnal, 1762–1809.* St. Petersburg, 1853–96.

Molebnov, M. P. *Penzenskii krepostnoi teatr Gladkovykh.* Penza, 1955.

Montefiore, Simon Sebag. *Prince of Princes: The Life of Potemkin.* New York, 2001.

Moon, David. *The Russian Peasantry, 1600–1930: The World the Peasants Made.* London and New York, 1999.

Mooser, R.-Aloys. *Annales de la musique et des musiciens en Russie au Xviiie siècle.* 3 vols. Geneva, 1948–51.

———. *L'opéra-comique français en Russie au Xviiie siècle.* Geneva-Monaco, 1954.

———. *Opéras, intermezzos, ballets, cantates, oratorios joués en Russie durant le Xviiie siècle, avec l'indication des oeuvres de compositeurs russes parues en Occident, à la même époque: Essai d'un répertoire alphabétique et chronologique.* Bâle, 1964.

Nikitenko, A. S. *Moia povest' o samom sebe: zapiski i dnevnik, 1804–1877.* 2 vols. St. Petersburg, 1904.

Nikolai Mikhailovich, Grand Duke of Russia. *Imperatritsa Elizaveta Alekseevna, supruga Imperatora Aleksandra I.* Vol. 2. St. Petersburg, 1909.

Bibliography

Nikulina-Kostiskaia, L. P. "Zapiski." *RS* 21 (1878): 65–80, 281–304, 609–24.

Nuvakhov, B. Sh. *Strannopriimnyi dom N. P. Sheremeteva.* Moscow, 1994.

Odna iz domashnikh bibliotek kontsa XVIII stoletiia. St. Petersburg, 1884.

Opisaniia Khrama Znameniia Presviatyia Bogoroditsy Sostoiashchago V Moskov-skom Novospasskom Monastyre Izhdiveniem Grafa Nikolaia Petrovicha Shereme-teva Vozdvignutago. Moscow, 1803.

Orlov, A. G. *Pis'ma grafa A. G. Orlova-Chesmenskogo i Vasiliia Vladimirovicha Sheremeteva s 1798 po 1804 g.* Moscow, 1911.

Ornatskaia, T. I., ed. *Rasskazy babushki: iz vospominanii piati pokolenii.* Leningrad, 1989.

Paget, Augustus B., ed. *The Paget Papers: Diplomatic and Other Correspondence of the Right Honorable Sir Arthur Paget, G.C.B. 1794–1807.* 2 vols. London, 1896.

Palmer, Alan. *Alexander I: Tsar of War and Peace.* London, 1974.

Passenans, Paul Ducret, de. *La Russie et l'esclavage dans leurs rapports avec la civilization européene.* Paris, 1822.

Pavlenko, N. I. *Ptentsy gnezda Petrova.* Moscow, 1994.

Petrov, A. N. "Palaty fel'dmarshala B. P. Sheremeteva i F. M. Apraksina v Moskve." In *Arkhitekturnoe nasledstvo* 6 (1956): 138–46.

Piriutko, Iu. M. "Lazarevskaia usypal'nitsa—pamiatnik russkoi kul'tury XVIII–XIX vv." In *Pamiatniki Kul'tury. Novye otkrytiia. Pis'mennost', iskus-stvo, arkheologiia. Ezhegodnik 1988* (1989): 485–97.

Plavil'shchikov, P. A. *Sochineniia.* Pt. 4. St. Petersburg, 1816.

Pobedonostsev, P. V. "Vospominaniia o P. A. Plavil'shchikove." *Novyi panteon otechestvennoi i innostrannoi slovesnosti* 4 (1819): 152–208.

"Podennaia zapiska o prebyvanii v Moskve grafa Fal'kenshteina, 1780 g." In *Shchukinskii sbornik* 10 (1912).

Pogozhev, V., comp. *Arkhiv direktsii Imperatorskikh teatrov.* 3 vols. St. Petersburg, 1892.

Poltoratskii, S. "Teatral'noe predstavlenie v sele Kuskove, podmoskovnoi grafa P. B. Sheremeteva v prisutstvii Ekateriny II 30 Iunia 1787 g." *Severnaia pchela* 203 (17 September 1858): 865–66.

Popova, N. *Krepostnaia aktrisa: Praskov'ia Ivanovna Kovaleva-Zhemchugova, grafinia Sheremeteva.* St. Petersburg, 2001.

Popova, N. I., and O. E. Rubinchik. *Anna Akhmatova i fontannyi dom.* St. Petersburg, 2000.

Porfir'eva, A. L., ed. *Muzykal'nyi Peterburg: Entsiklopedicheskii slovar'. XVIII vek.* 3 vols. St. Petersburg, 1996–99.

Potemkin, P. S. *Zel'mira i Smelon, ili vziatie Izmaila: liricheskaia drama.* St. Petersburg, 1795.

Poznanskii, V. V. *Talanty v nevole: Ocherki o krepostnykh arkhitektorakh, khudozhnikakh, artistakh i muzykantakh.* Moscow, 1962.

Priselkov, M. D. "Garderob vel'mozhi kontsa XVIII-nachala XIX vv." In *Zapiski Istoriko-bytovogo otdela Gosudarstvennogo Russkogo muzeia* (1) Leningrad, 1928.

Prokef'eva, L. S. *Krest'ianskaia obshchina v Rossii vo vtoroi polovine XVIII-pervoi polovine XIX veka. (Na materialakh votchin Sheremetevykh).* Leningrad, 1981.

———, and I. S. Sharkova. "O biblioteke Sheremetevykh." In *Kniga v Rossii v XVI-seredina XIX v.* Leningrad, 1985.

Prokopenko, L. I. "Istoriia sozdaniia i proektirovaniia teatral'nykh zalov Sheremetevykh." In *Starinnye teatry Rossii: XVIII-pervaia chetvert' XIX v. Sbornik nauchnykh trudov.* Moscow, 1993.

Prokopenko, L. I., and V. Iu. Asenov. "Istoriia proektirovaniia i stroitel'stva Ostankinskogo teatra-dvortsa." In *Novye materialy po istorii russkoi kul'tury: Sbornik trudov.* Moscow, 1987.

Puskhin, A. S. *Polnoe Sobranie Sochinenii.* 16 vols. Moscow-Leningrad, 1937–59.

Pyliaev, M. I. *Staryi Peterburg.* 1889. Reprint, Leningrad, 1990.

———. *Zabytoe proshloe okrestnostei Peterburga.* 1889. Reprint, St. Petersburg, 1996.

Rakina, Varvara. "Nikolai Argunov i problema zakazchika v russkoi portretnoi zhivopisi kontsa XVIII–pervoi chetverti XIX veka." Dissertation [Kandidatskaia stepen']. State Institute of Art History, Moscow. 2005.

———. *Zhivopisets Nikolai Argunov.* Moscow, 2004.

Razluka, ili ot'ezd psovoi okhoty iz Kuskova: Komicheskaia opera v dvukh deistviiakh s eia posledeovaniem v odnom deistvii. Moscow, 1785.

Reeder, Roberta. *Anna Akhmatova: Poet and Prophet.* New York, 1994.

Reinbeck, Georg. *Travels from St. Petersburgh through Moscow, Grodno, Breslaw, etc. to Germany, in the Year 1805.* In *A Collection of Modern and Contemporary Voyages and Travels,* edited by Richard Phillips. Vol. 6. London, 1807.

Reus, Klaus-Dieter, Markus Lerner, Gennadii Vdovin, Igor Dubinin. *Ocharovanie stseny.* Moscow, 2004.

Riddle, John M. *Eve's Herbs.* Cambridge, Mass., 1992.

Ritzarev, Marina. *Eighteenth-Century Russian Music.* Burlington, Vt., 2006.

————, and Anna Porfireva. "The Italian Diaspora in Eighteenth-Century Russia." In *The Eighteenth-Century Diaspora of Italian Music and Musicians,* edited by Reinhard Strohm. Turnhout, 2001.

Rogov, A. P. *Liudi shli: povesti.* Moscow, 1991.

————. *Davniaia pastoral': Praskov'ia Zhemchugova i Nikolai Sheremetev.* Moscow, 2004.

Roissard, M. le Abbé. *Uteshenie khristianina.* Translated by P. Karabanov. St. Petersburg, 1806.

Roosevelt, Priscilla R. "Emerald Thrones and Living Statues: Theater and Theatricality on the Russian Estate." *Russian Review* 50 (1991): 1–23.

————. *Life on the Russian Country Estate.* New Haven, 1995.

[Rosoi, Barnabé Farmian, de]. *Braki samnitian, geroicheskaia opera s peniem v trekh deistviiakh.* Translated by V. G. Voroblevskii. Moscow, 1785.

Rosslyn, Wendy. "Female Employees in the Russian Imperial Theatres (1785–1825)." In *Women and Gender in 18th-Century Russia,* edited by Wendy Rosslyn. Burlington, Vt., 2003.

————. "Petersburg Actresses on and off the Stage (1775–1825)." In *St. Petersburg, 1703–1825,* edited by Anthony Cross. New York, 2003.

Rostopchin, F. V. "Poslednyi den' zhizni Imperatritsy Ekateriny II—i pervyi den' tsarstvovaniia Imperatora Pavla I-go." *Arkhiv kniazia Vorontsova* 8 (1876): 158–74.

Rostovtseva, G. A. *Zelenyi teatr v Kuskove.* Perovo, 1958.

Rounding, Virginia. *Catherine the Great: Love, Sex and Power.* London, 2006.

Ruban, V. G. *Opisanie imperatorsgogo stolichnogo goroda Moskvy.* St. Petersburg, 1782.

Rudneva, L. Iu. *Ostankino v izobrazitelnom iskusstve: katalog vystavki.* Moscow, 1980.

Russkii biograficheskii slovar'. 25 vols. St. Petersburg, 1896–1918.

Sakhnovskii, V. S. *Krepostnoi usadebnyi teatr: Kratkoe vvedenie k ego tipologicheskomu izucheniiu.* Leningrad, 1924.

Sakulin, P. N. "Krepostnaia intelligentsiia." In *Velikaia reforma: Russkoe obshchestvo i krest'ianskii vopros v proshlom i nastoiashchem,* edited by A. K. Dzhivelegov, S. P. Mel'gunov, V. I. Pichet. Vol. 3. Moscow, 1911.

Savelov, L. M. *Lektsii po russkoi genealogii.* 1908. Reprint, Moscow, 1994.

[Sédaine, M.]. *Begloi soldat, liricheskaia drama.* Translated by V. G. Voroblevskii. Moscow, 1781.

Ségur, Louis Philippe, count de. *Memoirs and Recollections of Count Louis Philippe de Segur.* 3 vols. New York, 1970.

Selinova, T. A. *Ivan Petrovich Argunov, 1729–1802.* Moscow, 1973.

Semenova, I. G. *Ostankino: Dvorianskaia usad'ba.* Leningrad, 1981.

Senelick, Laurence. "The Erotic Bondage of Serf Theatre." *Russian Review* 50, no. 1 (1991): 24–34.

———. "Russian Serf Theatre and the Early Years of Mikhail Shchepkin." *Theatre Quarterly* 10, no. 38 (1980): 8–16.

———. *Serf Actor: The Life and Art of Mikhail Shchepkin.* Westport, Conn., 1984.

Sergeev. *Statistichesko-istoricheskoe obozrenie Strannopriimnago doma v Moskve.* [Moscow], 1843.

Shalikov, Prince Petr. *Puteshestvie v Malorussiiu.* Moscow, 1813.

Shamurin, Iu. *Podmoskovnye.* 2 vols. Moscow, 1914.

Sharandak, N. P. *Ivan Argunov, 1727–1802.* Leningrad, 1977.

Shchelkov, K. P. *Khar'kov.* Khar'kov, 1881.

Shchepelev, L. E. *Chinovnyi mir Rossii: XVIII-nachalo XX v.* St. Petersburg, 1999.

Shchepetov, K. N. *Krepostnoe pravo v votchinakh Sheremetevykh.* Moscow, 1947.

———. *Selo Ostankino i ego okrestnosti.* Moscow, 1952.

———. *Iz zhizni krepostnykh krest'ian Rossii XVIII–XIX vekov: Po materialam Sheremetevskikh votchin.* Moscow, 1963.

Shchepkin, M. A. *M. S. Shchepkin, 1788–1863 (Zapiski, pis'ma, rasskazy, materialy dlia biografii i rodoslovnaia).* St. Petersburg, 1914.

Shchepkin, M. S. *Zapiski aktera Shchepkina.* Edited by N. N. Panfilova and O. M. Fel'dman. Moscow, 1988.

———. *Zapiski aktera Shchepkina.* Edited by A. B. Derman. Moscow, 1933.

Shcherbatov, M. M. *On the Corruption of Morals in Russia.* Edited and translated by Antony Lentin. Cambridge, 1969.

Shenkman, G. *Fel'dmarshal Sheremetev (istoricheskie lichnosti Rossii XVIII veka i ikh potomki).* St. Petersburg, 2000.

Sheremetev, B. P. *Zapiski Puteshestviia . . . v evropeiskie gosudarstva.* Moscow, 1773.

Sheremetev, D. N. *Opis' biblioteki nakhodiasheisia v Moskve, na Vozdvizhenke, v dome grafa Dmitriia Nikolaevicha Sheremeteva do 1812 g.* St. Petersburg, 1883.

———. *Kalendarnyia zametki grafa Dmitriia Nikolaevicha Sheremeteva.* Moscow, 1904.

Sheremetev, N. P. "Dopolneniia k 'Perepiske grafa N. P. Sheremeteva'." *RA* 3 (1896): 526–35.

———. "Iz bumag i perepiski grafa N. P. Sheremeteva." *RA* 2 (1896): 189–216, 305–40, 457–520; 2 (1897): 497–521.

———. "Pis'ma grafa N. P. Sheremeteva k V. S. Sheremetevu." *RA* 1 (1899): 391–95.

———. "Pis'mo grafa N. P. Sheremeteva k grafu P. A. Palenu." *RA* 1 (1896): 326–27.

———. "Zametki po povodu pis'ma grafa N. P. Sheremeteva k V. S. Sheremetevu." *RA* 1 (1899): 675–78.

———. "Zaveshchatel'noe pis'mo grafa Nikolaia Petrovicha Sheremeteva maloletnemy syny svoemu." *RA* 2 (1896): 510–19.

Sheremetev, P. B. "K istorii Sheremetevskikh pevchikh: Ukaz grafa Petra Borisovicha Sheremeteva Peterburgskomu upraviteliu Petru Aleksandrovu." *RA* 2 (1911): 112.

Sheremetev, P. S. *Karamzin v Ostaf'eve. 1811–1911.* Moscow, 1911.

———. *Vasilii Sergeevich Sheremetev, 1752–1831.* N.p., 1910.

———. *Viazemy.* Petrograd, 1916.

Sheremetev, S. D. *Domashnaia Starina.* Moscow, 1900.

———. *Graf Dmitrii Nikolaevich Sheremetev.* St. Petersburg, 1889.

———. "Graf Dmitrii Nikolaevich Sheremetev (1809–1824)." In *Sochineniia grafa S. D. Sheremeteva.* N.p., n.d.

———. "Graf M. N. Murav'ev i ego doch'." *RA* 1 (1910): 112–25.

———. *Grafinia Sheremeteva.* St. Petersburg, 1889.

———. *Kuskovo do 1812 goda.* Moscow, 1899.

———. *Memuary grafa S. D. Sheremeteva.* Edited by L. I. Shokhin. Moscow, 2001.

———. *Mikhailovskoe.* Moscow, 1906.

———. *Ostafievo.* St. Petersburg, 1893.

———. *Ostankino.* St. Petersburg, 1897.

———. "Otgoloski XVIII veka. Kuskovskii zverinets." *Priroda i okhota* 1 (1897): 1–12.

———. "Otgoloski XVIII veka. Psovaia okhota grafa Nikolaia Petrovicha Sheremeteva." *Priroda i okhota* 4 (1896): 1–12.

———. *Polkovye vospominaniia.* St. Petersburg, 1898.

———. *Romanov dvor na Vozdvizhenke.* St. Petersburg, 1911.

———. *Skhimonakhinia Nektariia.* Moscow, 1909.

————. *Staraia Vozdvizhenka.* St. Petersburg, 1892.

————. *Starshii brat moi.* St. Petersburg, 1893.

————. *Tat'iana Ivanovna Shlykova, 1773–1863.* St. Petersburg, 1889.

————. *Ulianka.* St. Petersburg, 1893.

————. *Vasilii Sergeevich Sheremetev.* St. Petersburg, 1890.

————. *Vospominaniia 1853–1861 gg. (Semeinye).* St. Petersburg, 1898.

————. *Vospominaniia detstva.* St. Petersburg, 1896.

————. *Vospominaniia o sluzhbakh v domovoi tserkvi.* St. Petersburg, 1894.

————. *Vozdvizhenskii naugol'nyi dom sto let nazad.* 2 issues. Moscow, 1899, 1904.

————. *Zapisnaia Knizhka.* No. 1. Moscow, 1903.

————, ed. *Arkhiv sela Kuskova.* Moscow, 1902.

————. *Ikony semeinyia grafa S. D. i grafini E. P. Sheremetevykh.* St. Petersburg, 1899.

————. *Ostafievskii arkhiv kniazei Viazemskikh.* 3 vols. St. Petersburg, 1899.

————. *Otgoloski XVIII veka.* 11 vols. Moscow, 1896–1905.

————. *Pis'ma grafini A. S. Sheremetevoi k V. P. Sheremetevoi—tridtsatykh godov.* St. Petersburg, 1901.

————. *Stoletnie otgoloski, 1801, 1802, 1803.* Moscow, 1901–03.

Sheremeteva, V. P. *Dnevnik V. P. Sheremetevoi, urozhdennoi Almazovoi. 1825–1826 gg.* Moscow, 1916.

Shil'der, N. K. *Imperator Aleksandr Pervyi: ego zhizn' i tsarstvovanie.* St. Petersburg, 1904–05.

————. *Imperator Pavel Pervyi: Istoriko-biograficheskii ocherk.* St. Petersburg, 1901.

Shipov, N. I. "Istoriia moei zhizni: Rasskaz byshago krepostnogo krestianina N. I. Shipova, 1802–1845." *RS* 31 (1881): 133–48, 221–40; *RS* 32 (1881): 437–78.

Shishko, A. V. *Kuskovo.* Moscow, 1955.

Sholok, E. *Ostankino i ego teatr.* Moscow, 1949.

Sivkov, K. V. "Avtobiografiia krepostnogo intelligenta kontsa XVIII v." *Istoricheskii arkhiv* 5 (1950): 288–99.

————. *Kuskovo: Ocherk.* Moscow, 1927.

————. *"Shtat" sela Kuskova, 1786 g.* Moscow, 1927.

Smirnova, T. N. "Gde zhe vse-taki venchalsia graf N. P. Sheremetev?" *Moskovskii zhurnal* 6 (2001): 48–50.

Solovev, K. A. *Ostankino.* Moscow, 1958.

Springis, E. E. "Dvorets-teatr Ostankino: 'Bol'shoi i krasivyi dom.'" *Nashe nasledie* 43–44 (1997): 206–29.

———. "Usad'ba Zhikharevo i itogi stroitel'noi deiatel'nosti grafa N. P. Sheremeteva." *Russkaia usad'ba* 7, no. 23 (2001): 229–35.

———. "Vladelets-zakazchik i formirovanie usadebnogo kompleksa v kontse XVIII–nach. XIX v." Dissertation [kandidatskaia stepen'], Russian Institute for the Study of Culture, 1999.

Stakhov, A. "Klochki vospominanii." *RS* 86 (1896): 39–56, 347–68.

Stanislas II, Auguste, King of Poland. *Memoires du Roi Stanislas-Auguste Poniatowski.* Edited by S. M. Goriainov A. S. Lapp-Danilevskii, S. F. Platonov. 2 vols. St. Petersburg, 1914–24.

———. *Memoires secrets et inedits de Stanislas Auguste, Comte Poniatowski, dernier roi de Pologne.* Leipzig, 1862.

Staniukovich, V. K. *Biudzhet Sheremetevykh (1798–1910).* Moscow, 1927.

———. *Domashnii krepostnoi teatr Sheremetevykh XVIII veka.* Leningrad, 1927.

———. *Fontannyi dom Sheremetevykh. Muzei byta. Putevoditel'.* Petrograd, 1923.

———. "Krepostnye khudozhniki Sheremetevykh. K dvukhstoletiiu so dnia rozhdeniia Ivana Argunova, 1727–1917." *Zapiski istoriko-bytovogo otdela Gosudarstvennogo russkogo muzeia* (1). Leningrad, 1928.

———. *Materialy po staromu Kuskovu.* Moscow, 1926.

———. *Sem'ia Argunovykh.* Leningrad, 1926.

Starikova, L. M. *Teatral'naia zhizn' starinnoi Moskvy.* Moscow, 1989.

Stedingk, Curt Bogislaus Christophe, Comte de. *Un Ambassadeur ae Suède à la cour de Catharine II; Feld-Maréchal Comte De Stedingk: Choix de dépeches diplomatiques, rapports secrets et lettres particulières de 1790 à 1796.* Edited by La Comtesse Brevern de la Gardie. 2 vols. Stockholm, 1919.

Stites, Richard. *Serfdom, Society, and the Arts in Imperial Russia: The Pleasure and the Power.* New Haven, 2005.

Strannopriimnyi dom grafa Sheremeteva v Moskve. 1810–1910. Moscow, 1910.

Strannopriimnyi dom grafa Sheremeteva v Moskve. Konchina popechitelia grafa D. N. Sheremeteva. Moscow, 1871.

Struve, Johann Christian von. *Reise eines jungen Russen von Wien ueber Jassy in die Krim und ausfuehrliches Tagebuch der im Jahr 1793 von St. Petersburg nach Constantinopel geschickten Russisch-Kaiserlichen Gesandschaft.* Gotha, 1801.

Sukhodolov, V. N. "Graf N. P. Sheremetev i Praskov'ia Zhemchugova." In *Otechestvo. Kraevedchiskii al'manakh.* Moscow, 1994.

Svin'in, P. *Dostopamiatnosti Sankpeterburga i ego okrestnosti.* Vol. 2. St. Petersburg, 1817.

Tarasenkov, A. T. *Istoricheskaia zapiska o Strannopriimnom dome.* Moscow, 1860.

Tatlina, P. N. "Vospominaniia." *RA* 3 (1899): 190–224.

Thomas, Downing A. *Aesthetics of Opera in the Ancién Regime, 1647–1785.* Cambridge, 2002.

Tikhvinskii, N. *Vospominaniia o zhizni i trudakh Sviatitelia Dimitriia Mitropolita Rostovskago Chudotvortsa.* 1902. Reprint Rostov-Iaroslavskii, 1992.

Timofeev, N. *Izdaniia grafa S. D. Sheremeteva.* St. Petersburg, 1909.

Tomalin, Claire. *Mrs. Jordan's Profession: The Actress and the Prince.* New York, 1995.

Tret'iakova, L. "Teatr dlia krepostnykh aktris." In *Moi starinnye podrugi.* Moscow, 2001.

Tumanskii, F. "Opisanie kuskovskogo prazdnika v 1-yi den' avgusta 1792 g." *Rossiiskii magazin* 1, book 1, no. 2 (1793): 503–12.

Tydman, L. "Kuskovo." In *Dvorianskie gnezda Rossii: istoriia, kul'tura, arkhitektura.* Moscow, 2000.

"Ubiistvo fel'dmarshala gr. M. F. Kamenskago." *RS* 14 (1875): 212–13.

Uchrezhdenie i shtat Strannopriimnago v Moskve doma, zavodimago izhdiveniem deistvitel'nogo tainogo sovetnikna i ober-kamergera g. Sheremeteva. St. Petersburg, 1803.

Vasil'chikov, A. A. *Semeistvo Razumovskikh.* 5 vols. St. Petersburg, 1880–95.

Vdovin, G. V. *Ostankino.* Moscow, 1988.

———. *Ostankinskii teatr-dvorets.* Moscow, 1989.

———., ed. *Graf Nikolai Petrovich Sheremetev: Lichnost', deiatel'nost', sud'ba. Etiudy k monografii.* Moscow, 2001.

Vdovin, G. V., L. A. Lepskaia, and A. F. Cherviakov. *Ostankino. Teatr-dvorets.* Moscow, 1994.

Veiner, P. "Zhizn i iskusstvo v Ostankine." *Starye gody* (May–June 1910): 38–72.

Velizarii, M. I. *Put' provintsial'noi aktrisy.* Leningrad-Moscow, 1938.

Vel'tman, A. "Erotida." In *Povesti i rasskazy.* Moscow, 1979.

———. "Erotida." In *Selected Stories.* Edited by James J. Gebhard. Evanston, Ill., 1998.

Viazemskii, P. A. *Polnoe Sobranie Sochinenii.* Edited by S. D. Sheremetev. 12 vols. St. Petersburg, 1878–96.

Vigée-Lebrun, Elisabeth-Louise. *The Memoirs of Mme Elisabeth Louise Vigée-Le Brun, 1755–1789.* Edited by Gerard Shelley. London, 1926.

———. *Memoirs of Madame Vigée-Lebrun.* Translated by Lionel Strachey. New York, 1989.

Vigel, F. F. *Zapiski.* 7 pts. Moscow, 1891–92.

Vinogradov, K. *Muzei-usad'ba Ostankino. Dvorets-teatr.* 4th ed. Moscow-Leningrad, 1931.

———. *Ostankino: Krestiane i rabochie pri postroike Ostankinskogo "Uveselitelnogo doma" (Teatra-dvortsa). Istoricheskii ocherk.* Moscow, 1929.

Vodovozova, E. N. "Vospominaniia." *Minuvshie gody* 5 (May–June 1908): 242–77.

Voeikov, A. F. *Kratkoe opisanie sela Spaskogo, Kuskovo, tozh', prinadlezhashchago ego siiatel'stvu grafu Petru Borisovichu Sheremetevu. Sochinenie neizvestnogo. napechatano v 1787 godu, i progulka v sele Kuskove.* St. Petersburg, 1829.

[Voisenon, Claude Henri de, and Charles Simon Favart]. *Opyt druzhby, komicheskaia opera.* Translated by V. G. Voroblevskii. [Moscow, 1779].

Voroblevskii, V. G. *Kratkoe opisane sela Spasskogo Kuskovo tozh prinadlezhashchego ego siiatelstvu Petru Borisovichu Sheremetevu.* Moscow, 1787.

———. *Opisanie Ego Imperatorskogo Vysochestva blagovernogo gosudaria Tsesarevicha i Velikogo Kniazia Pavla Petrovicha v Berlin.* St. Petersburg, 1776.

———. *Liricheskie perevody.* Pt. 1. Moscow, [before 1780].

"Vyderzhki iz staroi zapisnoi knizhki, nachatoi v 1813 g." *RA* 3 (1875): 452–53.

Winkler, Martin. *Russische historische Miniaturen.* Feldafing, 1978.

Zaozerskii, A. I. *Fel'dmarshal B. P. Sheremetev.* Edited by B. V. Levshin. Moscow, 1989.

Zemenkov, B. S. *Pamiatnye mesta Moskvy. Stranitsy zhizni deiatelei nauki i kul'tury.* Moscow, 1959.

Zimnyi Dvorets. Ocherki zhizni Imperatorskoi rezidentsii. Vol. 1. St. Petersburg, 2000.

Zubov, V. P. *Russkie propovedniki: Ocherki po istorii Russkoi propovedi.* Moscow, 2001.

Zvonarev, Semen, comp. *Sorok sorokov: Al'bom-ukazatel' vsekh moskovskikh tserkvei v chetyrekh tomakh.* Vol. 2. Paris, 1988.

Index

Index

Index

Index